CURTAIN TIME!

CURTAIN TIME!

compiled & edited by
ZARA SHAKOW

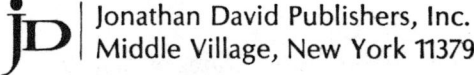
Jonathan David Publishers, Inc.
Middle Village, New York 11379

CURTAIN TIME!

Copyright © 1985
by
Jonathan David Publishers, Inc.

No part of this book may be reproduced in any form without the prior written consent of the publisher. Address all inquiries to:

Jonathan David Publishers, Inc.
68-22 Eliot Avenue
Middle Village, New York 11379

Original cloth edition published by Jonathan David Publishers, Inc., under the title *Curtain Time for Jewish Youth*. Copyright © 1968 by Jonathan David Publishers, Inc.

1988 1987 1986 1985
10 9 8 7 6 5 4 3 2 1

Library of Congress Cataloging in Publication Data
Main entry under title:

Curtain time!

  Originally published: Curtain time for Jewish youth. 1968. 1. Fasts and feasts—Judaism—Exercises, recitations, etc.
  I. Shakow, Zara. II. Curtain time for Jewish youth.
PN4305. J48C87 1985   808.8'98924   85-7057
ISBN 0-8246-0310-9 (pbk.)

Printed in the United States of America

Acknowledgments

The editor and publisher express their profound gratitude to the following authors, publishers and organizations who have kindly granted permission to use the material which originally appeared under their imprint.

American Jewish Congress, Women's Division, for "A Candle Lighting Script," "The Day Israel Was Born," and "Hanukkah" by Dorothy Ross.

American Jewish Historical Society for several items from the pamphlet *American Jewish History: Prose and Verse Selections*, compiled by Rabbi Philip Goodman.

Bloch Publishing Company for *Dance of the Hanukkah Candles*, by Zara Shakow and poem "Hanukkah Lights," by Shulamit Ish-Kishor.

Bruce Humphries, Inc. for poem "For Purim," by Zalman Shneour.

Brandt and Brandt for play "Children of Israel," by James Yaffe.

Dodd, Mead and Company for poem "The Jewish Cemetery at Newport," by Henry Wadsworth Longfellow, from *The Standard Book of Jewish Verse*.

Rabbi Sidney Greenberg, editor of *A Modern Treasury of Jewish Thoughts*, published by Thomas Yoseloff, for selection "Where Is Holiness."

Hadassah for documentary pageant "Seeds of Freedom," by Millard Lampell.

Houghton Mifflin Company for "Gifts" and "The Banner of the Jew" from *Poems of Emma Lazarus*.

Jewish Exponent for poem "Hanukkah" by Cecelia G. Gerson.

The Jewish Theological Seminary, Radio and Television Department (Eternal Light Program) for plays "Children of Israel," by James Yaffe, and "Come Under the Wings," by Grace Goldin, adapted by Virginia Mazer.

Jewish Reconstructionist Foundation for text of "What Is Torah," from cantata by Ira and Judith Kaplan Eisenstein; "Where God Is Found" and other selections from Reconstructionist Prayer Book, as well as a number of excerpts from *The Faith of America*, compiled by Dr. Mordecai M. Kaplan, Dr. J. Paul Williams and Dr. Eugene Kohn, published by the Reconstructionist Press.

The National Catholic Weekly Review, for poem "God Called It America," by Rabbi Abba Hillel Silver from magazine "America."

The National Conference of Christians and Jews, Inc. for play "Some of My Best Friends," by Robert Crean; poem "Some Children Are," by Jo Tenjford Oslo; and readings "And No One Asked," by Morris Reich, "What Is America," by Rabbi Samuel M. Silver, and "We Believe."

The National Recreation and Park Association for dramatic readings, "Americans All" by Frances Johnson and Jules Heller, "America Sings" by Margaret Morrow, "Freedom Means All of Us Everywhere," "I Hear America Singing," and "Who Are We of the United States?" by Ida Rosenfield and Rosalie Bissing.

National Young Judaea, for dramatic reading "How Is a State Born"; poems "The Voice Unto Pharaoh" by Arthur Guiterman; "Lincoln's Birthday," "Discovery of the Tu-key," "A Rhyme for Moon Months," and "Two by Two," by Dorothy Ross; "Why I Like Purim," and "Mattathias," by Elma Ehrlich Levinger; and "Hail the Maccabees," by Israel Goldberg.

Fleming H. Revell Company for text of songs "To Him from Whom Our Blessings Flow"; "Men Whose Boast It Is" by James Russell Lowell; and "Now Sing We a Song" by John W. Chadwick, from songbook *Hymns for the Living Age*, edited by H. Augustine Smith.

Schocken Books, Inc. for selection "The Omnipresence of God" from *A Jewish Reader: In Time and Eternity*, edited by Nahum N. Glatzer.

Synagogue Council of America for radio script "The First Passover in America," by Max Ehrlich.

United Synagogue of America, National Women's League for play "The Birth of a Queen" by Ann K. Glasner.

Viking Press for several lyrics from *The Book of American Negro Spirituals* compiled by James Weldon and Rosamund Johnson.

Dr. Meyer Waxman, editor of *History of Jewish Literature*, published by Bloch Publishing Company for poem "Melodies of Israel" by Zalman Shneour.

World Zionist Organization, Youth and Hechalutz Department, for play "Discovery" by Michael Elkins; and dramatic readings by Mila Ohel—"To Thee Will I Give It and To Thy Seed Forever," and "Israel Reborn."

The editor further wishes to convey her sincere appreciation to the following for their gracious cooperation:

Lillian Cohen, Director of Publications for the National Conference of Christians and Jews; Kathryn S. Cole, Manager, Department of Information, National Broadcasting Company; Rabbi Philip Goodman, Executive Secretary of the Jewish Book Council; Doris Gold, Editor of Young Judaean; Rabbi Emanuel S. Goldsmith, Assistant Executive Director of the Jewish Reconstructionist Foundation; Esther Kolatch, Executive Director of the American Jewish Congress Women's Division; Judith Levin of The Jewish Theological Seminary of America, Eternal Light Program; Dr. Isidore S. Meyer, Editor of the American Jewish Historical Society; Virginia Musselman, Director Program Services, National Recreation and Park Association; Miriam Ranan of the World Zionist Organization Information Office; Dorothy Ross; Julius Schatz of the American Jewish Congress; Bernard Weisberg, National Director of Young Judaea; and Helen Visconti for her assistance in typing the manuscript.

FOR
MY GOOD FRIENDS
ROSE AND HAROLD KOVNER
THANKS AND AFFECTION

Contents

MANUAL	1
HANUKKAH	43
PURIM	105
PASSOVER	139
ISRAEL INDEPENDENCE DAY	173
SHEVUOT	233
LINCOLN'S BIRTHDAY	279
JULY THE FOURTH	284
COLUMBUS DAY	320
THANKSGIVING DAY	322
AMERICAN-JEWISH HISTORY WEEK	329
BROTHERHOOD WEEK	367
BIBLIOGRAPHY	417

Manual

INTRODUCTION

This Manual is intended primarily for the teacher or leader with little or no practical experience in staging a dramatic presentation.

For those interested in pursuing the subject further, a comprehensive bibliography on Directing, Play Production, Stagecraft, Scenery, Lighting, Costume, Make-Up, Acting, Voice, Speech and Creative Dramatics is listed in the Appendix.

The contents of the anthology were expressly selected for their intrinsic dramatic-literary merit and are recommended unhesitatingly. Each category contains a number of possibilities for specific occasions. Since "the play's the thing," the problem of choice will partially be solved for the novice director.

When planning an entire assembly program, however, the teacher-leader has to exercise initiative in making selections so as to achieve an interesting, well-rounded, unified program that will stimulate, edify and entertain participants and audience. The following are important factors to consider:

1. Variety
2. Balance
3. Suitability
4. Potential capacity of players

5. Arrangement—sequential placement in terms of dramatic build-up
6. Program duration—playing time not to exceed the audience's interest span

The precautionary pointers, covering pitfalls to avoid—faults frequently seen in amateur productions—are based on observing and adjudicating school, center, camp, community theatre, kibbutz and Youth Drama Festival performances for years.

DIRECTOR'S FUNCTION AND APPROACH

The director's function in relation to the play is to be true to the playwright's intention, breathe life into the script, realize its basic theme and project it in such a way that audience empathy is evoked. If the director inspires the cast to contribute as *creative-interpretive* partners, the goal can better be achieved. "If you give inspiration to an artist he will give you inspiration," Josef Krips, renowned conductor, judiciously points out. This is doubly applicable to amateurs.

Staging a production is an exciting, challenging, creative process requiring the director to bring to the activity and the participants keen interest, dedication, genuine enthusiasm and love.

"It doesn't make any difference if the actor loves the director, but the director's love for the actors he's working with in a play is ten times more important than any love in the world," Broadway actress Brenda Vaccaro maintains. The validity of this statement is beyond question, for a director can perform veritable miracles by infusing the cast with love, and in turn, educe love from each one for the play, the company, production and audience.

The significance of the love factor in directing cannot be overemphasized. The fact that artists in different fields stress its pertinency is noteworthy. "The key word is love," according to Sir Laurence Olivier, "with actors and audience." In this connection, Josef Krips contends: "You've got to make the musician love the music he plays at the moment he's playing it because without love there is no music." Leonard Bernstein, world-famous composer-conductor, reminds us: "Communication is a way of making love to people . . . of reaching out to them. Love and art are two ways of communicating. That's why art is so close to love." And Jeanne Moreau, film star, aptly sums it up with: "Art is an act of love . . . the act of a lover of love. Love transfigures the act of acting . . . it becomes a generosity, a gift."

Dramatics can prove to be a "fun activity"—a truly joyful, enriching and rewarding experience for all involved—provided the director adopts the right psychological attitude and establishes a climate conducive to creative expression. By relating to the children with loving sympathetic understanding, inspiring, encouraging and guiding rather than imposing, the director cannot but elicit a reciprocal response, resulting in the entire cast giving its wholehearted cooperation.

When offering criticism, the director always has to be constructive, never destructive. The need for praising the children for creditable work done and instilling confidence in them must constantly be borne in mind. This not only serves as an impetus to continued improvement, but helps overcome self-consciousness and stage fright—a devastating condition. The fear of failure is rightly considered man's worst fear, and as we know, fear can paralyze. It is therefore imperative that the director avert the possibility of stage fright by assuring and reassuring the children that they will do well, and that fear is altogether groundless, since they are appearing before a friendly, receptive audience rooting for their success. The insecure, retiring child understandably requires even more encouragement and commendation.

DIRECTOR'S HOMEWORK

In order to facilitate the various phases of production and achieve smooth-running performances, it is necessary for the director to prepare sufficiently in advance of the first casting-call by formulating a well-organized plan of procedure. The following "homework" pointers on pre-production preparation may prove helpful:

1. Study and analyze the play to determine its theme and treatment.
2. Edit the text to suit your purpose and situation, but do not take undue liberty by making radical script changes.
3. Arrange for adequate copies of the entire play—one for each cast member, eight or more for the production staff and several extras to cover possible emergencies.

4. Develop a visual concept of the play to help you crystallize the milieu, atmosphere, characters, costumes, make-up and props, supplementing the script through research and illustrative material on the period.
5. Formulate specific production ideas based on the script and your research, so as to realize the play's inherent values and make them come alive.
6. Write a brief but incisive "portrait-study" of every character—the "inner" and "outer" man—describing outstanding characteristics and physical appearance.
7. Select pivotal scenes for each character, noting exact page and place in the script under the respective character's name in a casting notebook. List the requisite qualifications for each role.
8. Determine each character's basic motivating actions—why he behaves as he does and what he wants to achieve in each beat (separate moment of action).
9. If a realistic interior is to be built, when conferring with the Scenic Designer and planning the ground plan (basic outline of set), be sure to:
    a) Establish strategic placement of doors, windows, stairways, fireplaces, etc. to promote interesting dramatic entrances-exits and fluid stage movement.
    b) Arrange, if feasible, for a variety of levels by introducing platforms, steps and balconies.
    c) Plan placement of furniture so that it contributes to pictorially effective groupings.
    d) In subsequent selection of furniture, choose only essential pieces which are functional, in keeping with the period and atmosphere, as well as comfortable for the actors. Consider proportion, balance and harmony. Avoid massive furniture which dwarfs children. Use furniture sparingly to allow for ample acting area. Busy patterns in upholstery and drapery distract. Avoid them.
10. Follow similar procedure with an exterior set. Place pathways, housefronts, rocks, hills, trees, hedges, borders, trellises and outdoor furniture strategically to make for interesting, fluid movement.

Inasmuch as facilities, equipment and production budgets at most camps, schools and centers are usually limited, the realistic director adapts to conditions. The availability of adequate physical resources and technical equipment, while desirable, is not indispensable. The director need not be concerned about realism in detail under such circumstances, for striking effects are attainable through substitute backgrounds and symbolic costumes. It is all-important, however, to employ imagination and ingenuity in their execution. If the *illusion* of reality is created, the children will invariably assume the rest—their lively imaginations induce believability.

Simplified settings, consisting of multiple-section movable screens on wooden frames, covered with burlap, unbleached sheeting, cotton sacking, denim or even strips of heavy painted wrapping-paper can serve. When arranged effectively in pairs, or in a series, they can suggest walls, wings or doorways. Windows, mirrors, fireplaces and other wall decorations can be painted on wrapping-paper and fastened onto the screens.

Drops, combined with several flats or set pieces, also establish a background and prove pictorially effective.

Plastic units, such as arches, porticoes, steps or dais, used in conjunction with drapery and/or a cyclorama as well as drapery hung artistically, can produce a series of settings too.

If the theme of a play lends itself, a background can readily be established by posters, banners or placards with the locale artistically printed or written thereon, when displayed by pages, heralds or the equivalent of a "Chinese Property Man" or "Chorus."

Tapestry, maps, pictures, banners, pennants, shields, plaques or swords tacked onto the stage wall or backdrop adequately serve to suggest a setting too. Stencils for applying patterns to the back-wall or backdrop may also be used with good results.

11. In a costume play, consult with the Costume Designer and plan wardrobe with an awareness of color, cut, line, harmony and suitability. Strive to attain authenticity, appropriateness, practicality and comfort. Costume books, costume plates, engravings, paintings, encyclopedias, pictorial maga-

zines and production photographs of period plays furnish excellent reference material.

Simple inexpensive improvised costumes, even token costumes, suffice provided they symbolize the characters and authentically suggest the period and spirit of the play.

Helmets, armor, masks, animal heads and other objects requiring modelled surfaces and lightness of weight can be made out of papier mâché. Painted cardboard may also be used for a variety of period props and costume embellishments.

12. Outline the probable staff requirements, contingent on type of program, available facilities and personnel, namely:
    a) Assistant Director
    b) Stage Manager and assistants
       1. Prompter
       2. Lighting Man
       3. Sound Effects Man
       4. Prop Master
       5. Stage Crew
    c) Scenic Designer and Crew
    d) Costume Designer and assistants
    e) Make-up Head and assistants

    While some of these departments, understandably, will have to be relegated to faculty members, older boys are often keenly interested in the technical aspects of production—lights, sound, scene and prop construction—and may be equipped to handle them, or can be trained to do so.

13. Designate reliable individuals to manage the various categories and brief them on attendant duties, so they will efficiently discharge their responsibilities and properly coordinate the work.

14. Prepare a Property List—stationary and hand. Appoint a staff member to scout, collect and catalog props in readiness for performance, also "dummy" (substitute) props for book-free rehearsals. When props are otherwise unobtainable and must be rented or bought, be sure to order them well in advance.

15. Compile a Costume and Make-up Chart and list needs. Follow through as above.

16. Prepare Light and Sound Cue sheets and list needs. Allow ample time to order sound effect and music records, lighting equipment, gelatins, etc. If music and sound effects are to be taped, do so well in advance.
17. Arrange a Rehearsal Schedule, if only tentative; also, arrange for suitable rehearsal space for the entire rehearsal period.
18. Master basic stage terminology to aid you in visualizing the business recorded in script and to expedite the blocking.
19. Plan blocking (stage movement), at least the major large scale movements, with awareness of the stage acting area and the limitations of the auditorium's sight lines, in order to achieve maximum visibility for the audience. Establish a definite pattern of action, striving for fluid pictures. Make sure that each picture has a center of interest and the stage is well-balanced. Avoid movement for movement's sake, bearing in mind that every move and piece of business must be purposefully and logically motivated.

    Avoid straight lines, for a line of action is neither horizontal nor vertical, but diagonal, and the pivotal position, a triangle.

    As a general rule, move people *above* (up of) other people—away from the audience, not *below* (down of)—toward the audience.

    As the director subsequently observes rehearsals more objectively from the house (out front) and gets a better perspective, some changes in blocking may become necessary. Do not permit that to disconcert you, for it is inevitable at times. Professional stage directors frequently change blocking also.

    Additional inventive *business* to fill in details will invariably occur to you and the cast as book-free rehearsals progress. Encourage the players to suggest likely *business*.

GLOSSARY OF STAGE TERMS

It is expeditious to employ stage terminology consistently at rehearsals and performances. The following minimal stage terms are required to conduct rehearsals systematically:

AD LIB: To extemporize dialogue in an emergency, viz: to cover up a mishap—a delayed sound or light cue; an actor's belated entrance or an actor "blowing" or "going up on lines" —forgetting.

To improvise lines, as for greetings, in order to supplement the script's dialogue.

APRON: The stage space in front of curtain line. If there is no need for an orchestra pit, and auditorium space permits, a removable extension platform, or forestage, can be added to the stage floor to deepen the stage and use for street scenes, prologues or narrators.

AT RISE: The beginning of a scene, act or play.

BACK or BACKSTAGE: That part of the stage out of the audience's view. "Behind the scenes."

BACK WALL: The rear wall of the set or rear wall of the stage.

BLOCKING: Working out the play's movements and business, i.e.—entrances, exits, crosses, positions, activities; the process of giving the actors directions in this connection.

Stage directions are given from the actor's right and left, facing the audience. The abbreviations represent as follows:

    C: Stage Center
    R: Stage Right
    L: Stage Left
    X: Cross—a move from one position onstage to another
    D S: Downstage—towards the audience
    U S: Upstage—away from the audience
    U R: Up Right
    U L: Up Left
    D R: Down Right
    D L: Down Left
    U C: Up Center
    L C: Left of Center
    R C: Right of Center

Business noted in script as "U" of table, chair, etc. indicates "above." "D" of an object, person or place indicates "below."

STAGE AREAS

	BACK	cyc	WALL	
UP →	UP RIGHT	UP CENTER	UP LEFT	← DOWN
	RIGHT CENTER	CENTER	LEFT	
(wings)	DOWN RIGHT	DOWN CENTER / Curtain Line	DOWN LEFT	(wings) / proscenium

Apron

AUDIENCE

BUSINESS: Activities actors perform—e.g. reading, praying, sewing, knitting or setting a table. Also refers to stage movement or pantomimic action.

CLEAR STAGE: An order given to the cast and/or crew to get off the stage before curtain rise. Also a warning to actors to get off stage before the set and furnishings are struck.

CROSS: Indicated by an "X" in script or master prompt book, it denotes movement from one place onstage to another.

CUE: The last words or business preceding an actor's lines or business. In some instances, the cue may be a light or sound effect.

CURTAIN: The drape which shuts the stage off from the audience. In the text, it denotes the end of a scene or act. When used by stage manager, it is the signal for raising or lowering the curtain.

CYCLORAMA or CYC: A background effect of curtain, usually made of canvas and hung around three sides of the stage or only on the back wall. It may be used as a sky-cloth or a background for a draped stage.

DISCOVERED: The actors as designated in the script, are to be onstage when curtain goes up.

DROP OR BACKDROP: A canvas or muslin cloth of large dimensions fastened at the top and bottom, which serves as a backdrop.

ENT.: Enter—to come onstage.

EX.: Exit—to go offstage.

FLAT: A section of theatrical scenery, made by canvas stretched over a flat wooden frame.

GELATINS or GELS: Thin colored transparent sheets used to color stage lights.

GROUNDCLOTH: A canvas covering the entire stage floor. This is an asset, for it absorbs the sound of footsteps.

HOLDING FOR LAUGHS: Waiting for the audience's laughter to subside, but not completely die out, before continuing the dialogue.

HOUSE: A theatre or auditorium used by audience; a place of entertainment.

OFFSTAGE: Out of the audience's view.

ONSTAGE: In the audience's view.

PHYSICALIZE: Do physical activities using objects convincingly—relate to and handle given objects realistically in executing practical "business."

PLACES: The warning for actors to take their positions for the beginning of a scene or act before the curtain goes up.

POINTING LINES: Emphasizing an idea by pausing before a key phrase and thus pointing it up.

PRACTICAL: Usable in a realistic way. A piece of scenery or a prop which can be used by the actors. A practical window or a practical door has to open and close readily. A practical rock has to bear the actor's weight. A practical stairway unit has to hold the actors' weight safely, permit the graceful ascent and descent of the steps and provide a convenient exit place backstage, out of the audience's view. If practical books are called for, painted bookshelves cannot serve, unless some space is allowed for the insertion and removal of actual books, when the business so requires. Hand props, such as a parasol or fan, must be workable, if the business so demands.

PROMPT BOOK: A copy of the working script in which all business and blocking (preferably in diagram) as well as light, sound and curtain warnings and cues are noted. The "master prompt book" is the production's definitive record guide, by which the stage manager runs the performances.

PROPERTIES or PROPS:

Stationary: Stage furnishings, including furniture.

Hand Props: Properties which the players carry for use during a scene: flowers, books, suitcases, teacups, etc.

Personal Props: Articles required by an individual player, which he carries on his person: a letter, pen, wallet, gloves, handkerchief, fan, walking-stick, eyeglasses, etc.

PROPERTY TABLE: One or more tables placed conveniently offstage, on which hand props are laid out in readiness for the actors' use.

PROSCENIUM: The architectural frame separating the stage from the auditorium.

RING UP: Signal for the curtain to rise for the beginning of a scene or act.

RING DOWN: Signal for the curtain to close at the end of a scene or act.

SET or SETTING: The scenery—interior or exterior—for a scene or act.

SIDES: Half-sheets of typewritten manuscript, containing lines, business and cues for a role.

SIGHT LINES: The lines of vision from the extreme position in the auditorium; limit of visibility to the audience.

STAND BY: The command to be ready and await a signal.

STRIKE: Signal to remove props, furniture or scenery from the stage.

TAKING THE STAGE: Moving freely and using the stage area advantageously with stage presence.

WINGS: Two or three flats hinged together, used as entrances or as masks for the sides of the stage.

CASTING

The final objective of *formal dramatics* (public performance) is not to be confused with that of *creative dramatics*. Since the best possible show, the most artistic entertainment attainable, must be presented within the limitations of the particular set-up, the director has no alternative but to "typecast," even in a school or camp situation. The parts simply have to be given those children who, in the director's judgment, possess the physical attributes, voice, talent and potential to portray the characters most believably.

This, however, does not exclude use of the "open casting" method which affords every child interested in a part a fair opportunity to try out for it. A word of warning may not be amiss regarding overzealousness in this connection, since the exigency of time demands that tryouts be limited to three sessions maximum. In the last analysis, casting is predicated on intuition. Even professional stage directors rely on hunches in making decisions. After some experience in casting, the teacher-leader will be able to determine a child's capacity for a role when only a few sentences are read. He will learn to trust his intuitive reactions.

If the director is not well-acquainted with the group, it is wiser to cast only tentatively at first, with the understanding that final choices will be made by the second reading rehearsal, contingent on who manifests greater promise and fits into the ensemble better. For expediency and morale reasons, decisions ought not be deferred any longer.

When and if practical, leading or all roles may be double-cast. This has the advantage of making standbys available for understudies or replacements in the event children take sick. On the other hand, if only a single performance is scheduled, complications are bound to arise. Furthermore, rehearsing two casts obviously entails double work.

CASTING PROCEDURE

At the first open casting session, the director reads the entire play aloud to the candidates who responded to the casting-call, briefly comments on the play's story-line, basic theme and background, describes the characters and their relationships, and specifies the requisite qualifications for each role.

Before auditioning, it is desirable to clarify several matters to the prospective cast—interpret the actor's responsibility and attendant obligations in accepting a part; explain that potential talent and suitability are not the only factors which influence casting; outline stage conduct rules, and stress the urgent need for abiding by them.

This is also a propitious time to point out the impossibility of everyone getting a lead, why each character is equally important to the play and production, and that a part cannot be measured by the number of lines.

Children often resist playing "bad" characters, such as Haman or Antiochus. In such event, it is necessary to persuade them that it is more challenging actually to enact tyrants than heroic figures, and if they succeed in portraying them convincingly, they will contribute to a better understanding of the Jews' tragic plight during those eras.

Copies of the script can then be distributed to the candidates, and auditions started. Any method deemed desirable may be used. If the director does not know the group, a possible procedure in order to start the ball rolling, might be to read the volunteers first, and subsequently, the others, so that each child has a chance to try out. The problem of choice is, of course, markedly simplified when the children and their abilities are known.

Suitability for a role can more readily be determined when different children read the same key speeches. The director can then compare relative potential in terms of physical type, voice quality, talent and convincingness. Other important considerations are the candidate's capacity to capture the character's essential qualities and his ability to respond to direction.

It is also necessary to weigh how prospects will fit into the ensemble. Inasmuch as the visual element is important in casting, the director has to consider relative physical appearance—contrast in coloring and varied proportions—and project how the candidate will look onstage. Incidentally, the director may discover a candidate's possible fitness for another part, and make notations accordingly.

Every precaution must be taken against favoring those who recently played major roles, no matter how "right" they are for the parts or how well they might do. The "star system" has no place or justification in amateur theatricals, certainly not in school or camp dramatics.

A 3" x 5" card index containing identifying data and results of readings should be kept by the stage manager during auditions. The following information noted on each card enables the director to recall candidates to memory when making decisions:

a) name
b) address
c) telephone number
d) age
e) class or group
f) height, weight and coloring
g) voice quality
h) part read
i) summation of impression made

After casting is closed, the director reviews the cards, judges the candidates' relative merits to decide who will shape up best, and eliminates unlikely prospects. Uncertainty about some roles is inevitable, in which event, two possibilities are temporarily retained for each.

Adequate advance notice to report for the first company call is to be given the children selected. When they assemble, those definitely cast may be commended, and the tentative choices assured that decisions will be made by the second reading rehearsal, or sooner.

STAGE DECORUM AND DISCIPLINE

While discipline is, of course, essential from the first tryout through the final performance, it need not be overly stringent or so rigidly imposed that it inhibits the children. They must, however, be impressed from the beginning with the necessity for dependability, regularity in attendance, punctuality and loyalty, and made to understand that unless the basic rules of stage conduct are complied with, their parts will be revoked.

During the final rehearsals onstage and during performances, players not appearing in scenes should be within easy call in dressing rooms or awaiting entrance cues in wings, under the supervision of a teacher or Assistant Stage Manager. If the dressing rooms adjoin the stage, the actors must be warned to subdue their voices and in no way interfere with onstage proceedings. Talking backstage or peeking through the curtain should be prohibited. Nothing stamps a production more amateurish. Staff and crew members are not excepted. If and when they have to communicate with each other, they can use a pre-arranged signal system.

In administering discipline, the director must be guided by the incontrovertible fact that children work best in a friendly relaxed atmosphere, and not lose sight of one of dramatics' major aims, namely, to furnish release.

By encouraging the democratic process—investing each child with a sense of responsibility—an *esprit de corps* will inevitably develop. Every child, no matter how minor the role, should be made to feel an integral part of the ensemble, indispensable to the production as a whole. Members of the cast will then discharge their individual as well as collective responsibilities, and work harmoniously together towards the production's ultimate success.

If the cast is integrated as a happy family unit, engaged in a pleasurable, gratifying undertaking, rehearsing will not smack of arduous compulsory work, reminiscent in any way of school chores. It will, on the contrary, take the form of an exciting game of make-believe and rehearsal calls will be looked forward to eagerly.

REHEARSAL SCHEDULING

Amateur presentations invariably suffer because of too little or too much rehearsing. Since amateurs are inclined to grow stale, it is unwise to prolong rehearsals over too lengthy a period. Therefore, concentrate rehearsals, when practical, during a three to five week span.

> *For an average or long one-acter*: Playing time 30-50 minutes, which entails memorization, characterization and blocking—12-15 rehearsals of two hours each are recommended.
>
> *For a short sketch or playlet*: Playing time 15-25 minutes, schedule 8-10 rehearsals of an hour and a half each.
>
> *For dramatic readings and simulated broadcasts*: 3-5 rehearsals of an hour or 1½ hours each are adequate.

It is exceedingly important, however, to use every moment of rehearsal time advantageously and not waste any part of the session on maintaining discipline or other extraneous matters. Children enjoy rehearsing, provided they are activated and productively engaged. Otherwise, they understandably become bored and restive.

The problem of occupying them usefully can partially be solved by staggering rehearsals—having different members of the cast report only as needed, at different times. It is also helpful to divide the cast into small groups and designate assistant stage managers to conduct line rehearsals. When the group is so divided, it is best to have each subgroup within easy supervision, in an adjoining or nearby room.

Personally, I have found private rehearsals with both professionals and amateurs of inestimable value. When the actors are coached or rehearsed individually, in pairs, or small units for scenes which involve only a few characters, without the entire cast present, a great deal more is accomplished.

After eliminating conflicts, a Rehearsal Schedule noting specific dates, days, hours and place is made up for the entire period, a copy posted on a conveniently accessible Bulletin Board and copies distributed to the cast and staff. In the event of changes, sufficient advance notice is to be given.

A definite deadline for "off book," when scripts no longer will be allowed, must be stipulated early in rehearsals, strictly adhered to and not deviated from under any circumstances. Every cast and staff member must clearly understand this.

During this period it is advantageous for cast members to get together whenever possible by themselves and run lines on their own; also to conduct supplementary line rehearsals with the entire cast. A number of positive gains ensue—memorization is accelerated, the children become accustomed to pick up cues promptly and develop self-confidence.

Understandably, the more rehearsals held onstage in actual set with the actual props and wardrobe, the more assured the children will be by performance time. Six to eight onstage rehearsals are advocated. If unfeasible, because of the auditorium's unavailability, arrange for at least three rehearsals in actual set with the actual props and costumes. This minimum is absolutely essential, and no part of the time allocated may be used for any other purpose. In such event, technical run-throughs must be held before.

Final rehearsals should not be interrupted for any reason whatsoever. Instead, the director carefully notes all details which require correction. It is imperative for the cast, stage manager and technical crew to carry on independently. Furthermore, playing time has to be recorded. During these rehearsals, it is advisable that the director work from various parts of the auditorium in order to test visibility and audibility. When each rehearsal is over, the director meets with the entire cast and staff to give criticism and recommendations for changes.

READING REHEARSALS

Two or three sessions devoted to round-table readings during preliminary rehearsal period prove decidedly beneficial. The actors who are tentatively or definitely cast read their respective parts. If both tentative and positive prospects get a chance to read with the company, it is easier for the director to determine who would fit into the ensemble better. Seating the players involved in joint scenes near each other helps them establish a closer rapport and integrate relationships.

Everyone in the cast has to be given a complete script and cautioned not to lose or mar it. The use of "sides," containing only actual speeches and cues, is impractical and outmoded. The stage manager has to keep an accurate record of all scripts distributed, so that copies may be recalled from those eliminated.

The first reading rehearsal is opportune for assigning assistant stage managerial or other duties to the more mature members of the group, who have small roles.

Reading rehearsals are designed to familiarize the cast with the play, its background, setting, mood, characters and relationships. Group readings prove invaluable for clarifying and developing characterization, as well as unifying the company.

Discussion should be stimulated and all cast and staff members encouraged to contribute their ideas. Discussion will more readily be engendered if the director prompts the children to ask the following leading questions:

1. Who am I? (in terms of age, nationality, social group, religion, occupation, educational-cultural family background, status)
2. What do I want?
3. Why do I want it?
4. Where am I? (in terms of country, locale, specific place)
5. Why am I here?
6. Where do I come from?
7. When is it? (in terms of time of day, season, year and period)
8. What is he (she) to me? (relative to characters who appear during the course of the play, as well as those merely alluded to)
9. What do I want to get (give) him (her)?
10. Why do I want to do so?
11. Why do I say what I say?
12. Why do I do what I do?

This procedure cannot but produce a closer identification

with the characters and situations, besides sharpen awareness and believability.

If the children concern themselves with the relevant who, why, when, what, where and wherefore, rather than "how to," their acting will inevitably be meaningful and truthful. To paraphrase Shakespeare: "It must follow, as the night, the day, they cannot then be false to any role or character."

Encourage the cast to prepare biographies of the characters, by recreating their probable past lives and filling in details to supplement the playwright's contribution. They should be guided to work in specifics and particularize concretely. Generalities are dangerous and produce cliché caricatures instead of rounded, three-dimensional, life-like characterizations. If this procedure is followed, the children will acquire a more profound understanding of the reasons for the characters' present behavior, and as a result, motivate and justify their actions more convincingly.

Reading rehearsals offer a favorable opportunity to set exemplary speech patterns and stress the urgent need for listening. Accustom the children to establish connection, look at each other, talk *to* and *with* each other—exchange ideas, really converse and communicate. Encourage them to phrase rhythmically, stop only at the end of thoughts and enunciate distinctly throughout.

REHEARSAL PROCEDURE

First, a few suggestions: It is unrealistic to expect to accomplish everything at once. Therefore, aim for *one* specific, reasonable goal at each rehearsal and direct all efforts toward its attainment. Guard against making undue demands on yourself or the cast.

Avoid demonstrating stage business, promoting imitative gesturing or reproducing line readings insofar as possible. In most instances, the children will come through with the sought-for result, provided what is required has been clearly explained. Demonstration may be resorted to only after several attempts to stimulate creatively fail. In that event, the director has to make sure that the momentum eventually emanates from the player.

Occasionally, even a professional stage director with extensive experience, encounters a snag and is at a loss as to how to proceed. However, the cast is never made cognizant of this.

When working with children, it is doubly important to avoid conveying uncertainty or subjecting them to any pressure the director may undergo. If the project has been well-organized and adequate rehearsal time scheduled, there is no valid reason for frenzied nervous tension either during the period of rehearsal or performance, which, unfortunately, marks many amateur presentations.

A competent reliable stage manager on the staff is indispensable to a production's success. His function is to coordinate the separate facets of production, efficiently handle pre-production and rehearsal details and run performances smoothly. One of his major duties is to hold the script during rehearsals and record the business and blocking, the latter, preferably in diagram. If the master prompt book is to serve as the production's definitive guide, the stage manager must keep a complete accurate record of every detail. He is also responsible for marking the set's outline on rehearsal room and stage floors, in accordance with the Scene Designer's ground plan; he arranges placement of furniture, props and other essentials; supervises lights, sound effects, costumes and properties; maintains company discipline and takes over when the director is away. If no one in the group is equipped to discharge the duties of this key post, the aid of a faculty member should be enlisted.

Instruct the members of the cast to write their individual business in their own scripts. Since children memorize easily and business affects the rhythm of delivery, caution them not to commit lines to memory until scenes are blocked. They will better synchronize the business with the dialogue when they learn both simultaneously.

Persuade the children to take the following steps at rehearsals and performances. This will help in establishing and sustaining characterization.

1. *Relax*: sit, stand and move naturally, like a real person in real life.
2. *Concentrate*: focus your attention on the required point of interest and do not permit anything to intrude or divert you.
3. *Listen*: actively and actually, *not* simulatedly, merely awaiting cues.
4. *React*: always as if for the first time—to partners'

speeches as though you never heard them before, to events as though they never happened before.
5. *Believe*: implicitly in the reality of the character, situations, relationships and surroundings, in order to create the *illusion* of reality.
6. *Identify*: relate to the character and his experiences as though they were happening to *you*.
7. *Sharpen awareness*: of the place, time, period, relationships, etc.
8. *Motivate and Justify*: know the reasons for each action, speech, piece of business and movement—what you want to achieve and *why*.
9. *Make dialogue your own*: render your speeches with such conviction each time that it seems you are making them up yourself for the first time. Think, see, believe, feel, then say your lines and sustain to give the audience a chance to absorb what you convey.
10. *Add "sub-text"*: supplement the character's thoughts and feelings which are unexpressed in the dialogue. Add the lines between the lines.
11. *Visualize*: see vivid pictures in your mind's eye while talking, so the audience, in turn, sees graphic images.
12. *Realize, actualize* and *finalize*: bring everything to ultimate fruition; make everything happen in the *now*—the immediate present.
13. *Communicate*: convey ideas and feelings to your partners, impel them to hear and understand. Then, you will communicate with the audience too.
14. *Physicalize convincingly*: do physical activities actually, not synthetically, and handle objects as though they were real.
15. *Sustain characterization*: establish the character *before* entrance and sustain characterization until *after* exit, when completely out of audience's view.

DOING JUSTICE TO THE TEXT

The following pertinent quotations serve a director in good stead. When staging a production, they warrant being borne in mind as a constant reminder and guide.

"Drama is really a verb masquerading as a noun."
"Talk may be the crust of drama, but it can never be the core."—*Time Magazine*
"Judged by their words all men are the same. It is their deeds that unmask their difference. The only thing that counts with man is his deed. The whole conduct of man is a deed."—*Jean Baptiste Molière*
"A play is not constructed on lines of dialogue. A play is fundamentally a series of actions."—*Harold Clurman*

The validity of these cogent statements does not, however, nullify the text's importance. Notwithstanding the greater significance of actions—doing, being, happening—the text is another means for realizing the play, and it is incumbent on the director and cast to do justice to the text. The inner meaning must be extracted and communicated to the audience. Communication is, after all, a primary purpose of drama.

Amateurs, on the one hand, are prone to take the text for granted and fail to appreciate the magic or import of the word. On the other hand, amateurs tend to be so dependent on the text, actually bound by it, that except when verbalizing, they are at a loss for what to do. The director can help overcome these adverse tendencies by stimulating an awareness of the "sub-text" —the thoughts and problems behind the actual dialogue, the lines between the lines. Communication will thus be furthered.

In order to make the dialogue come alive, discard the script for part or a whole session and have the cast paraphrase the text, supplement the in-between lines, and improvise on probable situations preceding the play's opening as well as on situations referred to. This procedure warrants experimentation, for many positives follow. The improvisations serve a two-fold purpose— they enliven the text and warm up the cast to "tune" into character and mood.

Mechanical recitative delivery must be steered clear of at all times, for it vitiates the text's inherent meaning. Natural, conversational, convincing delivery, real talk as in real life, is the ideal to strive for. This can be achieved by encouraging the children to make the lines their own, and imbue them with conviction, color, variety, immediacy and spontaneity—"invent" them, as it were, each and every time, as if for the first time.

Descriptive passages, expository speeches of reminiscence, or conjecture about the future, require these qualities doubly.

It is a good idea to remind the cast that the dictionary defines *word* as: "A speech sound that symbolizes and *communicates* a *meaning*," and to point out that a word is intended to serve as a means of communication, *not* as an end in itself.

"The worst crime," virtuoso violinist Isaac Stern asserts, "is to play notes instead of making music." His apt observation is indeed applicable to dialogue delivery, for to speak empty words without feeling, and fail to interpret ideas and express emotions, does both the text and playwright a grave injustice.

The following excerpt from *Hamlet's Advice to the Players* is a most apropos warning to the cast:

"Speak the speech, I pray you, as I pronounced it to you, trippingly on the tongue: but if you mouth it, as many of your players do, I had as lief the town-crier spoke my lines."

PROJECTION

Projection, the act of communicating vividly to an audience, is largely a matter of being *willing to be heard,* concentrating on reaching the people in the last row and involving them. The children must realize that unless they are heard and understood by everyone in the auditorium, their performing is pointless. Clarity, audibility, and comprehensibility are essential. The voice has to be pitched to the balcony's back wall and ample resonant sound used. This does not imply mere loudness or shouting.

When facing upstage or seated on the stage floor, the actor has to take special care to speak more slowly and distinctly, and to intentionally amplify his voice. Otherwise, the dialogue is lost.

The amateur's anxiety to get the performance over with as quickly as possible partially accounts for his garbled, inaudible speech. Indifference, improper breathing, choppy delivery, lack of energy, as well as a lack of variety in color, emphasis and tempo are other contributory factors.

The problem of indistinct speech and resultant faulty projection can, to some extent, be obviated if the cast is trained to relax, breathe deeply, bring love, enthusiasm and vitality to the playing, give every syllable of every word its due value, phrase correctly, and enunciate distinctly. Distinct enunciation does not, of course, mean overly precise diction, which should under no circumstances be permitted, for it sounds affected and insincere.

Caution the children to refrain from distorting vowels, mispronouncing consonants, rushing speeches, running words together, mumbling and trailing off into an unintelligible monotone, as they are wont to do. Delivery will then be markedly improved and projection advanced.

PROPER PHRASING AND PAUSING

In order to make the sense of the words perfectly clear, it is necessary to phrase speeches properly and intersperse pauses at the end of thoughts. As in normal conversation, sentences have to be broken up into thought groups, and the groups set off from each other by pauses. A text's punctuation cannot adequately serve as a satisfactory guide for maximal interpretive delivery. Therefore, the director has to help the children make up their own punctuation, to simplify pausing at the end of thought groups. Understandably, the number of words in a group differs with the thought. On occasion, a single word may comprise a group. At other times, as many as ten words comprise a group, but on the average, five or six. Inasmuch as phrasing must always be smooth and rhythmic, never staccato or choppy, discourage unwarranted stops.

Pauses are often as significant as words themselves. In fact, a pause or dramatic silence, may well be more effective than words. Urge the cast to develop an awareness of the dramatic value of pauses and use them to advantage. Pauses must, however, be filled in by active thinking and feeling. An empty pause causes a blank spot, which is tantamount to a hole, detrimentally affects pacing and makes the scene drag. Pauses at the end of thoughts provide an opportunity to breathe in between groups, but more importantly, permit actualizing and finalizing, so that the meaning is clarified and more directly communicated to the audience for assimilation.

TRANSITIONS

According to the dictionary definition, a *transition* is: "A passage from one state, stage, place or subject to another; a change." This largely applies to acting too, for a transition is a change in subject, attitude, mood, feeling or relationship. Transitions necessitate variations in tone, pace, motivation and justification. Amateurs mistakenly rush transitions, anticipating what is to follow, instead of pausing and allowing one change to flow into the next. Any tendency to rush transitions has to be curbed.

QUESTIONS

When asking a question, the player should deliver it so that it rings out quizzically with a rising inflection that impels an answer. The question must be sustained until *after* the answer is given. This also holds true for abstract questions, the proverbial cry in the wilderness and the rhetorical question.

If questions are put with conviction and motivated to get answers, the right result will inevitably occur. In respect to questions, amateurs invariably are prone to think that they are finished before they actually are. The director, therefore, has to guard against this, and encourage the cast to sustain the question, actively listen to the reply, and react in accordance with the given circumstances.

INCOMPLETE INTERRUPTED SENTENCES

Sometimes a sentence in the script is expressly incomplete—to be broken in on. The actor who is interrupted has to finish the thought either mentally, or even verbally, ad-libbing the word or words. The actor doing the interrupting must come in very quickly with his speech. It is preferable that lines be stepped on, (both talk simultaneously) rather than have a meaningless empty pause. Leaving the thought unfinished, suspended in mid-air, not only creates a blank spot, but indicates a lack of identification with the character and a parrot-like mouthing of words.

TELEPHONE CONVERSATIONS

In order to make telephone conversations truly convincing, it is necessary to fill in the actual dialogue of the person supposedly at the other end of the line. If the player conversing on the telephone, while rehearsing, writes in and memorizes the imagined speeches of the other party, actively listens and reacts to them, the sequence when played will be more believable.

Counting to suggest the listening interval is wrong, for it results in mechanical responses.

PACING

The fact that a play acquires the right pacing by the prompt picking up of cues, and *not* through the rapid delivery of lines or rushing of transitions, must constantly be borne in mind. Picking up cues is, in some respects, like playing ping-pong. It is a matter of serve, return, serve, return at a fast clip; otherwise, the ball is missed. Similarly, unless cues are picked up with alacrity, the players continuously giving and taking, the actors have "missed the ball" and the timing suffers.

Comedy dialogue demands a quicker, brighter delivery than serious drama and an even faster picking up of cues. Comedy dialogue must be said with greater zest, sparkle and variety, and the give-and-take between fellow-actors and audience more consistently maintained.

POINTING UP FOR LAUGHS

Inflection is a most important factor in playing comedy. Laughter can more readily be provoked by pointing up a key laugh line in a seemingly casual manner, yet, hinting at the same time that it is funny. Under no circumstances should dialogue be continued while the audience is laughing. It is necessary for the player to defer the speech until the wave of laughter almost, but not completely subsides, and then resume.

Understandably, this is difficult even for professionals. It requires skill in playing, exposure to varied audiences through repeated performances, and a sharp awareness of audience reaction. However, children appearing in a comedy can at least be made to realize how unwise it is to step on an audience's laughter and thus squelch it. Obviously, bits of dialogue are bound to get lost when continued through laughter. Even worse, the audience's desire to laugh again is curbed, lest important lines be missed.

POINTING UP FOR EMPHASIS

An effective means of emphasis, infrequently used by amateurs, is the pause, before *or* after an important word or phrase, or before *and* after the word or phrase.

Both proper and family names require pointing up, so that

the audience can clearly catch them. It is necessary to enunciate the name distinctly, as well as pause before and after the name.

The more common forms of emphasis are: variations in force, duration and pitch—the latter being the most effective.

GESTURES

Children, as a general rule, find it difficult to sustain concentration for prolonged periods onstage, unless trained and experienced in professional theatre work. They tend to fidget, move about aimlessly, shift or swing their feet, wave their arms and indulge in other manifestations of restlessness. Since diffuse excessive movement distracts an audience, it is imperative to prevail upon the cast to refrain from extraneous gestures and movement.

Every gesture and move must be purposeful, appropriate to the character and occasion, and correlated with the speech. Cliché gestures stereotype rather than characterize and should be avoided. If a gesture is to convey meaning, it cannot be tentative, for a half-gesture is worse than none.

Encourage the children to stand or sit quietly, in repose, to actively listen and react while onstage, in order to remain a living part of the scene, even when not speaking.

In connection with gesturing, it is well to have them follow Hamlet's advice:

"Do not saw the air too much with your hand . . . suit the action to the word, the word to the action."

PHYSICALIZING

Physicalizing—doing practical physical activities with objects—relating to and handling the objects in a realistic convincing manner, as for example, weaving strands of yarn on a loom, painting a canvas with brushes and a palette, playing a musical instrument (a guitar, mandolin, violin, harmonica, etc.) engages the child's interest and keeps his hands occupied. Physicalizing can prove an invaluable aid in overcoming self-consciousness and solving the problem of nervous mannerisms to some extent. The physical activity must, of course, be suitable to the character, situation and period.

While the script usually suggests likely business, it is necessary for the director to supplement pieces of inventive business to fill in interesting details. The following possibilities may serve in good stead for different plays:

FOR INTERIOR SCENES

1. Reading a book, magazine, or newspaper.
2. Writing a letter or report; doing homework or accounts.
3. Doing handiwork: sewing, darning, embroidering, needlepoint, knitting, crocheting, weaving (cloth at a loom, or a straw basket).
4. Sketching, painting, drawing, coloring with crayons, carving, whittling, sculpting. Drawing or writing on a blackboard and erasing.
5. Practicing or playing a musical instrument of the period.
6. Working on a coin, stamp, butterfly collection or other such hobby.
7. Telephoning—looking up a number in a directory and making notes in conjunction with that activity.
8. Hanging a picture or curtains.
9. Winding and setting a clock or watch.
10. Sweeping, dusting, sorting laundry, washing, ironing, making a bed, rearranging furniture, washing dishes, stacking, drying, putting them away in the cupboard, and other likely household chores.
11. Building or stoking a fire in a stove or fireplace.
12. Washing and dressing young children, tucking them into bed, rocking a cradle, etc.
13. Activities connected with daily dressing ritual: selecting and arranging clothes, washing, brushing teeth, shining shoes, combing and brushing hair, manicuring nails, putting clothes on, removing outdoor garb.
14. Polishing brass or silver: candlesticks, trays, wine goblets, flatware, in preparation for a holiday.
15. Arranging flowers, watering plants.
16. Preparing a meal: peeling potatoes or apples, stringing beans, shelling peas, beating eggs, sifting flour, mixing ingredients for a cake, kneading dough, cooking.
17. Eating or drinking.
18. Setting a table for mid-week, Sabbath, holiday or Passover Seder and serving a meal. Conducting the Seder.
19. Lighting the Sabbath, holiday or Hanukkah candles and saying the prayer; preparing for the ritual.

20. Cutting the *chalah,* saying the blessing over bread. Washing hands prior to eating and saying the accompanying prayer. Reciting Grace after meals.
21. Pouring wine and saying "Havdalah," holding *havdalah* candle.
22. Praying—putting on phylacteries or prayer shawl.
23. Wrapping or unwrapping a parcel. Preparing *Shalah Manot* in readiness for *Mishloah Manot.*
24. Playing cards (solitaire or in a group), shuffling and dealing, dominoes, checkers, chess, Scrabble.
25. Playing with a ball, ball and jacks, marbles, nuts, blocks, toys, games, jig-saw puzzle, doll.
26. Making doll's clothes, dressing a doll; making paper cutouts.
27. Playing with and stroking a household pet; feeding fish in an aquarium, feeding a bird in cage, a cat or a dog.
28. Packing or unpacking a trunk, suitcase, school bag.
29. Using hand props such as a cane, parasol, umbrella, fan, bandana, handkerchief, eyeglasses.
30. Dancing.

FOR EXTERIOR SCENES

1. Washing at a well, pump or stream.
2. Drawing water or pumping water.
3. Carrying earthenware jugs to a watering-place and filling them.
4. Doing laundry at a stream or river.
5. Fishing—baiting hook, casting, reeling in.
6. Gardening—digging a hole in ground, planting, pulling up weeds, raking leaves.
7. Picking flowers, berries, or fruit.
8. Chopping and carrying wood.
9. Gathering twigs or wood for a fire.
10. Building a camp-fire.
11. Rigging up a tripod for a cauldron.
12. Marching and carrying flags or pennants.
13. Standing watch as a sentinel or *shomer* on lookout duty.

14. Exploring for snakes and other wild creatures.
15. Chasing butterflies.
16. Shooting arrows; playing with swords; playing at fencing, boxing, wrestling.
17. Flying a kite or balloon; spinning a top; blowing soap bubbles; bouncing a ball, playing catch, playing marbles; running; swinging and climbing a tree (if set permits); skipping rope; skipping; playing hide-and-seek.
18. Decorating a *Sukkah.*
19. Carrying *Shalah Manot,* a *Lulav,* groceries, baskets, wine jugs.
20. Loading a wheelbarrow, pushcart or other vehicle.
21. Wheeling a baby or doll carriage.
22. Dancing, preferably folk-dancing, so that hands are occupied with hand props: kerchiefs, bandanas, tambourines, castanets.

CHARACTER PARTS

Prevail upon those children cast as old men or old women to study the characteristics and behavior of old people and base their portrayals on firsthand observation. Caution them to beware of clichés—stereotyped, "phoney" voices and mannerisms—lest the aged appear ridiculous.

It is exceedingly important to arouse children's sympathy for the old, so they acquire a more profound insight into the inevitable deteriorative effects of aging. The children who play such character parts should be aware of the fact that advancing years invariably bring on a slowing-up process, an arteriosclerotic stiffening of the joints, which cause uncertainty of movement and dependency; that impaired vision and hearing contribute to slower reflexes and responses, and an attendant slackening in the rate of speech.

Point out that even the very old are not necessarily crippled, stooped, doddering or afflicted with palsy, neither do their bodies tremble, nor their voices quaver as a matter of course. The children will then delineate old people more truly.

Care must also be exercised in depicting the inebriated, for exaggeration produces ludicrous results and destroys audience believability.

As an aid in developing character, the director may find it helpful to suggest an image of a bird or animal which the character evokes. This proves a powerful impetus to the imagination, especially when children have to enact parts which are remote from their immediate life experiences.

BIT PARTS

The children cast in minor or non-speaking roles require special attention to aid them develop rounded characterizations. They are otherwise unrelated to the play and proceedings, work in a vacuum, feel and look bewildered while onstage. Nothing can be left to chance. Unless *supers* (walk-ons or bit players) concretely know what impels their being in a scene, it is impossible for them to function effectively and they unintentionally destroy whatever atmosphere is created. In order to circumvent this, it is necessary to assign each child specific things to do, and in some cases, specific dialogue to say—either *sotto voce* or loudly—depending on the circumstances.

Crowd scenes with soldiers, chamberlains, peasants and townspeople demand such treatment particularly. The director has to help the children personalize, individualize and particularize, by giving them definite details about the characters and the motivating reasons for their presence. Then, their acting will be convincing, integrated and contribute to the scene's dramatic impact.

DIALECT

When a part calls for the use of dialect, care must be taken to eliminate any exaggeration on the part of the actor, lest ridicule of a nationality, minority group or race be implied. A mere suggestion of the dialect is preferable, by far, than gross exaggeration, which distorts and caricatures. It is sufficient to capture the essential quality of the regionalism or native language —the indigenous rhythm and authentic inflection.

LIGHTING

Of all the technical aspects of production, lighting is, by far, the most effective means for creating atmosphere. Artistic lighting establishes mood, locale, time of day, season and weather, heightens dramatic values, and enhances scenery, costumes and make-up.

Its primary purpose, however, is to illuminate the actors and action for maximum visibility. If the audience is compelled to strain its eyes in order to see plainly, hearing and understanding will also be adversely affected.

The amateur director is usually handicapped in achieving appropriate effects because of limited equipment. Flexible modern lighting equipment, consisting of a portable switchboard with dimmers and borders, supplemented by spotlights and strategically placed baby spots, is a prime requisite for artistic results.

Lacking these essentials, the director has to make the most of whatever equipment is available, and advantageously use *point lighting*—illumination from light sources such as property lanterns, lamps, chandeliers or fireplaces. Point lighting serves adequately in a small auditorium, provided sufficient lamps are used.

Hanging several hooded lamps with reflectors just above the proscenium and acquiring (buying or renting) several baby lens lamps help immeasurably.

When rigging reflectors for these lights, care should be taken to concentrate the rays onto the acting area and justify the light as coming from natural sources—sky, windows, French or other doors, lamps.

Gelatin, the thin, colored, transparent sheets for covering stage lights, should be put in front of the lens or mouth of the equipment. In working out the color scheme, use a variety of colored gels. The more delicate tones are preferable. Gels can be obtained inexpensively in a wide range of colors from any theatrical electrician. The choice of colors requires careful consideration, for gels act as a filter and affect both color and texture of scenery, furnishings, costumes and make-up.

Colored silk, cellophane or paper can also serve as covering for light bulbs. However, they are not fireproof. It is imperative, therefore, to use wire-protectors with them, in order to avoid accidents.

Light rehearsals demand considerable time and patience. Aesthetic effects are attainable only through experimentation. Light rehearsals should be held after the set is completely dressed, but without the cast.

In order not to disturb the audience, light changes must be gradual—operated smoothly and unobtrusively. All lights have to be properly adjusted and checked from different parts of the auditorium to make sure they will not shine into the audience's eyes during the performance.

When a play has more than one scene, a subtle blackout of lights to indicate the termination of a scene is more desirable than drawing the curtain between scenes. It is inadvisable, however, to hold the blackout too long, for an audience tends to grow restive in total darkness. Blackouts have to be handled carefully—dimmed gradually to a fade-out and then blacked out—otherwise, they are disruptive.

Ingenious lighting equipment can be homemade at a minimal cost. The bibliography lists several excellent books on the subject. The director, on investigation, will usually discover several boys in the school, center or camp who have had shop or vocational training and are skilled along these lines. If activated in such a project under an electrician's supervision, they will capably construct the necessary equipment, and thus save the expense of buying or renting it. Their contribution will prove invaluable, for adequate lighting equipment is a great asset and indispensable to any drama group.

MAKE-UP

Make-up is an art which requires skill and patience to practice effectively. The make-up artist should have the facility of a portrait-painter, a knowledge of facial structure, and familiarity with the coloring and bone formation of various nationalities.

Make-up, if deftly applied, proves a decided asset to a production. When the physical characteristics of a role are emphasized, the actor automatically looks and feels more the type. It especially aids the child-actor to forget self and identify with the character.

Two types of make-up are used in the theatre: straight and character. Straight make-up is intended to improve the actor's appearance so as to create the illusion of greater attractiveness. The purpose of character make-up is to change the actor's appearance altogether, in order to establish middle or old-age, nationality, outdoor occupations (sailors, farmers, fishermen) or illness.

Unless adequate stage lighting and gelatin media are available, it is best to use make-up, whether straight or character, sparingly. Mere suggestion—a slight touching up of the face, combined with appropriate hairdos and headgear—suffices when lighting equipment is limited. Excessive make-up—chalk-white foundation, round spots of bright red rouge on cheeks, heavy eyeshadow, cupid-shaped lips—which I have all too frequently seen in amateur productions, must be avoided, for it makes the actors look more like clowns than human-beings. This kind of make-up does not add artistic values, but detracts. Make-up must be neither obvious nor obtrusive.

It is advantageous for every drama group to have a completely outfitted make-up kit, and a Make-up Director in charge of applying it. A staff member, preferably from the Art Department, should be designated to study the subject thoroughly and supervise this very important, but often neglected, phase of production. The simplified books on the art of make-up listed in the bibliography will prove helpful.

After mastering the fundamentals, the Make-up Director should, in turn, train others to share the responsibility. The cast can readily be taught to handle the elementary steps—application of cold cream and basic coat, as well as removal of make-up. The older girls in the group will, after a while, learn to make themselves up adeptly, and if asked, will gladly help with the younger children.

Since the burden of making up an entire cast usually falls on the shoulders of one, or at best, a few persons, provision must be made for adequate time to make up everyone, without creating tension prior to the performance and delaying curtain.

Under no circumstances should wigs be used. They are not only exceedingly expensive, but look ludicrous unless specially fitted for the individual. A fringe of white or grey crepe hair sewn to the edge of a period hat or cap can serve the purpose of a wig.

In order to achieve an illusion of maturity or old age with children, beards, especially little chin beards, are extremely helpful. While wigmakers rent and sell false beards and mustaches of human hair sewn onto gauze, it is both cheaper and better to make them of crepe hair. Caution should be taken to apply sufficient spirit gum so that the beards and mustaches stick firmly throughout the performance.

Besides lining the face with wrinkles, aging can be achieved by greying or whitening the hair. An application of white mascara, white grease paint or cornstarch at the temples, suggests middle age; silvery white aluminum powder on the entire head suggests old age. To make certain the application clings, it is advisable to oil the hair slightly first. Aluminum powder and cornstarch have drawbacks, however. The former is difficult to wash out, and the latter brushes off and dulls the hair's natural highlights. No matter what application is used, care must be taken to distribute the greying evenly, by combing it through the hair. The eyebrows cannot be neglected, but have to be treated similarly.

Since beards and mustaches affect clarity of speech, the cast requires ample opportunity to become accustomed to them. At least two rehearsals—"dress parade" and "dress rehearsal"—should be allocated for this purpose.

PRACTICAL HINTS FOR ACTORS

The following cautionary "don'ts" given to the cast before final rehearsals may serve as practical hints and prompt the right results at performance:

1. Don't step out of character from entrance until after exit.
2. Don't be worried, scared or nervous.
3. Don't get tired, bored or restless.
4. Don't move, gesture or say your lines without playing the reason.
5. Don't do or say anything tentatively, insincerely or without conviction, unless the character demands your doing so.
6. Don't anticipate what you are about to say or do.
7. Don't rush transitions.
8. Don't orate or declaim.
9. Don't use an artificial affected voice or diction.
10. Don't speak indistinctly or let your voice fall away at the end of sentences.
11. Don't clear your throat while onstage—swallow instead.
12. Don't stop in the middle of a thought, unless situation demands it.
13. Don't chop your speeches—phrase rhythmically.
14. Don't plod lines or drag scenes out.

15. Don't wait to pick up cues, unless there is a justifiable reason for hesitating or pausing.
16. Don't be through before you are finished.
17. Don't fluff lines or go blank (forget).
18. Don't go back if you make a mistake—carry on instead.
19. Don't lose stage awareness: sit on a book, a coat, knitting or other prop. Don't fail to cover up when a sound or other cue is late.
20. Don't do two things at the same time.
21. Don't permit props to clutter you.
22. Don't listen or do business simulatedly—do it actually.
23. Don't make unnecessary gestures or indulge in nervous movements or mannerisms, namely: swing feet, shift weight, twist fingers, lick lips, play with a ring or pendant, tug at dress or jacket.
24. Don't keep hands buried in pockets or hide them, unless business so requires.
25. Don't "hug" (hang onto) furniture.
26. Don't pull on your beard, mustache or wig.
27. Don't mask (cover) anyone onstage or let anyone cover you. Give—take a few paces—to right or left, so that you and your partner are always seen by the audience.
28. Don't "break" or giggle.
29. Don't "fake," "ham," or "mug." Don't overact, exaggerate facial expression or business, and "steal scenes" by resorting to tricks so that the audience will watch you instead of important happenings onstage. Don't overdo anything so that it is phoney or false. Don't distract the audience's attention by over-playing with a hand prop, such as a fan, handkerchief, etc.

PRACTICAL HINTS FOR DIRECTORS

The following cautionary "don'ts" are suggested as helpful reminders to the director:

1. Don't rehearse the first act at the expense of the last, if a long play; or, the beginning of a one-acter to the exclusion of the last part. In fact, the ending must be rehearsed more.
2. Don't fail to give special attention to the openings and finales of scenes.
3. Don't permit actors to be masked. Be sure they give (move

a few paces) as fellow-actors cross in front of them, so they are not covered at any time.
4. Don't bury actors behind furniture. Children's bodies seem to be cut off by furniture. Therefore, keep them right or left of sofa, chair, etc.
5. Don't have stiff straight lines across stage. When blocking, make certain to arrange for broken lines instead, to achieve pictorially interesting groupings.
6. Don't use unwieldy, clumsy properties.
7. Don't use wigs.
8. Don't permit excessive make-up.
9. Don't make last minute changes in blocking, business, interpretation, or anything else.
10. Don't forget to rehearse curtain calls.
11. Don't break in to correct at final rehearsals. Make notes instead.
12. Don't remain in one seat during final rehearsals. Change to different parts of auditorium to make certain of maximum audibility and visibility for the entire audience.
13. Don't have the children eat toast, crackers or other food irritating to throat. Don't be overly conscientious about business of eating or drinking. Eating hampers diction, and it is especially difficult for amateurs to manage and correlate swallowing with speaking. A mere suggestion to establish the fact of eating suffices.
14. Don't use water or other liquids unless absolutely essential for business. Colored glasses, opaque pitchers or wine-bottles are preferable, and avoid accidents.
15. Don't be careless about details, as for example:
    a) permit wristwatches or nail polish in a Biblical or period play.
    b) keds, socks or other inappropriate footwear with a royal costume.
    c) unpressed costumes or soiled, creased articles of apparel.
    d) uneven hem-lines.
    e) threads hanging from hems, sleeves, etc.
    f) safety-pins showing.
    g) old age make-up on face, but not on neck, back of ears and hands.
    h) props which are foreign to the period or locale, or which were not invented at the time.

i) use of theme-mood music or songs that are extrinsic to period.
   j) permit dolls (supposedly babies) to be naked or uncovered by blankets in mid-winter.
   k) permit anything which might be interpreted as desecration of a religious ritual:
      1. prayers not rendered with due piety.
      2. *chalah* or *matzot* not covered with a suitable cloth.
      3. prayer shawl or *siddur* handled irreverently.
      4. a pious man not wearing a *yarmulke*.
      5. a pious woman not donning a head-covering when kindling Shabbat or holiday candles.
16. Don't fail to have the stage manager soap or chalk all mirrors, so that reflection does not annoy the audience.
17. Don't forget to have final rehearsals as well as performances timed, in order to have an accurate record of playing time. If running time exceeds the time alloted, determine the cause of the lagging and rectify it.
18. Don't forget to check on all technical details with the stage manager considerably in advance of curtain opening at final rehearsals and performances:
    a) batteries in perfect working order for door-bells, telephone rings, sound-table hookup.
    b) light bulbs in lamps, and fireplace, properly connected.
    c) prop-tables with required props conveniently laid out.
    d) every piece of furniture on markings, as rehearsed.
19. Don't fail to visit dressing rooms to give cast a "pep talk" —thank everyone and wish them well. Include the stage manager, assistants and crew, make-up and costume department heads and assistants.
20. Don't, if at all possible, remain backstage during the performance. Rely on the stage manager to supervise physical aspects of the production. He is supposed to be in complete charge of the stage during performances and direct behind the scenes. Your presence will tend to make the cast and staff nervous.
21. Don't go backstage or into dressing rooms during the performance, except in an emergency.
22. Don't admonish the cast or staff when you do go back during intermission; compliment them instead to spur them on to better performances. While it is permissible to make sug-

gestions as to audibility or pacing, anything else burdens and confuses.
23. Don't fail to go backstage after curtain calls to congratulate the cast and staff members and thank them for their cooperation and for acquitting themselves so creditably, irrespective of how they did.
24. Don't ever permit your concern about the production's failure or success to be conveyed to the cast or staff.

CURTAIN CALLS

Regardless of how late the program concludes, the cast merits the gratification of receiving at least one curtain call, granting, of course, that audience reaction warrants it!

To deprive a cast of acknowledging an audience's applause is tantamount to not thanking a donor for a gift. To deprive an audience of expressing its appreciation is tantamount to a hostess summarily dismissing invited guests. It is frustrating to audience and actors alike.

Except in cases of emergency—illness, need to catch a train, or the presence of very young children who must be taken home—every member of the cast should remain in full costume and make-up to wait for curtain calls.

In the professional theatre, both union and management require *all* members of a cast to remain for curtain calls. This is a long-standing theatre tradition, in fact, an unwritten law, by which all performers are expected to abide unless excused because of another work commitment or some pressing personal business. To break this cardinal stage rule is considered an affront to the theatre-going public. Amateurs would do well to emulate it.

Curtain calls cannot be left to chance. They have to be rehearsed several times, so that the ensemble is groomed to take bows in a dignified, gracious manner and get into proper formation.

On final curtain, the stage crew is responsible for the speedy removal of any furniture downstage near the curtain line, which might obstruct the cast's formation. The cast then lines up in a semi-circle—the tallest children in the center, the shortest, stage right and stage left. Each child should know his or her place and quickly take the designated position, avoiding crowding and scrambling. Sufficient time must be allowed to enable the children to get into place briskly.

When the curtain is raised, the children slightly incline their heads in unison, then raise their heads, look towards audience in orchestra and balcony and together simultaneously smile in gratitude, whereupon the stage manager or assistant rapidly pulls the curtain closed. The cast retains its position until the curtain reaches stage floor. If applause continues, the cast is ready for a second curtain call. Otherwise, the children may break formation and return to the dressing rooms to remove make-up and costumes.

During curtain call, the children can join hands, keep them at their sides, clasp them in front, or if, in character, hold hands akimbo, on hips, or clasped in back.

Since children tend to be embarrassed when taking curtain calls, and even giggle self-consciously on occasion, it is advisable to warn them not to do so.

In the commercial theatre, stage hands resort to a tricky manipulation of the curtain called "milking"—raising the curtain very rapidly, to induce applause, with a view of eliciting more curtain calls. While such a procedure is to be frowned on naturally in amateur presentations, it does not follow that applause should be discouraged or curtain calls eliminated.

And now, it's
"CURTAIN TIME!"

So . . . on with the show, and good luck!

ZARA SHAKOW

Selections for Jewish Holidays

Hanukkah

	Classification	Title	Author	Age Level
1.	Poem	*Hanukkah*	Cecelia G. Gerson	8-11
2.	Reading	*The Observance of Hanukkah*	Joseph ben Ephraim Caro	11-16
3.	Reading	*The Miracle of Oil*	Babylonian Talmud	12-16
4.	Poem	*Mattathias*	Elma Ehrlich Levinger	8-12
5.	Reading	*I Maccabees*		12-16
6.	Reading	*Prayer*		8-16
7.	Dramatic Reading (Documentary)	*A Candle Lighting Script*	Dorothy Ross	13-16
8.	Dance with poem narration enacted through tableau	*Dance of the Hanukkah Candles*	Zara Shakow	7-10
9.	Poem	*The Banner of the Jew*	Emma Lazarus	13-16
10.	Story Reading	*Hanukkah Folklore*	Unknown	8-13
11.	Jingle	*Latkes*	Unknown	5-8
12.	Blank-verse Play	*The Dungeon in the Citadel*	Henry Wadsworth Longfellow	14-16
13.	Choral Reading—Poem	*Hail the Maccabees*	Israel Goldberg	10-13
14.	One-act Play	*The Night of the Eighth Candle*	Zara Shakow	8-14
15.	Dramatic Reading with choir and music	*Hanukkah*	Dorothy Ross	13-16

HANUKKAH
Cecelia G. Gerson

The hand of Time moves o'er the dial
    And guides the seasons through the years;
It drives the sorrow from our hearts—
    Behold—the Feast of Lights is here!

The Feast of Lights—old mem'ries stir,
    And pride within our breast soars high,
We live again in ancient days,
    When Judah's glory was the cry.

We see the Maccabees of old
    Bow low within the house of God;
Where Syrian hands defiled the halls,
    Where Israel's patriarchs had trod.

Now light we tapers for their deeds;
    Awak'ning in each heart a prayer,
That *we* may like the Maccabees
    The glory and the valor share.

The Feast of Lights—a time when hope
    Throws off the yoke of sorrow's rod,
To wing its way above the flames
    That leap to glory and to God!

The Jewish Exponent

THE OBSERVANCE OF HANUKKAH

For centuries the Shulchan Aruch has been the code of rabbinical Judaism for all ritual and legal questions that arose after the destruction of the Temple. Its author, Joseph ben Ephraim Caro, is the last of the great codifiers. The Shulchan Aruch was written in Caro's latter years, although its authority was not firmly established until the middle of the seventeenth century.

From this book have been taken the following injunctions for the observance of Chanukah:

I

Do not fast during Chanukah, nor on the day preceding the feast, nor on the day following.

II

Eat and be merry. Linger over your viands and punctuate your meals with jest and song, and relate miracles.

III

Buy yourself a lamp of silver to reflect the beauty of the flickering lights. Fill it with sufficient oil to burn at least half an hour. Set it in public view.

IV

Place the eight tapers in a straight row, since no day of Chanukah is superior to another. Only the kindler and guardian of the lights, the ninth taper, the Shamash, shall stand above them all.

V

Kindle the lights before any member of the household, child or adult, seeks sleep.

VI

Light the Shamash. With it kindle first the taper on the left. Move toward the right.

VII

Men, women and children may kindle the lamp of dedication. It is well for each member of your household to have a lamp to kindle.

VIII

Augment your contribution to the funds of the people.

PRODUCTION NOTE

More children can be activated in the rendition of this excerpt from the *Shulchan Aruch*, by breaking up passages I through VII, and assigning each to a different child—boy or girl.

As curtain rises, the eight members of the group are discovered standing stage center in a semi-circle—the tallest in center.

The Narrator steps forward and renders the "introduction" (Paragraphs I and II), then crosses downstage right and remains standing there, just above curtain line, throughout the reading. Readers I, II, etc. step forward in turn to say their respective passages, each returning to the line formation when finished. At finale, the Narrator joins the group, as he delivers VIII.

A suitable Hanukkah song sung by the entire group on curtain would enhance the effect.

THE MIRACLE OF OIL

Commencing with the twenty-fifth day of the month Kislev there are eight days upon which there shall be neither mourning nor fasting. For albeit the Greeks entered the temple and defiled the oil, it was when the might of the Hasmonean overcame and vanquished them that, upon search, a single cruse of undefiled oil sealed by the High Priest was found. In it was oil enough for the needs of a solitary day.

>Then it was that a miracle was wrought.
>The oil in the cruse burned eight days.

(From the Babylonian Talmud)

MATTATHIAS
Elma Ehrlich Levinger

He struck the traitor to the earth,
  He raised his sword that all might see;
    His words rang like a trumpet blast:
      "All who are faithful, follow me!"
From near and far all Israel came;
  They rallied to his battle cry;
They prayed unto the God of peace,
  And for their Law went forth to die—
To die—and yet today they live;
  Far down the centuries flaming see
    That beacon-sword! Hear that strong cry:
"All who are faithful, follow me!"

(From Poems for Young Judaeans)

I MACCABEES
(Excerpts from the Books of Maccabees)

And King Antiochus wrote to his whole kingdom, that all should be one people, and that each should forsake his own laws. And he sent letters unto Jerusalem and the cities of Judah that they should profane the Sabbaths and Feasts, pollute the sanctuary and build altars and temples and shrines for idols; and whosoever shall not do according to the word of the king, he shall die. And he appointed overseers over all the people, and he commanded the cities of Judah to sacrifice, city by city. And they did evil things in the land; and they made Israel to hide themselves in every place of refuge which they had. And they rent in pieces the Books of the Law which they found, and set them on fire. And whosoever was found with any Book of the Covenant, and if any consented to the Law, the king's sentence delivered him to death.

And in those days rose up Mattathias, a priest from Jerusalem; and he dwelt at Modin. And he had five sons, John, Simon, Judas (who was called Maccabaeus), Eleazar, Jonathan. And he saw the blasphemies that were committed in Judah and in Jerusalem, and Mattathias and his sons rent their clothes, and put on sack-cloth and mourned exceedingly.

And the king's officers, that were enforcing the apostasy, came into the city Modin. And many of Israel came unto them, and Mattathias and his sons were gathered together. And the king's officers spoke to Mattathias saying, "Thou art a ruler and an honourable and great man in this city, and strengthened with sons and brethren; now, therefore, come thou first and do the commandment of the king, as all nations have done, and the men of Judah, and they that remain in Jerusalem; so shalt thou and thy house be in the number of the king's friends, and thou and thy children shall be honoured with silver and gold, and many rewards." And Mattathias answered and said with a loud voice, "Though all the nations that are under the king's dominion obey him, and fall away every one from the religion of their fathers, yet will I and my sons and my brethren walk in the covenant of our fathers." And Mattathias cried out in the city with a loud voice, saying "Whosoever is zealous for the Law, and maintaineth the Covenant, let him follow me." So he and his sons fled into the mountains, and left all that ever they had in the city.

And then came unto him a company of Hassidaeans, who were mighty men of Israel. Also all they that fled for persecution. So they joined their forces and smote sinful men in their anger, and wicked men in their wrath; but the rest fled to the heathen for succour.

Then Mattathias and his friends went round about, and pulled down the altars; and what children soever they found within the coast of Israel uncircumcised, those they circumcised by force. So they recovered the law out of the hand of the Gentiles, and out of the hand of kings.

Now when the time drew near that Mattathias should die, he said to his sons: "Now hath pride and rebuke gotten strength, and the time of destruction, and the wrath of indignation. Now therefore, my sons, be ye zealous for the law, and give your lives for the covenant of your fathers. . . . Be valiant, and show yourselves men in behalf of the law; for by it shall ye obtain glory. And, behold, I know that your brother, Simon, is a man of counsel, give ear unto him always; he shall be a father unto you. As for Judas Maccabeus, he hath been mighty and strong, even from his youth up; let him be your captain, and fight the battle of the people."

So he blessed them, and was gathered to his fathers. And he died in the hundred forty and sixth year* and his sons buried him in the sepulchres of his fathers at Modin, and all Israel made great lamentation for him.

THE MACCABEE

Then his son Judah, called Maccabeus, rose up in his stead. And all his brethren helped him, and so did all they that held with his father, and they fought the battle of Israel. So he got his people great honour, and put on a breast-plate as a giant, and girt his warlike harness about him, and he made battles, protecting the host with his sword. For he pursued the wicked, and sought them out. Wherefore the wicked shrunk for fear of him, and all the workers of iniquity were troubled, because salvation prospered in his hand. Moreover he went through the cities of Judah, destroying the ungodly out of them, and turning away wrath from Israel; so that he was renowned unto the utmost part of the earth.

In the next year Lysias gathered together threescore thousand choice men of foot, and five thousand horsemen, that he might subdue them. And Judah met them with ten thousand men.

And when he saw that mighty army, he prayed and said: "Blessed art Thou, O Saviour of Israel, who didst quell the violence of the mighty man by the hand of Thy servant David, and gavest the host of strangers into the hands of Jonathan the son

---

* In the year 167 or 166 B.C.E.

of Saul, and his armourbearer; shut up this army in the hand of Thy people Israel, and let them be confounded in their power and horsemen. Cast them down with the sword of them that love Thee, and let all those that know Thy name praise Thee with thanksgiving."

So they joined battle; and there were slain of the host of Lysias about five thousand men, even before them were they slain.

Now when Lysias saw his army put to flight, and the manliness of Judah's soldiers, and how they were ready either to live or die valiantly, he went into Antiochia and gathered together hired soldiers, and having made his army greater than it was, he purposed to come again into Judea.

Then said Judah and his brethren: "Behold, our enemies are discomfitted; let us go up to cleanse and dedicate the sanctuary." Upon this all the host assembled themselves together, and went up into Mount Zion. And when they saw the sanctuary desolate, and the altar profaned, and the gates burned up, and shrubs growing in the courts as in a forest, yea, and the priests' chambers pulled down; they rent their clothes, and made great lamentation, and cast ashes upon their heads, and fell down flat to the ground upon their faces, and blew an alarm with trumpets, and cried toward heaven.

Then Judah appointed certain men to fight against those that were in the fortress, until he had cleansed the sanctuary. And he chose priests of blameless conversation, and they took those stones according to the law, and built a new altar according to the former; and made up the sanctuary, and the things that were within the temple, and hallowed the courts. They made also new holy vessels, and into the temple they brought the candlestick, and the altar of burnt offerings, and of incense, and the table. And upon the altar they burned incense, and the lamps that were upon the candlestick they lighted that they might give light in the temple.

Now on the five and twentieth day of the ninth month, which is called the month of Kislev, in the hundred forty and eighth year, they rose up betimes in the morning, and offered sacrifice according to the law upon the new altar of burnt offering, which they had made. Look, at what time and what day the heathen had profaned it, even in that was it dedicated with songs, and citherns, and harps and cymbals. Then all the people fell upon their faces, worshipping and praising the God of heaven, who had given them good success. And so they kept the dedication of the altar eight days, and offered burnt offerings with gladness, and sacrificed the sacrifice of deliverance and praise.

Thus was there very great gladness among the people, for that the reproach of the heathen was put away. Moreover Judah and his brethren with the whole congregation of Israel ordained that the days of the dedication of the altar should be kept in their season from year to year by the space of eight days, from the five and twentieth day of the month Kislev, with mirth and gladness. . . .

PRODUCTION NOTE

This excerpt from the apocryphal Book of Maccabees may be given in its entirety or in part. Two readers from the older age group can render the selection, alternating paragraphs. Readers could be costumed as Scribes of the period and hold books suggesting antiqued leather-bound volumes of history—their respective parts are pasted therein. If feasible, quoted passages by king's officers, Mattathias and Judah, should be pre-recorded on tape by adults, so that "speeches" will be authoritative and in character. Voices used should be mature and sonorous. In the event this is impractical, it would be advisable to use off-stage voices for quoted passages. Taped voices should be synchronized with readers' story-telling.

PRAYER
(After kindling the Hanukkah lights.)

Praised be Thou, O Lord our God, King of the universe, for the inspiring truths of which we are reminded by these Hanukkah lights.

We kindle them to recall the great and wonderful deeds wrought through the zeal with which God filled the hearts of the heroic Maccabees. These lights remind us that we should ever look unto God, whence comes our help.

As their brightness increases from night to night, let us more fervently give praise to God for the ever-present help He has been to our fathers in the gloomy nights of trouble and oppression.

The sages and heroes of all generations made every sacrifice to keep the light of God's truth burning brightly. May we and our children be inspired by their example, so that at last Israel may be a guide to all men on the way of righteousness and peace.

A CANDLE LIGHTING SCRIPT*
Dorothy Ross

NARRATOR

If it could speak, what would the Menorah say?
I have been honored, and I have been hidden away.
The Romans stole me from the Temple treasures and
Brought me with their spoils of war to Rome.
In Spain, my very presence caused arrest and trial.
Marranos hid me in their secret wall with Kiddush cups and
 precious Torah scrolls.
In Germany, they melted me to pay the cost of fascist war.
I am a symbol of my people's faith.
> The Wheel of Time revolves.
> Another Hanukkah. Another dedication.
> Twenty-one hundred Hanukkahs since Judah Maccabee
> restored the light.

Count up all the candles all the Jews have lit
Through all the centuries.
Count them by eight.
Count first the years in exile when the Jews lit furtive lights.
Include the candles which inspired Theodor Herzl to seek within himself
The Jewish flame which long had been unlit.

Pause now and listen to a Jewish girl, singing in
Holland while the Nazis searched. Her diary recounts that evening well.
Count in the lights that Israel has burned since '48,
When, with a flaming torch, a young Israeli lit the giant flame.
Compute this sum. The number may exceed the billion stars!

---

*Written expressly for Women's Division of the American Jewish Congress. Premiere performance at A.J.C. Hanukkah Reward Luncheon, December 7, 1964. Permission to reprint and present royalty-free granted by AJC on the proviso that school or center planning production, contact: Women's Division, American Jewish Congress, 15 East 84th Street, New York 10028. Please advise when, where and by whom (children, youth or adult group) script will be done. Copies of the script may be ordered through the AJC Office at a token charge.

What purpose do they serve us now, these flickering lights?
They still recall the Maccabees who fought for freedom in
   the ancient days.
They light our national memories and dispel
The darkness and the ignorance of our past.
In some of us they kindle with a glow
A personal memory of years ago . . .
When we were young, and in our parents' home, we lit these
Candles, and we sang these songs.

WHAT HAVE WE DONE WITH ALL THESE LIGHTS IN ALL THESE YEARS?

> We seize each Hanukkah with open arms.
> Into each light we read a noble thought:
> "To Peace," we cry. Aloud we quote Isaiah
> Whose words we carved on the United Nations.
> "The Day Will Come When They Shall Beat Their Swords
> To Plowshares And Their Spears to Pruning Hooks."

What would Isaiah say today, to each of us?

> We seize each Hanukkah with deep embrace.
> Into each light we read a noble word: To Liberty . . . To
>   Justice . . . To the oppressed.
> To Charity . . . To Righteousness . . . To Hope.
> We raise each candle with a measured word.
> But when the words demand an act of strength;
> When some with courage take upon themselves
> The burdens of our time,
> And speak like prophets of our century,
> They do not get the thundering support we give—Isaiah.
> We tremble; or we turn our heads;
> We close our ears; we shut our seeing eyes.
>
> We have forgotten we were Maccabees!

> > WHO WERE THESE MACCABEES?
> > THESE WERE THE MEN WHO PLACED UPON
> >   THEIR TIME THE CROWN OF GREATNESS.
> > THEY DID NOT BOW THEIR HEADS OR SHUT
> >   THEIR EYES OR CLOSE THEIR EARS.

>THEY READ THE SCRIPTURES AND THEY KNEW
>DEEP IN THEIR ROOTS
>THAT GOD CREATED MAN IN HIS OWN IMAGE
>AND MAN CAN BE A GIANT IF HE CHOOSE.

When they had won their freedom from the Greeks,
They lit their flickering light to last an hour, perhaps a day,
But we have learned it is a flickering light that never,
while man strives,
Can be put out.
In each of us one of these lights is lit.
It burns more brightly in the hearts of some.
When Anne Frank wrote, her flame was pure and high.
When Herzl dreamed, his light approached the sky.

IN EVERY POET WHO HAS SUNG HIS SONG,
    WHETHER OF HAPPINESS OR HOPE GONE WRONG:
IN EVERY STORY-TELLER WHO HAS WOVEN
    SOME STRANDS OF LIFE INTO A WONDROUS TALE:
IN EVERY CHASSID WHOSE SWEET MELODIES
    WITHOUT A WORD CONVEYS THE HUMAN HEART:
IN EVERY ARTIST WHO WITH BRUSH OR PEN
    CAN STIR A MAN TO BE ALIVE AGAIN—
THIS FLAME WILL NEVER DIM.

IT IS THE MIRACLE OF MAN WHICH IS
    THE MIRACLE OF HANUKKAH.
THEY HANDED US THE LIGHT AND WE—
    WE HOLD IT HIGH, OR WE EXTINGUISH IT.
IF MAN IS GREAT, AND WHO WILL QUESTION THAT?
WHOM DO WE HONOR WHEN WE KINDLE LIGHTS?
WE HONOR THOSE IN WHOM THE LIGHTS BURN HIGH!

(CANDLE LIGHTING CEREMONY)
(8 CANDLES—ARRANGE IN ANY ORDER)

READER—CANDLE NO. 1

Light then a candle to the valiant group
Who in time of apathy like ours
Turns not aside, but takes the burdens of our days upon its back.
We light this candle to Americans today
In fifty states, who keep the flame alive.

Reader—Candle No. 2

Jews of the U.S.A., we honor you!
Although in number a minority
Of all the population of this land,
You put your impress on this nation's heart
In science, music, law and art;
In every area where men have striven
The Jews both thought and energy have given.
This second candle we have lit for you.

Reader—Candle No. 3

Some women die, but nothing dims their lights.
The name of Emma Lazarus lives so long as in her hand
The Statue of Liberty holds aloft her torch.
Her words are carved upon the stone support.
And she reminds us, as we read the verse
That this land grew because our open doors
Invited all who fled oppression's shores.
This candle is a symbol of her torch.

Reader—Candle No. 4

There is an element in Jewish life which makes us different.
It is not suffering alone, though we have bled.
It shines through Holy Scriptures and the folk-lore of our centuries.
It is our Jewish humor, bitter sweet,
Which, at one time, can make us laugh and weep.
An affirmation of the will to joy.
    A candle for the laughter we create—even through tears!
    Imagine! Sholom Aleichem on TV appears!

Reader—Candle No. 5

You who were born in these United States,
Or came for refuge to our teeming shores,
How often do you pause to count the lands
Where meetings such as this could not take place?
Where Jewish culture is confined to books?
Or where the hate of anti-Semitism keeps Jews within the
Ghettos of their fears?

Let us remember, while we criticized to make it better,
That this land
Has given Jews the greatest opportunities to thrive.
We dedicate this candle to our land.

READER—CANDLE NO. 6
When Abraham was promised that his seed
Would multiply like sands beside the sea,
He didn't know that a heroic few
Would rise again like modern Maccabees
And light a flame in Israel anew.
No Jew who lives today can fail to see
How interwoven are our lives and dreams
With this democracy which rises green from barren desert soil.
    A light to Israel which feeds our flame!

READER—CANDLE NO. 7
There is a fantasy that comes to all
Who work for Israel's growth.
It is a vision that a day will come
When money for its needs will fall from the proverbial
Heavens that once sent manna to our ancestors.
But such a fantasy does not pay bills.
A candle to the purchasers of Bonds for Israel,
Who give to UJA, who help Youth Aliyah, support the ZOA.
Who recognize that love is not enough.

READER—CANDLE NO. 8
The continuity of Jewish life has been assured.
Let those who weep about our youth contain their tears
And take a better look.
Who go by hundreds to Israeli shores to test their heritage
In modern terms? Our Chalutzim.
Who work for peace? Who teach the underprivileged
In Africa or in the southern states?
The conflict of the generations goes way back to Abraham
Who left his father's house because their values differed
    Even then...

Our youth will not forsake our heritage if we believe in it,
And act on it. The Maccabean spirit burns in them.
   A candle to our youth!

(Narrator holds Menorah aloft for following, or points to it, fully lit.

If feasible, besides the Menorah with the lit candles, have each reader representing candles No. 1 through No. 8, carry a burning torch and form a "human" Menorah.

In the event this is possible, readers symbolizing the candles, should make their entrances from back of auditorium, marching up center or side aisles, ascend stage, render their lines, and after eighth reader has finished, get into formation for the "human" Menorah.

Readers should preferably be of similar height and dressed alike.
Then:)

NARRATOR

The miracle of Hanukkah is this:
THAT WHILE MAN STRIVES
THE LIGHT WILL NEVER DIM!...

   CURTAIN or
   BLACKOUT.

DANCE OF THE HANUKKAH CANDLES*
Zara Shakow

(With poem narration and musical accompaniment)
Music: *Prelude*. During the reading of poem, play music of "Chanukah Lights" from *Chanukah Songster*, by A. W. Binder, page 7, down and under.
Dance: "Mo-oz Tzur," same songster, page 10. First note of each bar should be sharply accented.
Reading: Poem "Hanukkah Lights," by Shulamit Ish-Kishor.

Nine little candles standing in a row
(The biggest one's the Shamash, that leaves eight, you know.)
Eight little candles, looking up to heaven,
Father lights the green for hope, then there are seven;
Seven little candles, with their small white wicks,
Joe lights red for bravery, then there are six.
Six little candles, soon will flame alive,
Rose takes pink for beauty, then there are five.
Five little candles—wish that there were more—
Ruth lights white for purity, then there are four.
Four little candles, pretty as can be—
Sammy lights the gold for luck, then there are three.
Three little candles,
Mother lights the blue—
That's for truth—the best of all,
Then there are two.
Two little candles, yellow as the sun,
David lights them both for wealth,
Then there are none!
Nine little candle-lights, old as ancient Rome,
Bring the gallant Maccabees to each Jewish home.
Nine little candle-lights ever dear and blest—
Now you shine in Is-ra-el
And Jewish hearts can rest!

Costumes for Dancers: Simple Grecian costumes made of voile, gauze or chiffon, dyed so that it matches color of candle

---
* Originally published by Bloch Publishing Company. Copies available at company's office.

which dancer represents—1 green, 1 red, 1 pink, 1 white, 1 gold, 1 blue, 2 yellow and 1 gold (Shamash).

Note regarding costumes: When dyeing costumes to match color of candles, an effort should be made to differentiate color of costume worn by dancer representing Shamash from that worn by dancer representing fifth candle—wealth.

As the curtain is raised, audience sees large Menorah on a table up stage center. Eight brightly colored candles, as follows: 1 green, 1 red, 1 pink, 1 white, 1 gold, 1 blue, 2 yellow, are in grooves in above order. In groove for Shamash, a gold candle topping the others.

Grouped around the table are seven children representing following characters in poem and dressed according to character they portray: Father, Joe, Rose, Ruth, Sammy, Mother and David. They form a tableau facing the Menorah upstage, their backs to the audience.

Extreme down stage, dancers form tableau. Eight girls, in so far as possible the same height, representing the spirits of the candles in Menorah, wearing colored costumes: green, red, pink, white, gold, blue, two yellow, pose—holding graceful sitting position; their legs are crossed to the right of their bodies; hands on left side of bodies; eyes are shut, heads resting on right shoulders. The dancers are supposedly asleep.

The Shamash, a girl taller than the others, wearing a gold-colored costume, is sitting in a similar position (stage center) in middle of semi-circle formed by other dancers.

The Reader, off stage, in a soft but resonant voice, reads "Chanukah Lights" to the piano's soft accompaniment.

>Nine little candles
>Standing in a row—
>The biggest one's the Shamash—

At the word "Shamash" the father in tableau lights Shamash in Menorah and the dancer representing Shamash slowly rises as though awakening from a deep sleep, looks dreamily about, opens her eyes, brings hands slowly and gracefully to eyes, rubs them, then brings hands out to side, shoulder level, jumps up joyously, pirouettes right over left, bringing hands down while doing the pirouette, as though about to gather up flowers, then brings hands out, and in a fluttering step approaches first dancer to awaken her.

Reader continues reading slowly, synchronizing with dancers. If dance and reading are properly rehearsed there will be no breaks or pauses.

> That leaves eight you know—
> Eight little candles, looking up to heaven,
> Father lights the green—

Father in tableau lights the green candle in Menorah with Shamash, giving Shamash to "Joe," who in turn gets ready to light his candle.

The dancer representing the Shamash lightly bends over dancer representing the green candle, awakening her. The dancer representing the Shamash then steps back, waiting for green candle to awaken. After spirit of green candle has been awakened, Shamash bends over red candle awakening her, and so on.

The first dancer, representing the spirit of the green candle, awakens as Shamash did before her, except that she holds her left hand, after completing step, ready to join with right hand of second dancer, representing the spirit of the red candle. The pose of the first dancer is this: Right hand outward, shoulder level, palms down, left hand outward left side, ready to join with right hand of second dancer. Her left foot is pointing sideward left and her head is turned extreme left looking toward left.

The dancers are all awakened similarly—when character in tableau lights respective candle in Menorah and Shamash approaches candle and awakens her spirit.

After all candles have been lit, during which time reader reads:

> Nine little candle-lights, old as ancient Rome
> Bring the gallant Maccabees to each Jewish home;
> Nine little candle-lights ever dear and blest
> Now you shine in Is-ra-el and Jewish hearts can rest.

the Shamash flutters back to her place in center of semi-circle, taking pose, her head back over left shoulder, hands outward, shoulder level, palms down, left toe pointing outward left. The characters in tableau walk off stage left, and dancers retain pose—hands linked, except for right hand of first dancer and left hand of last dancer, which are stretched outward. As dancers pose thusly, pianist finishes music of "Chanukah Lights" as reader completes reading of poem. Then chord; then pianist plays music for dance:

STEPS FOR ACTUAL DANCE

First dancer and eighth dancer join outstretched (unoccupied) hands, thereby forming circle. Shamash in center does same steps as other dancers except that she does them solo.

First Step: Going to right—right of first dancer. A polka step, starting with right foot, eight times to right accenting first step of polka into kick, thusly: kick right foot, step 2, 3, kick left foot, step 2, 3, etc., until eight steps (four left foot and four with right) going to right side have been performed. Then eight steps to left, beginning with left foot (left foot, right foot, left foot, right foot, etc.).

Shamash, facing audience throughout, does two steps to right, two to left, two to right, two to left, etc. Her hands are outstretched sideways, palms down, when starting each step lowers hands, then raises them in rhythmic co-ordination with step.

Second Step: Slide frontward sideward with right foot, hop back left foot, polka step in place 2-3-4. Then slide left foot, hop back right, step 2-3-4 in place. Repeat right, repeat left. Hand movements for this are as follows: On slide—outward and upward (in front) on hop back downward in front, on 2-3-4 down at side. Hands of dancers are linked throughout. When sliding right foot, heads and bodies facing diagonally right; when sliding left foot, hands and bodies facing diagonally left.

Hand movement for Shamash: On slide right foot, right hand upward front, left hand to side, on hop back, right hand across body criss-cross on left hand left of body holding that hand movement until slide left, then left hand is raised upward frontward and right hand is at side, then left hand is brought over to right hand at right side criss-crossing it, and hand position is held through polka step. Repeat right, repeat left.

Third Step: Arabesque—slide right foot to left over left and kick, then left foot to right over right and kick, then polka to left, step 2-3-4. This should not be done in place but moving toward right direction (right of green candle always). This step is done eight times toward right during which time dancers (in circle) will have circled stage. The Shamash does the same step in the same way except that she polkas in place and hand movement differs, thusly: When sliding on right foot over left she brings her right hand to left and on kick brings it back to right side; when sliding to right over left she does same with left hand, on polka, hands are outward sideward, palms down, and while doing polka step, lowers them, then raises them again shoulder level.

Fourth Step: Waltz in place—waltz right, waltz left, waltz right, waltz left, then waltz to right direction in circle, waltzing right eight times, then to left, waltz left, waltz right, waltz left, waltz right, eight times. Shamash, when others waltz eight steps right, she takes four steps right, then four steps left, then four right, then four left.

Fifth Step: Polka (in circle) toward Shamash, right, left, backward (to place), left, right. Then repeat. Retain circle formation.

Sixth Step: Repeat first half of *First Step*—eight polka steps to right accentuating beginning step into kick, then first and last dancer break (disjoining hands) and first girl polkas off-stage left, beginning with left foot, followed by the others doing the same step. After other dancers have gone off stage, the Shamash follows with a fluttering step, then breaks into a step, leap, turn, step and exits.

CURTAIN

THE BANNER OF THE JEW
Emma Lazarus

Wake, Israel wake! Recall today
    The glorious Maccabean rage,
The sire heroic, hoary-gray
    His five-fold lion-lineage;
The Wise, the Elect, the Help-of-God,
The Burst-of-Spring, the Avenging Rod.*

From Mizpah's mountain-side they saw
    Jerusalem's empty streets, her shrine
Laid waste where Greeks profaned the Law,
    With idol and with pagan sign.
Mourners in tattered black were there,
With ashes sprinkled on their hair.

Then from the stony peak there rang
    A blast to ope the graves; down poured
The Maccabean clan, who sang
    Their battle-anthem to the Lord.
Five heroes lead, and following, see,
Ten thousand rush to victory!

Oh, for Jerusalem's trumpet now,
    To blow a blast of shattering power,
To wake the sleepers high and low,
    And rouse them to the urgent hour!
No band for vengeance—but to save,
A million naked swords should wave.

Oh, deem not dead that martial fire,
    Say not the mystic flame is spent!
With Moses' law and David's lyre,
    Your ancient strength remains unbent.
Let but an Ezra rise anew,
To lift the Banner of the Jew!

---

* The sons of Mattathias.

A rag, a mock at first—ere long,
    When men have bled and women wept,
To guard its precious folds from wrong,
    Even they who shrunk, even they who slept,
Shall leap to bless it and to save.
Strike! for the brave revere the brave!

HANUKKAH FOLKLORE

Jews have always had a gift for escaping the mental torture of persecution through imaginative and speculative sorties into the lore and history of the past, seeking even in Holy Writ for hidden symbols. If Israel was the chosen of nations, possessed of a divine mandate, then somehow the shadow of coming events must be lurking in every page, in every letter of sacred writing.

Thus the medieval Jews amused themselves with anagram and word play and mystical interpretation of numbers and of letters; and with riddles and conundrums—all with that pinch of levity that made them true for the moment, but yet, as is any old man's tale, never to be accepted as "really true."

The Man-of-Old asked the Child-of-Today:

"Why did the first Hanukkah fall on the twenty-fifth day of the month of Kislev?"

The Child-of-Today made reply:

"Because Judah, the Maccabee, drove Antiochus from Jerusalem and rededicated the Temple, and the oil intended for one day burned for eight."

The Man-of-Old smiled and said:

"But why did all this happen on that particular day? You know, history has a way of repeating itself. Perhaps the victory and the dedication fell on the anniversary of a past event. Let us see."

Whereupon man and child travelled back until they found themselves at the beginning of time in the Garden of Eden. And lo and behold, they came upon an answer to part of the riddle! And the man set it down to be told again and again on Hanukkah to the little ones of Israel as "The Legend of the Winter Solstice."

The Garden of Eden was flooded with sunshine. The trees

grew and flourished. The birds sang. The flowers budded and bloomed, and the heart of Man was glad. At length there came a day when Adam paid heed to the whispers of Eve. He ate of the forbidden fruit. . . . And Man and Woman were driven from the Garden to eat bread in the sweat of their brow.

During the day the sun warmed the earth. When the coolness of evening came and the day's task was ended, Adam and Eve sat quietly in the shade to eat of the bread of their toil.

Suddenly Adam noticed that the sun set earlier. Darkness followed quickly. Nights became longer, days shorter.

Was this some new punishment? Alarmed, the Man and Woman fasted and prayed. A week passed—the sun withdrew yet earlier. Adam and Eve became terrified. Was darkness to creep further and further upon earth and devour all living?

Lo, a miracle! On the morrow the sun tarried longer, and on the morrow, and on the morrow after. Days grew steadily longer, nights shorter.

Then Adam laughed aloud at his fears. And he and Eve feasted and made merry. They kindled fires of thanksgiving. For they knew that all was as it had been, and would ever be—that the lights in the heaven were fixed in their courses for signs and for seasons, for days and for years, and that while the earth remained, seed time and harvest, cold and heat, summer and winter, and day and night would not cease.

Now the day that Adam celebrated by kindling fires of thanksgiving fell in mid-winter when the sun, they tell us, reaches a point farthest from the middle of the earth and appears to pause and then returns on its course.

And this day is the twenty-fifth of the month of Kislev. It is the Winter Solstice.

"This is only the first portion of our answer," said the Man-of-Old. "Let us move forward through the years." So they fared forth and joined their people in the wilderness on the trek from Egyptian darkness into the light of freedom.

And they beheld the children of Israel assembled, awed and expectant. For all the work of the tabernacle was finished. And Bezalel and the wise-hearted men who had wrought with him brought the tabernacle unto Moses, and all its furniture; the ark of the testimony, and the ark cover; the table, all the vessels thereof, and the showbread; the pure candlestick, the lamps thereof, even the lamps to be set in order, and all the vessels thereof, and the oil for the light—

And it was the twenty-fifth day of the month of Kislev.

So, with two portions of the answer to their riddle, the questing pair travelled farther, forward through the years to a second redemption, the deliverance from the night of exile in Babylon. And the people were gathered before Nehemiah and the priests. Upon the restored altar they put the slime that had remained in the pit. In it, seventy years before, the priests had hidden the sacred oil from the invader, and the earth of the pit had preserved this oil against what time the altar would be restored.

Suddenly the sun, which was hidden behind the clouds, burst forth in all its majesty. Its rays beat down upon the altar and lo, the residue of the oil burst into flame. Priests and people marvelled at this wondrous sight and Nehemiah decreed that henceforth a period of prayer and feasting and rejoicing should be held throughout all the generations of Israel on the anniversary of the day on which the altar and the rebuilt temple had been dedicated.

And this day was the twenty-fifth day of Kislev.

"Now," said the Man-of-Old, "let us seek in the time of the Maccabees for the final portion of our answer. Is it not possible that there was some event on the twenty-fifth day of Kislev from which Judah and his soldiers drew the renewed courage that brought the small band to victory, and the temple to its former state?"

And so they took up their quest, and found the people of Judaea in great distress. For the Syrian tyrant had declared a special feast, and had commanded that all the inhabitants of the land worship on the altars which he had set up in the holy places. The faithful among the Jews were tortured because they would not forsake the faith of their fathers.

And the King commanded that this day be called the Feast of Antiochus.

And it was the twenty-fifth day of the Month of Kislev.

And so it was that when the Child-of-Today had the four portions of the answer to his question, he found that the problem was solved.

"You see," said the Man-of-Old, "History does not explain everything. The day when the sun gave promise of renewed life to the sleeping earth, the Tabernacle was dedicated by Moses; and that also was a Hanukkah—a day of dedication. Centuries later, on that day, a redeemed people returned from Babylonia, beheld a miracle of sacred oil upon the restored altar. That likewise was a Hanukkah—a day of dedication.

"It was that day which the Maccabeans chose to re-dedicate the defiled altar, and so to turn the mourning of the Feast of Antiochus into the gladness of the Feast of Lights."

The Child-of-Today asks, "Is there any new portion for our own time? Has the twenty-fifth day of Kislev ever given occasion for a new dedication?"

The Man-of-Old said, "History does not explain everything. It was on the twenty-fifth day of the month of Kislev in our time—we call it the tenth of December of the year 1917—that a British general, by the name of Allenby, led the victorious forces of the Allied armies into the city of Jerusalem and delivered it."

PRODUCTION NOTE

This folktale can readily be dramatized by having a Storyteller, preferably an older boy, render the expository passages, and two boys—one with a mature voice to do the "Man-of-Old," and a boy, aged six or seven to be the "Child-of-Today."

The Storyteller need not memorize the lines, but the two boys portraying the "Man-of-Old" and the "Child-of-Today" should do so.

The entire script, triple or quadruple-spaced, should be bound in an attractive colored folder, and the Storyteller's passages carefully marked for cues and phrasing.

It would be advisable to place the Storyteller stage right, at the proscenium, just below curtain line. He can either stand, or sit on a high-backed period chair, or at a small antique desk, extreme stage right, to allow ample acting space for the two boys portraying the characters.

If feasible, have the "Man-of-Old" made up and costumed as Father Time; the boy who does the "Child-of-Today" dressed in a modern suit, shirt, tie and cap.

Three or four rehearsals of approximately two hours each are required to achieve a smooth presentation and synchronize the movement with the Storyteller's narration. The result will more than justify the time and effort expended.

LATKES

This is a pancake, made of flour or potatoes and eggs, with a pinch of salt and pepper. The recipe in rhyme says:

> If Latkes you would make
> Salt and eggs and flour take—
> Eat with jest and song and rhyme,
> At the festive Hanukkah time.

THE DUNGEON IN THE CITADEL
Henry Wadsworth Longfellow

(Excerpted from blank-verse play "JUDAS MACCABEUS"
Act II)

CHARACTERS:
The Mother of Seven Sons
Voices, her six sons
Antiochus Epiphanes, a tyrant
Sirion, Hannah's youngest son

SCENES:
Scene I: The ante-room of the torture-chamber
Scene II: The same

SCENE I

The MOTHER *is alone in the ante-room of the torture-chamber. She is listening.*

THE MOTHER

Be strong, my heart!
Break not till they are dead,
All, all my Seven Sons; then burst asunder,
And let this tortured and tormented soul
Leap and rush out like water through the shards
Of earthen vessels broken at a well.
O my dear children, mine in life and death,
I know not how ye came into my womb;

I neither gave you breath, nor gave you life,
And neither was it I that formed the members
Of every one of you. But the Creator,
Who made the world, and made the heavens above us,
Who formed the generation of mankind,
And found out the beginning of all things,
He gave you breath and life, and will again
Of His own mercy, as ye now regard
Not your own selves, but His eternal law.
I do not murmur, nay, I thank Thee, God,
That I and mine have not been deemed unworthy
To suffer for Thy sake and for Thy law,
And for the many sins of Israel.
Hark! I can hear within the sound of scourges!
I feel them more than ye do, O my sons!
But cannot come to you. I, who was wont
To wake at night at the least cry ye made,
To whom ye ran at every slightest hurt,—
I cannot take you now into my lap
And soothe your pain, but God will take you all
Into His pitying arms, and comfort you,
And give you rest.

A VOICE (*within*)
What wouldst thou ask of us?
Ready are we to die, but we will never
Transgress the law and customs of our fathers.

THE MOTHER
It is the voice of my first-born! O brave
And noble boy! Thou hast the privilege
Of dying first, as thou wast born the first.

THE SAME VOICE (*within*)
God looketh on us, and hath comfort in us;
As Moses in his song of old declared,
He in His servants shall be comforted.

THE MOTHER
I knew thou wouldst not fail! He speaks no more,
He is beyond all pain!

ANTIOCHUS (*within*)
If thou eat not,
Thou shalt be tortured throughout all the members
Of thy whole body. Wilt thou eat then?

SECOND VOICE (*within*)
No.

THE MOTHER
It is Adaiah's voice.
I tremble for him.
I know his nature, devious as the wind.
And swift to change, gentle and yielding always.
Be steadfast, O my son!

THE SAME VOICE (*within*)
Thou, like a fury,
Takest us from this present life, but God,
Who rules the world, shall raise us up again
Into life everlasting.

THE MOTHER
God, I thank Thee
That thou hast breathed into that timid heart
Courage to die for Thee. O my Adaiah,
Witness of God! If thou for whom I feared
Canst thus encounter death, I need not fear;
The others will not shrink.

THIRD VOICE (*within*)
Behold these hands
Held out to thee, O King Antiochus,
Not to implore thy mercy, but to show
That I despise them. He who gave them to me
Will give them back again.

THE MOTHER
O Avilan,
It is thy voice. For the last time I hear it;
For the last time on earth, but not the last.
To death it bids defiance and to torture.

It sounds to me as from another world,
And makes the petty miseries of this
Seem unto me as naught, and less than naught.
Farewell, my Avilan; nay, I should say
Welcome, my Avilan: for I am dead
Before thee. I am waiting for the others.
Why do they linger?

FOURTH VOICE (*within*)

It is good, O King,
Being put to death by men, to look for hope
From God, to be raised up again by Him.
But thou—no resurrection shalt thou have
To life hereafter.

THE MOTHER

Four! already four!
Three are still living; nay, they all are living,
Half here, half there. Make haste, Antiochus,
To reunite us; for the sword that cleaves
These miserable bodies makes a door
Through which our souls, impatient of release,
Rush to each other's arms.

THE FIFTH VOICE (*within*)

Thou hast the power;
Thou doest what thou wilt. Abide awhile,
And thou shalt see the power of God, and how
He will torment thee and thy seed.

THE MOTHER

O hasten;
Why dost thou pause? Thou who hast slain already
So many Hebrew women, and hast hung
Their murdered infants round their necks, slay me,
For I too am a woman, and these boys
Are mine. Make haste to slay us all,
And hang my lifeless babes about my neck.

SIXTH VOICE (*within*)
Think not, Antiochus, that takest in hand
To strive against the God of Israel,
Thou shalt escape unpunished, for His wrath
Shall overtake thee and thy bloody house.

THE MOTHER
One more, my Sirion, and then all is ended.
Having put all to bed, then in my turn
I will lie down and sleep as sound as they.
My Sirion, my youngest, best beloved!
And those bright golden locks, that I so oft
Have curled about these fingers, even now
Are foul with blood and dust, like a lamb's fleece,
Slain in the shambles.—Not a sound I hear.
This silence is more terrible to me
Than any sound, than any cry of pain
That might escape the lips of one who dies.
Doth his heart fail him? Doth he fall away
In the last hour from God? O Sirion, Sirion,
Art thou afraid? I do not hear thy voice.
Die as thy brothers died. Thou must not live!

CURTAIN

SCENE II
As the curtain rises the MOTHER *is standing before* ANTIOCHUS

THE MOTHER
Are they all dead?

ANTIOCHUS
One only lives. (*Draws her to the curtain to look behind it*)
Behold them where they lie;
How dost thou like this picture?

THE MOTHER
God in heaven!
Can a man do such deeds, and yet not die

By the recoil of his own wickedness?
Ye murdered, bleeding, mutilated bodies
That were my children once, and still are mine,
I cannot watch o'er you as Rispah watched
In sackcloth o'er the seven sons of Saul,
Till water drop upon you out of heaven
And wash this blood away! I cannot mourn
As she, the daughter of Aiah, mourned the dead,
From the beginning of the barley harvest
Until the autumn rains, and suffered not
The birds of air to rest on them by day,
Nor the wild beasts by night. For ye have died
A better death, a death so full of life
That I ought rather to rejoice than mourn—

> SIRION, *the youngest son, enters from the torture-chamber*

Wherefore art thou not dead, O Sirion?
Wherefore art thou the only living thing
Among thy brothers dead? Art thou afraid?

ANTIOCHUS
O woman, I have spared him for thy sake,
For he is fair to look upon, and comely;
And I have sworn to him by all the gods
That I would crown his life with joy and honor,
Heap treasures on him, luxuries, delights,
Make him my friend and keeper of my secrets,
If he would turn from your Mosaic Law
And be as we are; but he will not listen.

THE MOTHER
My noble Sirion!

ANTIOCHUS
Therefore I beseech thee
Who art his mother, thou wouldst speak with him,
And wouldst persuade him. I am sick of blood.

THE MOTHER

Yea, I will speak with him and will persuade him.
O Sirion, my son! Have pity on me,
On me that bare thee, and that gave thee suck,
And fed and nourished thee, and brought thee up
With the dear trouble of a mother's care
Unto this age. Look on the heavens above thee,
And on the earth and all that is therein;
Consider that God made them out of things
That were not; and that likewise in this manner
Mankind was made. Then fear not this tormentor;
But, being worthy of thy brethren, take
Thy death as they did, that I may receive thee
Again in mercy with them.

ANTIOCHUS

I am mocked,
Yes, I am laughed to scorn.

SIRION

Whom wait ye for?
Never will I obey the King's commandment,
But the commandment of the ancient Law,
That was by Moses given unto our fathers.
And thou, O godless man, that of all others
Art the most wicked, be not lifted up,
Nor puffed up with uncertain hopes, uplifting
Thy hand against the servants of the Lord,
For thou hast not escaped the righteous judgment
Of the Almighty God, who seeth all things!

ANTIOCHUS

He is no god of mine; I fear him not.

SIRION

My brothers, who have suffered a brief pain,
Are dead; but thou, Antiochus, shalt suffer
The punishment of pride. I offer up
My body and my life, beseeching God
That He would speedily be merciful
Unto our nation, and that thou by plagues

Mysterious and by torments mayest confess
That He alone is God.

ANTIOCHUS
Ye both shall perish
By torments worse than any that your God,
Here or hereafter, hath in store for me.

THE MOTHER
My Sirion, I am proud of thee!

ANTIOCHUS
Be silent!
Go to thy bed of torture in yon chamber,
Where lie so many sleepers, heartless mother!
Thy footsteps will not wake them, nor thy voice.
Nor wilt thou hear, amid thy troubled dreams,
Thy children crying for thee in the night.

THE MOTHER
O Death, that stretchest thy white hands to me,
I fear them not, but press them to my lips,
That are as white as thine; for I am Death,
Nay, am the Mother of Death, seeing these sons
All lying lifeless.—Kiss me, Sirion.

CURTAIN

HAIL THE MACCABEES*
Israel Goldberg

I

Hear Judea's mountains ringing,
   Hail the Maccabees!
Hosts from cleft and cave upspringing,
   Hail the Maccabees!
Shining shields and spear-heads glancing,
See the lion brood advancing.
   Hail the Maccabees!
   Hail the Maccabees!

II

Wild the battle din is beating,
   Hail the Maccabees!
See the tyrant hordes retreating,
   Hail the Maccabees!
Loud shall rave the tyrant-weakling,
Mad Antiochus, the Greekling.
   Hail the Maccabees!
   Hail the Maccabees!

III

See the bright procession wending,
   Hail the Maccabees!
Hear the songs of praise ascending,
   Hail the Maccabees.
Holy—great the dedication
Of a liberated nation:
   Hail the Maccabees!
   Hail the Maccabees!

PRODUCTION NOTE

This poem can be presented more effectively, by adding a group of ten to twelve boys and girls divided into:

   Boys' Voices: tenor
                 baritone
                 bass
   Girls' Voices: *soprano*
                 alto

and doing it as a choral reading—the group doing the reprise.

---

* Poems for Young Judaeans

A senior boy with a powerful resonant voice renders the main body of the poem. The "Choral Group" does the following, rising to a dramatic crescendo:

Stanza I: 1st "HAIL THE MACCABEES"—bass-baritone voices
2nd "   "   "   —soprano-alto voices

Stanza II: 1st "   "   "   —tenors
2nd "   "   "   —sopranos-altos

Stanza III: 1st "   "   "   —bass-baritones and tenors
2nd "   "   "   —sopranos-altos
Reprise of each stanza   —entire choral group

Suggested Costume:
    Girls: Navy blue or black full skirts; white or powder blue blouses
    Boys: Dark trousers; white or light-blue shirts; if ties are worn: royal blue

THE NIGHT OF THE EIGHTH CANDLE
Zara Shakow

CAST OF CHARACTERS:
Mr. Karl Kindermann, father, 43
Mrs. Eva Kindermann, mother, 37
Hannah, their eldest daughter, 16
David, their son, 13
Miriam, their youngest child, 7
Esther, the "little stranger," 12

PLACE:
The Kindermann home in Forest Hills, Long Island, New York.

TIME:
Hanukkah, night of the eighth candle, about 7 o'clock on December 7th, 1964, during an early severe winter. It is bitter cold. The ground is covered with a thick blanket of snow. The storm has not yet abated entirely—a sharp wind is still blowing, but the snow is falling only gently now.

SCENE:
The tastefully furnished dining and living room of the Kindermanns' private brick house in a desirable residential section of Forest Hills.

Wall to wall broadloom carpeting on floor.

Stage right, dining-room area, furnished with a round top oak table, leather-seat oak chairs, breakfront, server, lamps, tea-wagon, etc. Table is covered with an ecru lace banquet cloth. On table: a china tea-service with matching cups, saucers, sugar-bowl, sterling silver flatware, nappery, china plates, filled wine and brandy decanters, wine and brandy glasses, soda and tumblers, as well as variety of delicacies: petit fours, candies, bon bons, nuts, fresh fruit, etc.

Extreme stage right: a large picture window, hung with glass curtains and drapery, which not being drawn, form side panels on either side of window.

A handsome silver Menorah with eight colored lit candles (the Shamash having been extinguished) is on an end-table, facing window, from which the porch and a sweeping view of the deserted snow-covered street beyond can be seen.

Stage left: living-room area, containing built in bookshelves filled with books, a sofa, throw pillows on it, upholstered arm chairs, hassock, coffee table, lamps, etc. Paintings and etchings adorn the walls.

Stage left wall: a working fireplace, with burning logs. Above fireplace, a painting.

Off left, upstage, a stairway leading to upper floor—bedrooms, bathrooms, etc.

Upstage, off right, a foyer, leading to street door.

In foyer, visible to audience, a princess telephone on a telephone table, with a bench or chair beside it.

Off foyer, a door, leading to kitchen.

PRODUCTION NOTE

It would understandably be desirable and effective to have a realistic interior set with a stairway unit, as described. However, inasmuch as facilities and equipment are usually limited in schools and centers, constructing such a set may well be unfeasible.

In that event, the play can readily be staged in front of a backdrop, with entrances and exits managed through openings in backdrop curtain.

The importance of establishing the atmosphere of a lived in home and the presence of other rooms, the outdoors, etc. cannot be overemphasized. This can be accomplished by sharpening the awareness of the actors of an actual rather than a fictional setting, providing the necessary props—both stationary and hand—in order to help the actors relate to the surroundings of a home and physicalize business convincingly. Believability and identification on the part of the actors will promote involvement by the audience, notwithstanding the fact that the setting is suggestive rather than realistic.

SCENE I

AT RISE: The five members of the Kindermann family are seated at the table, finishing their Hanukkah dinner, eating the traditional potato latkes. A festive spirit of cheer and comfort prevails.

HANNAH: Oh, I'm *so* glad I came home! Everything's just super duper . . . one surprise atop of another—the recreation room and den, my own room redecorated as I always wanted with that beautiful canopied bed and the new spinnet—my Hanukkah presents—this delicious dinner—*everything!* . . .

MRS. KINDERMANN: And I had to *urge* you, *beg* you actually! Three letters weren't enough. I had to wire and phone. I don't know what's come over you, Hannah, not to be home for Hanukkah—your favorite holiday.

HANNAH: There were a couple of projects I had to finish, mother, and somehow—

MR. KINDERMANN: Somehow *nothing!* How could you put off coming until the very last day . . . barely making it by the skin of your teeth? You're spoiled, Hannah, that's what. (To Mrs. K.) I tell you, Eva, as I've told you time and again—you let her have her own way too often . . . give in to her every whim. She wants boarding-school, so off to boarding-school you send her . . . away from home, away from everyone and everything Jewish . . . (Deciding not to elaborate, he breaks off) I warn you, Eva, you'll rue the day you consented!

HANNAH: (Indignantly) How can you say that, dad, when Greylock's been so good for me? I've *grown* there . . . really blossomed! I was so mixed up before . . . just floundering. Greylock's helped me *find* myself. I know what I want now and where I'm going . . . have direction. The teachers—each and every one of them—inspire you. That's why I made such good grades. What's more, the program's accelerated. I'll get into college a year sooner, you'll see, by next September sure, right after I turn seventeen. At the rate I'm going I'll even be admitted into Radcliffe, Wellesley or any one of the seven sister schools. If I'd continued at Forest Hills with the overcrowding . . . the triple sessions—

MR. KINDERMANN: Don't sell Forest Hills High School short, Hannah! It's still rated one of the best in the city. Perhaps you're right about Greylock's Art Department. That's incidental, though. The important thing is that your attitude towards Yiddishkeit has changed, and I don't like it a bit. What's the sudden change due to *but* Greylock? Wanting to stay away for Hanukkah proves—

HANNAH: (Defensively) I *didn't want* to stay away, dad, honest, but leaving before all the other girls seemed . . . oh . . . uh . . . (At a loss for the right words) No one else was going until the Christmas holiday va—

MR. KINDERMANN: (Interrupting—incensed) *CHRISTMAS!* What have *you* to do with Christmas? But what can one expect when you live with a bunch of "shikses?"

MRS. KINDERMANN: (Intervening) "Shikses!?" Really, Karl, you *know* most of the girls are Jewish from fine Jewish families.

MR. KINDERMANN: (Sarcastically) Jewish from fine Jewish families! . . . Why, Judaism is more foreign to them than . . . Buddhism, yoga . . . or . . . *Zen!*

HANNAH: My, how you exaggerate, dad! I'll grant you they didn't all go to Hebrew School, but they had a good religious training just the same . . . everyone of them went to Sunday School until confirmation. They know Jewish history and all about the holidays. What's more, they observe too in their own way.

MR. KINDERMANN: (Heatedly) Don't tell *me* about them, Hannah! I know their kind all too well with their phoney fancy anglicized-Americanized names and their nose jobs to hide their Jewish origin. Ostensibly, they're reformed Jews, but they invariably tend to assimilate and intermarry. They're Americans first, last and foremost, Jews incidentally, accidentally, they say. What's the implication? Obvious . . . they can't be blamed for being born Jewish. They're no different, Hannah, no better, believe me, than those "pure" 100% German-Jews who denied their Jewish background or weren't aware of it even, until discovered and purged in the Nazi holocaust. Some of those "German first" Jews, as a matter of fact, even supported Hitler in the beginning. Many came from families who had lived in Germany for hundreds of years. Claiming to be "pure German" didn't save them from the concentration camps and gas chambers, as you know. (Heaves a deep racking sigh) My family, thank God, managed to escape to England in the nick of time, but I saw . . . *plenty!* (Pauses, shaken by his harrowing recollections) When I recognize the same symptoms among our reformed Jews here . . . the danger signals of a repetition of the same pattern, I. . . . It's frightening . . . makes one's blood. . . . (Shudders and pauses—deciding not to pursue the painful subject) I'm sorry I gave in to your going to Greylock—quitting your Hebrew classes and Center activities, but you and mother pressured me so, I finally agreed. No question but that you *needed* a change then . . . you were all sort of tangled up. Since you're doing so nicely, I won't insist on your switching now. After all, it's a matter of only another six months. However, I don't relish your being exposed to their false values and cockeyed ideas. (Urgently) *Please,* Hannah, don't be influenced by those girls or you'll lose your identity, become like them . . . a sport, a no-count don't belong! . . .

HANNAH: (Assuringly) I won't, dad, I promise . . . I *couldn't* . . . your upbringing's too deeply ingrained. I'll remain a good Baht T'zion—*always!* . . .

MR. K.: Remember who and what you are, dear. Remember your namesake . . . what the name Hannah signifies—a mother of martyrs—a true mother of Israel.

HANNAH: I shan't forget, dad, *ever* . . . I'm proud of my heritage.

MR. K.: (Touched and pleased, he rises, crosses to Hannah and kisses her on the brow) Then I shall always have reason to be proud of you, dear daughter. (In the interim, David and Miriam having finished their latkes, and disinterested in the adults' conversation, after excusing themselves to Mrs. K., cross into living-room area. Mrs. K. having cleared the dishes onto teawagon, has exited into kitchen stage right, wheeling tea-wagon off. David removes several throw pillows from sofa and sprawls on them, on floor, near fireplace. Miriam sits on hassock close to him.)

DAVID: (Extracts several crisp bills and a batch of coins from his jacket and trouser pockets, arranges them systematically on rug in piles) $10. from Daddy; $5. from Uncle Charley; $5. from Aunt Julia . . . and this haul from grandpa. I used to think grandpa got the new coins from the bank, but he *collects* them, Miriam, saves them for months and months until he has one for each year. He gets a real kick out of doing that. They gotta be bright and shiny though—like new—if not, they're n.g., he says. (Stacking the silver dollars and counting them) Thirteen . . . one for each birthday. And silver dollars are hard to find nowadays. I'll bet grandpa gets 'em from out west some place . . . Montana maybe . . . they use silver dollars there still, you know. (Stacking and counting the half-dollars) Thirteen . . . that makes six dollars and fifty cents—$6.50 and $13. is $19.50. (Stacking and counting the quarters) And thirteen quarters . . . three twenty-five . . . $22.75 so far . . . (Stacking and counting the dimes) Thirteen dimes . . . that's easy . . . dollar thirty . . . and thirteen nickels . . . sixty-five cents. (Struggles with mental arithmetic to arrive at total) Aw, I lost count . . . I'll need paper and pencil to get the total. Boy! . . . am I *rich!* Never got so much Hanukkah gelt before . . . this is the best Hanukkah I ever had.

MIRIAM: (Counting and re-counting her bills and silver as David does, but unable to make any headway with the figuring) A dollar from Daddy; a dollar from Mummy and a dollar from Hannah; seven half-dollars and seven quarters and seven dimes and seven nickels and seven golden pennies from grandpa. Together it makes . . . makes . . . (Pauses, completely at sea) Oh Davie, add it up for me, please. I *can't*.

DAVID: (Taking over in a quite business-like manner) Yours is a cinch. Three singles—$3. Seven half dollars—$3.50 and $1.75 in quarters and seventy cents in dimes and thirty-five cents of nickels and seven pennies . . . that makes . . . (Calculating) $9.37 altogether.

MIRIAM: You got more money, Davie, but I got a lot more Hanukkah presents . . . a walkie-talkie doll and a whole outfit for her and a big carriage like for a baby and a cooking-set and dishes and a fur-set . . . and . . . and . . . and . . .

DAVID: (Mimicking her) And . . . and . . . and . . . so what?! (Gathering his bills and coins and putting them away) My baseball outfit, football and that Raleigh bike Uncle Jack gave me beats anything you got. And how about those record albums from Uncle Joe . . . Dave Clark Five and the Beatles and Animals?

(Rises and crosses to dining-table for a candy. His attention is arrested by a face peering in at the window. It is a wan emaciated face of a slight pathetic-looking little girl. She wears a shabby leatherette jacket, a large woolen kerchief wrapped over her head and shoulders, a plaid woolen skirt, long wool socks and galoshes. Her hands encased in knitted gloves, worn at the finger-tips, holds a seemingly heavy suitcase.)

(Calling excitedly)
Dad!! . . . Dad! . . . Mom! . . . Hannah! . . . Look . . . *look!*

MR. K.: What is it, son?

HANNAH: Why do you shout like that, David? } simultaneously

MIRIAM: (Rushes to window) Ooooh! . . . Oh my!! . . .

DAVID: (Pointing and exclaiming) On the porch . . . there, at the window . . . see . . . a little girl . . . looking in . . . just see how she's staring! . . .

HANNAH: (Crossing to window) Poor kid ... she must be frozen stiff!...
MIRIAM: (Shivering in sympathy) Oooh ... 'tso cold outside ... it's freezing. Take her in, Daddy dear. She'll get warm here ... I'll give her my fur muff. (Imploringly) *Please* bring her inside, Daddy!...
MR. K.: (Affectionately patting Miriam—assuringly) I will, darling, I *will*. (Hurriedly exits, followed by David)
DAVID: (On exit) B'rrrrr ... sure wouldn't wanna be in that girl's boots! (Sound of street door opening and shutting. Hannah and Miriam remain at window. Hannah lifts Miriam so she can the better see. Sound of outer door opening and shutting again. Mr. K. re-enters, carrying the "little stranger" in his arms, followed by David, carrying her suitcase, which he places in a corner of foyer. She seems chilled or frost-bitten. Except for her black sparkling eyes, her rigid body and face show no sign of life. Mr. K. hurriedly crosses to sofa, and gently lays the "little stranger" on it. Hannah quickly removes her outer garments, galoshes, worn shoes and socks, then massages her hands and feet to bring on circulation.)
MR. K.: No wonder the child's frozen ... it's way below zero.
(The room's sudden warmth evidently overcomes her, for she closes her eyes and swoons. Noting the child's seeming loss of consciousness, Mr. K., to make her more comfortable, props several pillows up so she can lean against them.) Some brandy, Hannah, quick! She seems to have passed out. Hurry! That'll revive her. (Hannah hurriedly pours brandy from decanter on table, and hands glass to Mr. K., who presses it to the child's lips. She gulps it, opens her eyes, looks around, but does not react to anyone or anything except the Hanukkah candles in the Menorah, at which she wistfully gazes, then faintly mumbles:)

LITTLE STRANGER: Di Chanukeh lichteloch ... di dininke ... shayninke Chanukeh lichteloch!... (Then falls back weakly, her eyes shut)
MRS. K.: (On entrance) Who came in? (Then notices child on sofa with Mr. K. and Hannah hovering over her) Oh, my God!... How could anyone send a child out in this bitter frost?!! I wouldn't take the dog— (On approaching, recognizes the little stranger) Why, that's little Esther! (David and Miriam

have been fluttering about, trying to help. Their sympathetic identification with the little stranger is apparent. David has piled Esther's outergarments on a chair near fireplace to dry.)

MR. K.: You know her, Eve?

MRS. K.: Yes Karl, tell you later. First, must get some hot food into her. I'll wager she's starved. Wouldn't be surprised if it's hunger rather than the biting cold that's knocked her out. I'll heat some soup and warm up the roast-beef.

(Esther stirs, coming to partially, as Mrs. K. leans over and inspects her more closely.) Hannah, now that she's come to, take her upstairs and get her wet things off. She's drenched right through. Give her a good alcohol rub-down . . . use a heavy beach-towel. Your First Aid Course will come in handy. Then, have her put on something warm of yours. (Esther sits up. Hannah helps her rise and leads her off, up the stairs.)

MR. K.: Who *is* she, Eva? (Shocked) What kind of parents . . .

MRS. K.: She has no parents, Karl, only a stepmother. They get help from Welfare, I understand, and the stepmother earns a little doing alterations. She works for Mrs. Roberts occasionally and Esther usually delivers the stuff.

MR. K.: (Crossing to telephone, decisively) I'll give that Mrs. Roberts a piece of my mind . . . expecting delivery in this weather, knowing . . .

MRS. K.: No use phoning, Karl. They're out by now. Tonight's their Opera Night. They leave for Florida next week and this is a rush job, I s'pose. You know fashion-plate Mrs. Roberts! (Hurriedly crossing to kitchen) Don't delay me anymore, Karl dear. I must heat some food for her. She'll be all right, I'm sure, after she's had something nourishing.

(Mrs. K. exits into kitchen. Mr. K., distressed, crosses to window and stands looking out. David and Miriam join him at window. He tenderly embraces them both, as BLACKOUT or CURTAIN on Scene I to suggest time lapse.)

SCENE II

(Lights up or curtain on Scene II. The Hanukkah candles have burnt out. The dining-room table has been cleared except for a setting for Esther. Her own clothes have been removed.

She now wears a colorful quilted pegnoir, much too large for her—the sleeves rolled up, felt comfys, and woolen socks. She has just finished the meal. The food and drink obviously did her good, for a bright flush suffuses her cheeks and she is animated and energetic.

On rise, she is discovered relating her family's story. The Kindermanns, grouped around the table, are listening intently.)

ESTHER: Oh no, he was sick. He caught an awful cold . . . coughed by day and by night. Sometime, the whole night he couldn't sleep on account of coughing. My stepmother said it's only a cold, he'll get better.

DAVID: (Puzzled) Didn't he go to the hospital? What did your family doctor—

ESTHER: When we got a doctor it was too late. The doctor couldn't do anything. He didn't have no lungs left, the doctor said. My father once told me his mother died from t.b.—maybe he had it too and didn't catch it in time. Who knows? We didn't have anybody to help us. My stepmother wanted to go on relief, but my father wouldn't let. (Pause) Oh, he was so sick . . . such a terrible cough . . . I can still hear him coughing even now, and it's two years already . . . on the last day of Chanukah—the night of the eighth candle, he died. I was just ten. (Pause. The Ks are touched)

HANNAH: (In an attempt to divert her to practical matters) What kind of work did your father do?

ESTHER: He was a paintner, but he didn't belong to the union, so he got jobs only sometimes, you know. He never worked steady . . . never made enough money. The paint and walking up all those flights was no good for him, he used to say. We live on the top floor, see, the fifth.

DAVID: Where?

ESTHER: Downtown, on Cherry Street. Know where it is?

HANNAH: I do. Last year, our Social Studies Club went down to the Lower East Side to see the slum conditions in that neighborhood. Those tenements sure ought to be condemned. (Recollecting, but unsure) Cherry Street's near the East River, isn't it?

ESTHER: Uh-huh. I was born in the same rooms. My father used to promise to move to the Bronx soon as we could afford. It was so hard for him to walk those five flights, but we couldn't even pay the rent here until the Relief paid for us ... after ... (Pause; proudly) He wasn't only a paintner, my father, he was a Chaz'n too ... sang in the big schul on Madison Street. O, he used to sing something wonderful! Every Rush Ha'shuneh and Yum Kippur he sang in schul for the uhmid. In the house he sang too ... Kiddish and Zmires and Havduleh. He had such a sweet voice. You know, just before he died even, he tried to sing. I remember like it was yesterday, he said to me: "Esterl teirinke, breng mir dem Chanukeh luhmp, mir vel'n bentch'n Chanukeh licht." I brought him, put the eight candles in the Menorah, held the Shamish and box o' matches ready. He took it, but his hands were shaking so, he could hardly hold it. He began the Bruchuh with the niggin, but finished quick plain. He coughed so bad, like choking ... couldn't stop. He then made a motion I should light the candles. Then, he *made* himself stop coughing, sat up like, looked at the Chanukeh candles as if he knew he wouldn't ever see them again and in a tiny little weak voice—just like a baby's—said: "Di Chanukeh lichteloch ... di dininke shayninke Chanukeh lichteloch ..." and fell back on the pillow. He didn't move ... didn't say another word ... didn't say anything no more ... (Sobs brokenly) I cried ... I yelled: "Tahteh ... tahteh ... tahtenyu ... papenyu" ... but he didn't hear me. He *couldn't* hear me! I didn't know what to do ... I just couldn't believe. I cried ... I screamed ... ran to get my stepmother. She was by our next door. When she came in, she took a look, touched him and said: "Geshturb'n ... nu!" That's all she said ... that's all! ... (Cries bitterly, recollecting. The Kindermanns are profoundly moved. Pause.)

DAVID: (To distract her) Who makes the Bruchah now, Esther?

ESTHER: Nobody. My stepmother says: "S'nisht naytig ... ich ken zich bahgane uhn dem." But I miss it ... the Chanukah candles, the bruchuh, Nahrris Ha'luloo and everything! ... It's so ... so ... (Sighs nostalgically) I haven't heard Chanukah licht bentch'n since ... since ...

DAVID: (Suddenly inspired) Like to hear it now?

ESTHER: (Elated, but incredulous) *NOW?!!* ...

DAVID: Sure! Right away. I'll bentch for you. I can make the Bruchah. I can even sing it and Ha'nayrot Ha'lah'lu and everything. We learned it in Hebrew School long ago. (To Mr. K.) May I, Dad?

MR. K.: (Pleased) Of course, David. Good idea! Go ahead, son. (Hannah hands David box of Hanukkah candles. He takes nine colored candles out of the box, places eight candles in respective grooves of Menorah, and the Shamash in its niche, then puts on yarmelke. Chants and sings Bruchah.)

Transliteration of First Blessing:
Boruch ato Adonoy, Elohaynu melech ho-olam, asher kid'shonu b'mitzvo-sov v'tzee-vonu l'hadlik nayr shel Chanuko.

Translation of First Blessing:
Blessed art Thou, O Lord our God, King of the universe, who hast sanctified us by Thy commandments and commanded us to kindle the light of Hanukkah.

Transliteration of Second Blessing:
Boruch ato Adonoy, Elohaynu melech ho-olom, sheh-osu nissim l'avosaynoo b'yomim ho-haym b'zmahn ha-zeh.

Translation of Second Blessing:
Blessed art Thou, O Lord our God, King of the universe, who wroughtest miracles for our fathers in days of old, at this season.

(David then strikes match from matchbox Mr. K. gives him; kindles Shamash and two candles, then hands lit Shamash to Esther. She kindles a candle, then timidly asks:)

ESTHER: Can I light another one?
DAVID: Sure—light one more.
HANNAH: (Admonishingly) One! When you've lit so many!
DAVID: (Grandiosely) All right, Esther, light three, light *five* if you want!
ESTHER: (Delighted) Five!!! ... (As she kindles the next five candles)
DAVID: (As he transfers Shamash from Esther to Miriam) Here Miriam, for you—that's the last this year.
MIRIAM: (Disappointedly) Only *one?!!* ... No fair ... I wanna ...
DAVID: No more left. (Miriam lights the last candle in the Menorah and David places Shamash in its niche, then, sings: "HA-NAYRUT HA'LALOO.")

Transliteration of Ha-Nayrut Ha'laloo:
Ha'nayrut ha'laloo anoo madlikim ahl ha'nisim v'ahl ha'tshoout v'ahl ha'niflahot she'asitah l'avotaynu b'yamim ha'hem, b'zmahn ha'zeh, ahl yidai kohanechah ha'kdoshim. V'chul shmonaht y'may Chanukah ha'nayrut ha'laloo kodesh hem, v'en lanoo r'shoot l'hishtahmesh b'hem, elah l'rotahm bilvahd, k'day l'hodut oo'l'halel l'shimchah ahl n'sechah v'ahl y'shoo-atechah, v'ahl niflehtechah.

Translation of Ha-Nayrut Ha'laloo:
We kindle these lights on account of the miracles, the deliverances and the wonders that Thou didst work for our fathers in those days at this season, by means of Thy holy priests. During all the eight days of Hanukkah these lights are sacred, neither is it permitted us to make any profane use of them; but we are only to look at them, in order that we may give thanks unto Thy name for Thy miracles, Thy deliverances and Thy wonders.

NOTE TO DIRECTOR

For melody of "Ha-nayrut Ha'laloo," please refer to page No. 4 of S. Goldfarb's *Jewish Songster—"Bra-chot Shel Hanukkah."*
Singing of Hymn *"Ma'oz Zur Yeshu-ati"* is optional. However, it would prove effective with everyone onstage joining in except Esther, who because she is unfamiliar with the tune, hesitates to, but keeps time with the music, clapping her hands or tapping her foot and swaying in rhythm.
Understandably, rendition of blessings and songs in Ashkenazi or Sephardic pronunciation is contingent on which is used in particular school.

ESTHER: (Gratefully) Oh, thank you . . . *thank you!* You sing nice, David. My father sang different, but your way is nice too. Thanks a lot! . . .
DAVID: You're welcome. (Removes yarmelke) C'mon Esther, we'll show you our Hanukkah presents. (David leads the way up the stairs, followed by Esther and Miriam, hand in hand. Exit children. Mr. and Mrs. K. sit at dining-room table with Hannah, and converse in low voices, so as not to be overheard by children.)
MRS. K.: (Inspired) Know what I've been thinking, Karl dear? I'd like to adopt her.
MR. K.: Sure would be a "mitzveh."
MRS. K.: I'd just *love* to, if we could arrange it. Can't tell you what it would mean to me. (Rather self-consciously) Sounds

adolescent, I s'pose, but as far back as I can remember, I always wanted to adopt an orphan ... it's been my girlhood dream, sort of. That's what influenced me to be a volunteer with the Adoption Agency, I guess. If I hadn't met you then and we were married right away, I'd have gone in for social work no doubt.

MR. K.: Adoption's a pretty complicated business, Eve, isn't it—entails investigation—litigation and what not. Read something just the other day about the Family Court having exclusive jurisdiction—

MRS. K.: Don't know what the laws governing adoption are now, but we can find out easily enough. When I worked with the agency, as I recall, if the mother was willing to surrender and the Board of Child Welfare approved, it could be managed. Esther's a *full* orphan, after all, that woman's only a *step*mother. (Recollecting) There used to be some procedure too for placing a child on an experimental basis. Maybe *that* would be a solution. Oh, we'd have to be investigated and all that, but I believe we'd be accepted as foster parents. Of course, the fact that they're known to Welfare might make it more difficult, but ...

MR. K.: It's entirely up to *you*, Eve, granted her stepmother consents and the Welfare Department or whatever approves, as you say. If you feel you can take care of her—

MRS. K.: Take care of her? She's not an infant, Karl, she can look after herself. She's *twelve* ... mature way beyond her years. You can see how self-sufficient, practical and responsible she is—actually *adult!*

HANNAH: There you go again, mother, rushing intò things. She's a growing girl ... all sorts of problems can develop. Sure, she's better able to take care of herself than I was at her age, or Miriam is, having been on her own so much. But you'll have your hands full ... she'll keep you hopping. (Pauses, then becoming excited by the dramatic prospect, enthuses) Wouldn't it be *great* though if we could swing it?! ... It would mean the beginning of a new life for her, and what a different *better* life! ...

MR. K.: (Meditatively) Well ... we'll see ... we'll see. Doesn't depend on us alone, you realize. But let's take the necessary steps and inquire anyhow. (Children re-enter from upstairs. David brings on his football and baseball outfit—glove, bat, etc.; Miriam her walkie-talkie doll and fur-set—white scarf and muff. Esther helps Miriam carry the big doll down the stairs. The children sit on sofa, hassock and floor, facing the fireplace. David proudly shows his Hanukkah presents, but Esther is most impressed with Miriam's fur-set.)

ESTHER: (Lovingly caressing muff) Who gave you this, Miriam? It's ... it's *beautiful!* So soft and warm ... so snow-white ... like ... like a clean white pussy.

MIRIAM: Daddy.

ESTHER: Looks like ermine—is it?

MIRIAM: I don' know. Daddy gave me Hanukkah gelt too ... a dollar!

ESTHER: Money don't count so much. You know, Miriam, I like this best of all your Hanukkah presents ... yours and David's put together. (Gently strokes her cheek with muff, then puts her hands in muff and admires effect. The Ks and Hannah take in the cozy harmonious group.)

MRS. K.: (In hushed tones) Karl dear, do you suppose it would be wise to sound her out?

MR. K.: Whatever you think's right, Eve.

MRS. K.: (Calling) Children ... come over here, please. I want to talk to you. (Children cross to Mrs. K. She props Miriam on her lap and embraces Esther affectionately.) Would you like to be *our* little girl, Esther, live here all the time ... eat here ... sleep here ... go to school here ... our home should be *your* home?

ESTHER: (Incredulously at first, then slowly comprehending) You mean ... you mean ... you ... you'll be my mother ... and ... and ... (pointing to Mr. K.) Like my father?! ...

MRS. K.: (Patting Esther) That's right, dear, that's *just* what we mean.

ESTHER: (Tremulously eager) You'd really an' truly let me stay here every single solitary day and I won't have to be by my stepmother no more? (Earnestly) I'll be such a good girl if you'll only let me! I'll scrub the floors and clean and wash and polish and go on errands ... I'll do *anything*—anything in the world!

MRS. K.: Oh, we don't want you to work, dear, just be one of the family ... *our* little girl, like Miriam ... go to school and Hebrew School—dancing school if you wish, and grow up to be a happy healthy young woman same as Hannah. (David and Miriam slowly grasp the implication and seem thrilled by the prospect.)

MIRIAM: Is Esther gonna be my sister, mummy, stay here every day an'night and play with me?
MRS. K.: Would you like her to, darling?
MIRIAM: (Nodding assent, enthusiastically) Oh *yes*, mummy... very *very* much! And Esther won't tease me like David, will she?
MRS. K.: No dear, she won't. David shouldn't either, but older brothers somehow always do... teasing little sisters is their idea of fun. If Esther's auntie lets her stay with us, you'll have another sister. (To Esther) Try and understand, dear child, it doesn't depend only on us. Many things have to be taken care of... other people have to agree that it's best for you... best for you *now* and the future. Before we can do anything though, we need to know how *you* feel about it—whether you'd *prefer* living here.
MR. K.: When I take you back, Esther, we'll see what your stepmother has to say. That's important, but what *you* want is even more important. Are you *sure* you'd rather live here? That counts a great deal.
ESTHER: 'Course I'm sure... I'm very *very* sure... *positive!* You wouldn't ask me even if you knew how mean she is... how she screams on me... and hits me lotsa times. Always she picks on me... blames me for everything. She's awful mean, honest. I don't know why but she's always angry... from morning to night!... (Dwelling on her stepmother's mistreatment, she breaks down and sobs brokenly)
MRS. K.: (Placatingly) Come, come now, dear, don't cry!... Maybe we'll manage it so you'll have no reason to cry anymore. (Wiping away Esther's tears with her own handkerchief which she removes from her dress pocket) Let's hope everything will turn out all right. Come Esther, dry your eyes now and show us what a pretty smile you have. (Esther makes a concerted effort to smile) There... that's better!... Now *really* smile... a big broad smile!
ESTHER: (Notwithstanding her attempts to control herself, the spasmodic sobbing continues. Finally, she stifles sobs—determinedly) I won't cry no more, I promise. I won't cry no more... I *won't!*...
MRS. K.: (Lovingly strokes Esther's hair) That's a good girl!...
MR. K.: We really should get going, Eve. That woman must

be worried. Maybe we can call her or get a message to her, at least.

ESTHER: Nobody in the building's got a telephone, Mr. Kindermann. My next-door sometimes gets calls by Cohen's candy-store, but it's closed already. Ever since Cohen had a hold-up he closes early.

MR. K.: Hannah, get her ready, please. Find something warm for her to put on . . . her own things are hardly adequate. (Referring to his wrist-watch) It's after 8:30 . . . no idea it was that late. Really shouldn't have kept her so long. Even if her stepmother tried reaching Mrs. Roberts she wouldn't have gotten an answer.

MRS. K.: We'll dig up your fur-lined parka, Hannah, that'll be good.

MR. K.: (Crossing to outside door) The storm's let up, but I'd better put the snow tires on.

MRS. K.: (On exiting upstairs with Hannah) Careful driving, Karl dear.

MR. K.: (Taking suitcase Esther brought, on exit) You can play meanwhile, children.

DAVID: What d'you think of that, Esther? You're going to be part of our family!

ESTHER: It's too good to be true . . . I can't believe . . . like a dream, I'm afraid I'll wake up and . . . (disconsolately) Anyway, your mother said only *maybe* . . . 'cause it don't depend on—

DAVID: (Confidently) Oh, mother'll fix it! *She'll* manage, you'll see! . . .

ESTHER: (Sighing) I hope . . . I hope . . . I hope! . . .

DAVID: (To divert her) Wanna play a game, Esther?

ESTHER: (Shyly) H'mmm.

DAVID: You'll like this game, Esther, it's a play-acting game. Just make up your own words as you go along. We'll act out a scene from the Hanukkah play my club gave in the Center auditorium. I was Judah, the brave Maccabee. Now, I'll be Antiochus, the King of Syria. I was supposed to play that wicked tyrant madman Antiochus, so I know the part. Boy! was I glad I got Judah instead! *You* be Hannah, mother of the seven sons, and you Miriam, you'll be Sirion, her youngest son. Miriam knows the story from Sunday School. Do you?

ESTHER: O sure, my father told me about it lotsa times.

DAVID: Let's begin then, huh. Ready?

MIRIAM: Ready.

ESTHER: So'm I!

DAVID: We'll start from where your six sons were already tortured and killed because they refused to obey my orders—eat pig and bow down to my god Zeus. The soldiers are now dragging out Sirion, your last, only living son, before me. He was just a little kid, remember. (As he sits in arm-chair) I'm sitting on my throne. (Indicating) You stand over there, Hannah.

HANNAH: (Enters, carrying Esther's clothes and a bright red fur-lined parka. On overhearing last remark) What are you *talking* about, David?

DAVID: (Provoked) Whose talking to you?

ESTHER: (Explaining—apologetically) We're playing a Hanukkah game about Hannah and her seven sons. I'm Hannah and David was telling . . .

HANNAH: (Interrupting) This is no time for games, David. It's late and Dad has to drive you downtown Esther, . . . you've got to get dressed.

DAVID: (Annoyed) What are you butting in for? We wanna finish the game.

HANNAH: (Reprimandingly) Don't be rude, David, and silly *too*. It's late and Esther must get home right away.

DAVID: What d'you mean *home?* Thought *this* was gonna be her home!

HANNAH: We hope to arrange things so it *can* be, but first, dad has to talk to her stepmother and—

DAVID: What for?

MR. K.: (On re-entering, having overheard last remarks) You don't want people to say your Dad's a kidnapper, David, do you?

DAVID: 'Course not. He isn't and no one would ever say it.

MR. K.: O but they *will* if we keep Esther without her stepmother's permission and take other necessary steps to adopt her legally.

HANNAH: It's high time you were in bed, Miriam. Go . . . go . . . *go!* You too David, tomorrow's school.

MIRIAM: (Hugging Esther) Come back soon, Esther. Goo' night! (Exits reluctantly)

ESTHER: Good night, Miriam.

HANNAH: (Extending her hand to Esther) C'mon Esther,

let's hurry and get you dressed real fast. (Leads Esther off. Both exit)

DAVID: (Tarrying) O Dad, I don't want to go to bed yet. When you get back, I'll be asleep and won't know what happened ... not until tomorrow and I can't wait—

MR. K.: (Placing his hands on David's shoulders—man to man) Well son, I'll tell you what I'll do. Soon as I know what's what, I'll phone. You can stay up for my call if it takes all night.

DAVID: Thanks dad. That's great! Will you bring Esther back tonight?

MR. K.: O no ... definitely not! You must understand David, before we can adopt her there's a complicated procedure to go through. The one thing I may be able to accomplish tonight is get her stepmother's consent. That's the first step. Without that we can't go ahead at all.

DAVID: (Insistent) But her stepmother doesn't treat her right, so can't you *make* her agree. Esther's no square ... I'd like having her around. (Hannah re-enters with Esther, dressed for outdoors)

HANNAH: She's ready, Dad.

MR. K.: Thanks, Hannah. (As he takes Esther by the hand) Let's go, Esther. (To David) I'll ring you, David, soon as possible.

ESTHER: Goodbye, Hannah. Thank you for being so nice to me.

HANNAH: (Embracing Esther) Goodbye, Esther. Remember what mother told you.

ESTHER: (Nods in answer) 'Bye David. Sorry we couldn't finish the game.

DAVID: So long, Esther. See you ...

ESTHER: (Fervently) Hope so. (Exit Mr. K. with Esther. Sound effect of horn honking, motor starting and car driving off)

HANNAH: Why's Dad phoning you, David?

DAVID: (Cryptically, still offended by her treatment of him in Esther's presence) Because ... (Takes book out of bookcase and curls up on sofa to read) And I'm waiting for his call if it takes *all night!*

HANNAH: O *no*, you *don't!* Tomorrow's school, and you're going to bed *right now!*

DAVID: (Shrugging her off) Who cares what *you* say? (Adamantly) I'm *staying up!* Dad said I could.

(BLACKOUT or CURTAIN on Scene II to suggest time lapse.)

Scene III

(On curtain rise or lights up, the telephone bell rings. David rushes to answer, intercepting Hannah)

DAVID: (On phone) Hello ... Dad? Yep, it's me ... She said O.K. ... she's willing? Great!! ... (Disappointed) Esther's not coming back with you? ... I know you told me, but I thought —. .. Definitely not, huh? ... (Crestfallen) Oh! ... weeks ... maybe longer? ... But it's going to work out, you think? ... H'mmm ... Oke, I'll put her on. (Calling) Mom!! ... *Mom!* ... Dad's on the phone ... wants to talk to you.

MRS. K.: (Enters from kitchen, takes the telephone, and talks in hushed tones) ... Yes, Karl, I understand ... Didn't think it would be that easy ... Esther's such a great help ... Good! ... Once we have her signed surrender, we can go ahead ... Yes ... We'll follow through first thing tomorrow morning ... I'll expect you within the hour then ... Careful driving now, dear ... 'Bye. (Hangs up) I'd never have believed, Hannah, that she'd give Esther up so easily. Well, we're on our way! Her consent was all-important. We'll have to be investigated and approved, of course, but I don't think we'll have any trouble about that. It'll take some time before the adoption can be legalized though the Child Welfare Agency will have to sanction it, and—

HANNAH: (Curiously eager) Do you suppose Dad made a financial settlement?

MRS. K.: (Noticing that David's straining to eavesdrop) Shhh ...! David, why aren't you in bed where you belong? It's long after your bed-time! ...

DAVID: (Reluctantly crosses upstage toward stairway) G'night, Mom.

MRS. K.: Good night, David ... pleasant dreams.

DAVID: (On ascending stairs, excitedly calls) Miriam!!!! Mirrr ... eeeee ... ohhhm!!! ... Get up ... get up! Hurry, *WAKE UPPPP!* (At Miriam's door) Guess what, Mim? Esther's coming to live with us! (Then drones in a sing-song jingle) Esther's gonna be in our familee ... Esther's gonna be in our familee ... Esther'll be in the Kindermann clan!! ... O boy! What a terrific peachy plan! ...

MIRIAM: (Off-stage, voice sounding sleepy) Oh goody!...
I'm so glad, Davie, I can shout for joy!...

HANNAH: (Calling from down of stairway landing) Stop that racket, David! And get out of Miriam's room *this minute!* Why d'you wake her when it's—

DAVID: (Off-stage) Why *not?* Isn't it worth waking up for? She always wanted a sister 'stead o' me, and now her wish is coming true! (Enthusiastically) It's a Hanukkah present from God, I tell you, a Hanukkah present from God!...

MRS. K.: (Ascends stairs to calm David) Don't jump to conclusions, David. Nothing's settled yet. We hope it'll work out, but—

DAVID: (Off-stage keeps repeating) A Hanukkah present from God ... a Hanukkah present from God, that's what!...

MRS. K.: (Stops stock-still on upper landing, suddenly struck by the possible validity of David's statement, mulls over it) A Hanukkah present from God?!!... Maybe you're right, David. Maybe ... A Hanukkah present from God! (Relishing its import more and more as she slowly and meaningfully repeats:) A Hanukkah present from God!... Halevay!...

FINAL CURTAIN

HANUKKAH*

A dramatic reading for fourteen

Dorothy Ross

A dramatic reading in four parts with suggested songs for fourteen participants. Children from the lower grades can contribute the singing. Songs suggested are from *Songs We Sing*, by Harry Coopersmith.

The four readers may hold the script as a book, which should be bound in an attractive colored folder. Readers should be sufficiently familiar with text, so that they can get off book and relate to each other and audience.

On opening, Choir off-stage, humming *Mo-oz Tzur* (Rock of Ages). Please see page 129 in songster: *Songs We Sing*.

FIRST READER: Hanukkah is part of the experience of every modern Jew, but the story of Hanukkah is not to be found in the Bible. Those who wish to read it at first hand, must seek the source in the two Books of the Maccabees, in the Apocrypha. In the thirty-one chapters of these two books, the story unfolds —from the clash of ideology to the pitched battles, and finally, the victory in Jerusalem.

SECOND READER: What does the story mean to us today? LISTEN! Are these words familiar? (Each reader exhorts, as from a pulpit)

THIRD READER: If this trend continues, Jews as a group will vanish from this land!

FOURTH READER: Young Jews are changing their names and ways in order to assimilate!

FIRST READER: They are seeking jobs, concerned only about amassing wealth!

FOURTH READER: They are worshipping false values and false gods!

SECOND READER: Immodesty and nakedness are encouraged in the name of nature!

---

* Permission to reprint and present royalty-free granted by AJC on the proviso that the school or center planning production, contact: Women's Division, American Jewish Congress, 15 East 84th Street, New York 10028, to advise when, where and by whom (children, youth or adult group) the script will be done. Copies of script may be ordered through the AJC office at a minimal charge.

FOURTH READER: And the culture of the majority population is stamping out the Jewish way of life!

THIRD READER: Fellow-Jews, we appeal to you. Will *this* time in our history go down as the time of the Vanishing Jew? (Pause. Third Reader steps forward) Do these words sound familiar? Have you heard this cry in your Temple? Have you read these very words in our current magazines?

FIRST READER: Perhaps you have, but these very words were also spoken in the streets of Jerusalem over 2100 years ago, when *Greek met Jew* and the story of Hanukkah began.

SECOND READER: Hanukkah is not simply the story of the oil that lasted eight days.

FOURTH READER: Or of the courage of Judah Maccabee.

FIRST READER: Or of the latkes we eat, or the dreidel we spin. Hanukkah is not merely the celebration of a victory which took place in ancient Judaea in the years 167-165 B.C.E. (Before the Common Era).

THIRD READER: Hanukkah is a festival which has fired the imagination of the Jew in all times, till it has become in our age one of the shining gems in the crown of Jewish festivals.

SECOND READER: When Alexander the Great, two thousand three hundred years ago, conquered the entire eastern half of the ancient world, he brought with his army the culture of Greece—Hellenism—which made a deep impression on the development of Judaism and the culture of humanity.

FIRST READER: Under his rule, the Jews enjoyed political independence and freedom of worship.

FOURTH READER: But 150 years later, when Antiochus Ephiphanes became King of Syria, this cruel, mad king decided to prohibit the Jews, under penalty of death, from observing their faith.

SECOND READER: Instead, said Antiochus, the Jews were to worship the gods of the Greeks; and he placed a statue of Zeus in the Temple at Jerusalem.

THIRD READER: The Jews were not united. Hellenism had blinded many Jews and assimilation was popular.

FIRST READER: What was this struggle between Greek and Jew that led to the Maccabean revolt?

FOURTH READER: What was the historic clash between two philosophies—this duel between Zeus, the Greek god who lived on Mount Olympus, and Adon Olam, the Creator of the Universe?

SECOND READER: The Jew worshipped the Creator of Nature and sang praise to the spirit of God which hovered over the surface of the globe. (Background humming by Choir of "ADON OLAM". See page 75 of Songster)

FIRST READER: The Greek said: "God *is* Nature. *We* worship the material world."

THIRD READER: To the Hellenist, everything that was externally beautiful was good—nature, the body, the senses . . .

FOURTH READER: To the Jew, everything that was *inwardly* good, was beautiful.

SECOND READER: They were worlds apart—the Jews and the Hellenists—and the Jewish people were divided among themselves.

FIRST READER: Imagine a market-place in ancient Judaea. Imagine a debate between an Assimilationist Jew (Second Reader steps forward with a small sign "Assimilationist Jew") and a pious Chassidic Jew. (Fourth Reader steps forward with sign "Pious Jew." The two representing the Assimilationist Jew and the Pious Jew render the following lines dramatically, as though orating-debating)

ASSIMILATIONIST JEW: (By 2nd Reader)
There is no revelation; there is no God divine;
The only God is Nature—We worship him with wine.
Forget the Holy Temple. Embrace the shapely limb
Come join the Jewish-Hellenists. *We* worship at the gym!

PIOUS JEW: (Done by 4th reader)
The Hebrew Law is holy, at Sinai we received it.
We study all the holy writ, since Moses we've believed it!
Our conduct must be moral. In holiness is beauty,
The Hebrew people must fulfill a spiritual duty.

ASSIMILATIONIST JEW:
The Greek pursues a beauty which every eye can see,
In painting and in sculpture and in loose frivolity!

PIOUS JEW:
'Tis not so. All beauty is within. *Your* beauty will decay,
And we will live to celebrate our true Judaic way.

THIRD READER: Assimilation was at its height. Judaea was torn. Families were divided. The strict Jews banned all the alien culture, even the beautiful in Greek art. But the Hellenizers enticed the youth, the aristocracy, even some of the priests. Judaism was in grave danger of dissolution!...

SECOND READER: Then History worked one of its miracles!

FOURTH READER: Antiochus IV, King of Syria, wanting to spread Hellenism, wanting to indulge his vanity, decreed:

FIRST READER: "THE JEWISH TEMPLE IS NOW A TEMPLE OF THE GREEK!"

THIRD READER: "GOD is replaced by Jupiter-Zeus and pigs must be sacrificed to him in the Temple and in the public squares!"

FOURTH READER: For a few years, the people submitted in despair, until a false rumor spread that Antiochus was killed in Judaea. Riots and rebellion flared. But, Antiochus was very much alive, and furious with the Judaeans.

SECOND READER: He proclaimed war against Judaism!

FIRST READER: He began a systematic persecution of those who refused to become Hellenized!

FOURTH READER: He looted the Temple of all its treasures. Jews were tortured and killed without mercy.

THIRD READER: Hundreds of women and children were sold into slavery.

SECOND READER: Judaism itself was at stake. At first, dumb like cattle, many Jews submitted and suffered. Then, in the face of overwhelming odds, the Jews united to defeat their tyrants.

FIRST READER: The rest you know—the Chassidim, meaning the Pious, believing that life was not worthwhile without freedom of religion, died as martyrs "Al Kiddush Ha-shem," as Hannah did—the brave mother who sacrificed her seven sons for freedom of religion.

THIRD READER: But in the town of Modin lived a priestly family lead by Mattathias, who had five stalwart sons. Ordered to sacrifice a pig in the public square, Mattathias slew the enemy officer instead. Then he fled with his sons who united the Judaeans under the slogan "WHO IS FOR GOD, FOLLOW ME!"

FOURTH READER: In 165 B.C.E., the Maccabees, followers of Judah, marched into Jerusalem, cleansed the Temple, and celebrated for eight days the dedication of Hanukkah.

SECOND READER: Thousands had died that the nation and its faith might live!

FIRST READER: Listen to the martial tune set to the words of *Mo'oz Tzur*:

CHOIR: (Sings)
Rock of Ages, let our song
Praise Thy saving power;
Thou amidst the raging foes,
Wast our sheltering tower.
Furious they assailed us,
But Thine arm availed us,
And Thy word
Broke their sword
When our own strength failed us.

THIRD READER: This is the theme song of Hanukkah. Hear the words of the fifth stanza which tells in prose of the miracle:

"The Greeks gathered themselves together against me in the days of the Hasmoneans. They broke down the walls of my towers and defiled all the oils. But from the last of the remaining flasks, a miracle was wrought for the beloved, and men of understanding appointed eight days for song and praise."

FOURTH READER: *Mo'oz Tzur* is probably the best known melody among Jews next to the *Ha'tikvah*. It echoes the hope and confidence with which the Maccabees marched into battle. Here is the second verse:

CHOIR: (Sings)
Children of the Martyr-race,
Whether free or fettered,
Wake the echoes of the songs
Where ye be scattered.
Yours the message cheering
That the time is nearing
Which will see
All men free,
Tyrants disappearing.

THIRD READER: Nowhere is the word "Hanukkah" mentioned. What is the derivation of the word—*Hanukkah?* Is it the name of a man, a place, an event?

SECOND READER: It is a word, a Hebrew word, meaning several things. It is the word root of "chinuch," the Hebrew word for education, and for dedication; like the dedication of a new home or a new building, chanukat-ha-bayit. See the connection? A sound Jewish *education* can only be started in a sound Jewish *home* which lives by sound Jewish *values*.

FIRST READER: History is full of examples where the breakdown of home life endangered the nation. Didn't the Talmudists judge a city not by its defenses or its stone walls, but by the education given its children?

FOURTH READER: So we celebrate Hanukkah every year. For the adults, we remember the theme of the struggle of ideas —Hellenism vs. Judaism—and for the children, like all Jewish holidays, we celebrate in many different ways.

THIRD READER: We sing songs, like this: (see page 120 of Songster. Choir sings in Hebrew and/or English.)

CHOIR: (Song—"O Hanukkah—O Hanukkah")
O Hanukkah, O Hanukkah, a festival of joy,
A holiday, a jolly-day, for every girl and boy.
Spin the whirling trendels, all week long,
Eat the sizzling latkes, sing the happy songs!
Now light them, tonight then, the flickering candles in a row,
Retell the wondrous story of God in all His glory,
And dance by the candles' cheering glow.

SECOND READER: We grate potatoes and eat millions of latkes.

CHOIR: (Sings)

NOTE: (See page 113—Hebrew version—*"Kemah, Kemah."* If children or choral group are on stage, they can act out the song in pantomime as they sing the verse.)

Bring the flour from the bin,
Pour the oil from the tin,
Hanukkah is here,
Festival so dear,
La la la . . .

Mix the flour so snowy white
With the oil so golden bright

That's how Mother makes,
Hanukkah pancakes.
La la la . . .

FIRST READER: We play with the dreidel. Why? The guess is that when Antiochus forbade the study of the Torah, the Jews resorted to subterfuge either in card-playing or dreideldreying.

NOTE: (Choir sings "MY DREIDEL" page 109—or Hebrew version *"Svivon"* page 110.)

CHOIR:
I have a little dreydl,
I made it out of clay;
And when it's dry and ready,
Then dreydl I shall play.

O dreydl dreydl dreydl,
I made it out of clay;
O dreydl, dreydl, dreydl,
Now dreydl I shall play,
etc.

SECOND READER: And we recall for all time the miracle of Hanukkah, as we sing: Who can retell the things that befell us?

CHOIR: (Sings *Mi Y'Malel* in Hebrew or English)

NOTE: (Refer to page No. 118 of Songster—"Songs We Sing.")

Who can retell the things that befell us?
Who can count them?
    in every age,
      A hero or sage,
    Arose to our aid!
Hark! In days of yore, in Israel's ancient land,
Brave Maccabeans led the faithful band,
But now all Israel must as one arise,
Redeem itself through deed and sacrifice.

THIRD READER: Once it was Moses who made our people free; once it was Judah Maccabee; once it was Theodor Herzl who wrote in his diary how the eight Hanukkah lights inspired him in his dream for a Jewish State. More recently, it was Supreme Court Justice Louis D. Brandeis who said:

FOURTH READER: "As part of the eternal world-wide struggle for democracy, the struggle of the Maccabees is of eternal world-wide interest. It is a struggle of the Jews of *today* as well as of those 2,000 years ago. It is a struggle in which *all* Americans, non-Jews as well as Jews, should be vitally interested."

FIRST READER: But it was never the leaders alone. Behind them was the entire Jewish people joined in the struggle for spiritual freedom. (To audience) Join with us now in the last stanza of "Rock of Ages:"

Children of the martyr race,
Whether free or fettered,
Wake the echoes of the songs,
Where ye may be scattered.
Yours the message cheering
That the time is nearing
Which will see
All men free
Tyrants disappearing.

FINIS

Purim

Classification	Title	Author	Age Level
1. Poem	Why I Like Purim	Elma Ehrlich Levinger	5-7
2. One-act play with tableaux	A Purimdige Birthday	Zara Shakow	8-12
3. Poem—Reading with "toy orchestra"	For Purim	Zalman Shneour	5-8
4. Play—in 2 scenes	Birth of a Queen	Ann K. Glasner	12-16

WHY I LIKE PURIM
Elma Ehrlich Levinger

Now I like Hanukkah a lot,
    And Sukkot in the Fall,
And Pesach, But I think that I
    Love Purim most of all.

Maybe it's 'cause I like to watch
    My mother when she bakes;
And help her pound the shiny stuff
    She puts in Purim cakes.

The kitchen air smells awful sweet;
    I just won't go away,
Till she gives me a Hamantasch
    And sends me out to play.

Then father takes us all to Shul,
    Me, mother and the boys;
It's more fun than the reg'lar days,
    'Cause I can make a noise.

At home, we put on mother's clothes—
    Her oldest ones, I mean;
And cousin Rachel dresses up
    And tries to act a queen.

For then we give our Purim play
    And laugh and dance and cheer;
Say, don't I wish that Purim came
    'Bout twenty times a year!

(From *The Young Judaean*)

A PURIMDIGE BIRTHDAY
Zara Shakow

CAST OF CHARACTERS:
RUTH LEVY, 12
BESSIE, her friend and neighbor, 13
MRS. LEVY, her mother, about 38

KING AHASUERUS
HAMAN
MORDECAI
PERSIAN MAIDENS
ESTHER
QUEEN'S HAND-MAIDENS
COURTIERS
CHAMBERLAINS
SOLDIERS
THE SCRIBE

Non-speaking roles, appearing in tableaux scenes

SCENE:

Combination living-room and kitchen in the Levy home on the top (fifth) floor of a Pitt Street ill-kept tenement in a congested deprived section of New York's Lower East Side, near the Williamsburgh Bridge.

The room is sparsely furnished with an old worn brown leather couch, kitchen table, three imitation walnut chairs, small frig, kitchen cupboard, gas-stove, wash-tub, (which is also used for bathing purposes) built-in shelves with dishes, etc. An alarm clock and small transistor radio are on one of the shelves. A large brightly colored picture calendar is tacked on upstage wall. The table is covered with a floral plastic cloth, and in center is a fresh geranium flower-pot. A large grogger is on table. The floor is bare, but scrubbed immaculately clean. Hanging from center of ceiling, a large naked electric bulb with a string attached.

Upstage, off center right, a door leads to outer hall. Downstage left, a door leads to bedroom: only other room of apartment. Stage left, a window, curtained with a white swiss dimity cafe-curtain, crisply starched and ironed, faces street.

TIME:

Purim, also Ruth's 12th birthday, Thursday, March 18, 1965, about 7:30 P.M.

AT RISE: Ruth Levy, a lovable, sensitive, imaginative 12-year old girl, delicate of build, is discovered curled up on couch absorbedly reading. Engrossed in a beautifully illustrated deluxe gift edition of THE STORY OF PURIM, she seems completely identified with the characters, living through their lives' events, as though she were there . . .

Her father's sudden premature death five years ago, left the family penniless. Since then, her mother has been the provider, working as a seamstress—seasonal employment—part or full-time, in the garment district.

A "key child" and on her own since she was orphaned, Ruth is given to expressing her thoughts aloud—talking to herself for "company" in order to stifle her recurrent feelings of loneliness.

Several seconds after curtain rise, Ruth, on completing book for second time, closes it reverently, and sighs contentedly as she replaces it in box. Her bright eyes sparkle, her face is aglow with a joyous satisfaction.

RUTH: Oooh! . . . What a wonderful, wonderful story! It's better . . . *more* interesting . . . *more* exciting than any story I ever read. It's . . . it's . . . *terrific!!* . . . (Musingly) What a beauty Esther was, and how brave! And that wicked Haman, he got it all right, but *good*. Just what he deserved! And at last Mordecai was rewarded . . . a Jew made Prime Minister! Imagine! . . . And best of all, the last minute the Jews were all saved. A plain miracle, that's what. A miracle! . . . (Increduously, on noting the time) Half past seven??!! Can't be. I couldn'ta read so long. (Rises and crosses to alarm-clock, to verify) Really *is* half past seven! . . . What'sa matter then Mama isn't home yet?

(Crosses to window, opens it, anxiously looks out—up and down the street, then, disappointed not to find her mother anywhere in sight, she closes window.) What could be making her so late? She promised me for sure she wouldn't work overtime today . . . that she'd sure come home early! . . . (Paces nervously, then takes transistor from shelf, turns it on, but gets only static. The batteries have evidently been used up, for although she keeps turning dial, she cannot get reception from any station. Frustrated, she shuts the radio off and replaces it on shelf. Listlessly, she picks up grogger from table and mechanically twists it. The echo resounding through the room frightens her, so she quickly discards it. Then, on hearing footsteps, she eagerly rushes to the door, strains to listen, but hearing her neighbor's door open and shut, she resignedly returns to couch and sits—dejected) Someone for Mrs. Levenson. (Disturbed, and well-nigh panicky, she fidgets, swings her legs, kicks her heels against the couch, bites her lips, pounds her fists against couch; rises, sits again, gets up again and paces up and down the room. On the verge of tears, she fretfully repeats) Ain't she ever gonna come . . . aint she ever *ever* gonna come??!! . . . O, I *wish* she'd come quick! It's late . . . it's already dark outside . . . it's night . . . I'm afraid! . . . (Again hearing footsteps approaching her door, she stops short in her nervous pacing and listens intently. There is a sharp knock on her door. Frightened, but eagerly expectant, she asks:) Whooo *is* it?? (Hesitates to open door)

A CHILD'S VOICE: (Rather husky, off) It's me, Ruthie. Don't be such a 'fraidy-cat and open the door!

RUTH: (Hurriedly crosses to door—eagerly) Bess—eee?

VOICE: (Impatient-sounding) Yeah, it's me. *ME*, I told yuh. Let me in already! . . .

RUTH: (Quickly unlatches chain-lock and opens door to admit Bessie, her friend and neighbor, a matter-of-fact stockily-built tomboyish girl of 13, proud of her practicality; relieved) O Bessie, am I glad you came up! I was getting more an' more afraid every minute.

BESSIE: What are yuh afraid of? Nobody's gonna kidnap you.

RUTH: My mother didn't yet come from work and I can't imagine what'sa matter.

BESSIE: *Nuthin's* the matter. She must be working overtime again.

RUTH: O *no* . . . not today. She promised me for sure she'd come home real early because today's Purim and it's my birthday.

BESSIE: (Annoyed) Birthday . . . shmirthday! I know it's your birthday. You told me at least a thousand times already. Why d'you make such a "tzimmes" about your birthday? *I* don't. My birthday comes and it goes away every year like any other day. If I said to my mother it's my birthday, she'd say: "Nu . . . so what?" *Tohkeh* Ruth, so what, I ask you. With seven kids in the house, you don't make no fuss about birthdays, believe you me. You're an only child, so you think your birthday's a big deal. You told me today's your birthday so many times already, I'm sick an' tired of hearing. What's more, you said you'd have a birthday party with a birthday cake with 12 candles and candy and ice-cream an' everything . . . that the whole gang would come over. But, from what I see you aint gonna have a party, no nuthin . . .

RUTH: (Defensively) Well, I *thought* I'd have! I *hoped* I would, with a birthday cake and 12 candles and 12 . . . (Tearfully) but we can't afford, not this year anyway. (Wistfully) But *maybe* . . . I *will yet!* Like sometimes you read, the last minute something happens—

BESSIE: (Derisively) The last minute something happens! Honest, Ruth, what can happen, I ask you. If you haven't got a party by now, you won't have, that's all. It sure wont fall outa the sky! Sometimes you make me mad, Ruth, honest to goodness. You're always reading and you believe every word in books is true. My big brother Benny says even in the newspapers not everything is true. Stories for sure are nothing but make-believe, cock and bull stuff, just "bubbeh mieses!"

RUTH: (Indignantly) They're *not* "bubbeh mieses!! You're dumb, Bessie, plain ignorant to say such a thing. O.K. stories are make-believe, but that don't prove that it *can't* be true . . . that it couldn'ta happened some place sometime! Anyway, the story I just finished is true . . . *every single solitary word.* It's a history story, a Bible story about Purim.

BESSIE: Now you reminded me why I came up. I had to be absent from the meeting Tuesday, but Annie came over an' she told me—

RUTH: (Interrupting) That's another thing, Bessie, you're always absent. For a long time I didn't join Young Judaea even though I wanted because I was waiting for you. At last I got disgusted waiting so I joined December. *I* never once missed a meeting, but *you*, since you joined, you came to maybe two three meetings altogether.

BESSIE: (Defensively) It's not my fault, Ruth, so don't put the blame on me, *please*. I wanna go, but I gotta help my mother by the stand. You know how busy it gets in the market before a holiday, especially like Purim. (Anxious to change subject) Tell me already about the present Miss Isaacs gave you. Annie said it was a Purim book. Honest?

RUTH: (Nodding) H'mmm. That's the book I was talking about. (Crosses to take book out of box) THE STORY OF PURIM. Wait 'till you see the pictures! I never in my life saw such beautiful colored pictures except in color movies. (Carefully hands book to Bessie, who, impressed by the beauty of the handsome gift edition, handles it respectfully)

BESSIE: (On opening to fly-leaf, she reads written inscription slowly—rather laboriously) "To birthday girl Ruth Levy, a fine true Judaean for her 12th birthday. With my love and best wishes for a happy birthday. Miriam R. Isaacs, Young Judaea Club, Educational Alliance. Purim, March 18th 1965." (Impressed) You know, Ruthie, Miss Isaacs likes you. She likes you best of all the members.

RUTH: (Indignantly) Don't talk like a jealous-cat, Bessie! Miss Isaacs has no privilege characters. She's *fair* and likes everybody the same.

BESSIE: (Becoming engrossed in book, she sits on sofa. Ruth joins her. They hold the book between them. Bessie turns the pages, and on seeing a picture which attracts her especially, she pauses, and reads the caption) "AHASUERUS, KING OF PERSIA, AFTER DETHRONING QUEEN VASHTI, CROWNS ESTHER HIS QUEEN."

PRODUCTION NOTE:

The book's illustrations will be animated by the following tableaux. Only necessary episodes which are relatively simple to stage comprise tableaux. An effort has been made to capture the main high-lights of the Megillah, nevertheless.

A platform—raised level—placed upstage center, and a scrim, or a gauze curtain, behind which tableaux can be enacted, while desirable, are not essential. However, a raised platform would prove to be advantageous for the audience's visibility and a scrim would add a dream-like quality. It will not be difficult to manage the two simultaneous acting areas, provided Ruth and Bessie are seated extreme downstage right, on the couch.

Appropriate incidental mood music, either taped or on records, if played during the tableaux sequences would markedly enhance the effect. Understandably, the volume should be adjusted down and under so that the music does not obtrude and dialog is audible.

Simplified background "scenery" can be improvised by hanging banners, pennants, tapestry panels, etc. in order to establish the locale and period. The costumes and make-up should authentically suggest the place and time and suit the characters represented.

A spot is necessary to pinpoint and highlight the tableaux. Tableau I has to be blacked out to make way for Tableau II, and so on, one picture dissolving, as it were, to permit the next.

Entrances, exits and grouping formations have to be rehearsed adequately. Obviously, delays will detract from the presentation running smoothly. Each tableau has to be sustained—the picture held—for as long as the narration warrants. Smooth-flowing synchronization with the accompanying dialogue will then be achieved. If the participating actors believe that they are "playing statues," and realize the importance of holding their respective poses for the specified time, they will maintain the right positions and attitudes.

The possibility of handling the tableaux scenes through the use of a projection-machine with color slides, as a substitute for live actors, is offered as a possible solution, provided, of course, the School or Center has such equipment and the aid of the Art Department can be enlisted to sketch the required illustrations or color suitable engravings or prints. While this approach has the advantage of obviating the need for rehearsing the tableaux, it minimizes the number of participants. A decision as to whether to use actors or a projector with slides depends on the available facilities and the number of children to be activated in the production.)

TABLEAU I

AHASUERUS, KING OF PERSIA, CROWNS ESTHER HIS QUEEN

PLACE:
Palace throne-room.

CHARACTERS:
King, courtiers, chamberlains, maidens, Esther.

TABLEAU:
Haman, chamberlains, courtiers, Persian maidens and ladies of the Court look on as King Ahasuerus crowns Esther, Queen of Persia. Esther is a radiant Oriental-type beauty—young and graceful—dressed in a simple white flowing gown.

RUTH: Now, Esther is Queen of Persia. Vashti was the queen before, but once, when Ahasuerus commanded her to come before the Court, she refused. This made him very angry, so he punished her—took away her crown and everything. Pick the most beautiful Persian girl in the kingdom to be your queen, one of his advisors advised him, hold a Beauty Contest and you'll find her. That's a good idea, agreed the king, so he sent out messengers in all the provinces on a search. Of the hundreds and hundreds of beautiful girls who were brought to the palace, the king chose Esther, a poor Jewish orphan, to be his wife and queen because she was the most beautiful of all and he loved her best. (Pointing to picture of Esther in book) That's Esther.

BESSIE: Oh! . . . She's *gorgeous*—prettier than Elizabeth Taylor, even.

RUTH: See, it says: (Reads) "King Ahasuerus sets the royal crown upon Esther's head and makes her queen instead of Vashti. Henceforth, Esther shall reign as Queen of all Persia."

BESSIE: (Enthusiastically) This story's interesting—tell me more.

RUTH: First, I gotta find a picture of Haman, so you'll know the main part. All the troubles were on account of him. He wanted to get rid of the Jews . . . kill them all. As Prime Minister he had the power to do it too. Prime Minister was like Vice-President, *more* important really. (Finding illustration) Here he is.

BESSIE: What's the king giving Haman?

RUTH: His signet ring. Can't you see? It says: "And the King took his ring from his hand and gave it unto Haman."

TABLEAU II

KING AHASUERUS AWARDS HAMAN HIS SIGNET RING

PLACE:
Throne-room in the Palace.

CHARACTERS:
King Ahasuerus, Haman, courtiers, chamberlains, soldiers.

TABLEAU:
King Ahasuerus is seated on his throne. Haman kneels before him as he accepts the signet ring. Courtiers, chamberlains, soldiers, etc. in background, look on.

BESSIE: (Tentatively—self-consciously) Ruth . . . what's a signet ring?

RUTH: This should prove to you once and for all, Bessie, when you don't read you don't know anything. If you read a book sometime 'stead of watching TV you'd know what a signet ring is. Lots o' stories tell about it. It's a ring with a seal . . . of a signature or initials, could be, to stamp important papers, like state documents. When the king gave Haman that ring and Haman put the royal seal on something, it became a law right away. Haman had the power to do whatever he wanted because of that seal. He wanted the Jews destroyed, so they'd be, with the king's O.K.

BESSIE: But *why?* What did Haman have against them?

RUTH: Nothing but a grudge. First, you gotta know, Bessie, that Haman was a very wicked man—bad through and through, a *regular Hitler.* He was a liar and a hypocrite too. All the time he wasn't loyal even to the king, but the king didn't know, not yet, anyway. Ahasuerus trusted him . . . took his word for everything! Haman was Prime Minister, remember, the king's right hand man. Well, Haman hated all the Jews just because of this grudge against Mordecai, Esther's uncle. Nobody knew about her being a Jew and Mordecai's niece . . . not yet . . . it was a secret. Oh, you really gotta read the whole book straight through, Bessie, to know what happened. Imagine! Haman had it in for Mordecai because Mordecai refused to bow down to him. You know, it's against the Jewish religion. Well, ever since then Haman couldn't rest trying to figure out how to take revenge. So he decided to have all the Jews killed. He made up a pack o' lies about them . . . that they weren't good subjects, didn't pay their taxes or obey the laws and that it was dangerous to have them around. Well, after hearing this report, the king agreed the best thing was to get rid of them.

BESSIE: But how . . . how could the king fall for such dirty filthy lies?

RUTH: Because—didn't I tell you already—Ahasuerus trusted Haman a hundred per cent.

BESSIE: How awful!! . . . (Referring to text) Sure enough . . . it says here, the king said: "Do with them as it seemeth good to thee. And letters were sent out to every province in the name of King Ahasuerus and sealed with the king's ring, to destroy, to slay, and to cause to perish all Jews, both young and old, little children and women, in one day, even upon the thirteenth day of the twelfth month, which is the month Adar, and to take the spoil of them for a prey."

RUTH: See, I told you. Don't forget, Bessie, in those times a king's word was law. When the messengers delivered the letters stamped with the royal seal in all 127 provinces, and the Jews heard about Haman's terrible order, well, you can imagine! ... They cried and fasted and prayed that God should save them. Mordecai was just frantic—he tore his clothes, put on sackcloth with ashes and went around mourning. Dressed like that, he stood outside the palace gates, hoping he'd catch sight of Esther to tell her the awful news, so she'd go before the king and beg him to save her people. At last, Mordecai got a message to her, but what could she do? She was afraid to plead for the Jews because then the king might catch wise that—

BESSIE: (Incredulously) You mean to tell me that her *own husband* even didn't know she was Jewish?

RUTH: Didn't I tell you before it was a secret? *Nobody* knew, not in the court anyway. Mordecai warned her to keep it a secret. They wouldn'ta let her be queen maybe if they knew. I s'pose Mordecai had a hunch that some day she'd be able to help out the Jews then. (Referring to text) Sure enough, it says here: "And Mordecai said to Esther, 'For this wast thou made queen, that thou mightest plead with the king for thy people and save them.' But she was afraid." You gotta understand, Bessie, that she was afraid for two reasons, (Refers to text again and reads:) "All the king's servants, and the people of the king's provinces, do know, that whosoever, whether man or woman, shall come unto the king into the inner court, who is not called, there is one law for him, that he be put to death, except such to whom the king shall hold out the golden sceptre, that he may live."

BESSIE: (Concernedly) Did she ... did she go?

RUTH: Yeah, she went, because she knew the whole Jewish nation was depending on her.

BESSIE: Then Esther was really risking her own life!

RUTH: Sure, but she was brave and ready to sacrifice herself.

BESSIE: (Eagerly) Did the king hold out his golden sceptre right away?

RUTH: He did and what's more, he forgave her. She was his favorite, remember, and he loved her. Then, Esther invited him to a banquet and asked him to bring Haman along. She had a good reason for making this banquet and a better one even for inviting Haman. You'll soon see. The king promised he'd come with Haman. (Pause, during which Bessie turns pages of book, discovers the following illustration and reads caption:) "THE SCRIBE READS FROM THE BOOK OF CHRONICLES."

TABLEAU III

THE SCRIBE READS FROM THE BOOK OF CHRONICLES

PLACE:
The king's private chambers in the Court.

CHARACTERS:
King Ahasuerus, the Scribe, soldiers standing guard.

TABLEAU:
King Ahasuerus, perturbed and restless, reclines on a couch, listening as the Scribe reads a scroll from the Book of Chronicles.

BESSIE: What's chronicles, Ruthie?

RUTH: Like a history record . . . a book where happenings were written down—what happened, where, when and so on. That night the king didn't feel good, couldn't fall asleep, so he ordered his scribe to bring in the Book of Chronicles and read to him about what happened in the country lately. The Scribe read the part when Mordecai saved his life! . . .

BESSIE: You didn't tell me nothing about Mordecai saving the king's life.

RUTH: Oh, I forgot all about it. Not long after Esther was crowned queen, two of the king's chamberlains . . . they had funny names, I gotta look it up. (Refers to book and finds passage alluding to episode) Bigthan and Teresh they were called. Both o' them plotted to kill the king. It was late at night, and they talked real low, planning their scheme, but Mordecai overheard what they said. He told Esther, and she told King Ahasuerus. Then, the chamberlains were hanged. The whole thing was written in this Book of Chronicles the Scribe is reading from. (Points to illustration)

BESSIE: What did the king give Mordecai for saving his life?

RUTH: That's just it, he didn't give Mordecai anything. Always, whoever saves a king's life gets a big reward, you know. But for some reason, everybody forgot all about it, even the king. When the Scribe read about how it happened, the king reminded himself. He was sure he must'a rewarded Mordecai, but—(Pointing to relevant passage) see, it says: "And King

Ahasuerus asked: 'What honor and distinction have been done to Mordecai for this?' And the answer was 'None.' Then the king said: "Mordecai must be properly rewarded."

BESSIE: Was it a big reward?

RUTH: The biggest that could be! It's really funny, Bessie, because the whole idea was Haman's. When the king asked him what to do to honor some man, Haman was sure the king meant *him* of course—who else—so he answered: (Refers to book and reads relevant passage) "For the man whom the king delighteth to honor, let royal apparel be brought which the king useth to wear, and the horse that the king rideth upon, and on whose head a crown royal is set . . . array the man therewith and cause him to ride on horseback through the streets of the city, and proclaim before him: 'Thus shall it be done to the man whom the king delighteth to honor.' " Bessie, I bet you'll never guess who led Mordecai on the king's horse through the streets of Shushan and did the announcing!

BESSIE: Gimme three chances, Ruth, huh? (With trepidation, lest she make a mistake) It . . . it . . . it couldn'ta been *Haman!*

RUTH: (Pleased) Right, *Haman,* and on your first guess too! What's that expression about the tables being turned or something? It sure fits. When Mordecai rode through the streets, the people cheered him and bowed down to him, and Haman was like his servant. He felt so ashamed he couldn't get home fast enough to tell his wife how all of a sudden he wasn't anymore in the king's favor and his luck was changing. But that was only the beginning, Bessie, of the end for that wicked Haman. He was gonna get it right in the neck soon, and *how!!* . . .

BESSIE: (Leafing through the pages, she espies an illustration which enthuses her particularly) O Ruthie, *look,* just look at this picture here—what colors! . . . (Reads caption) "AT QUEEN ESTHER'S BANQUET—ESTHER PLEADS FOR HER PEOPLE."

TABLEAU IV

AT QUEEN ESTHER'S BANQUET

PLACE:
The queen's royal quarters in the Palace.

CHARACTERS:
Queen Esther, King Ahasuerus, Haman, queen's handmaidens and servants.

TABLEAU:
Queen Esther, beautifully arrayed, points to wicked Haman, exposing him as the enemy of her people. The king, enraged, stares at his Prime Minister with disdain and condemnation.

BESSIE: How—how did Esther manage to tell the king that she was Jewish?

RUTH: First, they all ate and drank, had a regular feast ... a real good time. Then, on the second day of the Banquet of Wine, when Esther saw the king was in a good mood, she said she wanted to ask something special. "Whatever thy request, even to the half of my kingdom, it shall be performed," Ahasuerus answered. So Esther begged him to save her people right away. She proved that Haman, because he hated the Jews, out of spite and on purpose, made up those lies about their not being good subjects, obeying the laws and paying taxes. She showed Haman up for the Jew-hater, hypocrite and trouble-maker he was. When the king realized Esther was telling the truth, he got angrier and angrier on Haman. He became angry with himself even, for being fooled like that. Then, he ordered Haman to be hung on the gallows he built for Mordecai. See ... (Leafing through pages) here's a picture where the soldiers are dragging Haman away to be hung. It says: "So they hanged Haman on the gallows that he prepared for Mordecai, and wicked Haman received his due punishment."

BESSIE: "Good riddance to bad rubbish" ... that saying fits all right! What happened after?

RUTH: Well, once Haman was gotten rid of, the worst danger was over, but Haman's order had to be changed. Esther pleaded for the order to be "reversed," it says. Then, the king called Mordecai to the palace to talk things over.

BESSIE: (Eagerly) Did he know already Mordecai was Esther's uncle?

RUTH: Not 'til just now. When Mordecai came, the king admitted he made a big mistake to trust Haman. Now, he wanted to "undo" the terrible things Haman did, but didn't know how. You see, Bessie, it was too late to get back Haman's letters ordering the Jews killed. So, Mordecai advised him to send messengers all over the kingdom with letters saying the Jews could and should defend themselves when attacked. That struck the king like a real good plan, so he gave Mordecai his signet ring to seal these letters. Wait a minute, there's a picture, I'm sure, showing the king giving Mordecai his signet ring.

BESSIE: (Finding illustration) Here! . . . (Reads from text) "King Ahasuerus gives his signet ring to Mordecai to repeal Haman's decree."

TABLEAU V

KING AHASUERUS GIVES HIS SIGNET RING TO MORDECAI TO REPEAL HAMAN'S DECREE.

PLACE:
Palace throne-room.

CHARACTERS:
King Ahasuerus, Queen Esther, Mordecai, courtiers, chamberlains, Scribe.

TABLEAU:
King Ahasuerus is seated on his throne with Queen Esther beside him. Members of the Court look on as the king presents his signet ring to Mordecai to seal the letters repealing Haman's death decree and permitting the Jews to defend themselves when attacked.

RUTH: The messengers delivered these letters in all 127 provinces as quick as they could. On the 13th day of Adar, when the Jews were supposed to get killed, they defended themselves against their enemies and were saved instead. Mordecai was promoted to Haman's place and became second in importance to the king. The Jews were protected then, and lived happily and peacefully in Persia thereafter.

BLACKOUT ON FINAL TABLEAU

RUTH: (Pointedly) Now you *can't* say *this* is a "bubbeh mieseh," Bessie.

BESSIE: *No,* this is no "bubbeh mieseh!" But this is *history,* not some fairy tale like you always read.

RUTH: (Carefully closing book and replacing it in box) And that's why we have Purim. Religious Jews fast on the 13th day of Adar—the Fast of Esther—it's called, to remember that our great great forefathers were supposed to die, and on the next day, the 14th, we celebrate Purim with a feast and rejoicing—we have to eat, drink and be merry, it says, because everything turned out all right and the Jews were saved.

BESSIE: Not until now did I know the real reason. All I knew was that people go to schule to hear the Megillah and we have to turn the grogger and make noise when they say "Humun."

RUTH: Now, you know *all* the reasons and I'll lend you my book, Bessie, so you can read about it by yourself. You won't get tired of it like from other stories, Bessie, believe me. I read it twice already and could read it over and over. No wonder they read the Megillah every single year.

BESSIE: It's history, that's why—*facts*—not bunk about a fairy-queen and what she did with her magic wand or foolishness about princes and princesses and that they lived happily ever after.

RUTH: You missed it, Bessie, but Tuesday in club, Miss Isaacs told us about Purim. She said every time before a holiday she's not only gonna tell us why we celebrate it, but we'll act out plays about it, sing songs, play games and everything.

BESSIE: I'm glad. From now on, I'm gonna come to meetings reg'lar, I promise. I always wanted to know why we have Hanukkah and Purim and Passover and other holidays. My father—I ask him, but he never explains it good, so I *really* understand. It's only right we should know the reason for American bolidays, but most o' the time we know more about Christian holidays even like Christmas and Easter than about our own, except we have to fast Yom Kippur, not eat bread Passover and like that. (Looking up at clock and noting the time) Say, ain't your mother *ever* coming? It's getting awful late.

(At this juncture, Mrs. Levy enters. She is a frail, slight woman of about 38, whose troubles have aged her beyond her years. Her black hair is prematurely thickly streaked with grey.

Her face is pale and emaciated. She is short of breath from the tiring climb up the five flights of stairs, and seems worn out,—has a weary stoop and a dragging step. Her clothes show signs of pathetic attempts at respectability, but obviously need replenishment. She carries two seemingly heavy shopping-bags and a large box under her arm.)

RUTH: (Rushes towards her, affectionately embraces and kisses her) O mamenyu . . . mamenyu . . . why d'you come so late? I didn't know what to think already, I was so worried.

MRS. LEVY: Sorry, darling, but I couldn't help it. (Gently pushes Ruth aside) Careful Ruthie, you'll yet break the— (Checks herself, lest she reveal the surprise)

RUTH: (Eagerly) What d'you bring . . . a present for me?

MRS. LEVY: (Placing shopping-bags in corner and cake-box on table; then removes her worn coat) No . . . no . . . not a present . . . a . . . a *surprise*. Close your eyes, darling, and— (On second thought, decides on a more effective way) Wait in the bedroom 'til I call you—I have to make ready.

RUTH: (Insistently) First, you gotta tell me why you came so late. 'Member you promised to come home early today for sure —that you wouldn't work overtime for anything?

MRS. LEVY: I didn't work overtime, Ruthie. Sorry it took so long, but I had to go to Suru Dvare. You know what a "shlepedige" trip it is, and "tzu ahle tzures," the subway got stuck yet . . .

RUTH: All of a sudden to Suru Dvare? What for?

MRS. LEVY: (Evasively) Because . . . never mind why. (Urgingly) Come, Ruthie, do as you're told, wait in the bedroom until I call you.

BESSIE: (Impatiently shoves Ruth into bedroom) G'wan, you slow poke! How many times does your mother have to tell you? (Closes the door leading to kitchen; crosses back to table and interestedly watches Mrs. Levy undo the mysterious package. Excitedly) What's inside, Mrs. Levy—a birthday present for Ruthie? Lemme see!

MRS. LEVY: (Admonishingly) Shhhhhh . . . Bessie, shhh . . . not so loud! She'll hear you yet. (Opens box and carefully removes an exceedingly large Hamantasch, topped with color icing, four colored birthday candles in grooves in each corner, and one in center for "good luck." It is indeed a unique original birthday-cake!)

BESSIE: (Enthusiastically) A *Hamantasch* birthday cake! Never, *never* in my whole life did I see a Hamantasch birthday cake!...

MRS. LEVY: (Places the cake on a large plate and hands it to Bessie to hold) Careful Bessie, don't drop. (Removes flowerpot and plastic cloth from table; takes a crisp white tablecloth out of kitchen table drawer, spreads it on table, places birthday-cake in center. Then removes box of ice-cream from the shopping bag and puts it in frig. Sets three places—paper birthday napkins, plates, glasses, etc. Takes several bags and boxes out of shopping-bags and empties contents—hard candy, chocolate, nuts, raisins, dates, etc. onto saucers and bowls; arranges a variety of fresh fruit in fruit-bowl. Then backs up several paces to examine the effect, rearranges everything somewhat, shakes her head and disappointedly heaves a sigh) Not so ai ai ai... but better than nothing. Maybe next year with God's help we'll better ourselves... but better than nothing it is.

BESSIE: (Has been fluttering about, trying to be of help; claps her hands delightedly, admiring the result of Mrs. Levy's efforts) I tell yuh, Mrs. Levy, that Hamantash birthday-cake is outa this world! Such a special odd birthday-cake, and so much "gutte zochen,"—a reg'lar party!... Ruth's sure gonna be surprised.

RUTH: (Off-stage, calling exasperatedly) Mammmahh!!... I won't wait no more... I'm coming out!

MRS. LEVY: (Placatingly) Just *one* more second, darling, *please*... only *another* second. (Hurriedly and nervously strikes a match from match-box above stove, lights the birthday candles and extinguishes the overhead electric light)

BESSIE: (Thrilled by the atmosphere the soft candlelight glow creates, shouts excitedly) Ready, Ruthie... *ready!* C'mon out.

MRS. LEVY: (Simultaneously with Bessie, in a tremulous voice) All right, "teirinke," *now!*

RUTH: (Enters, looks around, blinking her eyes. The unexpected darkness; the soft candlelight and shadows cast by the colored birthday candles momentarily bewilder her. She cannot quite grasp that her dream has come true. Gazing longingly at the Hamantash birthday-cake with the thirteen lit candles, she finally realizes that it is all intended for her, and stands transfixed for several seconds, overwhelmed... at a loss for words.

Then, she rushes over to Mrs. Levy, affectionately embraces and kisses her) Oh momenu, darling darling momenu! . . . I'm so . . . so . . . surprised, I don't know what to say. A Hamantasch birthday cake . . . a last minute birthday party! . . . (Profoundly grateful) Thank you, Mama darling . . . a million trillion thanks.

MRS. LEVY: You like, Ruthie darling? (Ruth nods. Hugs and kisses Ruth) Happy birthday, "mein liebe kihnd . . . biz a hoonderd und tzvontzig . . . nuhr gezund und glick!" Come, sit down, children, please. (Girls sit at table)

BESSIE: (Embraces Ruth shyly) Happy birthday, Ruthie my best friend. (Sings "HAPPY BIRTHDAY" Mrs. Levy joins in) Make a wish, Ruthie, make a wish and blow. (Ruth makes a wish and blows out all the candles in one breath)

MRS. LEVY: (Puts light on) Eat children, some candy, chocolate, nuts, fruit, whatever you like. We'll have the party first, Ruthie, then supper. Tomorrow's school—Bessie has to go home. I'll get the ice cream and we'll eat from the Hamantasch birthday cake . . . should be "ah emese meichel." Then, you'll drink milk and I'll make tea for me. (Puts kettle on gas-stove to boil water; takes box of ice cream out of frig; joins girls at table, dishes out heaping portions of ice cream, cuts birthday cake and serves them and herself) Before, Ruthie, it was a secret, but now, I can tell you why I came so late. I left the shop four o'clock, took Pelham Line to Mosholu Parkway to Suru Dvare's, so she'd help me make the cake. You know what a good baker she is. When I told her I want a fancy birthday cake—something *real special* for Ruthie's birthday, she said: "If already yes a birthday cake, why not a Hamantasch birthday cake lechoved Purim?" We never expected it would come out so "grutten." "Tohke gishmohk," no? (They eat the cake and ice cream)

RUTH: It's delicious, ma.

BESSIE: Just yummy, Mrs. Levy. Ruth, you didn't even show your mother what Miss Isaacs gave you.

RUTH: I'm so excited, I forgot all about it.

MRS. LEVY: (Pleased) Miss Isaacs gave you a present? (Simultaneously)

RUTH: Yes, ma, a Purimdige birthday present—a picture book about Purim. (Rises to get book to show to Mrs. Levy)

MRS. LEVY: (As she turns pages, admiringly) Oi, such pictures . . . such colors . . . beautiful . . . exact like paintings in a museum!

RUTH: (Meditatively) Isn't it funny, Bessie? I got a Purimdige birthday present and a Purimdige birthday cake and ...

BESSIE: (Summing it up) If you ask me, it's a Purimdige birthday altogether! ...

RUTH: See ... Bessie, I told you! Something *can* happen the last minute like a miracle. Never give up hope 'cause the last minute something happens! Maybe not every time, but lotsa times ... like tonight, this last minute birthday-party ... like for the Jews in Persia, like when the brave Maccabees beat all those Syrian soldiers and that tiny little bit of oil in the jar burned for eight whole days! ... A great miracle happened there!! ... (Grouped around the table, the three partake of the refreshments in celebration of Ruth's twelfth birthday. Mrs. Levy serves second portions of the Hamantasch birthday-cake, pours milk for Bessie and Ruth, and tea for herself

as
 S
  L
   O
    W
     CURTAIN
              descends).

FOR PURIM*
Zalman Shneour

1.
Oh, Haman lived in Shushantown,
    And he was most oppressive;
He wore a blue and purple hat,
    Three cornered and impressive.

2.
Knock, knockers, knock; knock, knockers, knock;
    And rattlers, rattle, rattle;
For Haman and his sons were hanged
    Upon a tree like cattle.

3.
With Mordecai was Haman grieved,
    And swore in his vexation
To hang him on the gallows high,
    And wipe out all his nation.

4.
Knock, knockers, knock; knock, knockers, knock;
    And rattlers, rattle, rattle;
For Haman and his sons were hanged
    Upon a tree like cattle.

5.
He sent out letters: "Rise and slay
    The Jews that they all perish,
The thirteenth day of Adar-month."—
    The Purim-day we cherish.

6.
Knock, knockers, knock; knock, knockers, knock;
    And rattlers, rattle, rattle;
For Haman and his sons were hanged
    Upon a tree like cattle.

---

* Reprinted by permission of Bruce Humphries, Publishers, Boston, Mass.

7.

But on that day a miracle
   God wrought, and sent salvation,
For we were saved, but Haman was
   Effaced from his creation.

8.

Knock, knockers, knock; knock, knockers, knock;
   And rattlers, rattle, rattle;
For Haman and his sons were hanged
   Upon a tree like cattle.

9.

In memory of the cornered hat
   Of Haman so ambitious,
We eat a cake resembling it,
   A *Hamantasch* delicious.

10.

Knock, knockers, knock; knock, knockers, knock;
   And rattlers, rattle, rattle;
For Haman and his sons were hanged
   Upon a tree like cattle.

PRODUCTION NOTE

It is possible to animate narration of this poem and also activate more children by organizing a "toy orchestra," consisting of five or six girls and boys.

Members of the "orchestra" should be dressed in colorful costumes, as clowns, Purim sprites or elves, and be seated on a bench, stools, or tripod chairs, preferably placed on a raised platform. The orchestra should be provided with a variety of simple, percussive noise-makers: groggers, rattles, gavels with blocks of wood, etc.

Two narrators may effectively be used—Narrator I, positioned downstage right renders stanzas 1, 3, 5, 7 and 9; Narrator II, stationed down stage left to balance Narrator I, does stanzas 2, 4, 6, 8 and 10. Lines must be memorized.

After Narrator II says: "Knock, knockers, knock; knock, knockers, knock; And rattlers, rattle, rattle . . ." the "orchestra" goes into action and performs business in accordance with lines; pound gavels on woodblocks, rattle rattles and turn groggers.

Members of the "orchestra" may then reprise lines: "Knock, knockers, knock; knock, knockers, knock; and rattlers, rattle, rattle . . ."

simultaneous with business, building up to a controlled dissonance. Their lines should, of course, be memorized and business done with genuine relish and gusto.

Narrator II then continues with the last two lines of stanzas 2, 4, 6, 8 and 10.

It is necessary to rehearse the members of "orchestra" a few times with Narrators so they promptly pick up cues, coordinate noise-making, and smoothly terminate business in unison, to enable Narrator to continue subsequent narration.

BIRTHDAY OF A QUEEN*

A one-act play in two scenes on a Purim theme.

Ann K. Glasner

CAST OF CHARACTERS:

RACHEL
ZIPPORAH
SHULAMIT
MORDECAI
HECKLERS IN CROWD
 (planted in house among audience)
HADASSAH
DAVID
DEBORAH

PLACE:

The city of Shushan in Persia.
Scene I: A Persian garden
Scene II: A room in Mordecai's home

TIME:

During the reign of King Ahasuerus

Scene I: A warm sunny afternoon
Scene II: Several days later, in the evening

PRODUCTION NOTE

To suggest locale of a Persian garden for Scene I, bench, greens and plants may be used.

Scene I: Before and after curtain rise, girls may sing or hum while sewing. Suggested tune: *Esther in Your Garden Fair*.

At finale of Scene I, Hadassah may pantomime her vision to background music of *Cantillation of Esther*.

Scene II: Low round tables, rugs, couch, earthenware pottery can help create the required Oriental atmosphere.

For finale of Scene II, the use of music of *Esther*, is suggested, but optional with director.

---

* Originally published by National Women's League of the United Synagogue of America. When presenting, kindly give due program credit.

Music suggested may be found in *Songs We Sing* by Harry Coopersmith, pages 159, 148 and 163, respectively.

AT RISE: Three girls, aged 16 or thereabouts, dressed in native costume of period, their long hair braided and tied with ribbons, are seated on a garden-bench, sewing.

RACHEL: Where is Hadassah?

SHULAMIT: (With a knowing smile) Where? Wandering in the fields, no doubt, with one of Mordecai's books clasped to her bosom. (Rises and crosses stage, walking in imitation of Hadassah, holding an imaginary book)

ZIPPORAH: Oft-times, I think Hadassah walks in her sleep, lost in her dreams.

SHULAMIT: I wonder are her dreams pleasant or—?

ZIPPORAH: Surely dreams will not complete her new garment. (Discards her sewing, rises, and crosses right to look out in the distance for a sign of Hadassah)

SHULAMIT: Have no fear, Rachel. (Confidently) Hadassah will not be lost for long. She will find her way back. Have you not heard Mordecai boast: "Who can compare to Hadassah?"

RACHEL: (Jealously) Who has *not* heard Mordecai boast, and to *our fathers!*

SHULAMIT: (Defendingly) Pray, let us be just. Hadassah is truly... (Breaks off—affectionately) She is all *I* would wish to be.

ZIPPORAH: Mordecai comes this way.

(Enter Mordecai—a tall, powerful figure. The girls hastily wrap up their sewing and retreat to a corner, huddling together, to listen to Mordecai as he addresses the townspeople. Mordecai speaks direct to the audience and is heckled by male voices—men planted in house.)

MORDECAI: My fellow-Jews, we cannot rest. We dare *not* rest, not while our enemies plot to destroy us. As I go about the city, I keep my eyes open, my ears attuned, watching and listening...

HECKLER: (Shouting) He who seeks trouble finds it. (Jeers from crowd)

MORDECAI: (More vehemently, over-riding the hecklers) And I say again, we must heed the danger signals before it is too late. At this very moment, Haman, the king's chancellor—

HECKLER: (Shouting) King Ahasuerus knows full well that

the Jews are a peaceful, law-abiding people. Do we not pay the taxes imposed, do we not obey—

MORDECAI: (More insistently) But we are an intransigent people. Haman whispers to King Ahasuerus: "These people do not bow down to any man, not even to you, the king." Thus, he plants the seed of suspicion that may well blossom to destroy us. We dare not ignore the forces which threaten us! We must prepare to combat—(As he moves off-stage, his voice gradually becomes fainter.)

ZIPPORAH: (Espying Hadassah) At long last, Hadassah returns.

RACHEL: (Following Zipporah's glance) It is as you said, Shulamit, Hadassah carries a book as is her wont. She has indeed forgotten her sewing.

(Enter Hadassah, smiling graciously at her friends. She is about their age, but taller, and unusually pretty. Veritably, she walks in beauty—carries herself with extraordinary grace and dignity. Clasped in her hand is a leather-bound volume.)

HADASSAH: When I awoke this beautiful morning, I thought on a day such as this, God smiles on all the world. (Rachel holds up Hadassah's sewing to show her how little progress she has made.) (Remorsefully) Oh!! . . .

RACHEL: (Indicating her own garment) See Hadassah, mine will soon be finished to wear at Shoshanah's wedding, while yours—

HADASSAH: Believe me, dear Rachel, I shall rejoice if I am unprepared and therefore cannot attend.

ZIPPORAH: (Surprised) But Shoshanah is the sister of Joel, he, whose father—(Looks to other girls for corroboration.)

SHULAMIT: Is it not true, Hadassah, that Joel's father has these many months beseeched Mordecai to arrange a match between you and Joel?

HADASSAH: Pray, do not speak to me of him. I do *not*—

ZIPPORAH: Surely, Hadassah, you cannot mean that Joel does not find favor in your eyes? Why, there is nary a maiden in all Shushan who would not consider herself fortunate to become his bride!

SHULAMIT: Do you not too dream of marrying, Hadassah, like other girls your age?

HADASSAH: Verily, I dream of marriage, as you all do, but it is not Joel I see in my dreams.

RACHEL: It seems to me, Hadassah, the time has come for you to renounce your dreams.

HADASSAH: That I cannot, for my dreams oft-times are more real than . . .

SHULAMIT: What is it you see in your dreams, Hadassah?

HADASSAH: Time and time again I dream I walk in a procession and I—(Demonstrates—walking with measured tread—head poised high. The girls exchange meaningful glances and shake their heads.)

MORDECAI: (Re-enters and smiles at the group) Shalom . . . shalom.

ZIPPORAH: Shalom. (The other girls greet him with smiles. Then, they all gather up their sewing, wave to Hadassah, and exit.)

HADASSAH: I heard your voice from way across the fields, Mordecai.

MORDECAI: Did it sound as the voice of doom?

HADASSAH: What is amiss? Tell me, Mordecai, has another burdensome tax been levied on the Jews?

MORDECAI: Far worse threatens us, Hadassah. (Paces—obviously distraught) And yet, our people go about tending their flocks, preoccupied, as though all's well . . . no one heeds my warnings! . . .

HADASSAH: Is it because of Haman, the king's chancellor? You have oft told me of his driving ambition and lust for power.

MORDECAI: Yes, my child, it is Haman who is responsible for this new danger which confronts us. He tells King Ahasuerus we are an alien people, worshipping an unseen god. (With increasing resentment) and paints us as traitors to the king's rule.

HADASSAH: Why do you not go before the king and plead in our behalf? And tell King Ahasuerus of the rumblings you've overheard . . . of enemies plotting against his life.

MORDECAI: Do you for a moment think the king will heed mere rumors? I must first ascertain the names of those who plot against him. But now, the whole court is buzzing with excitement . . . hearts are beating fast . . . all conjecturing as to who will be chosen queen.

HADASSAH: (Suddenly alert and keenly interested) King Ahasuerus is to be wed?

MORDECAI: Yes . . . very soon. And he will choose for wife

from among the most beautiful young maidens in the 127 provinces of the kingdom.

HADASSAH: (Puzzled) I do not understand...

MORDECAI: Messengers have been dispatched throughout the kingdom in search of the most beautiful damsels in all Persia. They will be brought to the palace and prepared to appear before the king. He will then select the one who pleases him most for wife. (Suddenly struck by an inspirational thought) If we Jews could but send a maiden to participate in the parade... and if God willed it and the king looked with favor on her—

HADASSAH: (Excitedly grabs his arm) Why can you not send *me*, Mordecai?

MORDECAI: (Recoiling, releases her grip) O no, Hadassah, *not you!*

HADASSAH: But pray, *why not?* Am I not fair? Have you not many a time said I am the most comely in all the land?

MORDECAI: That I have, and 'tis true, but I would not sacrifice you, Hadassah. No... no... I could not allow—

HADASSAH: (Decisively) I *choose* to go! (Mordecai, disturbed, turns away from her) I beg you, Mordecai, do not turn away from me. If... if by some miracle King Ahasuerus looked with favor upon me, a Jewess, think what it might mean for our people!...

MORDECAI: (Conflicted) But how... how can I sanction such a—

HADASSAH: Have you not day and night prayed for an advocate? *I* can *be* that advocate! (Determinedly) I shall join the parade and appear before the king!!...

MORDECAI: No Hadassah, my prayers were never intended for you. I cannot... I will not permit you to be thrown to those heathens!

HADASSAH: No matter what my destiny, Mordecai, I shall *always* remain a Jewess. That which you have taught me will ne'er be forgotten!

MORDECAI: You speak as a naive child... innocent of the ways of the world.

HADASSAH: (Dedicatedly) Remember your teaching me, Mordecai, that a good Jew must observe two principles: to live morally and to revere God? I shall always adhere to that. (Takes Mordecai's hand and smiles at him assuringly)

MORDECAI: (Gazing at her tenderly) May God be with you and watch over you, Hadassah.

CURTAIN
on
Scene I.

SCENE II

PLACE:
A tastefully, comfortably furnished room, the walls lined with books, in the home of Mordecai.

TIME:
Several days later—in the evening.

AT RISE: Mordecai is discovered, reading. His attention wanders, however. He seems to be awaiting someone. Two friends, David and Deborah—husband and wife—enter in a state of excitement.

DEBORAH: After we spoke, Mordecai, I surely thought you would reconsider and revoke your consent.

MORDECAI: Hadassah is adamant. I am unable to prevail upon her—

DAVID: Do you know what everyone says of you, Mordecai? That *you* are to blame... that it is your ambition which inflames the mind of your kinswoman, who is but a child.

DEBORAH: All her life Hadassah has been under your influence... read the books you gave her, been taught by you... listened to your every word. She has been exposed solely to your authority to the exclusion of—

MORDECAI: Therefore, she has learned too well, perhaps, that we Jews cannot passively stand by when danger threatens us, as now.

DAVID: They say too that only you, whose real name is Marduk, name of the Babylonian god, would thus cast a sweet innocent maiden into the heathen court.

MORDECAI: (Offended and shocked) You David, would question my true faith? Would I fight to preserve our religion and tradition were I not a loyal Jew, loyal with all my heart and all my soul? It is that faith which tears ... (Pauses, profoundly shaken) Hadassah is my nearest and dearest of kin, but truly, she was never like other children her age. Whilst they played with dolls and bits of cloth, Hadassah sought to spell out the print of my books.

DEBORAH: Verily... Hadassah is learned beyond her years, and always has been. However, to place herself upon a throne, to imagine herself, with your encouragement, Mordecai, crowned a queen, is beyond all—

MORDECAI: Do you not know the blood of kings courses through Hadassah's veins? We are the direct descendants of Kish—he, who was the father of King Saul. Can you deny, David, that Hadassah has the inborn grace, the beauty and the regal majesty of a queen?

DAVID: O, how you have fed those dreams of hers, Mordecai, and thus led her astray! We have watched Hadassah grow and love her as our own child. We assumed and hoped that one day she would walk with her eyes wide open ... so we smiled on her dreams.

MORDECAI: Hadassah dreams even as Jacob dreamed! (Paces and intones) "Jacob dreamed, and behold, a ladder set up on the earth, and the top of it reached to heaven."

DEBORAH: (Admonishingly) For shame, Mordecai! To compare the dream of a romantic young maid to Jacob's dream! I beg you, before it is too late, Mordecai, let not Hadassah be ensnared by her dreams!

DAVID: All this time, Mordecai, I have stood by you, warning our people of the disgruntled rowdy henchmen surrounding Haman. Knowing how evil they are have you once considered what they might do to a Jewish maiden?

MORDECAI: I have prayed.

DAVID: (Derisively) *Prayed!* ... Before King Ahasuerus views the procession, the beautiful maidens must be passed on by Hegai, keeper of the women. Has it occurred to you what Hadassah's fate will be if accepted by this Hegai ... that she may well become a concubine? (Breaks off, as Hadassah, Zipporah, Rachel and Shulamit enter. Hadassah carries a sewing-bag, which she hastily puts down. On overhearing the last remarks, she glances towards Mordecai solicitously.)

HADASSAH: (Embracing Deborah) I beseech you, Deborah ... (Turning to David) David ... do not reproach my cousin Mordecai. I have long dreamed of walking in a procession without fear.

MORDECAI: God is inscrutable and moves in mysterious ways . . . Hadassah will reign as Queen of Persia. I feel it in my bones.

DAVID: In your bones, Mordecai, methinks you feel only aches and pain.

(The three girls huddle together in a corner and laugh. Hadassah draws them into the room to be seated.)

HADASSAH: If I be chosen queen, then surely when I plead our people's just cause, King Ahasuerus will pay heed to me.

DAVID: (Impatiently) Mordecai, have you not yet told Hadassah why Queen Vashti was banished?

HADASSAH: I have long wondered why, but I do not know the reason. (The girls listen eagerly)

DAVID: The queen did dare publicly to defy the king, refusing to come at his commandment.

HADASSAH: Mordecai, pray do tell me just how Queen Vashti did defy the king.

MORDECAI: On the seventh day of an elaborate feast for his noblemen and army, King Ahasuerus was carousing with his guests. Besotted with wine, he ordered the proud and beautiful Queen Vashti to appear before them in a robe she deemed unseemly, so that she might dazzle them with her beauty and sparkling royal jewels.

HADASSAH: (Incredulously) Was it for disobeying so capricious an order that she was dethroned and banished?

MORDECAI: This was no small act of defiance, Hadassah. If Queen Vashti had not been punished for refusing to do the king's bidding, a dangerous precedent might be set. What man then in all the kingdom would be master and bear rule in his own house?

DEBORAH: The new queen, when she is chosen, will dare less than Queen Vashti.

HADASSAH: (Rebuffing Deborah) Hers was a truly courageous deed. It is ever a risk to be courageous! But, I shall have the advantage of Mordecai's counsel.

DAVID: (Sarcastically) Mordecai's counsel! (To Mordecai) Granted that it be God's will and Hadassah's destiny for her to be chosen Queen of Persia, how then, tell me, will you outwit the wily Haman?

MORDECAI: We take but one step at a time.

HADASSAH: (To David) No matter what you say, no matter what obstacle is put in my path, I shall nevertheless parade before the king. I am of the firm conviction that my fate was thus decreed. (Opens sewing-bag ond removes dress) This is the garment I shall wear, and no other! (Smiling at the three girls) My eternal gratitude to you for your help in finishing my sewing.

MORDECAI: Wait, Hadassah, I have brought you suitable raiment. (He beckons to Deborah, who after hesitating, reaches for the garments Mordecai hands her)

HADASSAH: I shall be clothed in the garment my friends and I have fashioned. (As she holds up a gown sheer as chiffon)

DEBORAH: (After comparing it with Mordecai's choice) No, Hadassah. Just see what beautiful things Mordecai has selected.

HADASSAH: (Briefly examining Mordecai's selections) These are indeed beautiful, but I cannot wear them.

MORDECAI: (Surprised and disappointed by her reaction) Why Hadassah, I have begged and borrowed to find garments like those worn by the others, splendid and suitable—

DEBORAH: If you join the parade, Hadassah, you should wear apparel fitting such an occasion. (As she picks up a glittering gown which Mordecai brought) These are appropriate indeed, while yours—

HADASSAH: I have no wish to shine as the stars in the night. Neither silk, satin nor tinsel are right for me.

RACHEL: Pray, Hadassah, how can you reject these? Yours cannot compare—

HADASSAH: It is not what I wear which will attract King Ahasuerus, but what I *am*. In these strange garments, I shall feel as a stranger.

MORDECAI: (Persuasively) In this simple garment you will ne'er be noticed. The eye is caught first by that which shines and glitters.

HADASSAH: Then the eyes turn away from the sun, for it is blinding. Oh, let me show you . . .

(The three friends surround Hadassah and assist her into the gown prepared for the Beauty Pageant, as Mordecai, David and Deborah cross to other side of stage. When the girls move away from Hadassah, she is revealed in an exquisitely simple gown, with flowing line, Grecian in style. She faces upstage. Before turning around to face audience, she loosens her hair. It falls about her shoulders—her raven-black tresses a startling contrast to the pastel color of her gown. She crosses to table for a garland of flowers and places it on her head. As Hadassah comes forward, she walks slowly, and gracefully with true majesty and superb confidence and poise. The three girls sing a marching song in a soft low register. The expression on the faces of Mordecai, David and Deborah soften. Mordecai obviously relents and makes a gesture of resignation.)

MORDECAI: (As he holds up a string of pearls) This, I thought to give you to wear and to keep, Hadassah. It is a gift.

HADASSAH: (As she takes it, gratefully) Ah, thank you. It is a gift I will treasure ... always! ...

SHULAMIT: Pearls do not glitter, Hadassah. (Takes pearls from Hadassah and fastens them around her neck)

HADASSAH: (Pleased) This suits me perfectly. (Mordecai gathers up the clothes he had selected for Hadassah to wear. The girls and Deborah crowd around Hadassah, admiring the pearls and her general beautiful appearance)

HADASSAH: (As she breaks away from group) Wait, Mordecai. There *is* something I would like. (Chooses a pair of sandals from the things Mordecai holds. Removes slippers she wears and puts on the new sandals) Oh! ... (She crosses stage)

MORDECAI: (Lightly) You will have long passed, my child, before King Ahasuerus' eyes reach down to those golden sandals.

HADASSAH: I believe, Mordecai ... (Pauses and stands quite still) you are mistaken. (Lifts the flowing skirt, looks down at the pretty new sandals, nods towards her friends and marches, as they smile at her, and sing softly)

MORDECAI: (Taking Hadassah's hand) Hadassah, you must now take a new name.

HADASSAH: Yes, Mordecai, I should. What shall it be?

MORDECAI: You will henceforth be called *Esther*, for star.

HADASSAH: (Mulling over the name with pleasure) (slowly) Es ... ther! ... (Stands in deep thought, repeats the name slowly, then crosses downstage—her face aglow with a prophetic light) Good! . . . I shall be called *QUEEN ESTHER!* . . . (She raises her arms high, in triumph. The girls sing. Deborah, David and Mordecai join in the singing.)

CURTAIN

Passover

	Classification	Title	Author	Age Level
1.	Dramatic Reading supplemented by songs	A Passover "Potpourri"	Dorothy Ross	13-16
2.	Reading	Quotations	From Bible, etc.	10-16
3.	Song (Spiritual)	Go Down Moses	Anonymous	6-16
4.	Choral Reading	Make Known His Deeds	Psalm 105	12-16
5.	Poem	The Voice unto Pharaoh	Arthur Guiterman	13-16
6.	Reading	When Israel Came Out of Egypt	Psalm 114	10-12
7.	Play	Children of Israel	James Yaffe	10-16
8.	Choral Reading with dance finale	The Song of Moses	Bible	12-16
9.	Song (Spiritual)	Great Day	Anonymous	10-16
10.	Simulated Radio Broadcast (Documentary)	The First Passover in America	Max Ehrlich	13-16

A PASSOVER "POTPOURRI"*
Dorothy Ross

A reading in four parts with musical selections. Suggested songs from: *Songs We Sing* by Harry Coopersmith (published by United Synagogue of America, 3080 Broadway, New York 10027); *A Treasury of Jewish Song* by Ruth Rubin (published by Schocken Books Inc., 67 Park Avenue, New York 10016).

PRODUCTION NOTE:

It is suggested that the four participants hold scripts as a book and sit on stools or chairs. The parts should be assigned in advance and the text rehearsed several times. Musical suggestions are for background humming, actual singing, (solo or group) as desired.

FIRST READER: When you hear the word Pesach—or Passover—what kind of images leap to your mind?

SECOND READER: Kneidlach and matzos and fish; borsht and wine; and all the special foods associated with the Seder. Spring cleaning, and the Pesach dishes, and Elijah's cup.

THIRD READER: For me, Peseach is family—the social festival—the gathering around the table; the participation of young and old, the telling of an ancient story; the wine-stained haggadahs, and my son singing for the first time Mah Nishtanah ... (sings) (*Songs We Sing*—Coopersmith, p. 176)

FOURTH READER: But for me Passover is still Warsaw 1943. Do you remember this poem written in the Ghetto of Warsaw:

> "Pesach has come to the Ghetto again.
> The lore-laden words of the Seder are said,
> And the cup of the Prophet Elijah awaits,
> But the Angel of Death has intruded, instead..."

(Background humming "Ani Ma-amin" (*Songs We Sing* p. 374)

---

* Written for the Women's Division of the American Jewish Congress. Permission to reprint in this anthology and present royalty-free granted by AJC on the proviso that school or center planning production, contact: Women's Division, American Jewish Congress, 15 East 84th Street, New York 10028, to advise when, where and by whom (children, youth or adult group) the script will be done. Copies of script can be ordered at a minimal charge through AJC office.

or "Jewish Partisan Song" (*Treasury of Jewish Song*—Rubin, p. 182 ending louder)

FIRST READER: Food, and history and custom and song. 3300 years of observing the sacred nature of freedom with great prayers and beautiful ceremonies while we eat, drink and rejoice in remembrance of the liberation from slavery. Have you ever paused to wonder at the hundreds of different communities of Jews throughout the world and the manner of their Passover celebration? In Spain after the Inquisition? In the Russia of the Czars? In Modern Israel? Among the Indian Jews? Does any community celebrate the Passover as Moses did, leading his people, as the Bible tells it, "eating the roasted meat with unleavened bread and bitter herbs, with their loins girded, their shoes on their feet, the staff in their hands, eating in haste?" (Background humming "Avadim Hayinu," *Songs We Sing* p. 177)

SECOND READER: I have read of a small Samaritan community in Israel, perhaps only 200 strong, who even today follow the Biblical Exodus. The entire community proceeds to Mt. Gerizim, and on a piece of land not far from the mountain, the lamb is roasted at sunset, after which, with loins girded, and their staves in their hands, they "eat in haste" and cry forth their prayers and sing of the departure from Egypt.

THIRD READER: In some communities in the Middle Ages, when the passage describing the crossing of the Red Sea was reached, a bowl of live fish was placed on the table to remind the celebrants of the fate which befell the Egyptians. ("VeHee SheAmdah," *Songs We Sing* p. 178)

FOURTH READER: Since the child is so important to the festival of Passover, the Oriental community loves to dramatize the Seder for the children. (Song—verse from "Chad Gadya" *Songs We Sing* p. 190 or "Echod Mi Yodaya" p. 188) The father literally carries a staff in his hand, wraps the three matzot in a bundle which he places on his back, and paces up and down the room. The children ask, "Whence do you come?" and he replies, "From the land of Egypt." "And whither are you going?" they ask, and he replies, "To the land of Israel." "And where is the food for your journey?" they ask, and he shows them the matzot wrapped in the bundle slung across his back.

FIRST READER: The Caucasian Jews of Southern Russia

greeted the Passover seated on the earth, dressed in their best clothes, with a spear close at hand, to portray the dangers that beset the Israelites in the hurried exodus from Egypt.

SECOND READER: And in the Eastern provinces of Portugal, near the Spanish border, descendants of Marranos who escaped the Spanish Inquisition hold a picnic in the country on Passover. All that is left of that Seder is a special prayer in memory of the Seder service their ancestors enjoyed, since not even a single matzoh could escape the eyes of the Inquisition. (Background humming "Borai Pri Hagafen," *Songs We Sing* p. 174)

THIRD READER: In some Jewish communities of Hungary and Poland, the Chassidim would assemble in a private home and dine together. After midnight they would take a pitcher of water and dance with it until the water spilled on the floor; or a pan of water would be placed on the floor and the Chassidim would jump over it and dance around it singing "Then Sang Moses." Even today, the modern Chassidim dance across an imaginary Red Sea. ("Eliyahu HaNavi," *Songs We Sing* p. 183)

FOURTH READER: And what of Pesach today in modern Israel, how does a Kibbutz celebrate?

FIRST READER: Here is a letter from a kibbutznik who celebrated in freedom: (Background humming modern "Mah Nishtanah," *Songs We Sing* p. 176) "The barley which has been cut in the fields is brought into the dining room, heaped in stacks in the center, a symbolic offering. The choir sings old and new songs, both much loved. Everyone has his own Haggadah, but reading is done in turn, each reader standing up in his own place. Readings are interspersed with songs, and some parts of the Haggadah are sung to melodies invented by the local folk. The food is better and more than usual and the watchword for the night is "gusto." By 11 o'clock the formal part of the festivity is over, but the young continue singing and dancing until 4 A.M. when the Passover night ends.

The emergence into freedom, which the tradition recalls, has a special meaning and poignancy here in this newly independent land, many of whose citizens have only been recently liberated from fear and from dread. This release, like the release of nature in the springtime, the kibbutz celebrates in song, in dance, and in the joy of the heart." (Modern version of "L'Shanah ha ba-ah BeYerushalayim," *Songs We Sing* p. 187)

SECOND READER: Of all the festival days, Passover has elicited unending stories of delightful fun. This is understandable, precisely because of what is at stake in Passover—love of liberty and devotion to freedom, the dignity of the human being and the hatred of tyranny. What more subtle way to fight the evils of slavery and dictatorship than to hold them and their works up to ridicule and mockery and blow away their pretensions in gales of laughter? The therapy of gaiety and laughter was as necessary as the air they breathed.

THIRD READER: The Bible reveals that Pharaoh commanded that every Hebrew male child should be cast into the river. If Pharaoh intended to annihilate the children of Israel, why did he not order the girls as well as the boys to be drowned? Pharaoh knew that if all the boys would be thrown into the river, the girls would jump in after them!

FOURTH READER: Neither persecution nor grief, nor the poverty of their dank ghetto prisons could keep the Jews from laughing:

FIRST READER: Several days before Passover a poor man came to the rabbi for advice. "Rabbi," he complained bitterly, "I'm in desperate circumstances. Passover is almost here and I haven't the means with which to observe it properly. I must get money for matzos, meat and sacramental wine. My family and I dare not show ourselves in the synagogue for the holiday services—we are all in tatters."

The rabbi tried to soothe him. "Don't worry, God will help you."

But the unhappy man was not to be comforted. "I've too many worries, Rabbi," he wailed. "I'm afraid they're too much for me." "In that case," said the rabbi, "let's see what your needs are." And he began to figure:

"How much do you need for matzos, meat and wine?"
"Sixteen rubles."
"Clothes for your children?"
"Eighteen rubles."
"A new dress for your wife?"
"Eight rubles."
"A new suit for yourself?"
"Ten rubles."

The rabbi then added up the various items and said: "You need altogether 52 rubles. Now at least you won't have to worry about matzos, meat, wine *and* clothing—you'll only have one worry—where to get the 52 rubles!"

SECOND READER: And here's a modern one for our times:

THIRD READER: A lover of art brought home a large canvas in an ornate frame. Displaying it to his wife with deep pride, he said: "Look at this beautiful painting I bought." The wife stared in amazement at the canvas, for it was completely blank. "I do not see anything on this canvas. Did you buy it at the Museum of Non-Objective Art? What is it supposed to be?"

"This is a painting of the Jews crossing the Red Sea," he replied condescendingly.

"But where are the Jews?"

"The Jews already passed through the sea and they are on shore."

"And where are the Egyptians?"

"The Egyptians are still pursuing the children of Israel and they have not yet reached the sea."

"And where then is the sea itself?"

"The waters of the sea are divided and have receded to the shores so that the Jews should be able to cross."

FOURTH READER: Jewish folklore reflects the attitude of our people toward the Jewish hero. It is not the warrior hero of other peoples, although we have our Maccabees, our Bar Kochbas, and our Warsaw Ghetto fighters, who fought for the preservation of their country with valor and an utter disregard for their lives. The Jewish hero is the tzaddik, the righteous man who stood up for their dignity and their beliefs.

FIRST READER: What kind of a hero was Moses, whose name is never mentioned in the Haggadah? Listen to what Heinrich Heine, the famous German poet, wrote of Moses:

SECOND READER: "Formerly, I felt little affection for Moses, probably because the hellenic spirit was dominant within me, and I could not pardon the Jewish Lawgiver for his intolerance of images ... I failed to see that despite his hostile attitude to art, Moses was himself a great artist, gifted with the true artist's spirit ... Unlike the Egyptians, he did not shape his works out of bricks or granite. His pyramids were built of men, his obelisks hewn out of human material. A feeble race of shepherds he transformed into a people bidding defiance to the centuries—a great, eternal, holy people, God's people, the prototype of mankind: he created Israel. With greater justice than the Roman poet could this artist, the son of Amram and Yochebed the midwife, boast of having erected a monument more enduring than brass."

THIRD READER: True, God through Moses discouraged and forbade images, as instructed in the Second Commandment, but the Jewish people in the past hundreds of years have expressed their art on beautiful Seder plates, wine cups for Elijah (low singing "Eliyahu HaNavi," *Songs We Sing* p. 183), paintings of the Seder, and particularly in the Haggadah. Artists found many subjects in the Haggadah they could illustrate: the four sons, the ten plagues, Jacob's ladder, the crossing of the Red Sea, the patriarchs, and the baking of the matzos. This festival has been a strong incentive for the artistic creativity of our people. Families had hand-illustrated Haggadahs handed down from father to son and kept for generations.

FOURTH READER: Although women are not mentioned in the Haggadah for the reason that in the early Mishnaic period the Seder was attended only by men and the Haggadah was created for fathers to relate to their sons, we find the medieval Haggadah showing the mother, the daughter, and even the servant girl participating in the Seder.

FIRST READER: Some Haggadahs show a woman reading a book, and a 16th century Haggadah shows a beautiful young woman, dressed in the taste of High Renaissance, standing before a seated older man and holding up a large book to him.

SECOND READER: Spanish Haggadot were gold lettered and ornamented;

THIRD READER: Amsterdam had copper engravings, while in Venice they were illustrated by woodcuts;

FOURTH READER: And museums throughout the world have parchment and manuscript Seder guides, including our own Jewish Museum in New York City.

FIRST READER: There is an amusing medieval engraving found in many editions of the Haggadah in which the wise man is portrayed as a scholar in the eloquent attitude of expounding the Torah. The wicked man, on the other hand, is represented as a fierce knight in armor running with spear in hand.

SECOND READER: I want to know about matzot. Doesn't that have a history?

THIRD READER: Yes indeed. In the days of the Talmud matzot were home baked, and even hand ornamented! Women illustrated birds and flowers on the dough, which was often an inch thick, or doves, fishes and other forms. But the rabbis later prohibited all personal designs unless they could be made with a comblike instrument and with perforated holes.

All matzot were round shaped, and baked by hand in private or communal bakeries until about 1850, when the demand in large communities exceeded the hand-baked supply.

FOURTH READER: And why the perforations in the matzot?

FIRST READER: To prevent the dough from rising during the baking!

And so,

SECOND READER: Even if Pesach only meant wine and kneidlach and fish and borsht, *dayainu*—it would have been sufficient;

THIRD READER: Even if Pesach only meant family, the old and the young together, the chanting of the Haggadah, it would have been enough;

FOURTH READER: Even if Pesach meant only liberation from the tyranny of Pharaohs and Hitlers, it would have been enough;

FIRST READER: But like the Passover "Dayainu" we all know so well and love to sing (two verses should be sung with chorus) Passover means all of this, and more.

SECOND READER: It is the holiday called the Feast of Unleavened Bread and the Season of our Freedom.

THIRD READER: It reminds us again and again that once we were slaves in Egypt.

FOURTH READER: It calls to mind the struggle to attain liberty, social justice and democracy not only for ourselves but for our fellow-man.

FIRST READER: While celebrating Passover the Jew is asked to think of the current needs of society and the individuals who comprise it.

SECOND READER: The hungry man cannot be free, so we restore his dignity by inviting "Let all who are hungry come in and eat"—testimony indeed that a healthy society can only be established when concern is shown for the needs of every one of its members.

THIRD AND FOURTH READER: When you hear the word Passover, how many are the images; and flavors; and customs;

and songs that leap to your mind! (All sing either "Adir Hu," or "Eliyahu Hanavi," from *Songs We Sing* by Harry Coopersmith.)

FINALE

QUOTATIONS

(NOTE: To be used when applicable, in introducing various selections.)

Thus said the Lord, the God of Israel: Let My people go ...
Exodus 5.1

Every person in every generation must regard himself as having been personally freed from Egypt.
Pesahim 10.5

THE FIRST ANNIVERSARY

And the Lord spoke unto Moses in the wilderness of Sinai, in the first month of the second year after they were come out of the land of Egypt, saying: "Let the children of Israel keep the passover in its appointed season. In the fourteenth day of this month, at dusk, ye shall keep it in its appointed season; according to all of the statutes of it, and according to all the ordinances thereof, shall ye keep it." And Moses spoke unto the children of Israel, that they should keep the passover. And they kept the passover in the first month, on the fourteenth day of the month, at dusk, in the wilderness of Sinai; according to all that the Lord commanded Moses, so did the children of Israel.
Numbers 9.1-5

THE EXODUS

And Moses said unto the people: "Remember this day in which ye came out from Egypt, out of the house of bondage; for by strength of hand the Lord brought you out from this place; there shall no leavened bread be eaten. This day ye go forth in the month Abib. And it shall be when the Lord shall bring thee into the land of the Canaanite and the Hittite and the Amorite and the Hivite and the Jebusite, which He swore unto thy fathers to give thee, a land flowing with milk and honey, that thou shalt keep this service in this month. Seven days thou shalt eat unleavened bread, and in the seventh day shall be a feast to the Lord. Unleavened bread shall be eaten throughout the seven days; and there shall no leavened bread be seen with thee, in all thy borders. And thou shalt tell thy son in that day, saying: It is because of that which the Lord did for me when I came forth out of Egypt. And it shall be for a sign unto thee upon thy hand, and for a memorial between thine eyes, that the law of the Lord may be in thy mouth; for with a strong hand hath the Lord brought thee out of Egypt. Thou shall therefore keep this ordinance in its season from year to year.

Exodus 12:1-3,6-8

GO DOWN MOSES

Go down, Moses,
'Way down in Egypt land,
Tell ole Pharaoh, to let My people go.
Go down, Moses, 'way down in Egypt land,
Tell ole Pharaoh, to let My people go.
When Israel was in Egypt land,
Let My people go,
Oppressed so hard they could not stand,
Let My people go.

"Thus spoke the Lord," bold Moses said:
Let My people go.
If not I'll smite your first born dead,
Let My people go.

Go down, Moses,
'Way down in Egypt land,
Tell ole Pharaoh, to let My people go.
O let My people go.

—Anonymous

MAKE KNOWN HIS DEEDS
Psalm 105

PRODUCTION NOTE:

This Psalm can be given effectively as a Choral Reading, by activating eight or more children. Two main readers (boys or girls, preferably boys) chosen for resonant voices and good diction, deliver stanzas marked for Reader I and II respectively. Six to ten boys and girls comprise the Chorus. Members of the Chorus should be selected for a wide range of voice quality.

The lines of the Chorus may be broken up and assigned to individual children, or the lines may be delivered in unison.

It is preferable to memorize the text. However, if the required time cannot be devoted to memorization and rehearsals, the Psalm can readily and more expeditiously be done as a Reading, with participants holding books. (Scripts should be bound in colorful hard covers.)

CHORUS

Praise the Lord! Call upon His name.
Make known His deeds among the peoples.

Sing to Him; sing praises to Him;
Recount all His marvelous works.
They who seek the Lord rejoice;
Let them glory in His holiness.

Look to the Lord and His might;
Seek his Presence continually.
Recall the marvels He has done,
His wonders and His judgments.

O children of Israel His servant,
O sons of Jacob, His chosen ones.
He is the Lord, our God;
He rules the whole earth.

READER I

He will always remember His covenant,
His promise to a thousand generations,
The covenant He made with Abraham,
The oath He reaffirmed with Isaac,

The unchanging compact with Jacob,
The everlasting bond with Israel,
Saying: "I give you the land of Canaan
As the portion which you will inherit."

READER II

When you were but very few in number,
Little more than strangers in the land,
When you passed from country to country,
Wandering from one kingdom to another.

READER I

He permitted no man to oppress you;
He rebuked kings on your account.
He said: "Touch not My anointed;
Do not do evil to My prophets."

He proclaimed a famine over the land;
He cut off the food that sustains life.

READER II

God sent Joseph before them to Egypt,
Joseph, who had been sold as a slave.

They tortured him with irons;
They imprisoned him with fetters.
Until that which he foretold came to be,
Until the Lord's promise vindicated him.

READER I

The king sent for him and released him;
The ruler of the people set him free.
He made him master of his palace
And ruler of all his possessions,

To instruct the princes as he wished
And to train the elders in wisdom.

READER II

Then Israel came into the land of Egypt;
Jacob came to live there as an alien.

Because God made His people fruitful
They very soon outmatched their foes.
The Egyptians turned against His people
And acted with guile toward His servants.

CHORUS

God sent Moses as His servant,
And Aaron whom He had chosen.
God wrought signs among the Egyptians
And produced miracles in their land.

READER I

At His command darkness was everywhere,
Yet His servants did not rebel against Him.
He turned their waters into blood
And He caused their fish to die.

READER II

Their whole land teemed with frogs
Swarming even in the royal chambers.
At His command flies overwhelmed them
And lice swarmed over all their land.

READER I

Instead of rain He gave them hail;
Lightning flashed through the skies.
At His command the locusts came
And grasshoppers beyond reckoning.

READER II

These devoured all their vegetation;
They consumed all crops of the soil.

READER I

He struck every first-born in the land,
The first fruits of their manly strength.

CHORUS

He led Israel forth with silver and gold;
There was not a straggler among His tribes.
Egypt rejoiced when they left;
Dread of them had fallen upon the land.

READER I

He spread out a cloud to cover them;
With fire He lit up the night for them.

READER II

When they asked for food, the quail came;
And He sated them with bread from heaven.

He opened a rock and water gushed forth;
It flowed through the desert like a river.

READERS I and II

Because He remembered His sacred promise,
The promise He made to Abraham His servant.

CHORUS

He led His people with song;
He led forth His chosen ones.
He gave them the lands of their foes;
He gave them the fruit of their labor,
So that His people shall keep His statutes
And shall observe His laws, Praise the Lord!

FINALE

THE VOICE UNTO PHARAOH
Arthur Guiterman

Pharaoh, Pharaoh, let my people go!
My fettered children toil with aching limbs
    And wearied fingers, brain and spirit bound,
Their puny forms are bent; the shadow dims
    Their straining eyes; their ears are choked with sound,
And thick with reek is every breath they draw.
    I gave them light to see and song to hear.
I gave them Truth for guide and Love for law;
    And thou hast given darkness, blight and fear.
Pharaoh, Pharaoh, let my people go!
In chains, unseen but strong, my children slave,
    Too dull for hopes or dreams, too dumb for prayers.
Thou hast robbed them of the youth I gave,
    The world I made, the joy that should be theirs.
Their lives are coined to swell thy shining store;
    Then darest thou plead, "Nay, Lord, I did not know,"—
Still heaping up their burdens more and more?
    The sand is running; let my children go.
Pharaoh, Pharaoh, let my people go!
Thy heart is hard. Be warned. The Plagues may come.
    The wrong thou dost may breed yet fouler wrong.
Those lips may speak in flame that now are dumb!
    Those feeble hands, through wrath and hatred strong;
May rend where they have wrought. Yea, once again
    Disease, Revolt and Crime may overthrow
The Selfishness that bred them. Sons of men,
    For dread of vengeance, let my people go!

From Poems for Young Judaeans

WHEN ISRAEL CAME OUT OF EGYPT
Psalm 114

When Israel came out of Egypt
And Jacob from an alien people,

Judah was God's sanctuary;
Israel was God's dominion.

Seeing it, the sea fled, the Jordan retreated;
Mountains leaped like rams, hills like lambs.

What frightened you waters, that you flee?
What terrified you Jordan, that you retreat?

O mountains, why do you leap like rams?
You hills, why do you skip like lambs?

Tremble, O earth, at God's Presence,
At the Presence of the Lord of Jacob.

He turns hard rock into water pools;
He transforms flint into fountains.

CHILDREN OF ISRAEL*
James Yaffe

We hear music—a children's chorus singing a traditional Passover song. Rather lively and spirited. The scene fades in slowly. We see a stage, with odd flats, bits of prop furniture, exits to the wings, etc. On the stage is the children's choir, singing under the direction of old Mr. Kaplan, the cantor. By his side is Mr. Feldman, a younger man, the assistant cantor. The chorus faces the audience.

As the singing goes on, one little boy in the front row keeps hitting the same wrong note. Finally Mr. Kaplan waves for the singing to stop.

KAPLAN: (He turns sternly to Stanley, the little boy, about nine) Stop it, stop it. Stanley, will you kindly sing us the melody please?

STANLEY: (Alarmed) All by myself, Mr. Kaplan?

KAPLAN: Why not? One—two—three—

(Stanley takes a breath and starts in. He goes along fine until he reaches that bad note he goes sour on. He stops embarrassed.)

KAPLAN: Exactly what I thought!

STANLEY: (Close to tears) I don't mean it, Mr. Kaplan. I've got the right note in my mind—but somehow the wrong one keeps coming out. I can still be in the Passover program, can't I? You're not going to make me—

FELDMAN: (Kindly) It's all right, Stanley. You're still in the program. One note isn't so important.

KAPLAN: But this has to be right, Feldman. The whole

---

* Reprinted by permission of The Jewish Theological Seminary of America, producers of *The Eternal Light* program, under whose auspices "Children of Israel" was originally presented March 18, 1956 on NBC-TV; the author James Yaffe, and Harold Freedman, Brandt & Brandt, Dramatic Dept., Inc., author's agent.

Permission to reprint this play and present it has been granted by author and agent only on the proviso that no admission is charged.

If given for a paying audience, permission must be obtained from the Brandt & Brandt Office, 101 Park Avenue, New York City, and a royalty paid.

Copyright © 1956 by The Jewish Theological Seminary of America.

synagogue will show up next week. The Board of Trustees. And my last concert before I'm retired—as cantor.

FELDMAN: Nothing will go wrong, Mr. Kaplan. Even the biggest tenors at the Metropolitan Opera occasionally miss a note.

KAPLAN: The Metropolitan Opera doesn't have to please our Board of Trustees.

(A serious-looking 12 year old steps forward from the choir. His name is David.)

DAVID: Please, sir—when he comes to that note, why can't Stanley just move his mouth and not make any sound?

FELDMAN: Now that's a good idea, Mr. Kaplan.

KAPLAN: (With a sigh; he pats Stanley on the head, and something like a smile comes on his face) All right, all right, you beat me down, as usual. So you'll be in the program next week—but don't let me hear any sour notes out of you!

STANLEY: (Beaming) Thanks, Mr. Kaplan. (He steps back into his place)

KAPLAN: (Looking at his watch) Now look what time it is! Three o'clock, and I'm due at my dentist in ten minutes! You made me forget all about it, with all this arguing. Feldman, you can take charge of things?

FELDMAN: Certainly, Mr. Kaplan.

KAPLAN: Remember, the Passover concert is their best chance to show off all year—so don't let them get away with anything.

FELDMAN: Not a thing.

KAPLAN: Well, I'll see you tomorrow, children. And nobody late.

(The children say goodbye to him, and Mr. Kaplan bustles off. They all wait until they hear the door closing backstage. Then the children all crowd around Mr. Feldman, talking excitedly)

FELDMAN: Wait a minute, wait a minute. One at a time. (The rest quiet down, and leave David to be their spokesman.)

DAVID: Here it is, Mr. Feldman, we've got the play written.

FELDMAN: (Taking a sheaf of papers from David) That's wonderful. Your committee acted fast. When I sat in on your meeting the other day, you hadn't written a word.

(Another boy, Irving, steps forward)

IRVING: Well, to tell the truth, Mr. Feldman, the committee

was doing so much arguing and everything—so Stanley just went home last night and wrote it all by himself.

FELDMAN: Stanley? (Surprised—Stanley is so small)

STANLEY: (Blushing) Yes, Mr. Feldman.

FELDMAN: You wrote this Passover play all by yourself?

STANLEY: I've done a lot of writing, Mr. Feldman. Last year I wrote a novel, while I had the measles. It's called "The Body in Aunt Harriet's Attic."

FELDMAN: You know how important this play is? We're charging admission for a very important reason.

STANLEY: We're going to give the money to Mr. Kaplan, so he can make a visit to Israel after he retires—I know all that.

FELDMAN: (Still uncertain) David—what do you think of Stanley's play?

DAVID: (After a moment's thought) It's a little immature in places, Mr. Feldman. But mostly it's pretty good.

IRVING: He's put in lots of stuff that the rabbi told us in Hebrew School.

(The other children raise their voices in approval of Stanley's play)

FELDMAN: (Laughing; he opens up the manuscript and glances at it) All right, all right, let's look at it. You've got the whole chorus on stage at the beginning, I see?

STANLEY: All the way through, Mr. Feldman. I wanted to be sure that everybody had something to do. (A little slyly) There's lots of singing in it for *you*, sir.

FELDMAN: (Clearing his throat, he looks through the script some more, then looks up puzzled) Yes—well, that's not really important, of course. But Stanley—you say here, "Moses enters with his brother Aaron. Moses is twelve years old, and Aaron is eleven years old. They are on their way to Egypt to free the Israelites from slavery."

STANLEY: What's wrong with that?

FELDMAN: Well—the way you've got it here, Moses and Aaron are only children.

STANLEY: Yes, sir. That's what they were, weren't they?

FELDMAN: I don't follow you—

STANLEY: That's what it says in the Bible. You know—the Children of Israel. Moses and Aaron, and the Israelites, they were *all* children. That's why it's so easy for us to act the parts.

FELDMAN: (Astonished) Children of Israel! Stanley when

the Bible says "Children of Israel," it doesn't mean they were really *children*.

STANLEY: You mean, the Bible isn't telling the truth?

FELDMAN: No, of course not . . . I mean—

DAVID: It's no use, Mr. Feldman. We've been trying to explain it to him all day. I told you it was a little immature.

IRVING: But it's a good play anyway, sir.

FELDMAN: (Smiling again) All right, let's hear it, I won't interrupt. Suppose you read it to us, Stanley.

STANLEY: (Eagerly; he takes the manuscript and starts reading) Yes, sir. Scene One: Music. It's the top of a hill. On stage is the burning bush. It burns for awhile, and then Moses enters. He is twelve years old—

Voices of the choir. They sing soft music which leads into the slightly unreal mood of the play. We see the scene set up, in a few props. In an open space below the choir, we see the burning bush—burning electrically. And then Moses—really David—appears. He stops in amazement as he sees the burning bush.

(Forestage, burning bush)

MOSES: Aaron, come quick! Look!—(Aaron enters, holding Stanley by the hand. Aaron is Irving)

AARON: (Seeing the bush) Golly! It's burning!

MOSES: Keep Stanley back, he might get hurt.

STANLEY: No, I want to look. What's making it burn?

AARON: (Holding him back) Stand back, Stanley. You know what Mama and Papa are always telling you, about playing with fire.

MOSES: I'll look at it. (He moves up the bush, stops short as the voice of the Lord—the voice of Mr. Kaplan—is heard from the bush)

THE VOICE: Moses, stop! This is the voice of the Lord!

MOSES: The Lord!

THE VOICE: Moses, I have work for you to do. I have heard the cry of the children of Israel. I have seen how the Egyptians oppress them. I am going to send you to Pharaoh, so that you can bring the children of Israel out of Egypt.

MOSES: But . . . why me? That's such a big job, bringing the children of Israel out of Egypt. And there's nothing special about *me*.

THE VOICE: I have chosen you as My messenger, nothing else is necessary. I will be with you every moment, so you don't have to be afraid.

MOSES: But Pharaoh won't believe me when I say I'm a messenger of the Lord. He'll laugh at me and send me away.

THE VOICE: Moses, have you so little confidence in Me? I will make sure that Pharaoh does not laugh at you. Do you see the rod in your hand?

MOSES: (Looking at his shepherd's crook) Yes.

THE VOICE: Cast it on the ground, and it will turn into a snake. *That* should convince Pharaoh that you are My messenger. Go ahead, cast it down. (Moses casts his rod on the ground. The voice of Mr. Feldman is heard.)

FELDMAN'S VOICE: Wait a minute, wait a minute. Stanley how do you expect us to turn the rod into a snake? The Lord can do miracles, but our property department doesn't have His experience.

STANLEY'S VOICE: We'll figure out some way, Mr. Feldman. Let me go on with the play right now. (Moses picks up the rod)

THE VOICE: Now pick it up again, Moses, and it will become a rod again.

THE VOICE: And now you are ready to set forth for Egypt.

AARON: (Aaron steps forward, polite but determined) Lord, please—can I go to Egypt with Moses? He's such a bad public speaker, you know. He might get shy in front of Pharaoh, and forget what he wants to say. But *I'm* never shy, so if I could be there to help him out—

THE VOICE: An excellent idea. You will take your brother Aaron with you, Moses.

MOSES: And what about Stanley, Lord? Aaron and I have always looked after him.

THE VOICE: Stanley will go with you too. And now I must leave you. (His voice fading away) But we will meet again in Egypt. (The voice fades away, and the burning bush stops burning.)

AARON: (Excited) He's gone! Come on Moses, let's start packing right away. Come on Stanley. Isn't it exciting? We're all going to Egypt!

MOSES: (Solemn and worried) Yes, you two hurry along, I'll follow.

STANLEY: (As Aaron leads him out) Aaron, how did the Lord make the bush burn? Do you think He'd teach me, if I'm a good boy— (Stanley and Aaron are gone. Moses, left alone, raises his eyes to heaven.)

MOSES: Oh Lord, I hope You didn't make a mistake, picking me. I'm only a child, you know.

(The choir, with Feldman as soloist, start singing. They sing music expressive of Moses' courage and determination as he sets out to encounter Pharaoh. Their voices grow softer, as Stanley's voice is heard above them.)

STANLEY'S VOICE: The next scene is in Pharaoh's throne-room. Pharaoh is about fifty years old, and he's terribly mean. He's dictating a letter to his secretary.

(The music rises briefly then ends. In the same place where the burning bush scene took place, we now see Pharaoh's throne-room—transformed by the addition of a throne and a couple of child-guards, holding spears. Pharaoh is dictating to his secretary, a girl of ten.)

PHARAOH: Take a letter, please. To all my overseers, foremen, and oppressors. Dear sirs: The building of the pyramids is taking too long and costs too much. From now on the Jews will not be allowed to use any more straw in the bricks. They will be required to make all their bricks without straw, and any Jew who produces even one less brick than his usual quota will be whipped and restricted to bread and water. Sincerely yours, Pharaoh, King of Egypt.

SECRETARY: Yes, your Highness, I'll send this out right away.

PHARAOH: *This* ought to put those Jews in their place. Always asking for their freedom and worshipping that God of theirs. Acting as if they weren't slaves at all—well, any other business this morning?

SECRETARY: Moses and Aaron want to see you, your Highness.

PHARAOH: My adopted son, the Jew. I thought he'd left Egypt for good. He said he'd never come back again. I suppose he wants to make things up with me. Well, I'm not a hard man. I was always fond of the boy, in spite of the fact that he is a Jew. I'll see him.

SECRETARY: Yes, your Highness. (She goes to the door and motions into the outer room. Moses enters, with Aaron and Stanley a little ways behind him.)

MOSES: (Bowing) Your Highness.

PHARAOH: (Looks at Aaron and Stanley) Rise, my boy, rise. Who are these two?

MOSES: My brother Aaron, and my little brother Stanley.

AARON: Pleased to meet you, your Highness. (He nudges Stanley who has been gaping around at the splendor.)

STANLEY: Er—pleased to meet you.

PHARAOH: Well, my boy, I'm delighted to see you. I think I can guess why you've come. You've got a favor to ask me, don't you?

MOSES: Yes, I do. But how did you—

PHARAOH: (Chuckling) Oh, I haven't been Pharaoh all these years without becoming a pretty good judge of character. Well, I'm in a nice mood today, so you may be surprised at the answer I'll give you.

MOSES: You mean—you might say yes?

PHARAOH: Ask away, and you'll find out.

MOSES: Your Highness, what I want—it means so much to me—

PHARAOH: (Beaming complacently) Of course it does. Come out with it.

MOSES: I want—I want—

(Aaron steps up next to him, smiles reassuringly.)

AARON: Go on, Moses. Don't be afraid.

MOSES: (Blurting it out) I want you to let my people go!

PHARAOH: (Blinking, taken off guard) Excuse me? What did you say?

MOSES: My people—the children of Israel. They want nothing from you, except to be allowed to live in freedom in their Promised Land. But you keep them here against their will, you beat them and starve them, you kill them if they dare to speak out for their rights.

PHARAOH: (Still stunned) The Jews? You're talking about my slaves, the Jews?

MOSES: (Proudly) My people. You must let them go. The Lord has commanded me to come to you.

PHARAOH: The Lord! How often have your cursed Jews plagued me with that Lord of theirs? And now *you* come to me

—you're sure you didn't come here for some *other* reason? This isn't some sort of a joke?

MOSES: A joke! The freedom of my people is no joke! I demand that you—

PHARAOH: (Really angry now) Demand! Who are you to demand anything from me? I am Pharaoh, King of Egypt, Nephew of the Sun, Cousin of the Moon, Brother of the Sacred White Cat! Get out of here at once, or I'll have my soldiers put an end to your demands!

MOSES: I'll get out when you give me your answer.

PHARAOH: My answer is No! Can't you understand plain Egyptian? Now get out!

MOSES: The Lord is powerful. He will bring plagues upon you and upon your people. He will punish your cruelty and injustice.

PHARAOH: Your Lord is going to punish *me?* Excuse me, that's funny.

MOSES: He has the power to punish all men. See my rod! (Moses throws his rod to the ground, while Feldman's voice is heard.)

FELDMAN'S VOICE: You're planning to turn it into a snake a *second* time?

STANLEY'S VOICE: Well, if we can do it *once*—

FELDMAN'S VOICE: All right, all right, go on with the play.

PHARAOH: (Jumping back from the rod) Take it away! I hate snakes!

MOSES: (Picking up the rod) Will you heed the commands of the Lord?

PHARAOH: (Recovering himself) Because of some silly parlor trick? I have a hundred magicians who can do better tricks than that. Your people are my slaves, and they're going to stay that way. I defy your Lord!

MOSES: (Angry, but quiet) Very well. The plagues must begin. I'm sorry. (He turns and strides out. Aaron starts after him. Stanley hangs back.)

STANLEY: Your Highness, you're mean. That's what you are—

(Aaron grabs Stanley and pulls him out after him.)

PHARAOH: (Glaring after them furiously) The Lord! What can their Lord do to *me?* I'm Pharaoh, King of Egypt!

SECRETARY: Yes, your Highness.
(The choir and soloist sing fast dramatic music, expressing the coming of the plagues. The voices drop into the background, and Stanley's voice is heard.)
STANLEY'S VOICE: Pharaoh was so stubborn that the Lord had to send nine plagues to the Egyptians. (As he says the name of each plague, the voices rise and sing a brief episode which suggests it.) Blood. Frogs. Lice. Flies. Blight. Boils. Hail. Locusts. Darkness.

(On the word "darkness" the light grows dim. The voices rise and sing mysteriously, suggesting the plague of darkness. The scene this time, a table and some chairs, suggests a room in Moses' house. Moses, Aaron, and Stanley are around the table eating. A candle gives them light. A loud knocking is heard. Aaron opens the door. Pharaoh is in the doorway, muffled up in a cloak, very stiff and pale.)

PHARAOH: May I come in?
AARON: (Surprised) Yes—of course. Moses, do you see who—?
MOSES: (On his feet) Your Highness.
PHARAOH: I've come alone. I slipped through the streets with my cloak over my face, so that nobody would recognize me. (With a short laugh) Not that I needed to worry about that. With the darkness outside—(With a pleading note) Moses, lift the darkness. I command you—No, no, I don't mean that. I ask you. I ask you as gently as the King of Egypt knows how. Free us from this terrible darkness.
MOSES: Free my people from the darkness of slavery in which you make them live.
PHARAOH: (A flash of anger) Your people again! I'll do it. Lift the darkness, and I'll let your people go.
AARON: Don't listen to him, Moses. He's said that before.
STANLEY: He's said it eight times.
AARON: And each time he's broken his promise. You can't trust him. Let the darkness go on, until he's really desperate.
MOSES: (Looking hard into Pharaoh's face) Is my brother right? How can I be sure of you?
PHARAOH: (Proudly) I am Pharaoh, King of Egypt. I keep my word. (Then, with a sigh, deflated) I've learned my lesson Moses, I know that I can't defy your God.

MOSES: Very well. I'll lift the darkness. (He paces forward and raises his arms slowly. As he does so the scene grows light.)

PHARAOH: (Blinking around) Light again! You've done it—

MOSES: And now my people will prepare for their journey.

PHARAOH: (Draws himself up imperiously) Your people will return to the stone works. I will instruct my overseers to whip them harder than ever.

AARON: I told you, I told you!

MOSES: Why do you talk like this? Pharaoh, King of Egypt, keeps his word, you said.

PHARAOH: Pharaoh, King of Egypt, does not consider himself bound by every casual remark he makes to Jews and slaves. (With great intensity) *I'm* the Law in Egypt, not you! It's time you found that out! (Turns sharply to go.)

MOSES: (As Pharaoh turns) Wait. Our Lord has still another plague for your people. Please don't force Him to use it.

PHARAOH: (Laughing) Another plague! Your Lord has emptied His bag of tricks!

MOSES: He has another plague—the worst of all.

PHARAOH: What can be worse than His lice, His locusts, His darkness? We have survived them all. We are stronger than your Lord.

MOSES: If you refuse to let my people go, the Angel of Death will come and smite all the first born in the land of Egypt. All, every one—from the first-born of the humblest servant to the first-born of Pharaoh himself. That's the plague the Lord has in store for you.

PHARAOH: (Brightened) The first-born—*My* son—(He shakes off the fear, grows haughtier than ever) Your Lord can't do it. He can destroy our cattle and our crops, but He can't touch my people. We are Egyptians, and our gods will protect us! (He turns on his heel and exits.)

MOSES: (Looking after him sadly) There is only one God, the God of light and justice. (He lowers himself wearily into a chair)

AARON: (Coming up to him) I knew it! You just can't trust them, these Pharaohs! Well, let's settle it once and for all, Moses. Raise your arms, call the Angel of Death to smite the Egyptian first-born.

MOSES: (He raises his arms, struggles for a moment with

the pain inside of him, then lowers his arms heavily) Yes, I'll call Him. Do we have to do it?

AARON: I don't understand you, Moses.

MOSES: The first-born—the children, who haven't done any harm to our people. They aren't the ones who keep us in slavery, and whip us and kill us. Why should they die for the sins of others?

AARON: But we haven't done the Egyptians any harm either. Why should *we* be whipped and killed?

MOSES: Yes, that's true. But still—

AARON: Pharaoh brought this on himself. It's his fault, not ours. So why do you hesitate?

MOSES: Because—if only there were some other way—

Aaron: But there isn't. This is the only way.

MOSES: (After a moment, he lowers his head, resigned; he rises to his feet, solemn and determined) Yes, it's the only way. (He sighs) God doesn't make it easy for His servants, does he? I'll call the Angel of Death.

(As Moses raises his arms, the choir and soloist, continue the mood of the last scene by singing a slow mournful lament for the first-born. At the end, their voices grow softer, the music continues under Stanley's voice.)

STANLEY'S VOICE: So the Angel of Death came, and the first-born were taken and Pharaoh's own son was killed too. So Pharaoh said that the children of Israel could go free.

(The music rises, happier, more energetic)

STANLEY'S VOICE: So the children of Israel got all packed, and started to leave Egypt. But Pharaoh still wasn't through being mean. He sent his soldiers after them to bring them back. But the waters of the Red Sea divided, and the children of Israel went through, and when Pharaoh's soldiers tried to follow, the waters closed up again and they were all drowned.

FELDMAN'S VOICE: I suppose you've thought of some way of doing *that* on the stage?

STANLEY'S VOICE: Well, no, sir. I thought we'd just announce it between the scenes.

STANLEY'S VOICE: So anyway, the next scene is on the other side of the Red Sea, and Moses is making a speech to his people.

(The music ends. Moses, facing front with Aaron and Stanley a little behind him. Moses speaks to the audience as if addressing a large group of people.)

MOSES: Children of Israel—we're free. The Lord has brought ten plagues on the Egyptians, and divided the Red Sea, and performed all sorts of miracles for us so that we may live in our Promised Land. Naturally we're very grateful to the Lord, and very proud that He's gone to so much trouble for us.

We mustn't get cocky and over-confident, though . . . we mustn't think that all our troubles are over now. The hardest part is still ahead of us. We have to wander through the desert for a long time, many years maybe, before we can enter our Promised Land. And we'll be on our own all this time too. Oh, the Lord may perform an occasional miracle for us, out of the kindness of His heart, but mostly He's going to leave it to us to earn our own freedom. So let's remember that—and while we're being happy as children, let's also be serious, like grown men. (He lowers his head, and is solemnly silent for a moment. Then he lifts his head and turns to smile at Aaron and Stanley)

MOSES: Come on. We'll go down to the people now, and begin the journey. (Moses takes Aaron by one hand and Stanley by the other. They start down to the people.)

(The music begins. The choir and soloist, sing in a manner that suggests the solemn yet inspiring experience that lies ahead. The chorus comes to the end of their song triumphantly. The empty stage again, with Stanley holding the manuscript and Mr. Feldman listening to it.)

STANLEY: (Turning over the last page) Curtain. The end.

(There is general applause, with Mr. Feldman joining in.)

DAVID: (Stepping forward) It's a good play, isn't it, Mr. Feldman?

IRVING: You'll let us put it on, won't you, sir? I'm sure it'll make lots of money for Mr. Kaplan's trip.

MR. FELDMAN: (Thinking it over) Yes—it's a good play. We will put it on. (A cheer goes up from the children.)

DAVID: Of course it *is* a little immature. We'll have to change some things.

MR. FELDMAN: (Smiling) No, I don't think so. I think

we'll leave it exactly the way Stanley wrote it. Now let's give out the parts.

STANLEY: Excuse me, sir—but I sort of saw David in the part of Moses.

MR. FELDMAN: Well, the author knows best. David you'll be Moses.

(And there is general confusion, talking, swarming around, as Mr. Feldman hands out the parts.

The scene fades out.

Darkness for a moment. Then loud applause.

Showing the stage. It is the end of the play, and the cast is taking its bows. The choir is lined up, and in front are Stanley, David, Irving, several others, in their biblical robes. Finally Mr. Feldman goes to the wings and pulls Mr. Kaplan out on stage, protesting.

But the applause rises at Kaplan's appearance. He bows quickly, embarrassed. Mr. Feldman raises his arms, and the applause quiets down.)

MR. FELDMAN: Ladies and gentlemen, we're glad you enjoyed our play. But the big treat of the evening is yet to come. Boys—children and now that we have our Mr. Kaplan here—let me introduce a man that we all know and respect, the Chairman of the Board of Trustees.

(From the wings comes the president of the trustees—a large pompous important-looking gentleman, no less than Pharaoh himself.)

THE CHAIRMAN: (After clearing his throat) Friends—children—fellow members of the Board of Trustees the Treasurer has made his tabulations, and it is my pleasure to announce that our little Passover production has achieved its financial goal. And so—with the heartfelt good wishes of all your friends and colleagues, and of course the members of the Board of Trustees, allow me to present to you our beloved cantor, Meyer Kaplan, this check, which should be more than sufficient to enable you to pay that little visit to Israel which you have long been hoping for. (He turns to Mr. Kaplan)

(As he takes the check from the president, Kaplan looks stunned. The applause rises up. Kaplan turns his head bewildered. The applause fades off, the president urges Kaplan to speak. But the old man can't keep his voice steady.)

MR. KAPLAN: I—I don't know—it's such—(Blurting out at the children) Fooling me like that! Hiding things from me! A fine state of affairs! (He breaks off, embarrassed. Then he pushes on most angrily) What are you waiting for? Sing the final song, will you! These people have to get home tonight!

(And he leads the choir, with Mr. Feldman, in the song of the play. As they approach the dangerous note, spotlight focuses on Stanley, singing away heartily. They reach the note, Stanley brings it out to the fear of David and the others around him. But the note comes out pure and true. Stanley beams happily, and Mr. Feldman gives a sigh of relief. The singing goes on, as the scene fades out.)

CURTAIN

THE SONG OF MOSES

PRODUCTION NOTE:

This selection from the Bible (Exodus 15:1-18,20-21), done as a Choral Reading can activate a group of teen-agers: a Narrator; a boy doing the lines allocated to Moses; a Chorus of 6-10, doing the lines in unison, or breaking up the passages thereof and assigning them to individual members; and a group of girl dancers portraying Miriam and the women.

For dance—see "Miriam's Dance of Triumph," in *Jewish Dances the Year Round*, by Dvora Lapson, published by Jewish Education Committee of New York.

NARRATOR

Then sang Moses and the children of Israel this song unto the Lord, and spoke, saying:

MOSES

I will sing unto the Lord, for He is highly exalted;
The horse and his rider hath He thrown into the sea.
The Lord is my strength and song,
And He is become my salvation;
This is my God, and I will glorify Him;
My father's God, and I will exalt Him.

CHORUS

The Lord is a man of war,
The Lord is His name.

MOSES

Pharaoh's chariots and his host hath He cast into the sea.
And his chosen captains are sunk in the Red Sea.
The deeps cover them—
They went down into the depths like a stone.

CHORUS

Thy right hand, O Lord, glorious in power,
Thy right hand, O Lord, dasheth in pieces the enemy.
And in the greatness of Thine excellency Thou overthrowest them
    that rise up against Thee;
Thou sendest forth Thy wrath, it consumeth them as stubble.
And with the blast of Thy nostrils the waters were piled up—
The flood stood upright as a heap;
The deeps were congealed in the heart of the sea.

MOSES

The enemy said:
"I will pursue, I will overtake, I will divide the spoil;
My lust shall be satisfied upon them;
I will draw my sword, my hand shall destroy them."
Thou didst blow with Thy wind, the sea covered them;
They sank as lead in the mighty waters.

CHORUS

Who is like unto Thee, O Lord, among the mighty?
Who is like unto Thee, glorious in holiness,
Fearful in praises, doing wonders?
Thou stretchedst out Thy right hand—
The earth swallowed them.

MOSES

Thou in Thy love hast led the people that Thou hast redeemed;
Thou hast guided them in Thy strength to Thy holy habitation.

CHORUS

The people have heard, they tremble;
Pangs have taken hold on the inhabitants of Philistia.
Then were the chiefs of Edom affrighted;
The mighty men of Moab, trembling taketh hold upon them;
All the inhabitants of Canaan are melted away.
Terror and dread falleth upon them;
By the greatness of Thine arm they are as still as a stone;

MOSES AND CHORUS

Till Thy people pass over, O Lord,
Till the people pass over that Thou hast gotten.
Thou bringest them in, and plantest them in the mountain of
    Thine inheritance.
The place, O Lord, which Thou hast made for Thee to dwell in,
The sanctuary, O Lord, which Thy hands have established.
The Lord shall reign for ever and ever.

NARRATOR

And Miriam the prophetess, the sister of Aaron, took a timbrel in her hand, and all the women went out after her with timbrels and with dances. And Miriam sang unto them:

MIRIAM
Sing ye to the Lord, for He is highly exalted;
The horse and his rider hath He thrown into the sea...

DANCE
as
FINALE.

GREAT DAY

Great day!
Great day, de righteous marchin',
Great day!
God's gwine-ter build up Zion's walls.

De chariot rode on de mountain top,
God's gwine-ter build up Zion's walls,
My God he spoke and de chariot stop,
God's gwine-ter build up Zion's walls.

Dis is de day of jubilee,
God's gwine-ter build up Zion's walls,
De Lord has set His people free,
God's gwine-ter build up Zion's walls.

Gwine take my breas'-plate, sword in han',
God's gwine-ter build up Zion's walls,
An' march out boldly, in-a de field,
God's gwine-ter build up Zion's walls.

We want no cowards in our ban',
God's gwine-ter build up Zion's walls,
We call for valiant hearted men,
God's gwine-ter build up Zion's walls.

Great day!
Great day, de righteous marchin',
Great day!
God's gwine-ter build up Zion's walls.*

—*Anonymous*

---

* The music for this song is to be found in *The Books of American Negro Spirituals* (volume 2, page 56), edited by J. W. Johnson and J. Rosamond Johnson, published by the Viking Press, New York.

Israel Independence Day

	Classification	Title	Author	Age Level
1.	One-act Play	Discovery	Michael Elkins	12-16
2.	Reading	Israel	Isaiah	13-16
3.	Choral Reading	The Vision of the Dry Bones	Ezekiel	12-16
4.	Reading	The Jews Shall Have a State	Theodor Herzl	12-16
5.	Documentary Reading with music and dances	How Is a State Born	Unknown	10-16
6.	Living Newspaper with Choir	"To Thee Will I Give It and to Thy Seed Forever"	Mila Ohel	12-16
7.	Reading	A Rendezvous with Destiny	David Ben-Gurion	14-16
8.	Dramatic Reading with Choir and Dancers	Israel Reborn	Mila Ohel	12-16
9.	Reading	Declaration of Independence		12-16
10.	Reading	Prayer for the State of Israel		10-16
11.	Documentary Reading with musical aids	The Day Israel Was Born	Dorothy Ross	12-16
12.	Reading	In Memoriam	David Ben-Gurion	12-16
13.	Poem	Two by Two—From the Ark to the House and the Zoo	Dorothy Ross	6-10
14.	Poem	Kfar Kennedy	Herb Brin	10-16

DISCOVERY

A Play in One Act

Michael Elkins

CHARACTERS:
(*in order of appearance*)

RAMI: A Bulgarian boy, about 15 years old
MOSHE: Also about 15, an American
RUTH: An American girl, about 14
DOV: A French boy, about 14, quiet in manner
ZVI:16, a Sabra

NOTE: If desired, the character Naomi can be substituted for that of Zvi. Naomi is an Israeli girl about 16.

RUNNING TIME: 18-22 minutes

PRODUCTION NOTES:

No attempt should be made to indicate national origin by accents. In the first scene the characters are dressed in clothes suitable for farmwork —heavy shoes, rough trousers. In the second scene they appear in clean after-work clothes.

The time is the present. The place—a kibbutz in Israel. The entire action takes place from the noon rest period to early evening of a single day. The only set is intended to suggest the interior of a wooden hut. There are no walls shown. On stage at curtain are six cots arranged along three sides of a rectangle—one cot stage left, four cots ranged across upstage centre, one act stage right. The open side of the rectangle is down-stage centre facing the audience. In this open side is a plain wooden table with six chairs. Under each of the cots can be seen a large wooden box filled with the clothes and miscellaneous possessions of the occupant of the particular cot.

Scene I

The interior of the hut; during the noon rest period.

Rami is seen crouching over the box partially pulled from under the cot at extreme left. He paws through it for a moment, takes a small object (not clearly seen by the audience) from the box. He examines it for a few seconds, stops—startled—to listen, then shoves the box hurriedly under the bed and crosses rapidly to his own cot, upstage right.

> As he goes he furtively conceals the object in his shirt. He flops down on his cot and Moshe enters stage left ...

RAMI: (Reading) L'aruchot boker anachnu ochlim ...
MOSHE: (Interrupts) ... anachnu ochlim gvina. And then we eat more cheese. And then, for a change, we have a little cheese. (He grins, sits on one of the cots upstage centre and starts to unlace his boots) Still I must admit it's good cheese.
RAMI: In Bulgaria ...
MOSHE: (Interrupts) Yes, I know. In Bulgaria you didn't eat cheese for breakfast. And if you did, it was better cheese than we have here. To hear you talk, everything was better in Bulgaria. (He holds a shoe in his left hand and shakes it at Rami) Look, Rami, you're not in Bulgaria, you're in Israel. You've been here for a month and a half and it's about time you got used to it. Like the rest of us.
RAMI: All I was going to say was that in Bulgaria we ate big coffee cakes for breakfast. I used to eat so much cake that I could hardly walk to school in the morning.
MOSHE: Is that so? From what I hear you never—(He snaps his fingers as he remembers something) Wow! I just remembered I haven't done the lesson for today. (He looks at his watch) I'll just have time to take a shower and knock out that composition. (He stands up and begins to take clothes, shoes and a towel, etc., from the box under his cot) It might help a little if I took a look at your composition. Let's see it, will you?
RAMI: (Hesitates) You can't do that, that's cheating.
MOSHE: What cheating? You still don't realize that in kibbutz education there aren't any marks or examinations. We aren't competing with each other. The only reason we get homework is to help us understand the lesson. So if it helps me understand by looking at your work, why not?
RAMI: (Stubbornly) You can't copy my composition.
MOSHE: Who wants to copy? I just want to look at it. Let's see it.
RAMI: I can't; I haven't done it yet.
MOSHE: Well, why didn't you say so. You'd better hurry up, too. It has to be handed in in an hour. Why didn't you do it this morning? You had half a Shabbat—no work. Why didn't you do it?

RAMI: (Embarrassed) Well, as a matter of fact, I can't do it. I tried. I just can't write a good Hebrew sentence yet.

MOSHE: (Looks at Rami silently for a moment) I don't understand you, Rami. All this fuss about cheating and it turns out the truth is you couldn't even write the composition. Why didn't you say so in the first place? And if you can't do something, why don't you admit it and let one of us help you? What do you think, a kibbutz is if not a place where people help each other? If you're having trouble with lessons, you should tell us. Why don't you ask Ruth to help? You know how good she is with Hebrew. Ruth would ... (Ruth and Dov enter stage left. Ruth is carrying flowers)

RUTH: She would not! ... Or maybe she would. (She puts the flowers in a small vase on the table) What do you want me to do, Moshe?

MOSHE: I don't want you to do anything. It's Rami. He wasn't able to do the lesson for today and I was telling him he could ask you for help.

RUTH: Of course, Rami, I'd be glad to help you. Why didn't you ask me?

RAMI: I didn't want to bother you.

RUTH: It's no bother. It's our job to help each other. That's why in a kibbutz we newcomers live, work and study in groups. So we'll be able to know each other's problems. I'd like to help you, Rami. (She takes the book Rami holds) Here, let's sit down and do it right now.

RAMI: (Stands up from the cot) No. I haven't got time now. I've got to do something. (He exits, stage left)

DOV: (Speaks for the first time; he speaks slowly) He's a strange fellow, that Rami.

MOSHE: You said it, Dov. For my money he's a misfit. I don't think he'll ever fit into kibbutz life. Like now, for instance. He's got no time to prepare his lesson, he's got something else to do. Here, even though field workers are badly needed, right now, the kibbutz gives all the youth groups half a day—every day—to study. The kibbutz thinks it's important to learn Hebrew and Jewish history and other things in addition to learning how to work. But none of this is important to Rami—he's got so many other things to take care of that are more important. (He nods his head positively) Nope, he'll never fit into a kibbutz.

RUTH: That's not fair. Why don't you give him a chance? He's only been here a month and a half ...

DOV: (Gently) You've only been here one month, Ruth. But you fit in already.

RUTH: That's different. It's not so new and strange for Moshe and me. We were in the Pioneer Youth Movement in America for three years before we came here. In another month the rest of our group is coming over and we'll be surrounded by old friends. We knew what to expect. For Rami, it's all new; and it's hard. Why he never even heard of Zionism until a couple of months ago!

MOSHE: What about Dov, here? He wasn't in any youth movement in France. It's all new to him, too. He never thought of Zionism either, until his parents came to Tel Aviv and decided to send him to a kibbutz. No, the difference is that nobody likes Rami and Rami doesn't like anybody.

RUTH: Rami never had anybody to like! You know his story. He's been an orphan ever since he can remember. Ever since the war he's been wandering around Bulgaria learning to steal to eat. How did you expect him to learn to like people? Until the Jewish Agency sent him here, no one had ever done anything to teach him to like people.

MOSHE: Okay, so he's had a hard life. But he makes it harder for himself. For example, why does he have to be such a liar? You should have heard him before about the cakes he used to eat in Bulgaria and the school he went to ... What a fibber!

RUTH: Don't talk like that, Moshe. He makes up those stories because he wants to be like everybody else who had a home and good things to eat and a school to go to. You've just got to discover what it is to be tolerant.

DOV: You're right, Ruth. Still he *is* a problem. It helps to know why people are the way they are; and we must try to understand and help them. But that Rami makes it hard to help him.

RUTH: It would help if that Dov would stop calling him "that" Rami.

DOV: (Apologetically) I didn't mean anything wrong.

RUTH: I know, Dov. I guess I'm a little excited.

MOSHE: One thing I've got to admit. Rami hasn't done anything really wrong since he had that fight with Bennie in the other group last month. And he certainly works better than he did when he first came. Boy, I never saw a guy take longer to do less than he did the first few weeks.

RUTH: (Laughs a little) You should talk, Superman! The first time you had to feed the bull you were so scared I thought they would have to tie you down to keep you from running all the way back to Philadelphia. It took you three hours to get up enough nerve to stand at the gate and throw corn husks at the bull piece by piece. And remember the first time you dug irrigation ditches? You had blisters on top of your blisters. For the next two weeks you did so little work that no one could tell you from the scarecrow.

MOSHE: (Laughing) Okay, okay. I give up. You win.

DOV: If the fight is over and Ruth is the winner, perhaps we can consider the question of the farewell party for Zvi. You remember, I suppose, that Zvi leaves for the music school in Jerusalem tonight!

MOSHE: Of course we remember. Did you get the candy, Ruth?

RUTH: Better than that, Eleesheva—you know her, who works in the bakery—is baking a cake for us. It'll be ready in time for the party. And the suitcase ...

MOSHE: It's hidden outside. Wait. I'll get it. (He exits, stage left)

DOV: Are you sure Zvi knows nothing of the surprise?

RUTH: I'm sure. He's been so busy I don't think he knows night from day.

MOSHE: (Enters stage left, carrying a new leather suitcase) Here it is. Isn't it a beauty? (He puts the case on the table and they all gather round to admire it)

DOV: It's very handsome.

RUTH: It's lovely, Moshe.

MOSHE: Should be ... costs about sixty pounds. Even with the kibbutz putting up two-thirds of the money, it will still take about half the holiday-money of our whole group. But it's worth it, isn't it?

RUTH: Certainly is. Zvi will be pleased.

DOV (Looks at his watch): Chaverim, let's go. It's one o'clock. We should be in class already.

MOSHE: Ow! My composition! (He picks up the suitcase and they all exit stage left)

Scene II

Same set. It is early evening. The table is covered with a tablecloth and set with some plates, silverware, and cups. In the centre of the table is a cake. On Zvi's cot (the one at far stage left from under which Rami had taken something in Scene I) is the new suitcase, tied with red ribbon and covered by a cloth.

Moshe, Dov and Ruth are on the stage. Ruth is completing setting the table. Dov and Moshe are at stage left looking into the wings.

RUTH: Where is Rami? Zvi will be here any minute.

DOV: Perhaps he did not remember Zvi was leaving tonight.

MOSHE: Of course, he remembers. I told him again in the shower. If Rami doesn't come to say goodbye after all Zvi has done for him, then I think we ought to ship him back to Bulgaria ... And I'd be glad to help him on the way with a swift kick in the pants.

DOV: (Looking off stage) Here he is!

RUTH: (Happily) I knew he'd be here! Rami wouldn't...

DOV: It is not Rami. It is Zvi. (Ruth's face shows her disappointment, but she quickly recovers and smiles her greetings as Zvi enters stage left and stops in surprise as he sees the others and the festively decorated table)

ZVI: (Pleased and grinning broadly) What is this? What is this?

DOV: It is our way of wishing you success with your music in Jerusalem. We hope you will do well there.

RUTH: (Comes forward and lays her hand on Zvi's arm) We will miss you, but we are happy the kibbutz agreed to pay for the music school. And just so you'll be able to go in proper style; this (She pulls the cover off the suitcase) is a present from all of us.

ZVI: (Sees the suitcase for the first time. He goes over, takes the ribbon off, opens the case. He is impressed and happy. He clears his throat) It is fine. It must have cost you much money. You—you shouldn't have done it ...

MOSHE }
RUTH } (Chorus, teasingly in time with Zvi) You
DOV   } shouldn't have done it!

ZVI: (All smiles) But I am glad you did. You all make me very happy. You all ... (He looks around) ... Why, where is Rami? Isn't he ... Is he ill?

RUTH: (Quickly) No, Rami's all right. He'll be here soon.

ZVI: I hope so. (He looks at his watch.) I would like to say goodbye to him. I have very little time.

RUTH: In that case, Zvi, why don't you start packing first and then we'll eat something. By the time you've finished packing, Rami will surely be here.

ZVI: Good. (He goes to his cot, pulls the box out from underneath and starts packing clothes into the suitcase.) It will be hard to be away from all of you for six whole months. Perhaps you will come to see me at school in Jerusalem on your holiday ... (He laughs) ... that is if you have any holiday money left after you have paid for this suitcase.

MOSHE: We'll be there. We'll be there when you graduate.

DOV: We will come to listen to you play your flute solo.

ZVI: (He has been looking through his now half-empty box) The flute ... Where is my flute? (Moshe, Dov and Ruth all crowd around to peer into the box)

ZVI: It was right here in the box. I put it here myself this morning after I had polished the silver and cleaned the mouthpiece. It was right here. (They all look at each other in bewilderment)

RUTH: Who could have taken ... ?

MOSHE: That little no gooder ...

RUTH: He couldn't have. He *wouldn't* ...

ZVI: Who?

MOSHE: Rami, of course.

RUTH: I don't believe it.

DOV: We can't say that. There's no proof.

MOSHE: Who else? You? Me? Ruth? Of course, Rami. That's why he isn't here, he didn't have the nerve to face Zvi.

ZVI: I wouldn't like to think that. It's not that the flute is so valuable—although it *is* worth quite a lot of money. It's not the value—no; I wouldn't like to think ... We'll ask Rami when he comes.

MOSHE: *If* he comes. Personally, I'd be surprised if he's still in the kibbutz.

RUTH: (Triumphantly) Well, be surprised then, Smarty, because here he is ...

RAMI: (Enters stage left hurriedly. He stops short as he sees the group) Oh! Hello, Zvi. I was hoping you wouldn't be here ... (Confused) I mean was hoping you would not be here *yet*. I'm sorry I'm late.

RUTH: (Gently) Rami, please sit down. (Rami sits on one of the chairs next to the table and looks around uneasily at the others)

RUTH: (Still speaking gently) Rami, you didn't ... Did you take Zvi's silver flute from his box?

RAMI: (Looks at the others ... then reaches slowly into his shirt and takes out a slender wooden case. He opens it and the flute is seen. He hands the flute—case and all—silently to Zvi)

RUTH: (Shocked and hurt) Oh, no! Rami, how could you?

MOSHE: (Steps towards Rami with his fists clenched) You little ...

ZVI: (Has taken the flute and is looking at the case) Wait a minute, Moshe. This is my flute alright, but this case is new. And on the inside cover of the case is carved: "To Zvi, who—with other good friends—is helping me to discover a new way of life. From Rami."

RAMI: (Sensing something wrong, he looks around bewildered) What's the matter? I know it's not very good, but it is the first time I have ever worked with wood. Don't you like it, Zvi?

ZVI: (Puts his arms around Rami's shoulders and speaks warmly) I like it very much. I like it more than you will ever know.

RUTH: (Looking significantly at Moshe) Well, it's been quite a surprise party, hasn't it?

MOSHE: (Grins sheepishly) You know, chaverim. I've just discovered something that will be very important to me. I've just discovered that I'm an awful fool. (He goes to the table and picks up a knife) Rami, let's eat, have a piece of cake. Have a real big piece. (He starts to cut the cake)

CURTAIN

ISRAEL

The Lord shall set His hand a second time to recover the remnants of His people. . . . And He shall set up an ensign for the nations and shall assemble the outcast of Israel and gather together the dispersed of Judah from the four corners of the earth.

Isaiah 2:12.

THE VISION OF THE DRY BONES

(The following selection may be presented as a combination of readings, dance and choral selections.)

Ezekiel, Chap. 37

FIRST READER
The Hand of the Lord came upon me, and carried me out with the Spirit of the Lord, and set me down in the midst of the valley, and it was full of bones.

CHORUS
And it was full of bones.

FIRST READER
And He caused me to pass by round about, and behold, they were very many upon the face of the valley, and behold, they were very dry.

CHORUS
And behold, they were very dry.

FIRST READER
And He said unto me:

SECOND READER
Son of man, shall these bones live?

FIRST READER
And I answered: Oh, Lord, Thou knowest!

CHORUS
Thou knowest!

FIRST READER
And He said unto me:

SECOND READER
Prophesy over these bones, and say unto them:
O ye dry bones, hear the word of the Lord.

Thus saith the Lord God unto these bones.
Behold, I shall cause breath to enter into you,
And you shall live.

CHORUS
And you shall live.

FIRST READER
And I will lay sinews upon you,
And I will bring flesh upon you,
And I will cover you with skin,
And I will put breath in you,
And you shall live.

CHORUS
And you shall live.

SECOND READER
And you shall know that I am the Lord.

FIRST READER
And so I prophesied as I was commanded.
And as I prophesied there was a noise,
And a great commotion
And the bones came together
One to the other.

CHORUS
And as I prophesied there was a noise
And a great commotion
And the bones came together
One to the other.

FIRST READER
And I beheld,
And lo, there were sinews upon them,
And flesh came up
And skin covered them above—
But there was no breath in them.

CHORUS
But there was no breath in them.

FIRST READER
And He said unto me:

SECOND READER
Prophesy unto the wind,
Prophesy, Son of Man,
And say unto the wind:

THIRD READER
Thus says the Lord God:
Come, thou wind from the four corners of the earth,
And breathe upon these slain
That they shall live.

CHORUS
That they shall live.

FIRST READER
So I prophesied as I was commanded,
And the breath came into them
And they lived,
And stood up upon their feet
An exceeding great host.

CHORUS
An exceeding great host.

FIRST READER
And He said unto me:

SECOND READER
Son of Man, these bones
Are the whole House of Israel.
Behold they say:

CHORUS
Our bones are dried up,
Our hope is destroyed,
We are lost!

SECOND READER
Therefore prophesy and say unto them:

FIRST READER
Thus says the Lord God:
Behold, I will open your graves
And cause you to come out of your graves
And I will bring you to the Land of Israel.

CHORUS
And I will bring you to the Land of Israel.

SECOND READER
And they will know I am the Lord,
When I open your graves
And raise you up from out of your graves,
My people,
And I will put my spirit in you,
And you shall live.

CHORUS
And you shall live.

SECOND READER
And I shall establish you upon your soil,
And you shall know that I am the Lord,
I have spoken, and I have performed it, sayeth the Lord.

CHORUS
And I shall establish you upon your soil,
And you shall live!

THE JEWS SHALL HAVE A STATE
Theodor Herzl

I believe that a wondrous generation of Jews will spring into existence. The Maccabees will rise again.

Let me repeat once more my opening words: The Jews wish to have a state, and they shall have one.

I do not bring you a new idea but an immemorial one. Yes, it is a universal idea—and therein lies its strength—old as our people which never even in the days of its bitterest need ceased to nourish it. This idea is the foundation of the Jewish State. It is extraordinary that through the long night of our history we Jews continue to dream this regal dream.... We plan for our posterity even as our fathers preserved the tradition for us.

We shall live at last as free men on our own soil, and die peacefully in our own home.

The world will be freed by our liberty, enriched by our wealth, magnified by our greatness.

And whatever we attempt there to accomplish for our own welfare will react with beneficent force for the good of humanity.

(The Jewish State)

HOW IS A STATE BORN
(From *Judaean Leaves*, Vol. II No. 5)

PRODUCTION NOTE:

This script can readily be presented as a simulated radio broadcast, members of the cast holding books and doing it as a dramatic reading. In that event, memorization of lines is unnecessary and little rehearsal is required. It is, however, advisable for participants to be sufficiently familiar with the text, so that they can look up from the script fairly frequently.

If time, facilities and personnel permit, the script can be more effective if it is staged, the players learning their parts and the director blocking movement and incorporating inventive business.

As with similar documentary readings, of this kind, the director may freely substitute or supplement lines, songs and dances best suited to the particular group undertaking presentation. However, caution should be exercised in their appropriate selection. While any of the "Shir Ha'Shirim" songs and accompanying ethnic folk dances would, for example, be suitable for the Yemenite sequence, the Hora or Polka would not be.

The number of roles may be increased or decreased, depending on the needs of the performing group.

Before calling the cast for first rehearsal, the director should have studied the entire script thoroughly.

CHARACTERS:

Narrator-s
Parents (A & B)
Abraham
Reader-s
Yaakov
Dina
Ephraim
Dudi } *members of Biluim kibbutzniks*
Batya
Yosef
Rachel
Radio Announcers
Choir
Dancers
Crowd

COSTUMES AND PROPS:

Work clothes (khakis or dungarees and sport shirts) for kibbutzniks

Authentic native dress for Yemenites
Modern street clothes for Narrators
Biblical costume for Abraham with shepherd's crook or staff
Old-fashioned table or cabinet radio (*not* transistor)
Posters, banners, flags, placards, etc.

The recording of "A State Is Born" is available at Banner Records Inc., 15 West 20th Street, New York 10011

NARRATOR: What were you doing eighteen years ago? And you—and you? Playing ball? Doing homework? Try to think back. Eighteen years ago—May 11th, 1948, the 5th of Iyar 5708 ... six thousand miles from here across two oceans, past three continents—in the midst of shootings, and bombings and sacrifices and prayers—the State of Israel was born. (Pause)
VOICE 1: How is a state born?
VOICE 2: How does it grow?
VOICE 1: What do you feed a new state?
VOICE 2: What does a new state do?

A and B (step forward)

A: We are the parents of the State of Israel ...
B: You say you never heard of a state having parents? Everything in this world has to have parents. Children ... dogs ... cats ... horses ... birds ... plants ... even ... even *ideas* ...
A: And that's all the State of Israel was at first ... an idea. An idea ... a hope ... a dream ... a prayer ... that we, the Jewish people parents of the State of Israel have had for two thousand years.
A and B: To be free people in our own land ... In Zion—and Jerusalem ... It all started with a promise and a vision ...
ABRAHAM: (In shepherd dress) I had a strange feeling ... it was as if God had spoken to me. I heard many strange and wonderful things. "Thy name shall be Abraham; for the father of a multitude of nations have I made thee, and make thee exceedingly fruitful, and I will make nations of thee, and be a God unto thee and to thy seed after thee. And I will give unto thee, and to thy seed after thee, the land of thy sojournings, all the land of Canaan, for an everlasting possession; and I will be their God."

MUSIC AND INTERPRETIVE DANCE ("Ali B'er" or other pastoral melody)

NARRATOR: And the words—the promise that was given to Abraham was repeated to Isaac and to Jacob was kept. And the children of Israel multiplied in the land of Israel. And we had a country, a homeland, a state.

But we did not always walk in the paths of righteousness and we were not strong—so first the Babylonians and then the Romans destroyed our land and banished us from Eretz Yisrael —and we were made to wander over the face of the earth. No sooner had we settled in one country and given our all to build it when we were forced to leave.

MUSIC—*HANODED*—DANCE

YAAKOV: I'm tired of being pushed around because I am a Jew. I'm tired of hearing: The Jew is a coward, the Jew is a usurer, the Jew ... and I want to go home.

DINA: Home? What do you mean—home?

YAAKOV: Home ... the home of our forefathers ... the Land of Israel. I want to rebuild my home so that my children at least will be free people in a free land ...

DINA: But Yaakov, how can we go? What will we do there? You're a student; Ephraim here runs a dry-goods store; what do *we* know of building a land?

EPHRAIM: Dina—we are young, we are strong, and we want to go. If we will it—we will succeed.

SONG ("Anu Banu Artza" or "Artza Alinu")

NARRATOR: In 1882 the Biluim—the first of the pioneers came to Israel. Soon, others followed in their path. They built and worked on the land—but still the land was not ours.

On November 29, 1947, the United Nations General Assembly gathered in Lake Success. After much debating and many investigating committees came to a momentous decision ...

(Play part of record—"A State Is Born"—If not available substitute the following:

RADIO ANNOUNCER: Ladies and Gentlemen—we interrupt this program to bring you a special news broadcast from the United Nations General Assembly—The General Assembly gathered today at Lake Success, New York, has arrived at a decision regarding the future of Palestine. By a vote of 33 to 13 the United Nations has decided to partition Palestine into separate autonomous territories for the Arabs and Jews and to end the British Mandate in Palestine on May 15, 1948.

The leaders and spokesmen for the Jewish State are at the United Nations now—Dr. Hayim Weizmann, David Ben-Gurion, Moshe Shertok, Dr. Emanuel Neumann, Rabbi Abba Hillel Silver, and a host of others. And, ladies and gentlemen, if you will forgive an editorial . . . a personal comment—one cannot help but share with them in this—their moment of rejoicing and thanksgiving—and wish them God-speed in the long and, it is feared, difficult road that lies ahead.)

NARRATOR: In New York the crowds went wild. Times Square was packed with Jews proudly and joyously celebrating.

SCENE: *Times Square in New York*

Crowds milling around and singing, newsboys shouting "Extra, Extra, read all about it—U.N. partitions Palestine. British to end Mandate. Extra, Extra!"

Some people dance Horas and others wave the Jewish flag, banners—and placards with slogans: "If you will it—it is no legend!" "We have a Jewish State!"

(If there is to be no live action substitute background roar, voices of newsboys and crowd singing.)

NARRATOR: And in Eretz Yisrael? How did the people react? Let's look at a new kibbutz—one of Israel's collective settlements, situated along the border.

DUDI: Chaverim—Rachel, Batya, Moshe—quick—the news broadcast about the U.N. is on. (Chaverim gather around the radio and listen intently to the announcement of the U.N. decision. Use morse code sounds—da . . . da . . . da . . . da . . .)

BROADCASTER: Kol HaYishuv M'daber. Kol HaYishuv M'daber.

Hayom nit-kayma yeshiva shel m'liyat ha-umot ha-m'uchadot b'Lake Success, N. Y. u-bah huchlat b'rov deyot shel shloshim v'shalosh neged shaloshesrei al hakamat medinah atzmayit l'am haYehudi b'eretz Yisrael.

This is the voice of Yishuv. This is the voice of the Yishuv.

The General Assembly of the United Nations decided today by a vote of 33 to 13 to establish an independent Jewish State in Eretz Yisrael. (A sigh of relief is heard)

BATYA: I don't know whether to laugh or cry or jump for joy—I'm stunned.

YOSEF: I'm *worried*. We know very well the Arabs will not accept the partition plan.

And what about our kibbutzim that will now be in Arab territory? What will happen to them?

NARRATOR: That night—the kibbutzniks had a joyous celebration—The Chaverim sang and danced and danced and danced. The oldtimers—those who had been in the Haganah for many years (the underground defense group)—danced too. But if you looked closely you could see tears streaming down their cheeks. (Pause)

That evening, the kibbutz doubled the number of Shomrim —(guards) who watched over the kibbutz at night. The very next day—busses carrying Jews from Tel-Aviv to Jerusalem were attacked—and Jews killed.

The Arab nations had decided not to accept the decision of the United Nations—the Organization for World Peace to which they belonged. (Palmach song)

VOICE: The war had started. The War of Liberation—the War of Jewish Independence where countless Jewish young men and women were to fight and suffer and die—so that the State of Israel would become a reality.

On Friday afternoon—May 14, 1948—the fifth of Iyar, 5708, in the Tel-Aviv Museum—at a special meeting of the Jewish Agency for Palestine—the following proclamation was made.

READER: (Background humming of Hatikva) We, the members of the National Council, representing the Jewish people in Palestine and the World Zionist Movement, are met together in solemn assembly today, the day of termination of the British Mandate for Palestine; and by virtue of the natural and historic right of the Jewish people and by the Resolution of the General Assembly of the United Nations, we hereby proclaim the establishment of the Jewish State in Palestine, to be called Medinath Yisrael (The State of Israel).

The State of Israel will be open to the immigration of Jews from all countries of their dispersion; will promote the development of the country for the benefit of all its inhabitants; will be based on the principles of liberty, justice and peace as conceived by the Prophets of Israel; will uphold the full social and political equality of all its citizens, without distinction of religion, race, or sex; will guarantee freedom of religion, conscience, education, and culture; will safeguard the Holy Places of all religions; and will loyally uphold the principles of the United Nations Charter.

We extend our hand in peace and neighbourliness to all the neighbouring states and their peoples, and invite them to cooperate with the independent Jewish nation for the common good of all. The State of Israel is prepared to make its contribution to the progress of the Middle East as a whole.

Our call goes out to the Jewish people all over the world to rally to our side in the task of immigration and development and to stand by us in the great struggle for the fulfillment of the dream of generations for the redemption of Israel.

With trust in Almighty God, we set our hand to this Declaration, at this Session of the Provisional State Council, and on the soil of the Homeland, in the city of Tel Aviv, on this Sabbath eve, the fifth of the Iyar, 5708, the fourteenth day of May, 1948.

SECOND READER: Baruch ata Adonai eloheinu melech Haolam, shehecheyanu v'kiy'manu v'higiyanu la-zman ha-zeh. Blessed art Thou, O Lord our God, King of the Universe, who has kept us in life, and has preserved us and enabled us to reach this season.

NARRATOR: The gates of Israel were flung open. Hundreds of thousands of Jews from internment camps in Cyprus, displaced persons camps in Europe, feudal and hostile Yemen and Iraq, poverty-stricken Morocco, from Turkey, India, South Africa, England, Chile, the United States, became part of the State of Israel.

And the people in Israel managed to fight and defeat the Arabs and welcome and care for the newly-arrived immigrants at the same time.

They came from Yemen—penniless, undernourished, but with a zeal to work in their land, and the land of their forefathers. They brought with them their lovely songs and dances —based on the Song of Songs.

DANCE—El Ginat Egoz etc. (if possible in costume—Yemenite)

They came from South Africa and brought with them their healthy minds and bodies—a sense of humor—and songs they had learned from the Zulu tribes.

SONG—Hold them down you Zulu Warriors $\Big\}$ 2
Hold them down you Zulu Chiefs
Hi ka zumba, zumba, zumba, mi ka zumba, zumba zae) 2

They came from the D.P. camps in Europe—Displaced persons—victims of Hitler's madness—and they were tired and bitter—and the people of Israel stretched out their hands and their hearts to these people and taught them to live again.

SONGS of work—DANCES (Lech, Lech Lamidbar)

A and B: For eighteen years now we, the parents of the Jewish State have watched it grow—have helped it grow, and have grown with it, and the State of Israel has helped us, the parents—Jews in Israel and all over the world. It has given us a sense of pride.

But we know that much remains to be done—real peace and friendship with the Arabs must be established, for we are tired of war, of fighting, of border attacks and recriminations—

SONG—*Lo Yisa Goy El Goy Herev*

BACKGROUND SONG *"AT ADAMA"*: The Negev—the future of Israel must be made to bloom—trees must be planted, industries developed, houses, and schools built—so that we may continue to grow and be strong and fulfill the promise and the prophecy.

READER: And Jacob dreamed; and beheld a ladder set up on the earth, and the top of it reached to heaven; and behold the angels of God ascending and descending on it. And, behold the Lord stood beside him and said: "I am the Lord, the God of Abraham, thy father, and the God of Isaac. The land whereon thou liest, to thee will I give it, and to thy seed. And thy seed shall be as the dust of the earth, and thou shalt spread abroad to the west, and to the east, and to the north, and to the south. And in thee and in thy seed shall all the families of the earth be blessed. And behold, I am with thee, and will keep thee whithersoever thou goest, *and will bring thee back into this land;* for I will not leave thee."

Hora—*V'korev p'zureinu* (slowly at first—build up and exit.)

INDEPENDENCE DAY SKETCH

To Thee Will I Give It and to Thy Seed Forever

*And the people willed it—
And the dream became a reality.*

Mila Ohel

A living-newspaper for Israel Independence Day

ON RISE: The stage is empty. There is music in the background. After some seconds, a boy enters, dressed as a shepherd and carrying a shepherd's staff. He stands and looks out into the distance.

A VOICE: (Off stage, awe-inspiring, impressive) Avraham, Avraham! Lift up now thine eyes, and look from the place where thou art northward, and southward, and eastward, and westward. For all this land which thou seest, to thee will I give it, and to thy seed forever.

And I will make thy seed as the dust of the earth, so that if a man can number the dust of the earth, then shall thy seed also be numbered.

Arise, walk through the land in the length of it and in the breadth of it: for I will give it unto thee. (The music grows loud and dominant. The boy advances a few paces. Then stands immobile.)

VOICE: Know of a surety that thy seed shall be a stranger in a land that is not theirs, and shall serve them; and they shall afflict them four hundred years. And also that nation, whom they shall serve, will I judge: and afterward shall they come out with great substance. (The music grows louder creating an atmosphere of enslavement and oppression. The boy exits. A choir enters.)

NARRATOR: And the Egyptians made the children of Israel to serve them with rigour.

NARRATOR: And they made their lives bitter with hard bondage, in mortar and in brick, and in all manner of service in the field.

NARRATOR: And the children of Israel sighed by reason of

the bondage, and they cried, and their cry came up unto God by reason of the bondage:

CHOIR: (Declaiming) Let my people go! Let my people go! (Again the music grows loud suggesting an atmosphere of revolution.)

NARRATOR: And it came to pass at the end of the four hundred and thirty years, even the self-same day it came to pass, that all the hosts of the Lord went out from the Land of Egypt.

CHOIR:
>Be-tzet Yis-ra-el mi-mi-tzra-yim
>Bet Ya-a-cov me-am lo-ez
>Hay-ta Ye-hu-da le-kod-sho
>Yis-ra-el mem-she-lo-tav.
>
>Ha-yam ra-a ve-ya-nos
>Ha-yar-den yi-sov la-a-chor
>He-ha-rim rak-du ke-e-lim
>Gva-ot kiv-ne tzon.

NARRATOR: And the children of Israel went armed to the land of Canaan.

NARRATOR: And the land, which was promised to Avraham, was given to his seed, as said the Lord.

NARRATOR: And the children of Israel inherited the land and settled in it.

NARRATOR: Joshua Ben-Nun, the Judges, King Saul, King David, King Solomon, the wisest of men, the kingdom of Judah and the kingdom of Israel—so it came to pass in the days when the people settled in their land.

NARRATOR: Yet Israel was but a little nation, and the nations around it were great and mighty. So they rose against Israel, and conquered it, and destroyed its Temple, and exiled the people from their land.

CHOIR: (Declaiming) By the rivers of Babylon, there we sat down, yea, we wept, when we remembered Zion.

We hanged our harps upon the willows in the midst thereof ... How shall we sing the Lord's song in a strange land?

NARRATOR: A very long and a very hard exile—

NARRATOR: But, in all its wanderings, the people never forgot their land.

CHOIR: (Declaiming) If I forget thee, O Jerusalem, let my right hand forget her cunning.

If I do not remember thee, let my tongue cleave to the roof of my mouth; if I prefer not Jerusalem above my chief joy. (The music loses the sad, depressing note that accompanied the last words, and becomes livelier.)

NARRATOR: O, house of Jacob, come ye, and let us walk in the light of the Lord.

NARRATOR: And Jacob shall return, and shall be in rest, and be quiet, and none shall make him a prey.

CHOIR: (Declaiming) Beth Ya-a-kov, le-chu ve-nel-cha! O, house of Jacob, come ye, and let us walk in the light of the Lord!

CHOIR:
Se-u Tzi-o-na nes va-de-gel, de-gel ma-cha-ne Ye-hu-da
Mi ba-re-chev mi ba-re-gel, na-as na la-a-gu-da.
Ya-chad nel-cha na ve-na-shu-va ar-tza a-vo-te-nu,
El ar-tze-nu ha-a-hu-va—e-res yal-du-te-nu.

NARRATOR: The ancient nation returns once more to its fatherland—

CHOIR: (Declaiming) Eretz Yisrael!

NARRATOR: At first one by one, then two by two, individuals, only a few. The First Aliyah—the Bilu. Later, in larger groups—the Second Aliyah, the Third Aliyah.

NARRATOR: Returning to the homeland. Living on the soil of Israel. Labouring by the sweat of their brows to raise bread from the land.

NARRATOR: In 1897 in Basle the Zionist movement was founded. And the First Zionist Congress resolved:

NARRATOR: "The aim of Zionism is to create for the Jewish people a home in Palestine secured by public law."

NARRATOR: And the great prophet, "the uncrowned King of the Jews," Dr. Benjamin Zeev Herzl, said:

CHOIR: (Declaiming) If you will it—it is no fable.

NARRATOR: And the people willed it and returned to Zion —the dream became a reality. The Jewish population in the Homeland grew larger and larger—

NARRATOR: Petah Tikva, Rosh Pinah, Rishon le Zion,

NARRATOR: Kibbutz Degania, Kvutzat Kinneret, Kibbutz Ein Harod—

NARRATOR: Tel Aviv, Haifa, Ramat Gan—

NARRATOR: New kibbutzim, new moshavim, new villages, new towns.

NARRATOR: Jewish farmers. Jewish industrial workers. Jewish builders and engineers.

NARRATOR: They came to Israel—to build and to be themselves rebuilt.

CHOIR:
A-nu ba-nu ar-tza
Liv-not u-le-hi-ba-not ba
A-nu ba-nu ar-tza
Liv-not u-le-hi-ba-not ...

NARRATOR: The Arabs in the country tried to interfere, to sabotage. They caused civil unrest, they rioted, and they burnt the fields—

NARRATOR: So the Jewish settlers formed the Hagana—
A Jewish army in the homeland,
An army without uniforms,
In secret, underground,
To defend the people and its work.

NARRATOR:
Never again—they said—shall we be destroyed,
Never again—they said—shall we be killed,
Never again shall we be evicted from the homeland.

CHOIR: (Declaiming) Never again will we let these things happen to us.

NARRATOR: They which builded on the wall, and they that bear burdens—stood firm.

NARRATOR: Everyone with one of his hands wrought in the work, and with the other hand held a weapon.

CHOIR: (Declaiming)
Come, and let us build up the wall of Jerusalem, that we
be no more a reproach ...
That the night may be a guard to us, and labour the day.

CHOIR:
Ba-ke-rem, ba-nir, ba-ir u-va-kfar
dom na-a-mod ve-ni-droch ha-me-tar.
La-nu ni-tan ha-a-dam pi-ka-don
an-she ha-mish-mar—hi-kon hi-kon.

> Na-a-se shri-re-nu e-shet
> ve-ei-nei-nu esh.
> Al o-yev ya-ez la-ge-shet.
> Kum sho-mer u-droch ha-ke-shet
> u-shmor al ha-yesh.
> Ha-ma-vet mu-le-nu—mo-ra la-nu zar
> la-nu kol re-gev ve-te-lem miv-tzar.
> Tzid-kat mif-a-le-nu la-nu ko-ach ve-on
> an-she ha-mish-mar—hi-kon, hi-kon.
> Na-a-se shri-re-nu e-shet
> ve-ei-nei-nu esh.
> Al o-yev ya-ez la-ge-shet.
> Kum sho-mer u-droch ha-ke-shet
> u-shmor al ha-yesh.

(Music accompanies the song of the Choir, and, after the Choir is silent, the music continues in the same spirit. Then the music changes to express an atmosphere of mourning, and diminishes to provide only a background.)

NARRATOR: The Second World War set the world in flames. Nazi Germany trampled across Europe in iron boots. Six million Jews were butchered, suffocated by gas, burnt.

CHOIR: (Declaiming) Six million Jews.

NARRATOR: And in the Land of Israel the British ruled and they closed the gates to the Land, which had been promised to the Jews as a home.

NARRATOR: Persecuted Jews, men, women and children were being murdered, without pity, in cold blood—and the gates of their homeland were closed to them—

NARRATOR: It was then that the movement of ha-apalah —the smuggling of Jews into Zion—was organized. Old, almost derelict boats were somehow obtained. Multitudes of immigrants boarded them. The young men of the Palmach became the officers of these boats which made their way towards the shores of Zion.

CHOIR: (Declaiming) Expending their ultimate reserves of strength, but with their last remaining hope—

CHOIR:
> Ba-cha-shai se-fina go-she-shet
> lel sha-chor, ha-yam za-ef.
> Hoy, shim-i, ad-mat mo-re-shet,
> shav e-la-yich ben a-yef.

Ba-cha-shai se-fina go-she-shet
Be-tik-va sham lev ho-lem.
Hoy, shim-i, ad-mat mo-re-shet
shav e-la-yich ben cho-lem.

Ba-cha-shai o-lim a-chai
al ad-mat mo-re-shet
u-ve-oz-nam hi sod lo-che-shet:
ko le-chai, ko le-chai.

(The music grows louder and there is a feeling of awakening.)

NARRATOR:
Ship after ship,
Boat after boat,
Big and small,
By day and by night,
In summer and winter,
In storm and gale...

CHOIR: (Declaiming) They returned and they settled. By force! There could be no surrender! They had nothing to lose and they wanted to live! (The music becomes loud and dominant.)

NARRATOR:
In Israel rebellion swept the country...
The Jewish population arose and said:
We have had enough of a hostile government,
We shall never agree to be imprisoned in a new ghetto,
We shall not remain a minority in our own land,
For this land—is our land.
We can—and we will—govern ourselves,
We will have independence!

CHOIR: (Declaiming)
We demand a Jewish State!
A Jewish State!

NARRATOR: And as the oppression of the British became more crushing, the movement of rebellion strengthened its resistance.

CHOIR:
Mi-sa-viv ya-hom ha-sa-ar
ach ro-she-nu lo yi-shach
lif-ku-da ta-mid a-nach-nu ta-mid
a-nu a-nu ha-pal-mach.

Mi-me-tul-la ad ha-ne-gev
min ha-yam ad ha-mid-bar
kol ba-chur va-tov la-ne-shek
kol ba-chur al ha-mish-mar.

Ne-tiv la-ne-sher ba-sha-ma-yim
Shvil la-pe-re ben ha-rim
mul o-yev dar-ke-nu ya-al
ben ni-krot u-ven tzu-rim.

Ri-sho-nim ta-mid a-nach-nu
le-or ha-yom u-va-mach-shach
lif-ku-da ta-mid a-nach-nu ta-mid
a-nu a-nu ha-pal-mach.

NARRATOR: And with the help of world Jewry, and the aid of many States, the great miracle took place.

NARRATOR: On the 29th of November, 1947, the 17th Kislev 5708, the United Nations of the world decided that the State of the Jews should be established in Eretz Israel.

CHOIR: (Declaiming)
Rouse yourself, rouse yourself,
Stand up, O Jerusalem,
You who have drunk at the hand of the Lord
the cup of his wrath, who have drunk to the dregs
the bowl of staggering.
I have taken from your hand the cup of staggering,
the bowl of my wrath you shall drink no more.

NARRATOR: But not so deemed the Arabs of Palestine, not so deemed the Arab states surrounding us. As the day dawned after the night of the great rejoicing, the great war of our nation began, the War of Independence.

NARRATOR:
We knew: independence is not given for nothing.
We knew: independence is not easily gained.
We knew: we must gather all our strength.
We knew: we must dedicate all our spirits.
This was our battle—for life or death.

CHOIR: (Declaiming)
Arise! To the aid of the people, arise!
With what? Do not waver! With what comes to hand!
With whom? Do not pause, for the man who doth grieve

> For the sake of his brother's pain, him let the band
> Gather up and recruit; to his kin let him cleave!
> Each sacrifice worthy, in all gifts rejoice
> The hour of peril permits of no choice!
> The salvage of good, and the remnant of light
> Let us gather together, to glow, brave and bright
> A banner, an ensign, for troublesome days!
> They will rise, then, and join us, from east and from west—
> A legion prepared, at its people's behest.

NARRATOR:
> Young men and women,
> brothers and sisters,
> from Eretz Israel and from the Gola,
> together they went forth into battle ...

CHOIR: (Declaiming) Unto life or death.

NARRATOR: Unto death—for the sake of life.

CHOIR: (Declaiming) Unto death—for the sake of life.

NARRATOR: Seven Arab states rose against us to exterminate us.

NARRATOR: We fought our way on 77 fronts.

CHOIR: (Declaiming) With our backs to the wall

NARRATOR: Many of us fell.

NARRATOR: A great many fell.

NARRATOR: Thousands ...

NARRATOR:
> But, deep in the night, as our fighters marched, grasping their poor weapons—
> The dead seemed to rise to go with us, in our lines they marched.

CHOIR:
> Kvar ha-la-yil yo-red ve-o-tef et ha-har
> ve-ha-tan me-yalel ba-ga-nim
> ba-mish-ol ha-ta-lul ha-yo-red el ha-kfar
> shuv tzo-e-det ki-tat cha-bla-nim.
>
> Ha-tar-mil al ga-be-nu ka-ved be-mit-an
> ve-ha-de-rech ka-sha u-te-ra-shit
> "Od shlo-sha ki-lo-me-ter, ma-a-lesh, ya cha-blan
> ve-a-zai te-da-ber di-na-mit."

NARRATOR:
    And, indeed, dynamite did talk.
    It talked everywhere.
    Risking their lives, in continual danger,
    They spoke with dynamite.

NARRATOR:
    For we had no other way
    But to blast our way to life
    By means of dynamite.

NARRATOR:
    So we broke through to Jerusalem,
    Our eternal capital,
    To our lovely Galilee,
    To the Negev—to Eilat.

NARRATOR:
    Step by step we fought,
    Step by step we conquered,
    A few against many,
    A small nation against millions
    with bare chests against armor.

CHOIR: (Declaiming)
    And so we attained our independence
    And so we founded our State,
    The State of Israel.

(Music again in the background.)

NARRATOR: On the 14th of May, 1948, the elected members of the National Council signed the Declaration of Independence, one by one. (Music dominates. If possible, bugles are heard.)

NARRATOR: And thus declared our elected leaders: "By virtue of our natural and historic right and of the resolution of the General Assembly of the United Nations, we do hereby proclaim the establishment of a Jewish State in the Land of Israel—the State of Israel."

CHOIR: (Declaiming)
    Arise, shine, for your light has come,
    And the glory of the Lord has risen upon you.

NARRATOR: The State of Israel has risen, renewing again the past days of our glory.
    The State of Israel was risen once more,
    Opening her gates to every Jew—

> To come to his own free land,
> To build and cherish a new life,
> For so says the Scroll of Independence.

NARRATOR: "The State of Israel will be open to Jewish immigration and the ingathering of exiles. It will devote itself to developing the land for the good of all its inhabitants. It will rest upon foundations of liberty, justice and peace as envisioned by the Prophets of Israel. It will maintain complete equality of social and political rights for all its citizens, without distinction of creed, race or sex. It will guarantee freedom of religion and conscience, of language, education and culture. It will safeguard the Holy Places of all religions. It will be loyal to the principles of the United Nations Charter."

CHOIR: (Declaiming)
> Lift up thine eyes round about and behold:
> All these gather themselves together, and come to thee,
> Your sons shall come from far
> And your daughters shall be carried in the arms.
> And they shall bring thy sons in their bosom
> And thy daughters shall be carried upon their shoulders.

NARRATOR: The gates of the State of Israel were opened wide.

CHOIR: (Declaiming) Wide open.

NARRATOR: Jews came from the four corners of the earth: from the east, from the west, from the north, from the south; by sea, by land and by air. Thousands of them, tens of thousands, hundreds of thousands. They came in an increasing flow, and they settled all regions in the land.

CHOIR: (Declaiming)
> Therefore thy gates shall be open continually.
> They shall not be shut day nor night.

NARRATOR:
> From seventy different nations and languages,
> From seventy traditions and cultures
> All of them return to their country ...

(From all sides of the stage a dance group bursts forth, their costumes expressing the different countries of their origin. They dance the dance of the Ingathering of the Exiles, ending with a hora.)

CHOIR: (As the hora is danced)
    A-nu ba-nu ar-tza
    liv-not u-le-hi-ba-not ba
    a-nu ba-nu ar-tza
    liv-not u-le-hi-ba-not ...

NARRATOR: Hundreds of new settlements were founded throughout the State.

Thousands of buildings appeared with amazing rapidity in the towns and villages. Whole new towns were built. New kibbutzim. Everything developed at an astonishing rate: agriculture, industry, building, transport, science, education. In a few years the face of the country was totally changed.

NARRATOR:
    The development caused wonders,
    The Jew achieved the incredible,
    He revived in the land of his forefathers.

CHOIR:
    Gal-ga-le ha-o-lam chor-kim shen ba-mif-al
    be-ri-na mit-ma-te-ach kol shrir
    kvar maz-hiv he-a-sif—ve-a-liz he-a-mal
    ba-sa-de ba-par-des u-va-nir.

    Kvar kub-du ha-gra-not um-tza-pot la-ye-vul
    tzuch-tze-chu me-cho-not ha-ka-tzir
    mit-ba-re-chet te-vel be-vir-chat ha-shich-lul
    be-shif-a uve-sov-a le-mach-bir.

    Ha-mo-to-rim shor-kim u-tru-ot ka-ta-rim
    mit-lak-dot le-hym-non ha-ye-tzi-ra
    di-na-mit me-ya-sher gav-nu-ne he-ha-rim
    ve-hat-mol ne-he-ras toch shi-ra.

    Ve-shi-rat he-a-tid mish-ta-le-tet ba-kol
    ve-ho-lech ve-nish-kach ha-ya-shan
    ve-tzo-ed dor tza-ir ve-so-lel ha-mish-ol
    le-o-lam shel be-ton me-shur-yan.

NARRATOR: A new Israel builds itself. Ploughs her lands and reaps her crops, plants her trees and gathers her fruit, manufactures her products and exports them; paves her roads and runs her trains, flies her planes and sails her ships, sends electricity through her wires and water through her pipes. In short, does all a healthy nation does in its independent state.

CHOIR: (Declaiming) By the people—for the people.

NARRATOR: But not for its own people alone—but for other nations too, as the Prophet said:

> And the Lord shall arise upon thee,
> and the glory shall be seen upon thee
> And the Gentiles shall come to thy light,
> and kings to the brightness of thy rising.

NARRATOR: For from the four corners of the earth the people come to see her. They see and are amazed.

And you—the young country, just born, that needs so much help in birth and in growth—already you are offering a helping hand to many different nations that are throwing off the yoke of a strange government. Just as you open your arms wide—to absorb your sons and daughters returning to their homeland—so you open them to developing nations in Asia, Africa and other parts of the world, who come to you to see and to learn.

CHOIR: (Declaiming)
> For out of Zion may go forth the law,
> And the word of the Lord from Jerusalem.

NARRATOR: And so Zion says to them: "Come unto me and behold, I am for peace and my face turneth to peace, for all my wishes are to live in peace and build in peace, for my own good and the good of all nations, for I demand peace from near and far."

CHOIR: (Declaiming)
> Peace be within your walls,
> and security within your towers!
> For my brethren and companions' sake
> I will say, "Peace be within you!"

CHOIR:
> He-ve-nu sha-lom a-le-chem.

FINALE

A RENDEZVOUS WITH DESTINY
David Ben-Gurion

Israel represents a great tradition and a universal ideal. It cannot be measured by the yardstick of territory alone. It must be seen against the background of four thousand years of history. Viewed in this light, the creation of the State of Israel is one of the great developments in the annals of mankind. And what's more, whoever looks back at the achievements of the Jewish people while it was struggling against tremendous odds, cannot but come to the conclusion that the future of that people will not be like that of all other nations and that somewhere in the higher reaches of the human spirit it has a rendezvous with Destiny....

The new epoch inaugurated by the rebirth of the State of Israel is but the beginning of its greatness. The vision of redemption which sustained us thousands of years had as its goal the complete redemption of the Jewish people and not of the Jewish people alone. There can be no redemption for the Jewish people without the redemption of all mankind. We can go on with our great and difficult task only by remaining true to our great vision —the vision of the Jewish Prophets which will be realized in the days to come.

ISRAEL REBORN

A Dramatic Reading For Independence Day

Mila Ohel

CHOIR:
>Me-al pis-gat Har Ha-tzo-fim
>Esh-ta-cha-veh lach a-pa-yim;
>Me-al pis-gat Har Ha-tzo-fim
>Sha-lom lach Ye-ru-sha-la-yim!
>Me-a do-rot cha-lam-ti a-la-yich
>Liz-kot, lir-ot be-or pa-na-yich.
>Ye-ru-sha-la-yim, Ye-ru-sha-la-yim,
>Ha-i-ri pa-na-yich liv-nech.
>Ye-ru-sha-la-yim, Ye-ru-sha-la-yim,
>Me-chor-vo-ta-yich ev-nech.

(Continues humming softly to the musical accompaniment in the background)

NARRATOR 1: (In time with the music in the background)
>From the summit of Mount Scopus,
>I bow me down before thee,
>From the summit of Mount Scopus,
>Jerusalem, I greet thee,
>A hundred generations I have dreamt of thee,
>Hoping once more thy face to see.

>>Jerusalem, Jerusalem
>>Shine forth upon thy son!
>>Thy ruins, O Jerusalem,
>>I will rebuild, each one.

>From the summit of Mount Scopus,
>Jerusalem, I greet thee.
>Thousands of exiles from afar
>Lift up their eyes to thee.
>A thousand blessings we will sing,
>City and Temple of our King.

>>Jerusalem, Jerusalem,
>>I will not stir from here!
>>Jerusalem, Jerusalem,
>>Come, O Messiah, come near!

CHOIR RECITING: (Not too loudly)
>Art thou not, Zion, fain
>To send forth greetings from thy sacred rock
>Unto thy captive train
>Who greet thee as the remnants of thy flock?
>Take thou on every side,
>East, west, and south and north, their greetings
>>multiplied.

NARRATOR 2: (Softly moves two to three steps forward as Narrator 1 finishes declaiming the last line. He spreads out his arms and says)
>They are coming. They are returning.
>After 2,000 years of exile
>They are returning.
>At first one by one, then by tens. Little by little.
>Soon, more and more. Their numbers are growing.
>They are returning to Zion. To the land of Israel.

NARRATOR 1: (Takes one or two steps forward, remaining slightly behind Narrator 2. Makes sweeping gestures as he speaks)
>From Eastern Europe. From Central Europe. From the Balkans. From North Africa. From South Africa. From the outposts of Yemen.

BOTH NARRATORS: They are coming. They are returning.

NARRATOR 1:
>From across the sea. From the Near East. From the far corners of the earth. From North America. From South America—

NARRATOR 2: (In ringing tones) To the land of Israel!

CHOIR RECITING:
>Wake and bestir thee, for come is thy light!
>Up! With thy shining the world shall be bright!

NARRATOR 1:
>They came. They settled.
>They plowed furrows.
>They founded villages.
>They built cities.

NARRATOR 2:
>They gave of their strength and their energy
>and their mettle and their blood.
>They built the land for their people.

BOTH NARRATORS:
    And they sang. They built and they sang.
CHOIR:
    Nivneh artzenu, eretz moledet
    Ki la-nu, la-nu e-retz zot
    Niv-neh artzenu, e-retz mo-le-det
    Zeh tzav da-me-nu, zeh tzav ha-do-rot.
    Niv-neh ar-tze-nu al af kol mach-ri-ve-nu
    Niv-neh ar-tzenu be-ko-ach re-tzo-ne-nu
    Ketz av-dut mam-e-ret, esh he-rut bo-e-ret
    Hod tik-vah me-za-he-ret—ba-nu yas-i-ru ha-dam!
    Tzim-e he-rut, Ko-me-mi-yut,
    Nitz-ad be-oz lik-rat shich-rur ha-am!
NARRATOR 1: Ten...
NARRATOR 2: Twenty...
NARRATOR 1: Thirty...
NARRATOR 2: Forty...
NARRATOR 1: Fifty years.

CHOIR RECITING: They came and they plowed and they sowed and they guarded and they suffered—and they waited.

NARRATOR 1: They waited for that one great day. For that one great moment.

CHOIR RECITING: And it came.

NARRATOR 2:
    On the evening of the 17th of Kislev 5708.
    On the 29th of November 1947 the signal was given.

NARRATOR 1: The General Assembly of the United Nations decided as follows: The Jewish People is entitled to establish its sovereign state in its historical land.

NARRATOR 2: At last the hour came for which they had been waiting. At last the hour came for which the Jews all over the world had been waiting. At last the vision of the great dreamer would be realized: The Jewish State would arise.

CHOIR RECITING: The Jewish State would arise anew.

NARRATOR 1: But the Arabs of Palestine thought otherwise, as did the surrounding Arab countries. On the morrow of that great day of joy, seven Arab nations together swooped down on the State, not yet born, to tear it apart.

NARRATOR 2: And there was war in the land. A new war of the Jews. A war of liberation.

CHOIR RECITING: Of Independence.

NARRATOR 1: They were not taken by surprise; they were not cowed by fear. They knew . . .

NARRATOR 2: They knew that they would not inherit their land again without a struggle.

NARRATOR 1: They knew that independence would not be handed to them on a silver platter.

NARRATOR 2: They knew that they had to recruit and be recruited, to volunteer and to sacrifice. They knew that they would have to give of their all in order to achieve victory. And they gave—

CHOIR RECITING: THEIR ALL.

CHOIR RECITING: (Alternating single voices and in unison)

>Arise! To the aid of the people, arise!
>With what? Do not waver! With what comes to hand!
>With whom? Do not pause, for the man who doth grieve
>For the sake of his brother's pain, him let the band
>Gather up and recruit; to his kin let him cleave!
>Each sacrifice worthy, in all gifts rejoice
>The hour of peril permits of no choice!
>The salvage of good, and the remnant of light
>Which God in our hearts has still left, let us raise
>Let us gather together, to glow, brave and bright
>A banner, an ensign, for troublesome days!
>They will rise, then, and join us, from east and from west—
>A legion prepared, at its people's behest.
>
>(*Ch.N.Bialik*)

NARRATOR 1: Brothers and sisters.

NARRATOR 2: Fathers and sons.

NARRATOR 1: Young men and women.

NARRATOR 2: From Israel and the Diaspora.

CHOIR RECITING: They joined forces in a mighty battle.

NARRATOR 1: Dozens fell in that battle. Hundreds fell. Thousands. But they kept on coming. A great host went forth into battle to help their people.

CHOIR:
>Ki-ta-te-nu ba-lai-la tzo-e-det
>Tov-la te-vi-lat esh ve-a-shan
>Be-chol har va-gai ba-mo-le-det
>Chel Tzi-yon lo ya-num, lo yi-shan.

La-ro-veh yad va-yad nitz-me-det
Ad ya-fu-tzu o-yev va-tzar
A-nach-nu dru-chim, dru-chim ba-mo-le-det
Nih-yeh la ma-gen u-miv-tzar.

CHOIR RECITING: WE SHALL REMEMBER.

NARRATOR 1: (As the choir sings softly in the background —see below)
May the people of Israel remember, in pride and in sorrow,
Its sons and daughters,
Strong in spirit and great in deed,
Who went forth as pioneers in the ranks of Israel
And fell in the fields of battle.
May their names shine forever,
And their souls have everlasting life.

CHOIR: (Sings softly in the background as the narrator reads the above. When he finishes, it bursts forth into song)
Kvar ha-la-yil yo-red ve-o-tef et ha-har
Ve-ha-tan me-ya-lel ba-ga-nim
Ba-mi-shor ha-ta-lul ha-yo-red el ha-kfar
Shuv tzo-e-det ki-tat chab-la-nim.
Ha-tar-mil al ga-be-nu ka-ved ba-mit-an
Ve-ha-de-rech ka-sha u-tra-shit
"Od she-lo-sha ki-lo-meter, ma-lesh, ya chab-lan
Ve-a-zai te-da-ber di-na-mit."

NARRATOR 2:
And in the midst of the smoke and the fire,
In the heart of the exploding dynamite—
There comes to life again—

CHOIR RECITING: The State of Israel!

NARRATOR 1: "By virtue of our natural and historic right and of the resolution of the General Assembly of the United Nations, we do hereby proclaim the establishment of a Jewish State in the Land of Israel—the State of Israel."

NARRATOR 2: On the fifth of Iyar, 5708, on the 14th of May 1948—members of the National Council, meeting at the Tel-Aviv Museum, signed the Proclamation of Independence.

BOTH NARRATORS: The State of Israel was reborn.

CHOIR RECITING:
Go through, go through the gates
Prepare ye the way of the people

Cast up, cast up the highway
Gather out the stones.
Lift up a standard for the people
Say ye to the daughter of Zion:
Behold thy salvation cometh.
Behold his reward is with him
And his work before him.

NARRATOR 1: And the Proclamation of Independence declared: "The State of Israel will be open to Jewish immigration and the ingathering of exiles. It will devote itself to developing the land for the good of all its inhabitants.

"It will rest upon foundations of liberty, justice and peace as envisioned by the Prophets of Israel. It will maintain complete equality of social and political rights for all its citizens, without distinction of creed, race or sex. It will guarantee freedom of religion and conscience, of language, education and culture. It will safeguard the Holy Places of all religions. It will be loyal to the principles of the United Nations Charter."

NARRATOR 2: And the country opened its gates to large immigration and to the ingathering of the exiles.

CHOIR:
El rosh ha-har, el rosh ha-har
Ha-de-rech mi yach-som lif-du-ye she-vi
Me-e-ver har hen zeh mi-kvar
Ro-me-zet la-nu e-retz tze-vi
Ha-a-pilu, ha-a-pilu
El rosh ha-har ha-a-pilu.

(The choir quickly leaves the stage, and in its place a *dance group* swiftly forms at the back, starting with slow restrained movements—serving as a background to the reading below—which become more pronounced towards the end until the group completely dominates the stage.

The dance group must represent in its costumes or in its dance patterns—or in both—the many communities which have immigrated to Israel.)

CHOIR RECITING: (Alternating single voices and in unison)
Lift up thine eyes round about, and see:
All gather themselves together, they come to thee:
Thy sons shall come from far
And thy daughters shall be nursed at thy side.

And I shall take you from the nations
And I shall gather you from all the countries
And I shall bring you to your own land
And I shall give you new heart, and a new spirit shall
I plant within you
And you shall live in the land which I gave to your forefathers.
Therefore thy gates shall be opened continually;
They shall not be shut day nor night.

DANCE GROUP: (Sweeping over the stage and dancing the dance of the Ingathering of the Exiles.)

NARRATOR 1: (As the dance group fades into the background and disappears from the stage.)
The gates of Israel were opened wide.

NARRATOR 2: Every Jew has the right to immigrate to Israel.

NARRATOR 1: Blessed be each son who returns to his homeland.

NARRATOR 2: Hundreds...

NARRATOR 1: Thousands...

NARRATOR 2: Tens of thousands...

NARRATOR 1: Hundreds of thousands immigrated to Israel in the years following the establishment of the State. They came from all corners of the earth, from 70 nations and tongues.

NARRATOR 2:
Each with his family; each with his customs;
Each with his culture; each with his dreams.

NARRATOR 1: But they all had one great goal:

CHOIR RECITING: To build this land.

(Now, one by one, boys and girls start filing onto the stage, each wearing a large printed sign with the name of a settlement in Israel. They arrange themselves on the stage, not necessarily symmetrically.)

NARRATOR 2: The period of absorption and development began.

NARRATOR 1: Thousands of new immigrants covered the face of Israel. They expanded the existing cities and built new ones. They joined existing kibbutzim and established new ones. They settled in existing villages and founded new ones.

NARRATOR 2: Hundreds of new dots were added to the map of Israel—hundreds of new settlements.

NARRATOR 1: They are working the land and growing wheat, vegetables and fruit.

NARRATOR 2: They are working in factories manufacturing machines, producing textiles, making cement for construction.

NARRATOR 1: They are working in the fields and at home, creating new industries large and small.

NARRATOR 2: They are doing everything—everywhere.

NARRATOR 1: Engineers and labourers; doctors and porters; merchants and farmers; statesmen and soldiers.

NARRATOR 2: Ports and airports; roads and railroads; waterworks and atomic reactors.

CHOIR RECITING: A people has been reborn. A State has been reborn.

NARRATOR 1: Within a few years the population trebled. Wastelands turned into gardens. Buildings sprang forth from sand dunes. Trees grew between the rocks.

CHOIR RECITING: A giant and painstaking task.

NARRATOR 2: The nations of the world took notice and were astonished. New states observed and said: here is a model example. The achievements of the young State became famous throughout the world.

NARRATOR 1: People from all over came to Israel to observe and to study, to learn how the nation worked and developed.

NARRATOR 2: From Asia....

NARRATOR 1: From Africa...

NARRATOR 2: From America...

NARRATOR 1: From Europe...

NARRATOR 2: From Australia.

NARRATOR 1: New states that attained independence and liberty, that sought to develop and to progress at a rapid pace, asked, "How did you do it?"

NARRATOR 2: And the State of Israel said to them:
   Come to us—and see!
   Come to us—and learn.
   We are ready to help you.
   We are ready to share our experience with you.

(As he speaks, the children turn their signs over and now show the names of all those countries in Asia, Africa, and America with whom Israel maintains various ties of aid and assistance.)

CHOIR RECITING:
> Arise, shine; for thy light is come;
> And the glory of the Lord is risen upon thee,
> And the nations shall come to thy light;
> And kings to the brightness of thy rising.

NARRATOR 1: As Israel has rejoiced in the help proffered her by others, so is she glad today to extend her assistance to other people. She sends experts to new states, and their students come to her.

NARRATOR 2: She is ready to help everyone—so that there may be peace for everyone. She seeks peace, pursues peace, awaits peace.

NARRATOR 1:
> For her peace is the peace of the world.
> Peace for near and far.

CHOIR RECITING: And they shall beat their swords into plowshares, and their spears into pruninghooks: nation shall not lift up sword against nation, neither shall they learn war any more.

> Peace be within thy walls and prosperity within they palaces
> For my brethren and companions' sakes I will now say:
> Peace be within thee.

CHOIR: (Which has entered and taken its place again during the reading of the above passage)
> He-ve-nu shalom alechem ...

FINALE

STATE OF ISRAEL
DECLARATION OF INDEPENDENCE

(1) The Land of Israel was the birthplace of the Jewish people. Here their spiritual, religious and national identity was formed. Here they achieved independence and created a culture of national and universal significance. Here they wrote and gave the Bible to the world.

(2) Exiled from the Land of Israel the Jewish people remained faithful to it in all the countries of their dispersion, never ceasing to pray and hope for their return and the restoration of their national freedom.

(3) Impelled by this historic association, Jews strove throughout the centuries to go back to the land of their fathers and regain their statehood. In recent decades they returned in their masses. They reclaimed the wilderness, revived their language, built cities and villages, and established a vigorous and evergrowing community, with its own economic and cultural life. They sought peace yet were prepared to defend themselves. They brought the blessings of progress to all inhabitants of the country and looked forward to sovereign independence.

(4) In the year 1897 the First Zionist Congress, inspired by Theodor Herzl's vision of the Jewish State, proclaimed the right of the Jewish People to national revival in their own country.

(5) This right was acknowledged by the Balfour Declaration of November 2, 1917, and re-affirmed by the Mandate of the League of Nations, which gave explicit international recognition to the historic connection of the Jewish People with Palestine and their right to reconstitute their National Home.

(6) The recent holocaust, which engulfed millions of Jews in Europe, proved anew the need to solve the problem of the homelessness and lack of independence of the Jewish People by means of the re-establishment of the Jewish State, which would open the gates to all Jews and endow the Jewish People with equality of status among the family of nations.

(7) The survivors of the disastrous slaughter in Europe and also Jews from other lands have not desisted from their efforts to reach Eretz Yisrael, in face of difficulties, obstacles and perils;

and have not ceased to urge their right to a life of dignity, freedom and honest toil in their ancestral land.

(8)   In the Second World War the Jewish People in Palestine made their full contribution to the struggle of the freedom-loving nations against the Nazi evil. The sacrifices of their soldiers and their war effort gained them the right to rank with the nations which founded the United Nations.

(9)   On November 29, 1947, the General Assembly of the United Nations adopted a Resolution requiring the establishment of a Jewish State in Palestine. The General Assembly called upon the inhabitants of the country to take all the necessary steps on their part to put the plan into effect. This recognition by the United Nations of the right of the Jewish People to establish their independent State is unassailable.

(10)   It is the natural right of the Jewish People to lead, as do all other nations, an independent existence in its sovereign State.

(11)   Accordingly we, the members of the National Council, representing the Jewish People in Palestine and the World Zionist Movement, are met together in solemn assembly today, the day of termination of the British Mandate for Palestine; and by virtue of the natural and historic right of the Jewish People and of the Resolution of the General Assembly of the United Nations, we hereby proclaim the establishment of the Jewish State in Palestine, to be called Medinath Yisrael (The State of Israel).

(12)   We hereby declare that, as from the termination of the Mandate at midnight, May 14-15, 1948, and pending the setting up of the duly elected bodies of the State in accordance with a Constitution, to be drawn up by the Constituent Assembly not later than October 1, 1948, the National Council and the National Administration shall constitute the Provisional Government of the Jewish State, which shall be known as Israel.

(13)   The State of Israel will be open to the immigration of Jews from all countries of their dispersion; will promote the development of the country for the benefit of all its inhabitants; will be based on the principles of liberty, justice and peace as conceived by the Prophets of Israel; will uphold the full social and political equality of all its citizens, without distinction of religion, race, or sex; will guarantee freedom of religion, conscience, education and culture; will safeguard the Holy Places

of all religions; and will loyally uphold the principles of the United Nations Charter.

(14)   The State of Israel will be ready to cooperate with the organs and representatives of the United Nations in the implementation of the Resolution of the Assembly of November 29, 1947, and will take steps to bring about the Economic Union over the whole of Palestine.

(15)   We appeal to the United Nations to assist the Jewish People in the building of its State and to admit Israel into the family of nations.

(16)   In the midst of wanton aggression, we yet call upon the Arab inhabitants of the State of Israel to preserve the ways of peace and play their part in the development of the State, on the basis of full and equal citizenship and due representation in all its bodies and institutions—provisional and permanent.

(17)   We extend our hand in peace and neighborliness to all the neighbouring states and their peoples, and invite them to cooperate with the independent Jewish nation for the common good of all. The State of Israel is prepared to make its contribution to the progress of the Middle East as a whole.

(18)   Our call goes out to the Jewish People all over the world to rally to our side in the task of immigration and development and to stand by us in the great struggle for the fulfillment of the dream of generations for the redemption of Israel.

(19)   With trust in Almighty God, we set our hand to this Declaration, at this Session of the Provisional State Council, on the soil of the Homeland, in the city of Tel Aviv, on this Sabbath eve, the fifth of Iyar, 5708, the fourteenth day of May, 1948.

• • • • • • • •

PRAYER FOR THE STATE OF ISRAEL

Our Father in Heaven, Rock and Redeemer of Israel, bless the State of Israel, the inaugural flowering of our redemption. Protect her with Thy love. Spread over her the tabernacle of Thy peace, and bestow of Thy light and Thy truth upon her leaders, governors and counselors, and endow them with Thy divine counsel.

O God, strengthen the hands of the defenders of Israel and lead them to triumphant victory. Grant peace to Thy Holy Land and tranquility to her inhabitants.

We beseech Thee, O God, remember our brethren, the whole household of Israel in all the lands of their dispersion. Speedily restore them in dignity to Zion, Thy city, and to Jerusalem, the abode of Thy name, as it is written in Thy holy Torah: "If any of thine that are dispersed be in the uttermost parts of heaven, from there will the Lord thy God gather thee, and from there will He fetch thee. And the Lord thy God will bring thee into the land which thy fathers possessed, and thou shalt possess it: and He will make thee more prosperous and numerous than thy fathers. And the Lord thy God will circumcise thy heart, and the heart of thy offspring, to love the Lord thy God with all thy heart, and with all thy soul, that thou mayest live."

Unite our hearts to love Thee, to revere Thy name, and to observe the precepts of Thy Torah.

"Shine forth in the majesty of Thy power over all the inhabitants of Thy world, that all with life's breath in their nostrils may proclaim: 'The Lord God of Israel is King and His dominion ruleth over all.'"

THE DAY ISRAEL WAS BORN*

A Documentary Reading

Dorothy Ross

Based on material from newspapers of Israel and United States. For three readers.

(Music)

FIRST READER: Some thought the day would come with a loud clap of thunder and a flash of light; with heralds blowing trumpets to proclaim.
(Chords) THE JEWISH STATE.

SECOND READER: It was not so. The sun in Palestine rose on that day like any other. Over Jerusalem the Arab shells exploded and the children shivered on their beds.

THIRD READER: Cut off, besieged by armies of Iraq and Jordan, Jerusalem defended itself under the booming of mortars and the crackle of gun fire.

FIRST: COMMUNIQUE: "At midnight tonight all clocks in Jewish Jerusalem will be advanced two hours in order to save fuel!"

SECOND: "The Jerusalem Electric Corp. will cut off current to the Jewish Quarters from 1 to 9 P.M. as of today."

THIRD: Today? The Calendar marked it May 14, 1948.
(Pause)

FIRST: At seven o'clock in the morning the British High Commissioner appeared on the steps of Government House wearing a full General's uniform. He stepped into his black Rolls Royce. The British flag came down the flagpole at the Allenby Barracks. The British motorcade swept down the pine-lined driveway. Did the British remember that, thirty years before, General Lord Allenby, bareheaded and on foot, had entered this

---

* Written expressly for the Women's Division of the American Jewish Congress. Permission to reprint and present royalty-free granted by AJC on the proviso that the school or center planning production contact: Women's Division, American Jewish Congress, 15 East 84th Street, New York 10028, to advise when, where and by whom (children, youth or adult group) the script will be done. Copies of the script may be ordered through the AJC office at a token fee.

city of peace? At exactly eight o'clock the motorcade reached the airport where two small military aircraft were waiting.

(Soft music: "Rule Brittania" several bars. Then)

THIRD: THE BRITISH MANDATE IN PALESTINE WAS TERMINATED.

SECOND: What did the British leave behind them? A country with no mail services; and all communications seriously impaired. For weeks before withdrawal they had stopped collecting taxes, registering cars, maintaining health controls. They had destroyed land deeds and dispersed all government records. For the Council of the People, set up before British withdrawal, there were no offices, no constitution, no civil services—and most crucial of all, NO ADEQUATE ARMY.

THIRD: No army? What about the Haganah?

(Background music: "Shir HaPalmach" continues through next paragraph)

FIRST: The Jewish forces of the Haganah consisted of 4 well-trained battalions of about 3,000 men known as the Palmach or shock troops, plus some 50,000 poorly trained reservists. There was no heavy artillery; a handful of anti-aircraft guns; some home-made mortars, and a people mobilized with a will to statehood! Against this ragtag establishment, five Arab nations had mustered armies of 80,000 men, including the crack British trained Arab legion.

THIRD: At eight o'clock in Jerusalem mothers ran for bread and risked being killed . . . they ran with water pails because the Arabs had cut the city's waterpipe line; but old wells had been cleaned, old pools from Solomon's time had been filled, and each inhabitant of Jerusalem was allowed one pailful of water per person per day—to be used for all purposes. Children of all ages filled sandbags for the barricades. The bread was baked out of barley that had been condemned as unfit for human use, and brought at great danger to the city.

SECOND: (Tender) "Why do they make the bread taste so good?" asked a child in Jerusalem. "When there is so little of it, they should make it taste bad."

FIRST: That was how it was in Israel's capital in the days of the birth of the nation. These were the people who made history, ordinary people, average people, who endured and stood fast. In Tel Aviv there was no siege. The people listened on the underground radio to the reports of villages and towns under air attack, and for word about the establishment of the new state.

THIRD: Golda Meir reported to the Peoples Council, that two nights before, disguised in Arab robes, she had driven beyond the borders of Palestine to Transjordan, hoping to reach some sort of agreement with Emir Abdullah that might avoid war. Over coffee, Abdullah told his visitor that war could only be avoided if the Jews *gave up,* or at least postponed, the idea of establishing a state of their own.

FIRST: In the United States, Secretary of State George Marshall pleaded with Moshe Sharett in Washington that the establishment of a Jewish State BE POSTPONED. But Ben-Gurion had decided to ignore both requests. He was determined to proclaim the existence of a Jewish State before the day was out ...

SECOND: The battle for Jerusalem raged. In the afternoon Jerusalem was subjected to shelling from the northwest ... In the cellars in Jerusalem bodies were being brought in to an underground hospital with every conceivable kind of wound ... A volunteer English missionary nurse wrote in her diary: "What a price in sacrifices and maimed young lives the Jewish State will have to pay for statehood."

FIRST: Tension was added by the failing of electric power in most parts of the city. A blackout had been ordered for the whole of Jewish Palestine. On top of the other hardships to a city without fuel, this meant no broadcast news, no newspapers, no piped water ...

(Pause) Music

THIRD: The matter of the proclamation was more complex than Ben-Gurion realized. A document of such importance could not merely be typed out and mimeographed, but should be inscribed on parchment ... One of his assistants searched all Tel Aviv for a piece of parchment, without turning up a single scrap. Tel Aviv's little Art Museum had been chosen as the setting for the independence ceremonies, partly because it could hold 200, partly because it was inconspicuous. For security reasons, the time and place were known only to the engineers of the secret Jewish radio, which would broadcast above ground for the first time, at the Museum proceedings ...

SECOND: Somebody raced about trying to get a flag. A few days before, it had been decided to use blue and white as colors of the new state, recalling the robes worn by the High Priest when he entered the Temple on the day of Atonement, and the colors adopted by the Zionist movement.

FIRST: At 1 P.M. in Tel Aviv the Peoples Council met in final session to debate the text of the proclamation of the new state...

SECOND: Somebody ran six blocks to cut a stencil and turn out copies at the Anglo-Palestine Bank...

THIRD: Another secretary dashed from store to store trying to buy a gold pen with which to sign the Proclamation, but there were no gold pens for sale on May 14, 1948 in Tel Aviv. All she could find was a gold-plated one.

FIRST: In the Museum, all pictures were removed which might offend the eyes of the pious. Pictures with Jewish themes were substituted. A large picture of Herzl was framed and hung, for had he not said: "If you will it—it is not a legend."

SECOND: Without parchment for the proclamation, substitute synthetic material was used. A secretary raced down six blocks to the Anglo-Palestine Bank to make sure it stayed open so that when the proclamation was signed, it could be safely hidden in the underground vaults of the bank. From all over Tel Aviv, people began to flock to the Museum. The Founding Fathers began to come, and people stood about silent, many of them weeping, many of them praying.

FIRST: Only fifteen minutes before the time of the meeting, the Proclamation came off the mimeo machine, but Zev Sharef, who had it, was blocks from the Museum. There were no taxis to be had. Sharef ran to a traffic cop, pleading "Stop a car! I've got to get to the ceremony." A car was stopped, and Sharef started to explain to the driver: "You have a rare honor. I hold in my hands the Declaration of the Independence of Israel." "That?" said the driver relieved. "I only stopped because I'm driving without a license."

THIRD: Inside the Post Office a new stamp was being issued, bearing the non-committal words DOAR IVRI—Hebrew mail, because the name of the new state had not yet been decided. The night before, the names of Zion and Judea strongly rivalled the name of Israel.

FIRST: Inside the Museum the future cabinet members sat at a long table on a dais, Herzl's portrait at their back. Facing them in the jammed hall sat the writers, artists, economists, rabbis and Haganah leaders who had played important roles in fighting for the Jewish state. Ben-Gurion, in tie and dark suit, his eyes riveted to the paper in his hands, read the proclamation. In a total of 979 Hebrew words which took less than 22 minutes, he read: "It is the self-evident right of the Jewish people to be a nation, as all other nations, in its own sovereign state."

[Music: HaTikvah (low background—keep playing until indicated)]

Then he reached the final paragraph. "With faith in Almighty G-d, we set our hands to this Declaration, at this session of the Provisonal State Council in the City of Tel Aviv, on this Sabbath eve, the fifth day of Iyar, the 14th day of May, 1948."

SECOND: And Rabbi Fishman, the 74-year old Minister to be for Religious Affairs, pronounced the Shehechianu—and 200 throats echoed AMEN. While Ben-Gurion, his eyes moist, read the first ordinances of the new government, the Palestine Philharmonic played the HaTikvah from a gallery upstairs and Ben-Gurion said to the people of the state of Israel and the people of the world: (Music louder and ending) "THE STATE OF ISRAEL HAS RISEN. THIS MEETING IS ENDED." Later, alone in his room at Haganah headquarters, he entered these words in his diary: "At 4 P.M. the Declaration of Independence. The people are profoundly happy. And *I*—am filled with foreboding."

THIRD: FLASH FROM THE PALESTINE POST: "The first independent Jewish State in 19 centuries was born in Tel Aviv as the British Mandate over Palestine came to an end on Friday, and it was immediately subjected to the test of fire. As Medinat Yisroel was proclaimed, the battle for Jerusalem raged, with most of the city falling to the Jews." At the same time

SECOND: In America, President Truman's announcement that the United States was proposing to recognize the new Jewish state reached newsmen before the American delegation itself knew about it ... All afternoon the Assembly had been tied up in knots. After much filibustering, it rejected the Franco-United States proposal for a special administration for Jerusalem.

FIRST: As the debate dragged on, correspondents sat with stop-watches to see whether a decision would be taken before the six o'clock deadline when the Mandate terminated. As zero hour was reached without a vote, they rushed to the booths, and, about 10 minutes later, the tickers in the local news agency offices flashed:

THIRD: *United States recognizes Jewish State . . . Washington—Quote . . . "Ten minutes after the termination of the British Mandate on Friday, the White House released a formal statement by President Truman that the United States government intended to recognize the provisional Jewish government as the de facto authority representing the Jewish State . . ."*

SECOND: Back in Flushing Meadow, the United Nations Assembly floor was half deserted and the American delegation had not been officially informed.

FIRST: The first to mention the Jewish State from the rostrum was Mr. Gromyko who said he saw no need for further action on the Franco-American proposal, since the Jewish State had been recognized as a reality by the United States.

FIRST: Russia and her allies had given early assurance of their intention to recognize the Jewish State, whoever else did or did not. As a result of Washington's action and the Eastern Bloc's stand, other countries are expected to extend their recognition to the newly-born state.

THIRD: *Medinat Yisroel*: A state of emergency in the Jerusalem area was declared to exist by the Haganah area commander, as from yesterday, in what is the first order of the day to be issued in almost 2,000 years by a Jewish military commander of the city.

SECOND: In Flushing Meadow there was an eerie atmosphere. The lights of the TV cameras played on the rostrum, lighting up one Arab speaker after another, who mounted the steps and in a low voice expressed frustration and anger. To the last minute, officials of the State Department were lobbying right on the floor against the Jewish State, even while the President's statement was already on the wires . . .

THIRD: *TV Flash*: "The creation of Medinat Yisroel, the State of Israel, was proclaimed at midnight on Friday by Mr. David Ben-Gurion, until then Chairman of the Jewish Agency Executive and now head of the State's Provisional Council of Government." The first act of the Council of Government was to abolish all legislation of the 1939 White Paper. In the Declaration of Independence, Mr. Ben-Gurion called on the Arabs of Palestine to restore peace:

Quote: "Even at this hour of bloodshed, we call upon the Arabs of Palestine to restore peace in this country. We call upon the Arab citizens to return to their homes. We assure them full civic rights on the basis of full representation in all governmental organs of the State. We are extending the hand of friendship to the neighboring Arab states in order to initiate mutual cooperation. We are ready to contribute our share to the revival of the Middle East. We call upon the Jewish people in all lands of its dispersion to stand fast and lend us every support in our struggle for the establishment of the State of Israel."

SECOND: In New York City there appeared a group of American Jewish youth carrying a blue and white flag and displaying the signs: "Our brothers in Israel are giving their lives for statehood. Will you give your blood?" and volunteers gave.

FIRST: The declaration states: "The state of Israel will open its gates to immigration of Jews from all lands. It will strive to develop the country for the benefit of all its inhabitants, in accordance with the social ideals of our Prophets."

THIRD: A ship from Cyprus was due at the Tel Aviv Harbor ... The *SS Teti* was coming in slowly. The bombardment of Tel Aviv was going on ... The city was in blackout ... An old man was helped into the incoming passenger's hall. "Look," he wept, waving a slip of paper. "Look. It reads: *The right to settle in the land of Israel is hereby given.*" An 80-year old survivor of the death camp of Buchenwald held the State's first immigration visa.

FIRST: The declaration states: "We declare that full civil and political liberty will be enjoyed by all citizens, regardless of religion, race or sex. ... There will be full freedom of religion, culture and language." "We declare that we shall safeguard the Holy Places of all religions within the area of the State of Israel."

SECOND: At Meah Shearim, a Haganah messenger arrived with the emergency news that roadblocks were needed in a hurry. Meah Shearim was an area of twisting alleys where Jerusalem's most devout Jews lived a life apart, awaiting the Messiah. (Chassidic background music) The soldiers of the Haganah were met with shrill curses. To these Jews, the State was an irreligious fantasy, attempted prematurely. However, the Haganah leader managed to muster 48 of the bearded men in their long black gowns and velvet hats. He organized them in working squads, giving his orders in Yiddish, explaining that this was a matter of life or death, and in such cases the Law even allowed them to work on the Sabbath. Gradually, the work quickened and the men began chanting their ancient chassidic melodies and swaying to the chants.

THIRD: (Tender, sensitive and triumphant—quiet background music like *Zug Nit Kaynmul*)

"*Editorial: Palestine Post*: May 14, 1948

Men, women, and children, are passing, in these hours, through the gates. You can hear them singing. You can see the shine in their eyes. You can feel the straining spirit that would burst from freed bodies to be quicker in the land. The gates are opened in Cyprus, Italy, in Germany, Bulgaria; the walls of the ghettoes and the wires of the concentration camps are coming down. The people stride over them and along the road that will take them home, set them upon their own soil, under their own sun, beside their own temples, among their own kin." "Never before has any people known so bitterly the years of detention or so joyously the moment of release. . . . It is in a man's soul and behind his smarting eyes that the miracle is felt. A miracle it is: not only that a people has come to free Statehood, but that the Jewish people has come to it, whose moral, social and often physical serfdom has been a burden on the civilized conscience."

SECOND: At 7:30 P.M. Ben-Gurion watched the ship come in. The refugees stepped ashore to the banner "Welcome Home." (Bruchim HaBaim)

FIRST: The Arabs were attacking with cannons and armored cars at the nearby Nirim Settlement. Ben-Gurion looked out to sea. Less than 24 hours had passed since the High Commissioner walked out of Government House and everything had gone on schedule so far—The British Withdrawal; The Proclamation of the State; And the invasion of the enemy. Whatever happened next, he thought, in those hours, the Third Jewish Commonwealth had become an accomplished fact.

THIRD: For the first time in twenty centuries, said Abba Eban, the destiny of our people had entered the autonomy of its choice. We had become the *agents,* not the *victims,* of our history.

(Triumphant last 2 lines of Hatikvah.)

· · · · · · · ·

IN MEMORIAM*

David Ben-Gurion

"LET US STAND SILENT in memory of our dearly beloved sons and daughters who gave their lives for the liberation of our homeland and the security of our people. They gave all they had. They poured out their very lifeblood for the freedom of Israel, even as the living waters quench the thirst of the arid soil. Not in monuments of stones or trees shall be preserved their memory, but in the reverence and pride which will, until the end of time, fill the hearts of our people when their memory is recalled.

"Our hearts are filled to overflowing with praise and thanksgiving to the Rock of Israel. But let us not delude ourselves that our work is finished. We are still at the beginning. The road stretching ahead is long and hard, and there are still many obstacles in our way.... The sword is still girded round our loins; let us not boast as men who have taken it off.

"On our festive day let us review in joy and thanksgiving the mighty deeds of the past and let us resolve to apply ourselves with all our might and all our heart to the new efforts of the future."

. . . .

---

* From an address on Independence Day, May 4th, 1949.

TWO BY TWO—FROM THE ARK TO THE HOUSE AND THE ZOO

Dorothy Ross

The Bible tells us many things of Israel's ancient days:
How people lived and worked and played, and differed in their
   ways.
The crops they grew; the foods they ate, so many facts; and yet,
The Bible never tells a thing about a household pet.

> Did Jacob have a pup or dog? Did Rachel love a kitten?
> Did David raise canary birds? These facts were never
>   written.
> When Samson caught the foxes and tied them by their
>   tails,
> Did he take his dogs along to sniff the ancient trails?

Camels moved in caravans, and donkeys filled the roads.
They couldn't have been household pets, they carried heavy loads.
But when the jackals howled at night, and leopards crept too
   near—
Did Judah keep a lion close to still his human fear?

> Hyenas, wolves and leopards in Galilee still roam,
> And new Israeli settlers spy them near their home;
> Fleet foxes still are numerous; the weasel and the lynx
> Will scare away a shy gazelle when she comes down to
>   drink.

The soldiers now in Israel train boxers for the border,
Policemen walk with wolfhounds and ride horses to keep order.
The Negev has its lizards—how they slither through the sand.
And birds? Four hundred different kinds fly high across the land.

> Jerusalem is very proud, and Tel Aviv is too,
> Each gathered Bible animals and placed them in a zoo.
> And Israeli children with their parents and their teachers,
> Make trips to see and learn about the living Bible
>   creatures.

The kibbutzim have rabbits, birds and animals they tame,
And very often puppies join a frisky running game;
But how will we discover, unless we find some clues,
What were the kinds of household pets among the early Jews?

From *Young Judaean*

. . . .

KFAR KENNEDY
Herb Brin

For him the trees of Israel
Will dance upon the holy hills
And clouds will leap from Lebanon
Across the Galilee.

And they will know of Kennedy
Who come in hope from distant place
To clear the stones and build the towns
And walk the hills of Galilee.

They will know that friend had died
Upon a distant Texas soil
To raise the cry that man is free
As free as winds in Galilee.

From *Wild Flowers*

Shevuot

Classification	Title	Author	Age Level
1. Reading	The Ten Commandments		7-10
2. Poem	Little Mount Sinai	Edna Bockstein	5-7
3. Choral Reading	What Is Torah?	Judith and Ira Eisenstein	12-16
4. Reading	Torah Light and the Stars	Unknown	5-8
5. Poem	God's Love	Meir b. Isaac Nehorai	10-14
6. Poem	Shechina	Herb Brin	12-16
7. Reading	Where God Is Found		13-16
8. Reading	The Omnipresence of God	Adapt. Nahum M. Glatzer	12-16
9. Reading	The Book	Heinrich Heine	14-16
10. Poem	Gifts	Emma Lazarus	13-16
11. Simulated Radio Broadcast	Come Under the Wings	Grace Goldin, Adapted by Virginia Mazer	13-16
12. Choral Reading	His Love Is Everlasting	Psalm 136	12-16
13. Poem	Melodies of Israel	Zalman Shneour	12-16

THE TEN COMMANDMENTS

1. I am the Lord your God, who brought you out of the land of Egypt, out of the house of bondage.
2. You shall have no other gods before Me.
3. You shall not take the name of the Lord your God in vain.
4. Remember the Sabbath day to keep it holy.
5. Honor your father and your mother.
6. You shall not murder.
7. You shall not commit adultery.
8. You shall not steal.
9. You shall not bear false witness against your neighbor.
10. You shall not covet your neighbor's house, nor anything that is your neighbor's.

LITTLE MOUNT SINAI
Edna Bockstein

The mountains quarreled jealously,
"Which one of us," said they,
"Will bear the Glory of the Lord
On the Holy Day?"

Only the tall ones quarreled,
The smaller ones were still,
The little mountain Sinai
Stood humble as a hill.

Mt. Tabor said: "When the flood
Swelled beneath the sky,
Nothing stood above the waves
But the Ark and I."

Said Hermon: "When the Israelites
Despairing, faced the sea,
I rose between the foamy shores,
And they crossed over me."

Mt. Carmel said: "Below me
You hear the ocean roar,
I shall be chosen, for I stand
Upon the sea and shore."

But God chose not among them—
The proud ones and the tall—
He chose the little Sinai,
The meekest of them all.

. . . . .

"COME UNDER THE WINGS"*

A Midrash on Ruth

Grace Goldin

Adapted for radio by

Virginia Mazer

* Reprinted by permission of The Jewish Theological Seminary of America, producers of *The Eternal Light* program, under whose auspices the play was originally presented on May 29, 1960 by the National Broadcasting Company.

VOICE

"SHOMER YISROEL" (ECHO) And the Lord spake unto Moses, saying, "Command the children of Israel that they bring unto thee pure oil olive, beaten for the light, to cause the lamps to burn continually in the tabernacle of the congregation, and it shall be a statute forever in your generations."

Our program today, "Come Under the Wings," a Midrash on Ruth, was written by Grace Goldin and adapted for radio by Virginia Mazer. This program marks the Festival of Shevuot which celebrates the revelation of the ten commandments at Sinai.

Guitar
Establish theme and down behind

NARRATOR

(Conversationally)
In the days the Judges judged in Israel
Two men of substance lived in Bethlehem,
Upright and canny, Bible millionaires.
Princes they seemed and all men swore by them,
By Boaz, second in strength to none;
By Elimelech, who was blessed with two tall boys....

ELIMELECH

Yes, indeed, my sons, Mahlon and Chilion!
Boaz, my brother, has no son.
        (With a trace of a sneer)
Though they do say
God's purpose is to make him ancestor of David, of the King.

BOAZ
(Regretfully)
That's a prophecy I'd give my life
To be one half so sure of as the witches are.

NARRATOR
Some thirty years these two lived side by side
Ruling or judging, laying up their wealth
And harvesting in honor from the town.
They were like two tall hills to Bethlehem
And only God (as His wise custom is)
Knew one of them to be a granite stone
And one no other than a heap of sand.
Then came a day, however, in the spring,
When God sent out, instead of rains and flowers,
A steadily hot wind that blew for hours.
And Boaz could see famine roll behind it.
He told his wife . . .

BOAZ
I think we are equipped
To care for all this summer through the fall.
Then, if the rains return to Bethlehem,
We shall lose neither man nor animal.

NARRATOR
In one more great establishment that night,
They feared the wind as much as it deserved,
For Elimelech was a farmer too.
He had lived through a famine once before
And with a bitter rind of thought recalled
Naomi's shrunken body, and the voice
Of undernourished beggars quacking "Bread."
He spoke

ELIMELECH
Naomi, Heaven in His righteousness
Claps down a sentence on our fellow men.

NAOMI
(Without unction, just a statement of fact)
Heaven's will is just.

ELIMELECH
Did I say *one* word
For you to take as censure of the Lord?
My thought is this: That by this wind He speaks
To those of us with wit to understand.
"Rise up and flee," He says, "as fled from Sodom Lot
To Moab's healthy meadows; rise and flee,
You and your wife, your wealth, your family."

NAOMI
No. If famine comes again
To smite our citizens of Bethlehem,
Would not God's word beseech you to remain
To save His folk whatever way you can?
You and your brother Boaz stand as one.
Boaz will scarcely think as you have done.

ELIMELECH
Let's let the rabble seek out Boaz then.
He has to gain by being generous.
An old man, Boaz, sixty if a day.
And that, Naomi, makes him old enough
To be my father—if he had it in him.
But by the Lord's inscrutable decree
He will not father be to any man.
All moonshine and burnt magic is the talk
Of sir great-grandson king and emperor.
If Boaz had the sons God granted us,
He'd find it hard to be magnanimous.

NAOMI
But if our sons go out of Israel,
I cannot tell
How you imagine you are planning well.
With what composure can you buy them bread
Ground in the mills of sin and uglihed?
I think the stuff will poison them instead.

ELIMELECH
Ha. . . . Where there's no bread at all
There'll be no Torah. Comfort yourself, Naomi.
When we're in Moab, I shall build you courts
Richer by far than these in Bethlehem,

And wall them round with flower and with vine
And hide them in the hiding of the hills.
There we shall dwell as dwelt our ancestors
To God more dedicate than here.
I say this bitter wind is Heaven-sent. . . .

              NARRATOR
                (Sardonically)
And so they went. And so they went.

Guitar
Accent and segue to accompaniment for

               SINGER
When Elimelech quit the land
He thought he fled starvation;
He had no mind to desecrate
The customs of his nation.

But camping in a pagan place
He did what pagans do;
He broke their bread, he drank their wine,
He tipped their retinue;
And when the great cup came around,
He poured libations too.

Till it was so, his very life
Interpreted the text:
In innocence, in innocence
Will Israel be vexed;
A Jew that left the Holy Land
Will serve Baalim next.

Guitar
Up and fade behind

               NARRATOR
It happened in the seventh year in Moab
Of Elimelech that he grew increasingly morose.
He would not trade,
Withdrew from court and market place, and built
In a rude bare burnt place out behind his lot
An altar high as any pagan god's

And there he set up sacrifice the way
Israel did, and prayed. Nobody knew
How he sought God—sought, but he never found,
Prayed, and he never heard.

ELIMELECH
(Wildly)

Naomi, tell me what you think.
As the sheep caught fire, the smoke would not rise straight.
Did the Lord reject my sacrifice as he rejected Cain's?

NAOMI
(Non-committally)

Cain was bloody born, a murderer.
He slew his brother Abel with his hand.

ELIMELECH

While I, Elimelech, never yet have killed
One soul save cattle.
Word has been sent that famine, after all,
Was not so bad in Judah as one feared.
It was not actually very bad.
No Jew has died by reason of our swift departure.
None even hungered very much.

NAOMI

No. *Boaz* made haste to care for all.
Boaz redeemed his brother Elimelech.
Who is now, no, not in any sense a murderer.

ELIMELECH
(Low ... from his heart)

But, just because of this, though the rains fall
And seasons move again in Bethlehem
That sorry Elimelech and his wife
May not go home.

NAOMI

Moab must be their home.

ELIMELECH

How could I look Boaz in the face?

Guitar
Quick bridge and behind

NARRATOR
So matters stood; and one evening the sons
Of Elimelech brought great news home with them.
As men they prospered, living now in town,
Serving King Eglon as his bodyguard.

MAHLON
Father, in all good cheer we come, with news—
Good news—to reassure you past all doubt.

CHILION
Your God did not abandon us in Moab
Nor hide His countenance, as you in saintly
Overanxiety supposed.

ELIMELECH
(With little interest)
Prosper in God, my word has ever been
Or perish. What's the news?

MAHLON
The King of Moab,
Our royal master Eglon, he whose strength
Throughout Transjordan is the law, has viewed
Your Jewish sons with quite unusual favor.

ELIMELECH
How so? What now?

CHILION
Make yourself quieter, dear Father.
Eglon has chosen us (A dramatic pause) to *wed his daughters!*

ELIMELECH
Oh, so I feared. Oh, so my heart foretold!
Is it not enough we lent you to the King,
Saved you from harvest and inheritance....

NAOMI
Gave our consent—God knows how fearfully—
That you be soldiers in the troops of Moab....

ELIMELECH
Soldiers, murderers!

MAHLON
Dear Father, Mother. All has been arranged. We pray you
Add your voice to our blessedness, and bless us.
We marry well: the purest blood in Moab.

ELIMELECH
Speak me no sorrow. Will you be foresworn?
To join our good blood with the blood of Lot!

MAHLON
You speak of royal blood as if it were
The brine of fishwives.

CHILION
You have seen the maidens
Some years ago at court. You must recall them.
They are as they were then, but quieter.

MAHLON
(Excitedly)
Ruth is like some slender damsel of fourteen.
I never saw in Israel *or* Moab
Woman of such hushed gracefulness!
Low in her speech and marvellous in motion,
The dancer tamed.

NAOMI
The dancer at *what* altar?
Profane! Idolatrous!

CHILION
Father, do Jews
Monopolize this wide world's decency?

MAHLON
Our father Moses married a black woman:
Whereas my Ruth is fair as is God's sun,
More gold than gold is, golden through and through.

ELIMELECH
O miser, miser,
This beauty blinds you. Let you not be led
Astray by beauty in these godless folk!

CHILION
There rose a prophet out of Moab once,
As great in God's eyes for the needs of Moab
As Moses was, to speak for Israel.
God's spokesmen both. They called their prophet Baalam.

ELIMELECH
O heart of Elimelech, break
That I should live to hear my sons invoke
The wicked Baalam for their evidence!
You obstinate asses! Baalam me no more!

NAOMI
Elimelech, let us go.
Let us go home once more, where your sons may wive
Congenial daughters of our Jewish parents.

CHILION
But, Mother,
We never learned the Hebrew love-words
To speak to women such as these.

MAHLON
Mother, if we marry
In Israel or Judah, we will take
Some stranger to be mother of our children
Rather than *Ruth*.

CHILION
There was a time you wanted us in Moab.

ELIMELECH
Moab or no Moab,
Your inmost natures, Chilion and Mahlon,
Are Jewish. I begot them so myself.
And howsoever you will stubbornly temper
Your Jewish natures in the fires of freedom,
Such freedom was not meant for us, my boys:
We thrive best in the bondage of the Lord.

CHILION
Return, sad heart, return,
Go back to Bethlehem where you were born,
Where the men talk as you would want them to,
And worship in the way you always wanted to.

MAHLON
Your sons,
Mahlon and Chilion, have come of age
To make their choice. We will remain in Moab,
Marry our princesses, and lead such lives
As shall, by reason of their decency,
Silence this argument.

CHILION
We ask, Father, only your consent.
             (A long pause)

ELIMELECH
Shall I obey, dear Lord? I'll not obey.
Shall I give them my fatherly consent?
I will not give them my consent.
Not in my lifetime, by the name of God!
Some curse I'll find to curse them, as I live,
And break apart their Jewish-planted pride!

NARRATOR
That night, Naomi's husband left their bed,

Guitar
Sneak

NARRATOR
He climbed his altar of the rough-hewn stone,
Cast himself bodily down from it . . . and died.

Guitar
*Theme up . . . establish well . . . we need at least
a quarter of a minute to set stage for passage of time
. . . guitar under*

NARRATOR
Mahlon and Chilion, our sources read,
Died, both of them. But no book tells us why.
There lived two men in Moab . . . but they died
Of some disease peculiar to their nation
That neither one had virtue to resist.
In spice-bark and in laurel and in myrrh,
With the pomp a royal setting would require,
Moab laid two young Jews inside their grave to rest.

Neither the gold, nor incense, nor the bells
Comforted Ruth and Orpah—who had been their wives
Not in the least.
They looked to right, to left; then up the street
They saw a woman coming all in grey.
Barefooted, with a bundle on her back,
And in their hearts the princesses were glad
To see at last the sign of so much grief.

NAOMI
(The sound of her weeping a second or two)

RUTH
Mother!

ORPAH
Mother!

NAOMI
I am a woman whom the Lord has cursed;
Cursed are all who ever dwelled with me.
Whatever I took into my hands to do
The Lord has brought it to calamity.

RUTH
No!

NAOMI
My daughters, tell me how to comfort you.
To the dead you were at all times kind.
Because of you, they both found burial
Not without honor, though of such rude nature
As never Jew in his right mind would suffer.
When was a Jew decked out in spikenard?
And what Jew wore tiaras when he died?
Nevertheless, I know your hearts, I know
The love you bore my sons, and for your sakes
More than my own I grieve. Oh, princesses,
I cannot counsel you. I cannot bless.
I pray that Moab somehow give you wisdom
And that your father's gods bring happiness.

NARRATOR
With that Naomi kissed them, raised her pack,
And turned along the duty road to Judah.

Behind her went her daughters. When she saw
That they still followed her, Naomi spoke
Once more to them with rising urgency.

NAOMI

My daughters, that are nobly born in Moab,
Why would you follow me?
I am a bitter woman, have no sons.
Return!

RUTH

You say my mother is a bitter woman,
Salty and sulphurous. But I bear witness:
To me you are like musk or lavender.
Your spice has from the first gone to my head.
Deep below you, I hear a rushing from
The wells that wait there of salvation.

NAOMI

Would it were so!
No, Ruth.
I am a salt abandoned sea, I lie
Too deep for you. Let me beseech you
For your own sake, Ruth, not to follow me.

RUTH

Consider: I had stood so many years
Like some great statue hammered up in gold,
Encased and shuttered; when I saw your face
The spiral round me split; and I looked out
To see—I cannot tell you what I saw.
I cannot focus clearly yet. I cannot
Put you within the limits of a word.
But this I know. I saw no curse.

NAOMI

If you will not credit my words, and for
Your own sakes go, then for Naomi's sake
I pray you flee the curse that cleaves to me!

RUTH

Once again, no! Not curse! Not punishment!
No, blessing, blessing was what your God meant.
Why did He send you forth? A miracle!

The purposes of God are merciful;
He had put many blessings in your load
For you to scatter out upon the road,
That grew, and spread, and flourished till this hour:
Know by our loves, your blessing came to flower!

NAOMI

Kind and courteous
It is on your part, Ruth, to comfort me
When you have greater need for comforting.
It is uncanny how you know
That the Lord punishes, and He forgives;
Breaks, and makes whole again; and resurrects:
You might have made a very subtle Jew.
However, Ruth, I beg you pardon me.
No dialectic does me any good.

ORPAH

I, Orpah, up to now have held my peace.
No longer. Mother, tell me this:
If God be all you say, both mean and great,
And for no sin nor slipping on your part
Withdrew from you and left you desolate;
And piled down plagues upon your kindly head
What kind of God is He? Our Baalim
Are *this* one fair, that one ominous.
I cannot in a word imagine HIM
Who with one body must be all to us.

NAOMI

Orpah, child, turn aside.
You ought not dabble in such speculations;
The kernels of religious thought reside
Neither in Orpah's heart nor in her nation's.
Wife of my Chilion, Orpah, go your ways;
I am returning to my own far country.
(A pause) And it were well for Ruth to go with you
Back to the atmosphere you always knew.
What can I give you, girls? I am rock poor.
I cannot dress you, cannot shelter you.
You will be stoned as an idolator
Or taken coolly when you turn a Jew.

And you'll not find in Judah anywhere
The courtliness you are accustomed to.

NARRATOR
Then Orpah kissed her mother, and shed four—
Four little tears she shed, for Chilion's sake;
And turned away reluctantly, to take
The road to Moab, to her father's door.
But Ruth went on, her eyes like some gold lake,
Holding Naomi's elbow as before.

RUTH
You were too harsh with Orpah.
Had you but coaxed her as she dared you to
She might have gone the difficult way with you.

NAOMI
We are forbidden bribery, my Ruth,
Since only those who come with extreme love
For heaven and heavenly things, and love of God,
Are welcome to be Jews.

RUTH
(Urgently) Naomi, Mother, will you make my soul,
Will you become my mother in all truth?

NAOMI
I am afraid, Ruth. I foretold this not,
Nor am I worthy of the power to do it.

RUTH
I beg—

NAOMI
No, listen to me.
Ruth, can the daughter of a king conceive
What it is like to be an outcast people?
In their own land, for their own laws, they are slain:
What does it matter who the stranger be
So long as he shall have more strength than we?
Oh, Ruth, my Ruth, while you can do so, flee!

RUTH
Dear Mother, whither you go, I go.

NAOMI
A Jewish daughter, Ruth, will never go
To drunken theatres or circuses
Or any pagan show.

RUTH
Whither you go, I go.

NAOMI
A Jewish daughter will not dwell
In a house where they have not put mezuzas
On every door.

RUTH
Where you shall dwell, I dwell.

NAOMI
You must eradicate idolatry
Within yourself; we have one God, one law.
Our Torah is our one word of command,
And the Eternal God is our one God.

RUTH
I am not worthy of these obligations:
Yet if you will permit me, Naomi,
I would accept your people for my people,
And I would want your God to be my God.

Guitar
A few chords for accent and to introduce singer

SINGER
(Guitar accompaniment)
My God is this world's King
Before all else He was;
He was my root and cause
And now my flowering;
My God is this world's King.

I yield to Heaven here
My body with my spirit,
So I may disinherit
The body of this fear.
Lord God, I will not fear!
I yield to heaven here.

Guitar
Up and down behind
NARRATOR
How deviously God moves
To bring fulfillment after trial
And indirection, to the man He loves!
For fifty years, Boaz had had a wife
Whom God had set like Hagar at his side
To comfort him the while
Ruth ripened down in Moab, and the life
Of Mahlon had been wasted, and he died.
This wife of Boaz bore no child. The day
Naomi came with Ruth to Bethlehem,
Wore out with years the woman passed away
So that her funeral first welcomed them.
And Boaz mourned, and rose, and then through tears
Spoke with the Holy One, blessed be He....
Guitar
Keep low behind
BOAZ
Look down upon your subject, O my King.
I have not crossed your will in any thing,
Concerning which our Sages say this thing:
The son of his son's son shall be the King.

Good Father, who the entire earth hast fathered,
My Harvester, grant that my seed be gathered.
Then, if you will, let Boaz's life be gathered
And let me never see the son I fathered.
Guitar
Out
NARRATOR
When they were in the town a month or so,
Ruth told Naomi:
RUTH
This will never do!
I'd rather chill all winter in a hut
Than listen to such-like commiseration
From cousin this and great-uncle that.
Let me go out and glean as poor girls do.
We need at least not *eat* out of their hand.

NARRATOR
Naomi did not tell Ruth where to go.
Naomi left the details to the Lord.
Some say there was in Bethlehem but one
Great field, that Ruth was bound to fall upon.

BOAZ
What woman is this woman
With my petitioners?
There's not a maid among them
Of courtesy like hers....

SINGER
(Without guitar)
They wink the eye
And they shake the hip
They heave a sigh
At his widowship;
They hike the skirt
And they bare the thighs
And they show famine
In their eyes....

BOAZ
But this new woman gleans with them for hours
Like a queen's daughter gathering in her flowers.

MAN
(With a sneer)
My lord, the girl is Ruth,
Naomi's daughter.

BOAZ
This shall be Boaz's word concerning her.
Let me not hear of one Jew spurning her.
Nor shall you grant her less grain than her due
On the pretext she was not born a Jew.

Guitar
Chords and gaily to accompany singer

SINGER
(Recitative)
Said the maidens and the mothers of the maidens
And the widows with their ten good years ahead;

May the Lord provide a suitor for each woman born in Judah
When Boaz prefers a pagan girl instead.

Have you ever seen the like of it, my sister?
Prince Boaz scarcely knows that we exist.
Regardless of his danger, he revolves around the stranger
Till the stranger has to beg him to desist.

Guitar
Out

NAOMI
Ruth, as your mother, let me speak frankly to you.
How long, Ruth, can you and Boaz play your little game?
Lo, it is seven weeks, Ruth, since the crop began,
And seven weeks, Ruth, you have gone harvesting.

RUTH
(Demurely)

Yes, Mother.
Behold the harvesting is over and done,
Tonight they winnow wheat on the threshing-floor.

NAOMI
Rise up, my daughter; adorn yourself.
Put Sabbath raiment on, undo your hair.

RUTH
Undo my hair!

NAOMI
And some sweet scent apply to your garment's hem
Such as my sons desired you wear for them. . . .
Then, cautiously, when the night's work is done
And revelry drops silent, creep about
To where among his reapers Boaz sleeps.
Uncover his feet, my daughter; crouch down there. . . .

RUTH
And then, Mother? What then?

NAOMI
(Quickly) Let Boaz tell you what you ought to do.

Guitar
Sneak softly in background

NARRATOR

That night the moon rose late. As Boaz dreamed
A dozen Ruths skimmed past him single file,
Each like the Ruth who graced the barley-rows,
But each one bolder than the living Ruth.
Had he stored seed through half a century
To spill it in a dream upon a slut?
What of the legend? God had promised him
Son of his flesh; begot upon what woman?
Would such a convert be God's messenger?
Then Boaz slept, a heavy drunken sleep,
And when he woke again it was to find
The body of a woman at his feet....

BOAZ

Who art thou?
Art thou spirit or woman?

RUTH

I am a maid.

BOAZ

Art thou clean or unclean?

RUTH

I am in a purer state than thou art now, my lord.
Yes, I am clean.

BOAZ

Who art thou?

RUTH

I am Ruth, thy handmaid.

BOAZ

Ruth! So the dream was not a dream,
But flesh and blood.
Tarry, my love.

RUTH
(Sings softly)
Not by day and not by darkness
Not by truth and not by falsehood
Not to play and not in earnest
I come to you, my love....

BOAZ

Ruth! This is no time for singing!

RUTH
Boaz, remember yourself. Think what you are.
To you God gave the legend of a saint.
Men ought to sing of Boaz near and far
And praise his steadfastness and his restraint.

BOAZ
Ruth. Tarry with me.

RUTH
Boaz, remember me. I am no light
Gleaner. I am a woman of some frame,
Born royally in Moab and tonight
Seeking the promise of far greater name.
(Proudly) I shall not cast my legend down, nor pour
Myself away like wine on a barn floor.

BOAZ
Forgive me, Ruth.
Tarry this night. I am an old man,
I think I have not very long to live.
But, by my faith, you may be comforted.
Before tomorrow night you shall be wed.
Boaz is yours now, Ruth, living or dead.

Guitar
*Accent and segue to theme, continue long enough
to indicate a passage of time and under*

SINGER
(Recitative)
If a man has died at the measure of his days,
And the man was senile and spent;
And on his wife's breast, thoroughly well content
He came to death
In the simplest way, by letting go his breath,
Silence the dirge-singers, bid them be gone,
And let the bier be brought and carried on,
The earth be scattered and the garment torn . . .
But do not mourn. . . .

Guitar
Out

WOMAN I
Poor Ruth, poor soul, she is not what she was.
She seems to walk on twigs and she looks her age.

WOMAN II
And her hair does not shine as it did.

WOMAN I
Do you think she is sick in body as in mind?
Might she be with child by Boaz?

WOMAN II
I think it likely—considering the manner
Of Boaz's death.

WOMAN I
(Thoughtfully)
If Ruth's with child, and she bear
Boaz a son, then the rest of the story of King—of
Messiah—will equally come true. Whatever we say...

WOMAN II
But not in our day. Not in our day.

Guitar
Chords and behind

NARRATOR
From Boaz until David came, Ruth slept
While the world worked, saw, sorrowed and begot,
And Obed and Jesse were her sons, but not,
Not for the likes of these have women wept.
(A pause)
Then David came and David was made King
And one brought word to Ruth of him....

RUTH
His time has come then. Shall I stand amazed
Or shall I feign honest bewilderment?
But royal blood has found out royal blood.
I am not one to dazzle at a crown.

MAN
They say
David's mouth is ever at God's ear.

WOMAN
He's so familiar with God,
Much of the time he never even thinks of him.

MAN
And David's prayer goes up delightfully,
Not as a burden to him, but a song.

RUTH
That gift of singing David had from me.
His charm I likewise know ...
But as a sin most subtly dangerous
To his friends, his nation, and his character.

MAN
He's not only King they say, but hath in many a
Creditable source been named Messiah!

RUTH
(Wonderingly) Messiah! (Pause) What are his traits
To serve as witnesses? What *is* Messiah?

NARRATOR
Alone now, Naomi long since dead, Ruth held dialog with herself.
    ... With God if you prefer, then call it prayer.

RUTH
What is Messiah? He is more than me.
Whom might we find more royally equipped
Than David? Lived there such a one?
Never in this world! Shall a man be born
And have no spot in him? ...
But then Messiah must be a denial of fact.
All rests with God; this too may come to pass.
It must be possible, or prophecy
Had been proved false at the beginning of time
And prophecy is known for coming true!
When is Messiah? Not till the future to come.
Reason will not abide the thought of him
In the present tense.
Messiah is salvation for our children's
Children's, children's children, never for us.
(A pause)
What then shall I do?

I shall spread out my skirts, and sit, and wait. . . .
Waiting—for whom? For David's seed?
Even my people might not live so long!
Sense of the ultimate is what I need
And no more to be bankrupt by a song.
(A pause . . . she sighs)
Truly the one for whom I wait is God.

MAN
(Quietly, ever so slight echo)
Quietly, Ruth, though you wait for the Lord
And He continues to hide His face from you,
Has He not waited equally long for Ruth?

Guitar
A few chords . . . sneak behind

RUTH
I looked for Him to come from afar off.
I waited for His footsteps in the square.
And all the time He was as near to me
As David, and I could not see Him there.

I was thick-witted but ready of heart.
It took the Lord a century to pierce
My stubborn mind, but I would have you write
That though I met with no response for years
Morning and evening it was my delight
To follow my God's reason out of sight.

Guitar
Some very strong chords of affirmation and down behind

SINGER
Neither for David nor for Ruth, but for
His glory only, hath the Lord done this.
Whatever he does, be sure His reason is
That all men may perceive Him, and adore. . . .
Extolled and blessed be the Name of the Lord;
Honored, exalted, glorified, adored!

Guitar

NARRATOR

The story of Ruth is timeless, for at its core are the ever-present issues of the human heart. And chief of these are the capacity for love, the possibility of loyalty, and the hunger for God, or, in the author's phrasing, "the sense of the ultimate." Clearly, these three are related one to the other, much as the seed finds fulfillment in the plant, and as the plant flowers into bloom. Of this progression, our poem is dramatic, vivid illustration.

Ruth's love for Naomi prompts her to plead, "Will you become my mother in all truth?" This is no barren sentiment. It issues into her insistent resolve to share, no matter what the burdens. Naomi's reminders of these are powerless to dissuade. To these, Ruth replies: "Whither you go, I go. Where you shall dwell, I dwell." And, finally, "I would accept your people for my people, and I would want your God to be my God." Thus, out of the seed of love, there grows the sturdy plant of loyalty, and loyalty unbounded must needs seek the presence of its ultimate source and goal—God, as the river must run down to the sea.

In faltering, broken rhythm, of which the story of Ruth is the perfect rhythm, we live our lives. Love, if it be authentic, ripens into loyalty and responsibility. Those whom we truly love and the things profoundly precious to us, we would make ourselves responsible for. And yet, loyalty is no displacement of love. It holds it within its embrace. But if it be loyalty and not mere partisanship, it tends to grow and will not cease until in its outreaching it nears the precincts of God. Thus Ruth concludes, "Truly, the One for whom I wait is God."

Many of us, alas, have lost the way to God, and stumble now in paths that are no paths. A world at dead end, where else can it go but back—and pick up the trail again—a trail that begins within the confines of the heart and leads on to the broad places where the spirit of God hovers over a humanity held in His embrace.

CURTAIN

PRODUCTION NOTE:

Though living in antiquity, these people of the Bible are as real as our own neighbors. The dialog, though blank verse, should be treated as ordinary speech. *Boaz* is a pious, upright man who has lived with and made friends with disappointment. His brother, *Elimelech*, is glib and somewhat unctuous, only at the end when he faces the tragedy he has wrought does he put aside the hypocrisy that cloaks him. *Naomi*, his wife, is a woman of stern purpose in painful contrast to the weakness of her husband and sons. The sons, *Mahlon* and *Chilion*, are likeable but shallow. Ruth is a poem, "more gold than gold is, fair as is God's sun." The *Narrator* should be able to handle blank verse as if he were talking to you in your living room.

A *guitar* is the only music. It is lyric with a trace of the Oriental, but of this world rather than mysterious.

WHAT IS TORAH?

Judith and Ira Eisenstein[*]

"and gave us the Torah"...
—Torah...
—Torah... what's that?...
—what's the Torah...
—Is it a book?...

NO—not exactly...
—Is it a law...
NO—not exactly...
—Is it a story...
      more than that...

Torah is a book, yes, it's an idea, a code, a law, a vision, a history... a way of life...

Torah is *THE CREATION OF THE WORLD*

—the chaos of matter lying inert until the breath of a divine spirit moves over it, stirring it to life, to harmony, to form, creating the hills and valleys, the rivers, streams, oceans, the birds, the fish, the beasts, the fowl, the trees and grass, the desert and lush foliage, the stars, the moon, the sun, corn, the fruit... and man, fashioned in the image of the Creator, creature and co-worker with God...

—Torah is the Sabbath, the day when heads are lifted from the grindstone, from the lathe, from the typewriter, when aching limbs are stretched in languorous ease, when the soul comes up from its lethargy and sees the world again... sees that it is good, very good... despite the tumult and the shouting that is momentarily gone...

      and the candles?
      and the hallah?
      and the kiddush cup that is full to the brim?
      and the soft chanting of a tune?

---

[*] This is only the verbal text of a Cantata with complete musical score for unison chorus and piano, published by the Jewish Reconstructionist Foundation and available through its office for $1.50.

WHAT IS TORAH?
—the Torah is a pastoral life, of ancestral shepherds, pushing on slowly . . . eastward to fertile lands . . . where the grass is greener and taller . . . resting in the cool of night . . . and round a fire dreaming dreams of a people that shall arise . . .

>AND I WILL MAKE THEE A GREAT NATION
>AND I WILL BLESS THEE
>AND MAKE THY NAME GREAT
>AND BE THOU A BLESSING . . .
>
>UNTO THY SEED WILL I GIVE THIS LAND . . .
>BE THOU A BLESSING . . .

WHAT IS TORAH?
It is the anguish of a people enslaved . . .
—building bricks without straw . . .
—baby boys thrown into the Nile . . .
—taskmasters . . .
—whippings . . . huge stones rising as pyramids . . . storehouses
—groaning . . .
—crying aloud to God for rest, for peace . . .

>FOR FREEDOM . . .

It is the soul of a man who went out to see his people, to share their sorrows, to lift their burden . . .
To feel burning in his marrow, the fire of FREEDOM . . . the fire that warms, and energizes, but does not consume . . .

It is the defiance of Pharaoh . . .
—the obstinate heart . . .
—the determined leader . . .
—the people bowed down . . .
—the cruel oppressor . . .

IT IS THE PEOPLE ON THE MARCH . . . away, away from the pit, the chains, the sweat and the toil . . . free . . .

—ADONAI IS THE GOD OF FREEDOM . . .
—HE IS THE REDEEMER . . .

WHAT IS TORAH?
—It is Abraham's compassion for the innocent of Sodom...
—It is Jacob's love for Rachel, that made the years fly by...
—It is Joseph's forgiveness, when his brothers had wronged him
—It is...
  THOU SHALT LOVE THY NEIGHBOR AS THYSELF...
  THOU SHALT NOT TAKE THE NAME OF GOD IN VAIN...
  REMEMBER THE SABBATH DAY TO KEEP IT HOLY...
  HONOR THY FATHER AND THY MOTHER...
  THOU SHALT NOT MURDER...
  THOU SHALT NOT COMMIT ADULTERY...
  THOU SHALT NOT STEAL...
  THOU SHALT NOT BEAR FALSE WITNESS...
  THOU SHALT NOT COVET THAT WHICH IS THY NEIGHBOR'S...

—Remember: you were slaves in the land of Egypt...
—The stranger that sojourneth with you shall be as a native among you...
—If thy brother become poor, thou shalt uphold him...
—Ye shall not deal falsely... nor lie to one another...
—The wages of a hired servant shall not abide until the morning...
—Thou shalt not curse the deaf... nor put a stumbling block before the blind.
—IN RIGHTEOUSNESS SHALT THOU JUDGE THY NEIGHBOR...
—Thou shalt not go up and down as a tale bearer among thy people...
—Thou shalt not take vengeance nor bear any grudge...
THOU SHALT NOT HATE THY BROTHER IN THY HEART...
—Ye shall be holy...

WHAT IS TORAH?
Torah is a scroll... some rolls of parchment with writing on it...
—Sometimes it is wrapped in a simple cloak...
—Sometimes it is bedecked with jewels and breastplate, and a solemn crown...

The scroll is proudly held aloft for all the congregation to see... The scroll is carried around the crowded synagogue... for little children to kiss... for grandmothers to weep over... for straight young men to salute...

It is a flag... leading an army of peace...
—dance with it... sing with it... and on Simhat Torah, clasp it in your arms, whirl in ecstasy of joy, singing, shouting, dancing, dancing...

It is a scroll...
—when the mad, sadistic foe throw firebrands into the sacred place, and flames roar and crackle, they wrap the tallit about their faces, crash into the blazing sanctuary, rip the doors of the ark apart, and take that scroll into their scorched arms, to their burning breasts...

> All else may perish...
> All else is nought... the scroll is saved...
> And Israel bears it to a new abode...

WHAT IS TORAH?

It is a little room with many little boys... and a man who teaches them...
—kometz, alef, oh...
Yes, my little ones, the holy letters... they flew to heaven when the Temple was destroyed...
> The letters flew to heaven?

Yes, floated in the air... the letters floated in air...
Again, little ones, again: KOMETZ ALEF OH...
Learn the letters well, for they are drenched with tears...
They are carved out of the flesh of martyrs...
Learn them well...
KOMETZ ALEF OH...

Torah... is a dim bet hamidrash... a lone kabbalist, in mystic contemplation, searches out the hidden thought... he gropes for the infinite, the En Sof, the ineffable one... striving, straining to reach out, to grasp the hem of the garment, the edge of the divine throne... to wrest the secret of the Almighty...

Torah ... it is the modest study of the Rav who sways in slow and pious rhythm over the Talmud,

> he is the judge,
> the scholar,
> he is humble, and calm and wise ...

Torah ... it is the mother crooning over her babe ... soothing him to sleep ... "grow to learn Torah,—it is the best of all the worldly goods that you may have ..."

Torah ... it is the prayer of every Jew that learning may abide with him, and with his children after him ... that the word of God may not depart ... that the spirit of knowledge may blossom and flourish ...

WHAT IS TORAH?

Torah is the land, the soil, mother earth ...
—Eretz Yisrael ...
> the land that binds Israel to God ...
> the land that Moses could not see except from afar, from the heights of Neboh ...
> the land flowing with milk and honey ...
> the land of Joshua, Samson, David ...

—It is the land that empires covet ... Pharaoh, Nebuchadnezzar, Alexander, Titus ...
—It is the Temple site, in ruins, as Jeremiah sighs over the glory that is departed ...
—It is a small band of exiles sitting by the river's edge in Babylon, without a song on their lips ...
—It is fiery Ezekiel, stirred by the vision of a valley, filled with dry bones which come to life again ...
—It is the marching song of triumphant exiles returning, returning ...
—It is the hushed throng watching the foundations of the new Temple laid ...
—It is the Maccabean guerillas ...
—It is a relentless Roman phalanx ...
—It is a flaming Temple again ... and little Yabne gathering to study ...

—It is Bar Kokhba...
—It is the long, long exile, filled with dreams of Yerushalayim shel ma-aloh.

WHAT IS TORAH?

It is the great awakening... It is
THEODOR HERZL...

—the Zionist Congress... Jewish State... Max Nordau... Menachem Mendel Ussishkin... Chaim Weizmann... halutzim ... Henrietta Szold... Daganiah... Hadassah... the Balfour Declaration... Tel Aviv... industry... University... Nahalal... En Harod... Keren Kayemet... halutzim... halutzim...

The Torah of work... of sturdy limbs... of hardened hands ... of bronzed faces... AVODAH...

WHAT IS TORAH?

The Torah is Israel's gift to humanity .. the inspiration of poets, statesmen, religious leaders, scholars...

The Torah is the impress of Israel upon the civilization of mankind...

The Torah is the cornerstone of the great western religions...

The Torah is the inspiration of modern ideals of freedom, equality, justice...

Torah is the hope of the Negro people, plunged into poverty and despair...

In all their tragic years upon this continent, the memory of Israel's struggle has kept their faith alive...

It is Lincoln's "fourscore and seven years ago..."

It is Franklin Delano Roosevelt saying, "We are inspired by a faith which goes back all the years to the first chapter of Genesis: 'God created man in His own image.' We on our side, are striving to be true to that divine heritage. We are fighting, as our fathers fought, to uphold the doctrine that all men are equal in the sight of God."

WHAT IS TORAH?

—Torah is the Creation of the world ...
—Torah is the Sabbath ...
—Torah is the pastoral life ...
—Torah is the epic of Egyptian slavery and emancipation ...
—Torah is ethical idealism ...
—Torah is a parchment scroll ...
—Torah is a study room, a lullaby, a prayer ...
—Torah is a land ...
—Torah is a light unto the nations ...

WE THANK THEE O OUR GOD FOR THE TORAH WHICH THOU GAVEST UNTO OUR FATHERS. MAY WE EVER CHERISH IT ... GUARD IT ... LEARN IT ... PROTECT IT ... ADVANCE IT ...

FOR IT IS OUR LIFE AND THE LENGTH OF OUR DAYS ..

FINALE

TORAH LIGHT AND THE STARS
A Legend

"Come, my child," grandfather said to me on Shevuot night, "let us go outdoors for a little while."

I put my hand in his warm hand and we walked out.

"Look up, my son," grandfather said. "See the stars. They are small but they have always existed. If we understood them they would tell us many wonderful things which have happened in the heavens above and on the earth below since the world was created. They saw with their eyes of light the giving of the Torah on Mount Sinai. The stars did not want the Torah to be taken down to earth, and they pleaded with God. 'Here in heaven it is bright and holy,' they said. 'Here there are kind, pure angels, shining stars, the sun with its golden rays that gives light and warmth. The earth below is a dark ball, black as night. There is little light on the earth, little warmth, and there are many people upon it who are wicked.'

"Morning came and the stars were silent," grandfather continued. "Then the voice of God was heard: 'The earth is cold and dark. Therefore I am giving the Torah, that it may be warm and light. It has no stars. Therefore I am sending the Torah to the earth. The people will study my Torah, and there will be wise, learned men among them who will bring light and wisdom to the people, and they will be like stars among them. There are no angels on the earth. Therefore, will I raise up children who will be as good and pure and full of love as angels. Then the cold dark earth will be like paradise and it will shine as brightly as the sun and the stars in heaven.'

"And the voice of God was heard from one end of the world to the other. The children of Israel standing at Mount Sinai heard the voice of God. They heard the Ten Commandments. Then, Moses went up on Mount Sinai and brought down the Two Tablets of the Law on which the Ten Commandments were written. Since that time, the stars look down upon the earth every night with sadness and longing. They long for the light of the Torah."

PRODUCTION NOTE:

This legend can readily be dramatized simply and effectively by having an older boy with a deep resonant voice portray the grandfather (preferably in character make-up) and a boy, aged five or six, act as the child.

The narration lines can be enacted; the scene placed in an outdoor setting—a park or garden. A backdrop with a bench prop would serve adequately.

The scene, if possible, should be lit by bright moonlight.

On opening, the grandfather and child are found strolling hand in hand. They pause and stand, gazing up at the sky, grandfather embracing the child, his arm around child's shoulders.

Then, on the line: "The stars did not want the Torah to be taken down to earth" the grandfather sits on the bench, and the boy sits beside him, either on the ground or on a rock, looking up at him—fascinated, absorbed, listening intently.

The actors should, of course, face front. Grandfather establishes the sky and stars by pointing to the ceiling of the auditorium's back wall, and involves the audience, as though he were relating the legend to them too.

GOD'S LOVE
Meir b. Isaac Nehorai

Could we with ink the ocean fill,
Were every blade of grass a quill,
Were the world of parchment made,
And every man a scribe by trade,
   To write the love
   of God above
Would drain the ocean dry;
   Nor would the scroll
   Contain the whole,
Though stretched from sky to sky.

SHECHINA
Herb Brin

Upon the wild wind, Shechina
Upon the cold wind, Shechina
Upon the slant of a lonely hill
Upon a shadow: Shechina!

Upon the tall grass, His Presence
Upon the wild grass, His Presence
Upon the seed in a gnarled hand
Cast upon earth, His Presence.

Upon the shattering thunder: Shechina!
Upon the churning sea
Upon the frost of a day in birth
Upon the wing of a distant bird ...

Shechina, on the face of a child
The smile in beauty, Shechina
The caress of a tender night,
The sigh of love, Shechina.

Shechina, in the beginning
And in the end
Shechina.

From *Wild Flowers*

WHERE GOD IS FOUND

God, where shall I find Thee,
Whose glory fills the universe?
Behold I find Thee
Wherever the mind is free to follow its own bent,
Wherever words come out from the depth of truth,
Wherever tireless striving stretches its arms toward perfection,
Wherever men struggle for freedom and right,
Wherever the scientist toils to unbare the secrets of nature,
Wherever the poet strings pearls of beauty in lyric lines,
Wherever glorious deeds are done.

From the *Reconstructionist Prayer Book*

THE OMNIPRESENCE OF GOD*

Adapted by Nahum N. Glatzer from the Midrash

THE BURNING BUSH:
    And the angel of the Lord
    appeared unto him in a flame of
    fire out of the midst of a bush.
    A heathen asked Rabbi Joshua ben Karhah:
    "Why did the Holy One, blessed
    be He, choose to speak
    to Moses out of the midst of a
    thornbush?"
    The rabbi answered him:
    "Had it been out of the midst of
    a carob tree or out of the midst
    of a sycamore, you would have
    asked the same question.
    Still, I cannot send you away empty-handed.
    Well then: Why out of the midst of a thornbush?
    To teach you that there is no place void of the
    Presence of God, not even a thornbush!"

---

*Reprinted by permission of Schocken Books Inc. from a *Jewish Reader: In Time and Eternity,* edited by Nahum N. Glatzer, copyright 1946, 1961.

THE BOOK
Heinrich Heine

The Bible, what a book! Large and wide as the world, based on the abysses of creation, and peering aloft into the blue secrets of heaven; sunrise and sunset, promise and fulfillment, birth and death, the whole drama of humanity are contained in this one book. It is the book of God. The Jews may readily be consoled at the loss of Jerusalem, and the Temple, and the Ark of the Covenant, and all the crown jewels of King Solomon. Such forfeiture is as naught when weighed against the Bible, the indestructible treasure that they had saved. That one book is to the Jews their country, their possessions—at once their ruler and their weal and woe. Within the well-fenced boundaries of that book they live and have their being; they enjoy their alienable citizenship, are strong to admiration; thence none can dislodge them. Absorbed in the perusal of their sacred book, they little heeded the changes that were wrought in the real world around them. Nations rose and vanished, states flourished and decayed, revolutions raged throughout the earth—but they, the Jews, sat poring over this book, unconscious of the wild chase of time that rushed on above their heads.

(Trans. by Ludwig Boerne)

GIFTS

Emma Lazarus

"Oh, World-God, give me Wealth!" the Egyptian cried.
　　His prayer was granted. High as heaven, behold
Palace and Pyramid; the brimming tide
　　Of lavish Nile washed all his land with gold.
Armies of slaves toiled ant-wise at his feet;
World-circling traffic roared through mart and street;
His priests were gods; his spice-balmed kings enshrined,
　　Set death at naught in rock-ribbed charnels deep.
Seek Pharaoh's race today, and ye shall find
　　Rust and the moth, silence and dusty sleep.

"Oh, World-God, give me Beauty!" cried the Greek.
　　His prayer was granted. All the earth became
Plastic and vocal to his sense; each peak,
　　Each grove, each stream, quick with Promethean flame,
Peopled the world with imaged grace and light.
The lyre was his, and his the breathing might
Of the immortal marble; his the play
　　Of diamond-pointed thought and golden tongue.
Go seek the sunshine-race, ye find today
　　A broken column and a lute unstrung.

"Oh, World-God, give me Power!" the Roman cried.
　　His prayer was granted. The vast world was chained
A captive to the chariot of his pride.
　　The blood of myriad provinces was drained
To feed that fierce, insatiable red heart.
Invulnerably bulwarked every part
With serried legions and with close-meshed Code;
　　Within, the burrowing worm had gnawed its home;
A roofless ruin stands where once abode
　　Th' imperial race of everlasting Rome.

"Oh, Godhead, give me Truth!" the Hebrew cried.
　　His prayer was granted. He became the slave
Of the Idea, a pilgrim far and wide,
　　Cursed, hated, spurned, and scourged with none to save.

The Pharaohs knew him, and when Greece beheld,
His wisdom wore the hoary crown of Eld.
Beauty he hath forsworn, and Wealth and Power.
 Seek him today, and find in every land;
No fire consumes him, neither floods devour;
 Immortal through the lamp within his hand.

Psalm 136
HIS LOVE IS EVERLASTING

Give thanks to the Lord; He is good;
    His love is everlasting!
Give thanks to the Supreme God;
    His love is everlasting!

Give thanks to the Supreme Lord;
    His love is everlasting!
To Him who alone performed great wonders;
    His love is everlasting!

To Him whose wisdom made the heavens;
    His love is everlasting!
To Him who suspended the earth over waters;
    His love is everlasting!

To Him who made the great luminaries;
    His love is everlasting!
The sun He made to rule by day;
    His love is everlasting!

The moon and the stars to rule by night;
    His love is everlasting!
To Him who smote the Egyptian first-born;
    His love is everlasting!

Who delivered Israel from their midst,
    His love is everlasting!
With strong hand and upraised arm;
    His love is everlasting!

To Him who split the Red Sea;
    His love is everlasting!
Who led Israel through its waters;
    His love is everlasting!

Who drowned Pharaoh and his host therein;
    His love is everlasting!
To Him who led His people in the desert;
    His love is everlasting!

To Him who brought low renowned rulers;
His love is everlasting!
To Him who struck down mighty kings;
His love is everlasting!

He smote Sihon, King of the Amorites;
His love is everlasting!
He humbled Og, King of Bashan;
His love is everlasting!

He gave their lands as a heritage;
His love is everlasting!
As a heritage to Israel, His servant;
His love is everlasting!

He remembered us when we were low;
His love is everlasting!
He rescued us from our enemies;
His love is everlasting!

He provides sustenance for all flesh;
His love is everlasting!
Give thanks to the God of heaven;
His love is everlasting!

PRODUCTION NOTE:

Six or more participants can be activated in the rendition of this Psalm, by doing it as a choral reading.

Two narrators with good resonant voices, from the older age group, recite the main body of the Psalm. Narrator I, placed down stage right, at proscenium, delivers stanzas 1, 3, 5, 7, 9, 11 and 13. Narrator II, downstage left, does stanzas 2, 4, 6, 8, 10 and 12. The text, of course, should be memorized, and two or three rehearsals should be held.

A "chorus" of 4 to 6 younger children, placed upstage center in a semicircle, say the second and fourth lines of each stanza: "His love is everlasting!" in unison, slowly and with dedicated conviction. During the lines given by Narrators I and II, members of chorus should stand quietly in repose, listening, and pick up their cues rapidly.

"Chorus" should be chosen for clearness of diction and a wide range of voice quality.

MELODIES OF ISRAEL
Zalman Shneour

Where is there a holy book in which
    you do not hear
The swish of Jordan's waters and the
    rustle of the Lebanon?
Where is there a chapel or a shrine
Wherein you do not catch the echo
Of the son of Amram's voice or
    Psalms of David's praise?
Where is the canvas, marble or
    the bronze
Which does not speak the language
    of the ancients—
The low-voiced stirring of awakening
    matter
That heartfelt something of my
    treasured prophets
And the dreams and visions of
    their light,
The gentle dropping of Creation's
    dew
From out the pages of our Genesis,
The sad-sweet vintage of Kohelet
The exultation of the Song of Songs?

    . . . .

Selections for American Holidays

American Holidays

Classification	Title	Author	Age Level
LINCOLN'S BIRTHDAY			
1. Poem	Two to Remember	Dorothy Ross	8-13
2. Reading	The Significance of the Day	Mordecai Kaplan J. Paul Williams Eugene Kohn	12-16
3. Reading	The Gettysburg Address	Abraham Lincoln	12-16
4. Reading	The Emancipation Proclamation	Abraham Lincoln	12-16
JULY THE FOURTH			
1. Poem or Song	To Him from Whom Our Blessings Flow	Anonymous	8-14
2. Reading	Declaration of Independence		10-16
3. Reading	The Significance of Independence Day	Mordecai Kaplan J. Paul Williams Eugene Kohn	12-16
4. Dramatic Reading with music	Freedom Means All of Us Everywhere	Unknown	12-16
5. Poem for Song	Men, Whose Boast It Is	James Russell Lowell	12-16
6. Dramatic Pageant with musical interludes	Americans All	Frances Johnson Jules Heller	12-16
7. Reading	Prayer That America Fulfill the Promise of Its Founding		12-16
8. Poem	God Called It America	Abba Hillel Silver	10-14
9. Dramatic Reading with musical interludes and dance sequences	America Sings	Margaret Morrow	10-16
10. Reading	I Am an American	Stephen S. Wise	12-16
11. Dramatic Pageant with musical interludes	I Hear America Singing!	Unknown	10-16
12. Reading (Prayer)	The Spiritual Heritage of America		12-16
COLUMBUS DAY			
1. Reading	The Significance of Columbus Day	Mordecai Kaplan J. Paul Williams Eugene Kohn	10-16

Please refer to:
AMERICAN-JEWISH HISTORY CATEGORY
for suitable material, viz:
    A TWO-FOLD BLESSING
    FROM THE DAYS OF COLUMBUS
    THE DISCOVERY OF THE "TU-KEY"

Classification	Title	Author	Age Level
THANKSGIVING DAY			
1. Reading	The Significance of Thanksgiving Day	Mordecai Kaplan J. Paul Williams Eugene Kohn	10-16
2. Poem for Song	Now Sing We a Song	John W. Chadwick	8-14
3. Choral Reading	Thanks for the Blessings of Home	Mordecai Kaplan J. Paul Williams Eugene Kohn	12-16

Lincoln's Birthday

TWO TO REMEMBER*
Dorothy Ross

There were thousands of years between them,
And miles and miles of space;
Yet both are remembered as leaders
Who inspired the human race.

> The first was plucked from a river
> And saved by a princess' hand—
> The second grew up in a cabin
> Loving his people and land.

> Each tried to create out of many
> A people united as one;
> Each started his folk on their journey;
> Each died before it was done...

There were thousands of years between them,
Yet both had the vision to see
That each man must care for his brother
And all men on earth must be free!

*From *Young Judaean*

PRODUCTION NOTE:

If facilities permit, superimpose blow-ups of photographs, or reproductions of paintings of Moses and Abraham Lincoln on a screen, as a background during reading of poem. If this is not possible, hang large photographs or reproductions of portaits of Moses and Abraham Lincoln on backstage wall or backdrop.

THE SIGNIFICANCE OF THE DAY*
Mordecai Kaplan, J. Paul Williams and Eugene Kohn

This day is gratefully dedicated to the remembrance of Abraham Lincoln, who led the United States through four years of civil strife to keep the nation one, and who used the power of his office to free the Negroes from slavery. His memory is both an inspiration and a challenge. It inspires us to dedicate our lives as he did his, to freeing the bound. It challenges us to make of our country a land in which all men are accepted by their fellow men for what they are and for what they can make of themselves.

We are wont in family life to accept our brother; we assume his right to be himself, to seek his own welfare in his own way; we ask of him only that he share with us a common devotion to the family. So let us in our public life accept our fellow man in brotherhood. Let us acknowledge his right to his own interests, his own beliefs, his own loyalties. Let us ask of him only that he share with us a common devotion to the cause of all humanity.

Ours is a nation built by men of different races, different faiths, different cultural traditions. To recognize all of them as our brothers is to show respect for their right to be different from us. It is to learn to value the special contribution which each can bring to the common cause. It is to welcome his cooperation in the building of a common civilization. That civilization should be great enough to embrace all the diversities among us. Let us make America safe for differences and liberate all those who today are oppressed by unbrotherly prejudice and rancor. Thus and thus only can we honor the memory of Abraham Lincoln and bring victory to the cause for which he lived and died.

---

* From *The Faith of America* published by Jewish Reconstructionist Foundation.

THE GETTYSBURG ADDRESS

Fourscore and seven years ago our fathers brought forth on this continent a new nation, conceived in liberty, and dedicated to the proposition that all men are created equal.

Now we are engaged in a great civil war, testing whether that nation, or any nation so conceived and so dedicated, can long endure. We are met on a great battlefield of that war. We have come to dedicate a portion of that field as a final resting-place for those who here gave their lives that that nation might live. It is altogether fitting and proper that we should do this.

But, in a larger sense, we cannot dedicate—we cannot consecrate—we cannot hallow—this ground. The brave men, living and dead, who struggled here, have consecrated it far above our poor power to add or detract. The world will little note nor long remember what we say here, but it can never forget what they did here. It is for us, the living, rather, to be dedicated here to the unfinished work which they who fought here have thus far so nobly advanced. It is rather for us to be here dedicated to the great task remaining before us—that from these honored dead we take increased devotion to that cause for which they gave the last full measure of devotion; that we here highly resolve that these dead shall not have died in vain; that this nation, under God, shall have a new birth of freedom; and that government of the people, by the people, for the people, shall not perish from the earth.

THE EMANCIPATION PROCLAMATION

The crowning achievement of Abraham Lincoln's career was the emancipation of the Negro slave. That emancipation was not achieved at one stroke. Indeed, there is still much that remains to be done before the Negro can be said to enjoy the same freedom of opportunity as the white man. The great initial step, however, in the liberation of the Negro from slavery was the Emancipation Proclamation. Let us read the salient portions of that proclamation.*

Whereas, on the twenty-second day of September, in the year ... one thousand eight hundred and sixty-two, a proclamation was issued by the President of the United States, containing, among other things, the following, to wit:

"That on the first day of January, in the year ... one thousand eight hundred and sixty-three, all persons held as slaves within any state, or designated part of a State, the people whereof shall then be in rebellion against the United States, shall be then, thenceforward, and forever free."

Now, therefore, I, Abraham Lincoln, President of the United States, by virtue of the power in me vested as commander-in-chief of the army and navy of the United States, in time of actual armed rebellion against the authority and government of the United States, and as a fit and necessary war measure for suppressing said rebellion, ... do order and declare that all persons held as slaves within said designated States and parts of States are, and henceforward shall be, free; and that the Executive Government of the United States, including the military and naval authorities thereof, will recognize and maintain the freedom of said persons.

And I hereby enjoin upon the people so declared to be free to abstain from all violence, unless in necessary self-defense; and I recommend to them that, in all cases when allowed, they labor faithfully for reasonable wages.

---

* Introductory note by Mordecai Kaplan, J. Paul Williams and Eugene Kohn from *The Faith of America* published by the Jewish Reconstructionist Foundation.

And I further declare and make known that such persons of suitable condition will be received into the armed service of the United States to garrison forts, positions, stations, and other places, and to man vessels of all sorts in said service.

And upon this act, sincerely believed to be an act of justice, warranted by the Constitution upon military necessity, I invoke the considerate judgment of mankind and the gracious favor of Almighty God.

July the Fourth

TO HIM FROM WHOM OUR BLESSINGS FLOW*

Anonymous

To Him from Whom our blessings flow,
Who all our wants supplies,
This day the choral song and vow
From grateful hearts shall rise.

'Twas He who led the pilgrim band
Across the stormy sea;
'Twas He who stayed the tyrant's hand.
And set our country free.

Be Thou our nation's strength and shield
In manhood and in youth;
Thine arm for our protection wield,
And guide us by Thy truth.

---

* The music for this poem can be found on page 228, in *Hymns for the Living Age*, published by Fleming H. Revell Company, Westwood, N. J.

DECLARATION OF INDEPENDENCE

On the fourth of July, in the year 1776, a new nation was born, the United States of America, conceived in liberty and dedicated to the proposition that all men are created equal. Their faith and vision the Founding Fathers expressed in a solemn Declaration of Independence. That Declaration set forth the principles which moved them to establish the former British colonies as an independent union of states. It is well that on the anniversary of this event we be reminded of the spiritual foundations of our Republic, and that we renew from year to year our allegiance to them. Let us then rise and listen to the words of that epoch-making Declaration.*

The assembly rises

WE HOLD THESE TRUTHS TO BE SELF-EVIDENT: that all men are created equal; that they are endowed by their Creator with certain unalienable rights; that among these are life, liberty and the pursuit of happiness; that to secure these rights, governments are instituted among men, deriving their just powers from the consent of the governed; that whenever any form of government becomes destructive of these ends, it is the right of the people to alter or to abolish it, and to institute new government, laying its foundation on such principles and organizing its powers in such form, as to them shall seem most likely to effect their safety and happiness. ...

"We, therefore, the representatives of the United States of America, in general congress assembled, appealing to the Supreme Judge of the world for the rectitude of our intentions, do, in the name, and by the authority of the good people of these colonies, solemnly publish and declare that these United Colonies are, and of right ought to be, free and independent States.

---

* Introductory paragraph by Mordecai Kaplan, J. Paul Williams and Eugene Kohn from *The Faith of America*, published by the Jewish Reconstructionist Foundation.

... And for the support of this Declaration, with a firm reliance on the protection of Divine Providence, we mutually pledge to each other our lives, our fortune and our sacred honor."

The assembly is seated

THE SIGNIFICANCE OF INDEPENDENCE DAY*

Mordecai Kaplan, J. Paul Williams and Eugene Kohn

Our fathers' God, Author of Liberty, who desirest that all men be free to serve Thee and that none be constrained to serve other masters, we thank Thee for the liberty that our nation achieved in the war for independence. Thou hast endowed all men equally with the right to life, to liberty, and to the pursuit of happiness. Teach us to respect the rights of others and to assert our own rights in accordance with Thy will. May we never abuse our liberties by employing them to our own advantage while depriving others of the opportunity to realize their just desires and hopes.

May we never forfeit our liberties by permitting our minds to be enslaved to error, superstition, or prejudice, or our wills to yield to the promptings of cowardice or self-indulgence. May we ever expand the area of human freedom by developing to the utmost and using for the good of all whatever powers Thou hast bestowed upon us. Let us ever cherish our nation's independence and the freedom of its institutions, so that our nation may serve Thee and Thy law of love and justice. AMEN.

---

* From *The Faith of America,* published by the Jewish Reconstructionist Foundation.

FREEDOM MEANS ALL OF US EVERYWHERE

CAST
Leader
Several Men
Several Women
Several Boys
Several Girls

America the Beautiful sung by the audience.
Pledge of Allegiance to the Flag by the audience.

LEADER: (Conversationally) Well, the parade is over. It was a good parade—as it should be. It should be good because this is the people's day. It is being celebrated in every city and every town and every hamlet all over the country. This is the day when we, the people—all the people—of the United States pay tribute to all the men and women in all the years of our history who have made our freedom. This is the day when we remember that freedom isn't easy. It isn't easy to get. And it isn't easy to keep.

MAN: (Clear and vigorous) Eternal vigilance is the price of liberty.

LEADER: Eternal vigilance—and the cold, sharp memory of the winning, the stern, cold duty of the keeping of liberty and justice—for ALL. It hasn't been easy and it hasn't been cheap. Let us remember how it began. Let us remember 1775 to 1783.

BAND: *Yankee Doodle*

MAN: (Thoughtfully) When in the course of human events, it becomes necessary for one people to dissolve the political bands which have connected them with another, and to assume among the powers of the earth the separate and equal station to which the Laws of Nature and of Nature's God entitle them, a decent respect to the opinions of mankind requires that they should declare the causes which impel them to the separation. We hold these truths to be self-evident, that all men are created equal, that they are endowed by their Creator with certain inalienable rights, that among these are Life, Liberty, and the pursuit of

Happiness. That to secure these rights, Governments are instituted among Men, deriving their just powers from the consent of the governed.

LEADER: Tom Jefferson didn't make freedom. The signers didn't make freedom. And the Liberty Bell didn't make freedom when it

WOMAN: (Triumphantly) Proclaimed liberty throughout the land.

LEADER: Freedom was the job of the people.

MAN: It took the people five long, struggling years; years of cold and death, years of raggedness and fear and homesickness and killing and discouragement. It took all these years and all these things and more—much more—to set our feet on the freedom road.

WOMAN: (Grumbling) It took longer because some were selfish and greedy and careless—because some couldn't see beyond their own noses.

MAN: It took longer because some didn't agree with Patrick Henry.

BOY: (Quickly—showing off a little) Give me liberty or give me death!

WOMAN: It took longer because some people didn't always remember that we all had to hang together or we'd all hang separately.

LEADER: It took longer because everybody didn't think that liberty means all of us. It took a long time. But in the end we were free.

BOY: Were we really free as soon as Cornwallis surrendered?

LEADER: You've got something there, son. We weren't free because we couldn't decide what was good for us. It took a lot of wrangling and bickering and quarreling before even the preamble to the Constitution was written—before we could put down on paper—

GIRL: (Reciting a lesson) We, the people of the United States, in order to form a more perfect Union, establish justice, insure domestic tranquility, provide for the common defense, promote the general welfare, and secure the blessings of liberty to ourselves and our posterity, do ordain and establish this Constitution for the United States of America.

LEADER: It took more years and more uncertainty before

we could write that and before we had the sense to make ourselves a Bill of Rights.

WOMAN: Freedom of religion and speech; freedom of the press and assembly and petition.

BOY: (Reading quickly, but clearly) Congress may make no law respecting an establishment of religion, or prohibiting the free exercise thereof; or abridging the freedom of speech or of the press; or of the right of the people peaceably to assemble and to petition the Government for a redress of grievances.

WOMAN: The right to bear arms

BOY: (Reading as above) A well-regulated militia being necessary to the security of a free State, the right of the people to keep and bear arms shall not be infringed.

WOMAN: Freedom from search and seizure.

MAN: The right of trial by jury.

LEADER: We wrote ourselves those liberties and then, I guess, we thought we had freedom for sure and we sat back to enjoy it—to make some kind of use of it. But we found it wasn't so easy. We, the people of the United States of America, had to *stay* free. We were a small country, not very strong, and there were plenty of other people who thought they could take advantage of us. Some people across the world thought they could make us pay to carry on our trade.

GIRL: (Stubbornly) Millions for defense, but not one cent for tribute.

LEADER: We said that and we made it stick. And, then, somehow, we got mixed up in a quarrel between England and France along about 1812. We didn't like the idea of our ships being searched and our sailors—peaceable men going about peaceable business—being taken off our ships and impressed into somebody else's navy. We didn't have much of a navy ourselves, but we did pretty well with what we had because the people meant to stay free.

BOY: I have not yet begun to fight!

LEADER: And all that time we were growing, pushing out westward. After 1815 other people left us alone awhile. But we were so busy expanding our nation that we forgot that freedom means everybody. We forgot in those years that we had put our name to a document that said ALL men are created free...

(*Each of the next phrases should be staccato, following quickly on one another and building in tempo and volume*)
BOY: Missouri Compromise
WOMAN: Dred Scott Decision
MAN: John Brown
WOMAN: States Rights
MAN: Secession
BAND: *Battle Hymn of the Republic*
LEADER: (Quietly and slowly) We couldn't seem to settle those disputes peaceably. We had to fight again—fight among ourselves with guns and swords, not just with words.
(*Same staccato and building technique as above*)
BOY: Bull Run
GIRL: Chickamauga
WOMAN: Lee and Jackson
MAN: Sherman and Grant
WHOLE CAST: LINCOLN!
LEADER: (Quietly and slowly) Yes, Lincoln. Lincoln and Douglas. Lincoln and the inaugurals. Lincoln—and Gettysburg.
BOY: Fourscore and seven years ago our fathers brought forth on this continent a new nation, conceived in liberty and dedicated to the proposition that all men are created equal. Now we are engaged in a great civil war, testing whether that nation or any nation so conceived and so dedicated can long endure. We are met on a great battlefield of that war. We have come to dedicate a portion of that field, as a final resting place for those who here gave their lives that that nation might live. It is altogether fitting and proper that we should do this. But, in a larger sense, we cannot dedicate—we cannot consecrate—we cannot hallow—this ground. The brave men, living and dead, who struggled here, have consecrated it, far above our poor power to add or detract. The world will little note, nor long remember, what we say here, but it can never forget what they did here. It is for us the living, rather, to be dedicated here to the unfinished work which they who fought here have thus far so nobly advanced. It is rather for us to be here dedicated to the great task remaining before us—that from these honored dead we take increased devotion to that cause for which they gave the last full measure of devotion—that we here highly resolve that these dead shall not have died in vain—that this nation, under God, shall have a new birth of freedom—and that

government of the people, by the people, for the people, shall not perish from the earth.

BAND: *Battle Hymn of the Republic*

LEADER: That bitterness passed and we started to grow again. The north and the south pushed out together and built the west. We built machines and railroads. Telegraphs and steamboats. Factories. We harnessed the winds and the waters to make our standard of living. We conquered space to bridge a continent and a world. But we still had to learn that liberty means ALL OF US—EVERYWHERE. We still had to learn that "freedom is a hard-bought thing."

(*In the following sequence the historical statements by the boy should be excited and quick, the responses bored and slow*)

BOY: 1914: Archduke Ferdinand assassinated!

WOMAN: Who's he?

BOY: Germany invades neutral Belgium!

MAN: None of our business. We're busy in Mexico. Don't let's mess with Europe's wars.

BOY: England declares war on Germany!

WOMAN: Another European squabble.

BOY: 1916: Verdun! Jutland! Submarine warfare!

MAN: Re-elect Woodrow Wilson. He kept us out of war.

BOY: 1917: Germany begins unrestricted submarine warfare!

WOMAN: This means us! War's declared.

BAND: *Over There*

LEADER: This was war. War to keep our freedom. Many of us—the people—were still not very much concerned with other people's troubles. We talked about making the world safe for democracy. But Czechoslovakia was just a long name nobody could spell.

MAN: (Considering and slow) Some of us were selfish and greedy and careless.

WOMAN: A lot of us couldn't see beyond our own noses.

BOY: Most of us forgot that all means everybody.

GIRL: (Quickly) A few of us remembered.

WOMAN: (Defensively) The boys who were fighting in France remembered.

MAN: (Belligerently) Woodrow Wilson didn't forget.

LEADER: No, Wilson didn't forget. Woodrow Wilson had ideas about the peace.

(*The next section should be taken at moderate tempo*)
GIRL: Open covenants openly arrived at.
BOY: Freedom of the seas.
BOY: No economic barriers.
MAN: Reduction of armaments.
WOMAN: A general association of nations to keep the peace.
GIRL: Territorial integrity.
BOY: Self-determination of people.
WOMAN: (Puzzled, as if to herself) That sounds familiar. I wonder why?
MAN: Maybe because of this. "That to secure these rights, Governments are instituted among Men, deriving their just powers from the consent of the governed."
WOMAN: That's it, the consent of the governed.
LEADER: We had fought a war. We had written a peace. We had honored the dead—the men who had come to know that freedom has to keep on growing, who had learned on the battlefields the stern, cold duty of keeping liberty and justice—for all. But a lot of us didn't believe—really believe—in what we had done. We only believed with our lips. A lot of us couldn't be bothered to keep the peace.
WOMAN: (Apologetically) It wasn't that we *wanted* another war.
MAN: (Thinking it out) It was just that we were too busy here at home. We were too busy about the business of high standards of living to bother about keeping the peace. I guess we kind of thought the peace would keep itself while we went about our jobs.
WOMAN: (Rather sadly) We drew back behind our ocean barriers and left the rest of the world to wag along in its own way.
WOMAN: (Angrily) You who talked about standards of living. It's plain to see that you didn't go through the depression.
WOMAN: You never lived in a slum or share-cropped a farm. Did you ever hear of Tobacco Road?
MAN: Don't you know that there are such things as underprivileged people, submarginal people, substandard living? Right here in the U.S.A.?
LEADER: Even at home we hadn't learned that freedom means all of us.
MAN: (Defensively) We learned a lot from the depression.

WOMAN: (Bitterly) We learned—or we ought to have learned, though some of us didn't seem to—that a Bill of Rights isn't much good to the hungry.

GIRL: To the homeless.

MAN: A Bill of Rights doesn't put clothes on your back or take despair out of your heart when you can't get work.

LEADER: We were beginning to learn. We were beginning to know that democracy spells responsibility as well as rights —responsibility for the other fellow—at home and abroad. It took another war to drive that lesson home.

BOY: It was a long time coming, but we didn't pay much attention.

WOMAN: Hitler becomes Chancellor of Germany!

MAN: (In a monotone) More automobiles.

WOMAN: Hitler reoccupies the Rhineland!

MAN: (Monotone) More radios.

WOMAN: Hitler persecutes the Jews!

MAN: (Monotone) More washing machines.

WOMAN: Austria! Czechoslovakia! Appeasement! Munich!

MAN: (Rather cynically) Peace in our time anyway.

LEADER: We the people were shocked. We the people shook our heads. We the people were smug behind our ocean barriers. We the people continued to do business with Hitler. This didn't touch us—not yet.

MAN: Poland invaded. Denmark. Norway. Holland and Belgium. France.

LEADER: It was coming closer.

WOMAN: No entangling alliances. Keep out of Europe's wars.

MAN: Dunkirk!

LEADER: Closer.

MAN: (Rich, full voice—slowly) We shall fight on the beaches. We shall fight in the hills. We shall fight in the streets. We shall never give up. Blood, sweat, and tears.

LEADER: That was England speaking. Not we the people of the United States of America.

WOMAN: Yes, that was England speaking. But the bombs and the blitzes and the concentration camps, the beatings and the starvings and the killings were getting under our skins. We were beginning to learn that England's peril was our peril; that

Europe's suffering was our suffering; that the enslavement of any people anywhere in the world was our problem.

MAN: Enough of us knew that. Enough of us wanted to assume that responsibility.

(*The next sections should be staccato*)

BOY: Destroyers for bases.

GIRL: Lend-lease.

WOMAN: Draft boards.

BOY: Trainees.

CAST: Pearl Harbor.

LEADER: (Slowly and quietly) Pearl Harbor shook us—the people, all the people. A Japanese submarine shelling the West Coast, air-raid spotters searching the skies for German planes, shattered the protection of our ocean barriers. Civilian Defense, war industries, broke open the barriers of money and class between man and man. We, the people, were glimpsing a better world through the dirty haze of war.

(*The next three speeches should build to a climax*)

WOMAN: Freedom from want.

MAN: Freedom from fear.

WOMAN: For everybody—everywhere.

WOMAN: The walls that shut us in are down ... blown out and away by the bombs dropped on London, the explosives in Amsterdam, the incendiaries at Manila, the jets over Seoul. Most of all—by the great mushrooming cloud over Hiroshima.

MAN: The walls are down. We, the people, know that there are many nations—but one world!

BOY: We, the people, know that freedom is for everybody everywhere.

LEADER: All the men and all the women who have fought and struggled, who have lived and died that liberty might be preserved have taught us that. This is their day. This is the day when the people in every city, in every town, in every village and hamlet and crossroads' store remember those men and those women. This is the day when we ... remembering them ... keep the cold sharp memory that

ENTIRE CAST: (Triumphantly) FREEDOM MEANS ALL OF US EVERYWHERE!!!

(*Star Spangled Banner* by audience)

PRODUCTION NOTE:

Freedom Means All of Us Everywhere is designed to be presented very simply. It should be tailored on the spot to fit the needs of the given group. It can be made into a longer, more elaborate production by using costumes and adding tableaux at likely points in the script. If a band is unavailable, the musical interludes can be tape-recorded or omitted. If a speech choir can render the music, the dramatic effect will be enhanced.

The participants can all stand on the stage, or the leader may appear there alone, with the rest of the cast "planted" in the audience and speaking from their places.

Special permission to include this script has been granted by the National Recreation Association on the proviso that it will not be reproduced. Copies are available at a minimal cost through the Association's Office.

MEN, WHOSE BOAST IT IS*

James Russell Lowell

Men, whose boast it is that ye
Come of fathers brave and free,
If there breathe on earth a slave,
Are ye truly free and brave?
If ye do not feel the chain
When it works a brother's pain,
Are ye not base slaves indeed,
Slaves unworthy to be freed?

Is true freedom but to break
Fetters for our own dear sake,
And with leathern hearts forget
That we owe mankind a debt?
No! true freedom is to share
All the chains our brothers wear,
And, with heart and hand, to be
Earnest to make others free.

They are slaves who fear to speak
For the fallen and the weak;
They are slaves who will not choose
Hatred, scoffing, and abuse,
Rather than in silence shrink
From the truth they needs must think;
They are slaves who dare not be
In the right with two or three. Amen.

---

*The music for this poem is to be found in *Hymns for the Living Age* (page 289), edited by H. Augustine Smith, published by The Fleming H. Revell Company, New York.

AMERICANS ALL*

Frances Johnson and Jules Heller

PRODUCTION NOTE:

A pageant emphasizing the contributions various nationalities have made to American culture. In communities where there is a concentration of nationality groups other than those mentioned here, additions or substitutions should be made to honor those groups.

The part of the Citizen, who reads all the lines, is taken by a narrator who stands at a lectern at one side of the stage. A soft light should be provided so that this narrator can see his script even though the stage is in darkness.

The Indian Council Fire tableau may be arranged at the back of the stage, behind curtains which part to reveal it at the proper time. At the end of the Indian dance, the braves seat themselves around the fire once more, and the curtains close. This arrangement will make it possible for the next scene to go on without a delay for clearing the stage.

A Citizen Speaks

Hello there. Nice evening, isn't it? Oh, don't bother looking around for me—I'm sitting right beside you. I'm the man in the row behind you wearing the straw hat, the boy up front with the baseball cap, the woman on your left in the light blue dress. I'm one of you. I'm all of you. Know why I came here tonight? Heard there were some goings on about all of us Americans. Isn't that why you came?

I'm a Frenchman, a Belgian, an Irishman, an Englishman, an Italian, an Indian; I'm all of you people. I've come from the smallest village and the largest city in any and every part of the world. Poland, Scotland, Switzerland, Holland, Spain. Why did I come?

I came because there is in the soul of every man a lifelong desire to obtain freedom—freedom of mind, of body, of spirit, of heart, of conscience. I couldn't get that freedom where I was; I found it in America; I'm an American, and the cultures I brought from all these different countries have been fused.

(Beat of tom-tom in background)

I am an Indian. I'm a Pawnee, a Mohawk, an Iroquois, a

---

* Obtainable from National Recreation Association in pamphlet—"Pageants and Programs."

member of the Blackfeet tribe. I lead a simple and a happy life; I hunt, fish, weave blankets, make religious objects, paint colorful pictures, and wander over the face of what you call America. My dances are a real part of my life. They personify my experiences in the great woods, my tribal life, my thoughts.

(As chief raises hands to Great Spirit, a Council Fire flares up lighting the seated forms of an Indian group, who slowly get up to dance. Upon the completion of the dance, the fire disappears.)

(The spotlight will pick out and follow one individual as group walks behind. When all are on stage, the lights go up.)

(Band plays softly)

I am a Pole. My hopes for building a greater America lie in the able bodies and alert minds of my youth. I bring you simplicity of living; a love of freedom, and of the land—its soil and grain. My statesmen and engineers have helped to build your country. My scientists, especially Madame Curie, have given radium to the world. I bring you great music and renowned musicians—Chopin and Paderewski. My soul-stirring martial music personifies the strength of my people.

(Polish dance and drill)

(Spanish music—softly)

I am a Spaniard. I'm a Spaniard from the Old World—a Spaniard from the New World—from old Madrid and Barcelona—from Buenos Aires and Tampico. Pan-American artists, musicians, sculptors, scholars, teachers are exchanging ideas and ideals to acquaint us better with each other's culture. My dark hair and flashing eyes, my clicking castanets, my innate sense of rhythm, my intricate dance steps are yours.

(Spanish Dance)

(Italian music—softly)

I am an Italian. I have given the world some of its greatest artists, sculptors and musicians; Michelangelo and Leonardo Da

Vinci are but two of many. Who can forget Caruso and his powerfully beautiful voice—or the melodious music of "O Sole Mio?"

Little is known of my statesmen. Mazzei came to America before the Revolutionary War. A good friend of Thomas Jefferson's, he wrote many articles on liberty and democracy which Jefferson translated into English. And the famous phrase about our being "created equal," which Mazzei used, found its way into the Declaration of Independence.

(Italian Chorus and Tarantella)

(Swiss music—softly)

I am from Switzerland. I am from the land of snow-covered peaks, beautiful lakes, and mountains that defy the hardiest climbers. I am the patient Swiss clockmaker. I am the skilled woodcarver whose figurines grace your mantels. I am the Swiss engineer who answers your call. I am the yodeler high on the mountainside, whose songs you know so well.

(Swiss solo)

(Bagpipes—softly)

I am a Scotsman. You know me by my kilts, my vivid plaids, the music of my bagpipes, my tam-o' shanter. I gave you the game of golf. My thrifty habits and economical management are known to everyone. The humorous, homespun poems of Robert Burns take their place with the great poetry of the world.

(Scotch dance)

(Irish music—softly)

I am an Irishman. I wanted to see my children grow up in a land where there is enough for all, and so I brought them to the New World—brought my children and also my gay songs, my lilting laughter, my buoyant sense of humor, and my Irish jigs. I brought the plays of Sean O'Casey, which you have produced here. I brought Irish players to entertain you.

(Irish dance)

(English music—softly)

I am an Englishman. My land was once looked upon as the mother of your country. I am an industrialist. We share the same language. Years of tradition form the basis upon which you have built many institutions. Your rivers, mountains, states and your large cities bear English names. I gave you the nucleus of a race.

(English folk songs)

(Negroes hum—softly)

I am a Negro. I bring the spirit of happiness and service. I, too, have my great scholars, surgeons, sociologists, athletes and other professional men. My spirituals and my sense of rhythm have been adopted by modern musicians and incorporated into contemporary American music.

(Negro spirituals)

(Greek music—softly)

I am a Greek. I gave you the poetry of Homer, the drama of Euripides and the philosophy of Socrates. Your greatest museums display the beauty created by my sculptors. I gave you the word "democracy" and the ideal it embodies. No people have ever valued liberty more highly than the Greeks, or fought for it more courageously. The lively strains of my music personify the free and venturesome spirit of my people.

(Greek dance)

I am an American—yet I am every one of these people you have seen. I am the fusion—the result of 190 years as a nation —of peoples who have come from near and far to find the light they were seeking. I am the crystallization of the cultures of the world united in a democracy whose culture reaches everyone no matter what his position in life. It is basic and understanding as well as appreciative of the ideals, hopes, and aspirations of the average man. America has the potentialities to become a far greater seat of culture, provided we acquire a better understanding of each other. And through the unity that will naturally follow, we will help make this idealistic concept of greater happiness in this democracy a living reality!

Fanfare of Trumpets

(The band plays a solemn processional. Spotlight on Columbia, who wears a white robe.)

(Columbia is borne in by Boy Scouts from rear center, carrying an unlighted torch. All nationality groups enter from left and right carrying lighted torches and marching in V formation. The spearhead person carries the torch. They all form a star-shaped group about Columbia and one by one cross torches until there is a blazing fire. From this fusion Columbia's torch is lighted.)

(All lights on)

"The Star-Spangled Banner" is sung by cast and audience.

FINALE

PRAYER THAT AMERICA FULFILL THE PROMISE OF ITS FOUNDING

Jewish Reconstructionist Foundation
Sabbath Prayer Book

O GOD, who art Liberator and Redeemer, Lawgiver and Judge, who rulest over all mankind and presidest over the destinies of nations, we invoke Thy continued blessing on our Republic, which Thy grace called into being and Thy love has sustained to this day.

> May America remain loyal to the principles of the Declaration of Independence and apply them to ever widening areas of life.

Keep us from all manner of oppression, persecution, and unjust discrimination; save us from religious, racial, and class conflicts; preserve our country as a haven of refuge for the victims of injustice and misrule.

> Instruct us in the art of living together. Teach us to respect differences, to reconcile clashing interests, and to help one another achieve a harmonious and abundant life.

Give us the wisdom to choose honest and capable leaders who will govern us according to Thy law of righteousness.

> Bless Thou the enterprise of the American people, that they may utilize the resources of the land for the good of men.

May our nation be ever receptive to new revelations of truth in science and philosophy, ever sensitive to the appeal of beauty in nature and art, ever responsive to the call of duty and the spirit of religious consecration and worship;

> And may Americans so love their country that they shall withhold no sacrifice required to safeguard its life and to fulfill its promise.

GOD CALLED IT AMERICA*
Rabbi Abba Hillel Silver

God built Him a continent of glory
    and filled it with treasures untold;
He carpeted it with soft-rolling prairies
    and columned it with thundering mountains;
He studded it with sweet-flowing fountains
    and traced it with long winding streams;
He planted it with deep-shadowed forests
    and filled them with song.

Then He called unto a thousand peoples
    and summoned the bravest among them.
They came from the ends of the earth,
    each bearing a gift and a hope.
The glow of adventure was in their eyes,
    and in their hearts the glory of hope.
And out of the bounty of earth
    and the labor of men,
Out of the longing of hearts
    and the prayer of souls,
Out of the memory of ages
    and the hopes of the world,
God fashioned a nation in love,
    blessed it with a purpose sublime—
And called it America!

---

* Reprinted with permission from *America*, The National Catholic Weekly Review.

AMERICA SINGS*
Margaret Morrow

Prologue

Reader:

Walk around the blocks of any city square,
Or down the stretch of a country lane;
Ride in a coal car in a Pennsylvania mine,
Or an iron car in a Minnesota pit;
Follow the hod carrier on a bricklaying job,
Or the planter in the cotton field;
Watch the mechanic in a midwestern garage,
Or the fisherman on the Pacific coast.
Anywhere—everywhere—watch America at work....
And listen!
Listen to America sing—work songs, play songs.
Sad songs, gay songs—
You hear America sing!
Whence came these songs?
Down through the centuries endlessly singing comes the great song.
You are part of it as I am, and from the centuries comes our song.
It is a song of strength—of fight—of courage—of love—of unconquered people.
It is a song washed with the tide, roaring against the rocky coast of Maine,
And washed with the wind through the magnolia trees of the deep South.
It is a song borne over the prairies in cumbersome wagons and etched with the blood of the pioneers.
It is a song of the loneliness of the plains and a campfire outlining a solitary sleeper.
It is a song of the majesty of the mountains and the fearful thunder of water pouring down canyons.

---

* Special permission to include this script was granted on the proviso that it will not be reproduced. Available in pamphlet "Pageants and Programs" at a nominal cost from National Recreation Association, 8 West 8th Street, New York 10011.

It is a song of the soft-footed men of God, chanting their solemn Te Deums in the monasteries of the west.
It is a song of those in bondage struggling to be free, and the free struggling to keep free.
It is a song of gaiety and laughter and life today, for tomorrow might not come.
It is a song of people struggling to keep afloat a pennant of idealism in a morass of untruths.
It is our song, and it began long ago—before the white man's pale face scattered birds in the thick forests of Maine.

Scene I: Indian Tableau

Reader:

When the land was young, it began—
When the virgin forests covered the land from east to west and silently the red man glided through the forest to his lodge,
There in the evening's blue, he rested, told his day's adventures, and listened to the nightbird's call, shrill against the moon.

(Girls' trio: "From the Land of the Sky Blue Water")

Scene II: Pilgrims

Reader:

Relentless is the push of civilization.
Westward and still westward came the white man, sailing into the bays of Massachusetts, with the sun glinting from the ships' sails.
Fearless people, and protected by a faith so great that the destruction of half their number could not daunt them.
They had a song.

(Mixed chorus: "Prayer of Thanksgiving")

Scene III: The Flag

Reader:

The faith that grew in the hearts of those determined men became an ideal of a young nation-to-be.

And the cry for freedom rang along the shores of the Atlantic with never-diminishing strength, until a new nation was born.

They borrowed a tune and made a song that has rung through the years—a challenge to those who scorn the strength of the strong in heart.

Their song made a nation and a flag to fly wherever flags are flown—

A flag of freedom and refuge, and life as life was meant to be.

(Mixed chorus: "Yankee Doodle." Girls' chorus: "Hail Columbia," modulating to the last part of the last stanza of "The Star-Spangled Banner," beginning with "Praise the power that hath made and preserved us a nation.")

Scene IV: The South
Reader:

And the nation grew and prospered.

America was born in a thousand places—a cove in Maine, an island in New York, a plantation in Virginia, a cabin in Kentucky.

But the nation, united in purpose, dissented in ideals, and there came a race baptized in bondage and paying homage to a material king.

They had songs, too.

(Minuet—dance. Mixed chorus group: "Go Down Moses.")

Scene V: Westward Expansion
Reader:

Meanwhile the nation struggled forward.

Out went the people.

The prairie grass blazing didn't hold them.

The mountains towering didn't hold them.

The plains were not wide enough.

Out they went with their wagons and their rifles—their cattle and their homespun tablecloths—their prayers and their loneliness.

Out they went until the mighty, heaving breast of the Pacific
    gathered them close, and they stretched their lungs to
    shout the freedom that was theirs.
They left a trail of broken wagon wheels and bleached bones,
But they left a song, too.
    (Banjo solo: "Oh, Susannah")
    (Boys' chorus: "Bury Me out On the Lone Prairie")
    (Girls' chorus: "Cielito Lindo")

Scene VI: The Building of the Nation

Reader:

Then came the time of building.
Out of the wilderness they forged a trail—by land—by water.
They dug ditches, and left their hearts on the iron spikes of
    a railroad.
There was a nation to build—and they sang.
There were friends to meet, weddings to be held, and requiems
    to be sung;
There was a life to be lived, and they had a song for all of it.
    (Mixed chorus: "Erie Canal")
    (Boys' chorus: "Workin' on the Railroad")
    (Square dance to violin: "Turkey in the Straw")

Scene VII: The Civil War

Reader:

But an ideal takes a long time to blend.
One purpose, two ideals—and he who walked tall and gaunt
    among them rebuked them and reminded them that a
    house divided shall fall.
Dark days, and the blood of brothers spilled and soaking into
    the earth—and freedom caught in the quagmire of de-
    struction.
There was a song for that, too.
    (Mixed chorus: "Battle Hymn of the Republic")

Scene VIII: The Gay Nineties

Reader:

A bullet fired in a theater made us a nation.

Overnight America leaped forward and grew and grew until it seemed the very shores must give way to the demands of the youthful struggle.
This was America.
The land of plenty!
Gaiety became characteristic.
Gold and satin—diamonds and tandem bicycles—plush chairs and leg-o'-mutton sleeves.
And could they sing!

(Mixed quartet :"Strolling Through the Park"; "Bicycle Built for Two")
(Small instrument group: "The Band Played On")

Scene IX: The World War
Reader:

The band played on and on.
Baseball and Coney Island, waltzing and revival meetings, picnics in the park—this was America.
America sang and grew rich.
And then again the despots threatened to crunch an iron heel upon the nation, and the lusty youths threw away their bicycles and climbed into orange crates that flew—and went off to make the world safe for democracy.
They sang. They sang as they marched and fought and died.

(Girls' chorus: "Keep the Home Fires Burning")
(Boys' chorus: "Pack Up Your Troubles in Your Old Kit Bag")

Scene X: The Roaring Twenties
Reader:

Then again the nation needed building.
And so they built it.
But this time they overlooked the solidarity of firm foundations.
Castles rose in the air—towering high like multi-colored bubbles, floating far above the earth.

The roaring twenties with their hectic mad dash to live today,
  lest tomorrow never come.
They sang—deliriously.

> (Girls' trio: "Ain't We Got Fun")
> (Modern dance orchestra: "Jumping Jive")
> (Dance: Jitterbug)

Scene XI: The Thirties

Reader:

Then the bubble burst—the paper fortunes vanished—
And a humbler, wiser people built anew—
On a firmer foundation.

> (Boys' chorus: "Brother, Can You Spare a Dime?")
> (Mixed chorus: "Happy Days Are Here Again")

Scene XII: The Second World War

Reader:

There were those who shook their heads and watched the dark thunderheads gather on the horizon and flash ugly streaks of lightning.
But America was safe and snug deep in the hinterlands of complacency, with the waves of two oceans washing oil on her beaches.
Still they danced and sang,
And the old songs yellowed and cracked in the attics.
The lights in the prairie homes went out to light the Atlantic shore and the Pacific shore.
And suddenly, with the ominous portent of a summer storm, there burst the roar of cannon on the beaches, and thunder boomed, and lightning burned the hearts of those who danced.
But America has always sung.
There was a song for the cannon and the thunder and the lightning, too.

> (Boys' chorus: "Praise the Lord and Pass the Ammunition")

Scene XIII: Midcentury

Reader:

At last the thundering cannons were still
And America and all the free world stood together—more closely united than ever before.
But a curtain of iron lay over half of Europe, its lengthening shadow threatening country after country.
As the atom yielded up its secrets—as the arsenals were filled with more and more terrible weapons—
America turned to a higher Power, with an ancient song on the lips of her people.

(Mixed chorus: "God Bless Our Native Land")

Epilogue

Reader:

And now it is today.
This is still America.
And it is still the voice of America we hear singing its various carols.
Whence came these songs?
Not from the waves of the Atlantic,
Nor the drawing rooms of Virginia;
Not from the mountains of the west,
Nor the railroads;
Not from any of these.
The songs came from the hearts of those who knelt in Plymouth.
And those who drove the spikes,
And those who felled the trees and built the homes—
Each one singing of the freedom that is his.
These are the songs that mean America.

Finale

(Audience and cast: "The Star-Spangled Banner")

—Reprinted from *Lagniappe*

I AM AN AMERICAN*
Rabbi Stephen S. Wise

I am an American. I thank God that my parents brought me to this country. I thank God that my children and children's children have been born in this country. They have entered into and become sharers in the most precious heritage which can fall to the lot of man, and I have faith that they will prove equal to and worthy of the high opportunities of life which American citizenship affords. They, like me, will give their deepest, truest loyalty to the America which is today, to the greater, freer, nobler America that is to be on the morrow.

I am an American, an American Jew who, because he is a Jew, proudly recalls that on the Independence Bell, which, on the fourth day of July, 1776, proclaimed the gladdest tidings that human ears ever heard, there were inscribed the words of the Hebrew Bible, "And ye shall proclaim liberty throughout the land unto all the inhabitants thereof." On this, "I Am an American" day, I know, and I thank God because I am permitted to know, that the Bible verse "And ye shall proclaim liberty throughout the land unto all the inhabitants therof" has, since the seventh day of December, 1941, yea since the third of September, 1939, yea since the fourth day of March, 1933, translated itself into the larger term, "And ye Americans shall proclaim liberty throughout the lands unto all the inhabitants thereof."

I am an American. Because I am an American, I am free. Because I am an American, I shall live and labor to the end that all men be set free and that the spirit of American freedom rule over all the sons and daughters of men.

---

* From *As I See It*

I HEAR AMERICA SINGING!*

CAST

Boy
Girl
Poet
America
Indian
Pilgrim Father
Pilgrim Mother
Pilgrim Child
Quaker Maiden
Thomas Jefferson
Negro Woman
Oriental Man
Hebrew Immigrant
Glee Club

(Curtain opens revealing the American poet, Walt Whitman, dressed in plaid shirt and jeans. He is sitting with scratch pad and pencil, writing, thinking, dreaming—)

(Enter boy and girl in school clothes.)

GIRL: There he is again! I have seen him sitting there, looking at the sky, every afternoon for the last week. I wonder who he is!
BOY: I asked the teacher about him. She says he is a poet!
GIRL: A real poet? Let's ask him what he has written! (To the poet) Hello! What are you doing?
POET: I am thinking, children—thinking about America.
GIRL: I am an American. My father belongs to the Sons of the Revolution, my mother to the Colonial Dames.
One of my ancestors pitched tea overboard in Boston Harbor.
Another hungered with Washington at Valley Forge.

---

* Special permission to include this script was granted on the proviso it will not be reproduced. Copies are available in pamphlet "Pageants and Programs" at nominal cost from National Recreation Association, 8 West 8th Street, New York 10011.

My forefathers were America in the making:
They spoke in her council halls;
They died on her battlefields;
They commanded her ships;
They cleared her forests.
Staunch hearts of mine beat fast at each new star
In the nation's flag.
Keen eyes of mine foresaw her greater glory;
The sweep of her seas;
The plenty of her plains;
The man-hives of her billion-wired cities:
Every drop of bood in me holds a heritage of patriotism;
I am proud of my past.
I am an American.
—*Elias Lieberman*

    BOY: I am an American.
My father was an atom of dust.
My mother a straw in the wind,
To his Serene Majesty.
One of my ancestors died in the mines of Siberia;
Another was crippled for life by twenty blows of the knout.
Another was killed defending his home during the massacres.
This history of my ancestors is a trail of blood,
To the palace of the Great White Czar.
But then the dream came—the dream of America.
In the light of the liberty torch,
The atom of dust became a man
And the straw in the wind became a woman
For the first time.
"See," said my father, pointing to the flag that fluttered near,
"That flag of stars and stripes is yours!
It is the emblem of the promised land.
It means, my son, the hope of humanity.
Live for it—die for it!"
Under the open sky of my new country I swore to do so
And every drop of blood in me will keep that vow.
I am proud of my future.
I am an American.
—*Elias Lieberman*

(Poet stands—walks slowly to stage left. The children follow—the poet speaks dreamily.)

POET: I heard ... I heard America ... singing.
(Poet sits, continues to write and dream throughout the pageant, ignoring the children who watch the pageant over his shoulder.)
(At the words "I heard America singing" Glee Club sings *America* while character, America, in starry robe, moves up center aisle, up central stairs of stage.)

AMERICA: Two American children! Yet how different are the stories of my children—many as my stars. From all races, all churches have come "Americans." The Indian—native of my lands.

(Indian ascends central stairs and speaks.)

INDIAN: The Great Spirit above has appointed this place for us, on which to light our fires. Sell a country! Why not sell the air, the clouds and the great sea as well as the earth? Did not the Great Spirit make them all for the use of his children?

—*Words of Tecumseh, famous Shawnee Chief*

AMERICA: The Pilgrims from England seek the freedom of my wilderness.

GLEE CLUB: (Sings "Faith of our Fathers" as Pilgrim Father, Mother and small child approach. Pilgrim Father carries a large family Bible.)

Faith of our fathers, living still
In spite of dungeon, fire and sword!
Oh, how our hearts beat high with joy
Whene'er we hear that glorious word!
Faith of our fathers, holy faith,
We will be true to thee till death!

PILGRIM FATHER: For summer being done, all things stand upon us with a weather-beaten face; and the whole country, full of woods and thickets, presents a wild and savage view. If we look behind us, there is the mighty ocean which we have passed, and which is now a bar and gulf to separate us from all civil parts of the world. What can now sustain us but the spirit of God and His Grace?

—Words of William Bradford,
Second Governor of Plymouth

(Pilgrims move upstage, Quaker maiden moves up center aisle to stage.)

GLEE CLUB: (Singing)
"Faith of our fathers, faith and prayer,
Have kept our country brave and free,
And through the truth that comes from God,
Her children have true liberty.
Faith of our fathers, holy faith,
We will be true to thee till death!"

AMERICA: The Quakers, Friends, come to live in Pennsylvania.

QUAKER MAIDEN: Let us then try what love will do. For if men do see we love them, we should soon find they would not harm us.

God is better served in resisting temptation to evil than in many formal prayers.

—Words of William Penn, founder of
the state of Pennsylvania.

AMERICA: And a clear voice from Virginia is raised in words that echo around the world. Thomas Jefferson speaks for the colonists.

THOMAS JEFFERSON: We hold these truths to be self-evident, that all men are created equal,
That they are endowed by their Creator with certain inalienable Rights,
That among these are Life, Liberty, and the pursuit of Happiness.
That to secure these rights, Governments are instituted among men.

—Thomas Jefferson,
Declaration of Independence

AMERICA: And so my gates were declared open to the humble and oppressed of the old world. The Scotch kept alive

their Presbyterian faith as they pushed sturdily into my frontier.
The Germans—Lutherans, Dunkers, Mennonites, found homes on my farms.
French Huguenots sought security and tolerance here.
Irish, Celtic in race and Catholic in faith, fled to my shores bearing scars of an age-old struggle.
Italians, dark-eyed and happy.
Norsemen, fair and strong.
They come! They come!
And while they come the cries of a race long dwelling within my shores are heard.

GLEE CLUB: Sings "Deep River," while Negro Woman moves forward.

NEGRO WOMAN: (Recites)
You got to cross that River Jordan
You got to cross it foh yohself
There cain't nobody cross it foh you.
You got to cross it foh yohself.
Cain't yoh brothoh cross it foh you.
You got to cross it for yoh-self.
—American Negro Spiritual

GLEE CLUB: Sings "Battle Hymn of the Republic."
AMERICA: Hard-working people of the Orient turn my soil, lay my rails, live by their teachings of wisdom and patience.
ORIENTAL: The Master said: A man should say, I am not concerned that I have no place; I am concerned how I may fit myself for one. I am not concerned that I am not known. I seek to be worthy to be known.

What the great man seeks is in himself. What the small man seeks is in others.
—Confucius

AMERICA: And the Hebrew, persecuted wanderer, finds rest, brings courage and a strong faith in God.
HEBREW IMMIGRANT: This is my latest home and it invites me to a glad new life. The endless ages have throbbed through my blood but a new rhythm dances in my veins. America is the youngest of the nations and inherits all that went before

in history. I am the youngest of America's children. Mine is the whole majestic past. Mine is the shining future.

—*Writer Anonymous*

CAST AND GLEE CLUB: Sing first stanza of "America the Beautiful."

O beautiful for spacious skies,
For amber waves of grain,
For purple mountain majesties
Above the fruited plain.
America! America! God shed His grace on thee,
And crown thy good with brotherhood
From sea to shining sea.

(America leaves followed in dignified line of march by other characters while Glee Club continues singing "America the Beautiful." Poet, boy, and girl are left on the stage, poet still writing.)

POET: (Standing and walking to stage center)
I hear America singing
The varied carols I hear!

—*Walt Whitman*

THE SPIRITUAL HERITAGE OF AMERICA*

We thank thee, O Lord, for having imbued the Founding Fathers of our nation with that faith in Thee which moved them to proclaim truths of great moral import:

> That all men are created equal, that they are endowed by their Creator with certain inalienable rights, that among these are life, liberty, and the pursuit of happiness.

Thou didst guide them in the framing of a constitution designed to promote the general welfare and to secure the blessings of liberty to themselves and their posterity.

> They made provision that all men should be free to serve Thee as their own conscience dictates.

They sought to keep far from these shores the old-world prejudices and fanatical hatreds by which men have profaned Thy name.

> America was to be a nation that, in the words of Washington, "gives to bigotry no sanction, to persecution no assistance."

We thank Thee, O God, for having taught the founders of our Republic laws that safeguard the equal rights of all citizens and impose equal obligations upon all.

> Thus is the happiness of every American bound up with the welfare of the nation by a solemn covenant of citizenship.

Yet not always and not in all ways have we been true to the high purposes of the Founding Fathers; but when we went astray, Thou didst summon us back to the path of righteousness.

> Thou didst send us leaders of prophetic stamp who recalled us to our duty, and who taught us to behold Thy

---

* *Sabbath Prayer Book*—Jewish Reconstructionist Foundation

chastening hand in the sufferings and trials brought on by our sins.

O God, help us to keep America true to its faith in democracy and to fulfill the promise of its nationhood.

Unite the hearts of all Americans, whatever be their race, religion, or part in the nation's economy, and help them preserve and enrich the American heritage of liberty and justice, of democracy and brotherhood.

Protect us from all enemies who, knowing not Thy way of justice and freedom, would seek to destroy or enslave us.

And protect us also from our own inclination to seek personal, partisan, racial, or sectarian aggrandizement.

Give us love and understanding; may we recognize one another's needs, and help one another in achieving all the worthy purposes we cherish for ourselves and for our people.

Help us to respect and value the heritage of every community in our land, and enable each community to give of its best to the service of all.

May our nation be privileged to prove, both in its own life and in its dealing with other nations, how good and how beautiful it is for brethren to dwell together in unity.

Columbus Day

THE SIGNIFICANCE OF COLUMBUS DAY*

On August 3rd, 1492, three small sailing ships under the command of Christopher Columbus set sail on a voyage fraught with more consequences than any other which history records. On October 12th, after almost six weeks of perilous adventure on the high seas, the vessels of Columbus at last reached land, a new land of whose existence even he had had no inkling. Thus was America discovered.

That is the event which we celebrate today and well may we do so. For Columbus to have undertaken that westward journey in the kind of ships available to men in those days was a great act of faith. The notion that the world was round and that one could reach the east by sailing toward the west had indeed been propounded before that time. The arguments were known to Columbus. But no one had yet put the theory to the test. How many well-reasoned theories have foundered on the rocks of hard fact! Columbus had the faith that the results of sound reason would be verified by experience. He had the courage to express his faith in action, in defiance of dangers both real and fancied.

And God blessed the faith of Columbus by rewarding it with a success beyond his dreams. His voyages uncovered a new continent in which the ancient civilizations of Europe could take root in virgin soil, renew their vigor, and yield a civilization such as the world had not yet known. That is what makes Columbus Day worthy of celebration.

It behooves us, the heirs of Columbus, to ask ourselves what use we have made of the opportunities that his discovery opened to mankind. Are the standards and ideals of our life here a mere replica of those by which our fathers lived in the old world? If so, Columbus dared and suffered in vain. Or have we here

---

* From *The Faith of America* edited by Mordecai Kaplan, J. Paul Williams and Eugene Kohn, published by the Jewish Reconstructionist Foundation.

in America really discovered a new world, achieved a new way of life, developed a new type of civilization?

Let us set out today on a journey not unlike that of Columbus. Let us seek to rediscover America, to examine what the experience of the men who have taken up their home in this country has contributed and can continue to contribute to the welfare of mankind. And may God guide us in fulfilling the promise which the discovery of America by Columbus has held out to all humanity.

Thanksgiving Day

THE SIGNIFICANCE OF THANKSGIVING DAY*

OUR GOD AND FATHER, it is good to give thanks to Thee and to acknowledge Thy blessings. Only thus can we savor them to the full. In the hurried pace of our lives and in our preoccupation with the petty and the trivial, we are prone to take Thy gifts for granted. Oblivious of Thy bounties, we sinfully waste the opportunities they afford us for living the good life. Therefore, do we set aside this day for thanksgiving.

We thank Thee for the land and for its fruits by which we live. We thank Thee for the vigor of body and mind that enables us to exploit the fertility of our country's fields and forests and the buried treasures of its mineral wealth. We thank Thee for the varied beauty of its landscape, for the grandeur of its mountains, the hospitality of its plains and prairies, and the gleaming vistas of ocean from its coasts.

We thank Thee for the inspiration of our country's history —for the courage and hardihood that sustained its explorers and pioneers, for the heroism that inspires its fighters for freedom and equality, for the enterprise that builds its teeming cities, for the arts that express the beauty and meaning of its way of life, for the just laws and free institutions that enable its people to work together in peace and harmony.

Grant, O God, in Thy grace, that we may perfect our national life to the measure of Thy bounty. Grateful for the gifts Thou hast bestowed upon us, may we use them to extend the area of freedom, justice, and good-will among men. May our use of Thy gifts bear witness to mankind that life is good when lived according to Thy benign will, O gracious Giver of all good. AMEN.

---

* From *The Faith of America* by Mordecai Kaplan, J. Paul Williams and Eugene Kohn, published by the Jewish Reconstructionist Foundation.

NOW SING WE A SONG*
John W. Chadwick

Now sing we a song for the harvest;
Thanksgiving and honor and praise,
For all that the bountiful Giver
Hath given to gladden our days;

For grasses of upland and lowland,
For fruits of the garden and field,
For gold which the mine and the furrow
To delver and husbandman yield.

And thanks for the harvest of beauty,
For that which the hands cannot hold;
The harvest, eyes only can gather,
And only our hearts can enfold.

We reap it on mountain and moorland,
We glean it from meadow and lea,
We garner it from the cloudland,
We bind it in sheaves for the sea. Amen.

---

* Music for this poem is on page 81 of *Hymns for the Living Age*, edited by H. Augustine Smith, published by Fleming H. Revell Company, Westwood, N. J.

THANKS FOR THE BLESSINGS OF HOME*
Mordecai Kaplan, J. Paul Williams and Eugene Kohn

OUR FATHER, to whom we look to make us at home in this strange and mysterious universe, we thank Thee on this day of national Thanksgiving for the blessed homes of America.

> For the love and affection, the comfort and security, the reverence and holiness that marked the family life of the early generations of our people.

Most of us carry in our hearts some happy memories of the home in which we were born,

> In the shelter of which we learned our first lessons of loyalty, helpfulness, truth, and honor.

May our homes afford us a haven of rest away from the swirling currents of life, a retreat of privacy where we and our families can be ourselves and shut out the clamorous voices that stupefy our feelings, disturb our thinking, and distract our will and purpose.

> May our children find in the home a warm and sheltered nest, where they can grow to wholesome maturity.

But let us not in the comfort of our homes forget the homeless,

> Or those whom human folly and greed have condemned to live in unwholesome hovels or huddled in wretched tenements amidst filth and squalor.

Help us to make America's homes fit abodes for beings created in Thine image.

> Worthy shrines for all that hallow American life.

---

* From *The Faith of America*, published by Jewish Reconstructionist Foundation.

May our homes, through the sacred memories of our forebears, link us with the past and, through the birth and rearing of children, link us with the future, so that we may know ourselves to be children of the Eternal,

> That our lives may ever serve ideals which shall outlive us and shall abide with our posterity when we are no more.

As we thank Thee on this day for the blessed homes of our childhood, so may our children in the days to come have occasion to rejoice in their memories of home and offer Thee thanks and praises for Thy unfailing love. AMEN.

PRODUCTION NOTE:

This selection can effectively be done as a Choral Reading. However, if adequate time is not available for rehearsal, a simplified rendition follows:

Divide the passages among four readers—two boys and two girls.

Allocate Paragraphs I, III, V, VII, VIII, IX, X to the boys—alternating voices; Paragraphs II, IV, VI, XI, XII to the girls—alternating voices. Have the entire group—both boys and girls—render passage XIII in unison.

Lines should, of course, be memorized.

*Selections for
Special Occasions*

American-Jewish History Week

Classification	Title	Author	Age Level
1. Reading	*Prayer*		12-16
2. Documentary Pageant	*Seeds of Freedom*	Millard Lampell	12-16
3. Reading	*A Two-Fold Blessing*	Joseph Krauskopf	10-16
4. Poem	*The Jewish Cemetery at Newport*	Henry Wadsworth Longfellow	10-16
5. Reading	*From the Days of Columbus*	Lee M. Friedman	10-14
6. Poem	*The Discovery of the "Tu-key"*	Dorothy Ross	8-14
7. Simulated Radio Broadcast (Documentary)	*The First Passover in America*	Max Ehrlich	12-16

PRAYER

O Lord, our God, God of our fathers, Ruler of nations, we worship Thee and praise Thy name for Thy mercy and for Thy truth. On this day of our rejoicing we will make mention of Thy loving kindness according to all that Thou has bestowed on us and we will proclaim Thy great goodness toward the house of Israel. For Thou didst say, Surely they are My people, children that will not deal falsely; so Thou hast been our Savior.

Throughout the past ages Thou hast carried Israel as on eagles' wings. From the Bondage of Egypt, through the trials of the wilderness, Thou didst bring us and didst plant us in the land which Thou didst choose. In the sorrows of Babylon, Thy love and pity redeemed us; and when dispersed in every land, Thy Divine Presence accompanied us in every affliction. Yea, when we passed through the waters, Thou wast with us, and through the rivers, they did not overflow us; when we walked through fire, we were not burned. From nation to nation Thou didst lead us, until the hand of the oppressor was weakened and the day of human rights began to dawn. Wherever we found a resting place, and built Thee a sanctuary, Thou didst dwell in our midst, and cleaving unto Thee, O Lord, we are alive this day.

We thank Thee that Thou has sustained us unto this day, and that in the fullness of Thy mercy Thou hast vouchsafed to us of the seed of Israel a soil on which to grow strong in freedom and in fidelity to Thy truth. Thou hast opened unto us this blessed haven of our beloved land. Everlasting God, in whose eyes a thousand years are as yesterday which is past and as a watch of the night, we lift up our hearts in gratitude to Thee, in that well-nigh three hundred years ago Thou didst guide a little band of Israel's children who, seeking freedom to worship Thee, found it in a land which, with Thy blessing, became a refuge of freedom and justice for the oppressed of all peoples. We thank Thee that our lot has fallen in pleasant places. Verily, O Lord God of Israel, Thou hast given rest unto Thy people, rest from our sorrow, and from the hard bondage wherein we were made to serve.

O Lord, look down from Thy holy habitation from heaven and bless this Republic. Preserve it in the liberty which has been proclaimed in the land, and in the righteousness which is its foundation. Bless it with prosperity and peace. May it advance from strength to strength and continue to be a refuge for all who seek its shelter. Imbue all its citizens with a spirit of loyalty to its ideals. May they be ever mindful that the blessings of liberty are safeguarded by obedience to law, and that the prosperity of the nation rests upon trust in Thy goodness and reverence for Thy commandments. Bless the President and his counselors, the judges, lawgivers, and executives of our country. Put forth upon them the spirit of wisdom and understanding, the spirit of counsel and the spirit of might, the spirit of knowledge and the fear of the Lord. May America become a light to all peoples, teaching the world that righteousness exalteth a nation.

Our Father in Heaven, Who lovest all nations, all men are Thy children. Thou dost apportion tasks to peoples according to their gifts of mind and heart. But all are revealing Thy marvelous plans for mankind. May the day speedily dawn when Thy kingdom will be established on earth, when nations shall learn war no more, when peace shall be the crowning reward of a world redeemed by justice, and all men shall know Thee, from the greatest unto the least. Then shall loving kindness and truth meet, righteousness and peace kiss each other, truth spring forth from earth and righteousness look down from heaven. May all hearts serve Thee with one accord and recognize that Thou art One and Thy Name is One. Amen.

(From American Jewish Historical Society pamphlet.)

SEEDS OF FREEDOM
(Capsule Version)

Millard Lampell

All of the major characters in this pageant were actual people. In many cases, the words they speak here are direct quotations from their letters and diaries, and the episodes are based upon events of their lives. See *Historical Note* at back of script.

Directives

CAST

(Minimum) *five women, one man, a boy* (the part can be changed to a girl's role.)

If more performers are available, the parts indicated as doubles can be distributed among them.

CHAIRMAN (can double as ERNESTINE ROSE)
SPEAKER
MRS. ASSER LEVY (can double as MRS. BRECKEN-
                RIDGE; FIRST PIONEER WOMAN)
BACKWOODSMAN (can double as CIVIL WAR SOLDIER)
ESTHER HAYS (can double as MRS. TRAGER)
JOSHUA HAYS a boy of about 13.
MRS. PATTERSON (can double as EMMA LAZARUS)
(ALSO: Non-speaking Extras to double as Early Manhattan Immigrants.)
CHORAL GROUP
A FEMALE VOCAL SOLOIST to sing the lullaby, and other
    numbers.

The double roles indicated are quite possible as far as costume change, time, and general age level are concerned. But other combinations of doubled roles are possible, and it will be up to the director to determine the way doubled roles can best be distributed.

There are a number of important women's speaking roles. If it appears difficult to get women capable of handling them all, some of the speeches of Esther Hays (her diary excerpts), and Augusta Levy (excerpts from her letter) can be taken by the Chairman, who will in that event remain onstage with the Speaker throughout.

A *professional Director* is advisable, or one of your own people *experienced* in production.

SETTING

There are two major playing areas: Stage Right, and Stage Left. If spotlights are available, they should be used to pinpoint these two areas. When the Center Stage is used (as in the "Sweet Betsy from Pike" dance, and the Finale), full stage lights are all right.

SOUND

In halls where microphones are needed, it is best to have two; one at Stage Right to be used by the Speaker and Chairman, and the other at Stage Left to be used by all others. Take care in routing entrances and exits, so that there is no awkwardness in a new character reaching the mike.

If a third mike is available, it would be excellent to use it for the offstage solos—"Sweet Betsy from Pike," etc.

Only two sound effects are indicated: *scattered rifle fire* (in the Colonial scene), and *distant cannon fire* (in the Civil War passage). These can be obtained from your local radio station —or by writing to: Standard Radio, 444 Madison Avenue, New York, N. Y. Describe the effects you want, and enclose $2.00 for each record.

PROPS

Sets are only suggested by props. A table (for the Colonial and Frontier scenes) ... three low stools and a high one (so that Esther Hays, when seated, can reach the mike) for the Chanukah scene. Where other period props are available (such as a spinning wheel for the Colonial scene), they should be used for added effect.

MUSIC

If the male soloist can play a guitar or banjo (or if one can accompany him offstage), it will strengthen the folk songs. Piano or accordian may be used to accompany Chorus, if available. For additional directives on Music, see "Production Chart" at back of script.

AT CURTAIN: At stage right is speaker's rostrum.
Near it is a chair in which sits a woman—the Chairman. At curtain rise the speaker enters, carrying a pile of papers and books.

SPEAKER: (With a nod toward the woman) Madam Chairman ... ladies and gentlemen. It is more than 300 years since the first Jewish Community was founded in America. As an historian, I've been asked to make a few remarks on the subject. The facts are not hard to find. You come across them on the dusty pages of old documents. The date being September, 1654. And the place: the village of New Amsterdam. Windmills along Wall Street, and sheep grazing on the green hills of the Bowery. Down at the dock, a ship has just arrived. A tiny, battered vessel named the St. Charles, up from Brazil with twenty-three Jewish voyagers ... (At stage left, the voyagers enter. Spotlight picks out the tableau: people in 17th century dress, loaded down with trunks, bundles and household possessions; the last woman cradling a baby in her arms.)

There have been individual Jews in America before—including five or six with Columbus on his first voyage. But this is the first community. (Poking among his papers: opening a heavy book.) In the ancient city archives you find the record of their promise that "the poor among us shall not become a burden to the community." (Fumbling amongst his papers) In connection with the leaders there are certain documents which ... (He becomes aware that the Chairman is stifling a polite yawn) Am I boring you?

CHAIRMAN: I'm sorry. It's not you. It's just ... history. (Gesturing toward tableau) Those figures—I've seen them a thousand times—pictures in my school books when I was a kid. The way they pose there, as though cut out of cardboard.... I could never believe they were once alive.

SPEAKER: (Groping toward his books) Oh yes, I assure you, there exists documentary ...

CHAIRMAN: (Passionately) I mean *alive!* That's another thing about history. It's always the leaders, the important names, the big heroes! (With a disarming smile—a little awkwardly) Everybody's always so ... noble. "Give me liberty or give me death!" Okay, sure, that's important ... only, where are the people like me? Telling their kids, "go wash your face before you sit down to eat," cooking, scrubbing ... The ones whose words never get into the history books. Never mind the leaders. Just for once, what I'd like to know is ... (Pointing toward tableau) ... who was that one? That woman back there at the end—who was she? (The woman has begun to croon a gentle, wordless song of comfort to her baby.)

SPEAKER: (Leafing his books) Well, I ... I don't seem to find any ... there doesn't seem to be any mention of ...

CHAIRMAN: Was nothing she ever did worthwhile remembering? It would make it so much more real to me if there were just a footnote saying: "All the time she wandered from Holland to Brazil, from Brazil to New Amsterdam, she dreamed of having a set of dishes she could call her own." Or, "such and such were the words of the lullaby she sang to her baby . . ."

WOMAN: (Has moved forward. And now she sings a brief, simple old lullaby: "Yoheved's Lullaby"*)

> Sleep my darling, peacefully sleep,
> Yoheved, your Mother, watch will keep
> As you belong to Israel's daughter,
> I will tend you, so do not weep!
> Though in strange lands you may be,
> Tales of Israel you'll hear from me.
> Grow up strong and wise
> And try to set your people free.
> Now sleep peacefully.

CHAIRMAN: (After song, as woman fades out, humming) Three hundred years ago, she was one of the first to come to America.... Who was she? What was her name?

SPEAKER: (Reluctantly shuts his book) I'm sorry. It doesn't seem to be recorded.

CHAIRMAN: (Pointing out another woman) And what about that one? I like her face. I'm sure she must have quietly done something worth remembering. (The immigrant woman—Mrs. Asser Levy—has stepped forward. She holds a cooking pot in her hands.)

MRS. ASSER LEVY: It was just after the first year we

---

* See "Production Chart" at end of script.

came. 1655. My husband had set himself up as a shochet ... I remember the baby had a terrible cough ...

CHAIRMAN: (To Speaker) Who *is* she? What's her name?

SPEAKER: (Searching) It doesn't seem to be recorded. Wait, wait ... here ... husband a shochet ... it doesn't list her name, but that would be the wife of Asser Levy ... (Light fading on Speaker—holding on Mrs. Levy.)

MRS. LEVY: After having run halfway around the world, we were praying, please God, let this new land be the place where we can live free and equal. And then the Burgomasters passed this law ...

SPEAKER: (In dim light ... we needn't see him clearly. Unrolls proclamation scroll and reads ...) "All male inhabitants of New Amsterdam capable of bearing arms shall be enrolled in the Burger Guard for the protection and defense of the city. *Except Hebrews,* who shall remain exempt from guard duty, on condition that each male person over sixteen and under sixty contribute sixty-five stivers each month ..."

MRS. LEVY: I remember, I was just taking the soup off the fire that night when my husband came home. He looked weary, his lips tight and bitter. "So," I said to him, "... it's beginning again. They pass a law setting us apart from everyone else. You'll let them start like this, and soon it will be Spain all over again!" He shrugged his shoulders. "What can I do?" "You can put on your hat and march down there and tell them you're going to stand guard duty. Let them know we'll do our part, just like the others." (Firmly) "Go on!—Please." (A faint, proud smile) And he went ... (She seems to be watching him go ... her hand rising to her lips to blow him a soft kiss for luck.)

MRS. LEVY: (Continuing) I remember, I called after him ... "I'll keep the soup hot!" (Light at left blacks out. Tableau exits.)

SPEAKER: Do you imagine that equality springs full-grown out of the air? No ... the beginnings are slow and painful. A word, a nervous decision, a quiet act of courage. A woman urging her husband to stand up for his rights. A tired man insisting on taking his turn at guard duty along the walls of a village.

April 21, 1657. Asser Levy becomes the first Jewish citizen in America. In 1680: he is one of the founders of the first congregation, Shearith Yisroel. (Offstage voice sings chant of synagogue service.)

And from these beginnings, the Jews spreading out across the Colonies, rooting their institutions deep as hickory in the American soil. 1750: the synagogue Beth Elohim dedicated at Charleston, South Carolina. 1763: the synagogue Yeshuat Yisroel dedicated at Newport, Rhode Island. (Light, left, has come up revealing a figure in colonial dress wearing a tallith and holding a prayer book—his voice rising now, the chant up full, then fading down again as he moves away.)

SPEAKER: (Continuing) (Cue at fading of chant, above) And the first Jewish colonists spreading out into the wilderness of Pennsylvania, Georgia, Kentucky ... And then it was planting time ... wheat in Virginia and apple trees in Vermont. (Dramatically) And one more new seed sown in the earth ... in the wild duck marshes of Jersey ... in the streets of Philadelphia ... seed for a crop called Freedom.

And in Boston, New York, Charleston, South Carolina—the Sons of Liberty meeting to organize the defiance of tyranny. And among them, the descendants of a young shepherd named David who, in his day, knew a thing or two about defying giants. Find their names among the lists of the Continentals ... Haym Solomon, Asher Pollock, Francis Salvador ...

CHAIRMAN: And the ones like me ... the anonymous ones, the ordinary, everyday women ... the nobodies ... What about them?

SPEAKER: (Slamming a book shut) No one seems to have recorded (Laughs) nothing about nobodies in these official records.

CHAIRMAN: (Breaking in) ... never mind those dead documents ... where are the diaries, love letters, recipes ... the faded bits of paper found in old hope chests ... marriage records put down on the cracked pages of family bibles ... memories of great-grandmothers ...

SPEAKER: (Voice sounds far away) In the rolling green slopes of New York State, in an old farmhouse in Westchester County, you find a cherry-wood chest in the attic. And in the drawer, an ancient diary ...

CHAIRMAN: (Taking it up and reading) December 15, 1779. Today marks three weeks my husband has been gone ... and my brother in Maryland, a prisoner of the British.

SPEAKER: The ink is faded now. But there was a time the ink was new, and the hand that held the pen was slim and lovely. The hand of a woman named Esther Hays. The wife of a farmer in the village of Bedford.

ESTHER'S VOICE: Three long, lonely weeks since my David left to try and slip through the British lines with supplies for the Continentals. No word from him as yet. At night I lie awake in the darkness, half out of my mind with worry. Still, today is Chanukah, and little Joshua expects to celebrate. (The lights come up, left. There is a bare table, and three three-legged stools, two high and one low. If a spinning wheel is available, it will make an excelent background prop ... or any other suitable piece of early Americana. A child is covering the table with a cloth, and setting out a menorah and a dish of biscuits. He is in colonial costume.)

ESTHER: He keeps asking me, "When will father be home?" And all I can answer is "Soon, soon ..." It seems so strange to celebrate the holiday with my husband off God knows where ... and no one here but me and the boy ... (Turning) Joshua, are your hands clean? (The child offers them for inspection.)

JOSHUA: (Pointing off) Mama, Look! Smoke ... a whole cloud of it going up into the sky. What is it?

ESTHER: I don't know. Come ... (She gently urges him toward a stool) Since Papa isn't here, it's up to me to tell the story. I'll do my best. (Joshua has taken the stool—the child looks up expectantly) So. Once upon a time—long, long ago—in the land of Israel, in the village of Modin, there lived a priest ...

JOSHUA: Mattathias.

ESTHER: (Nods) And his five sons. Simon, John, Eleazar, Jonathan ...

JOSHUA: And Judah.

ESTHER: And the Syrians ruled over the land. And it came to pass, one day ... (Under the above, a voice is heard, offstage, calling excitedly. And then Mrs. Patterson, Mrs. Breckinridge, rush in. Mrs. Patterson wears a shawl over her head—the other lady a bonnet and cloak.)

MRS. PATTERSON: (Excitedly) The British ... a whole regiment of them! Here, here in Bedford! They say they've got information that our men are out with the patriots. They want to know where they are. They say if we won't tell ...

MRS. BRECKINRIDGE: They've set fire to the meeting-hall already. And Tom Jackson's house ... They set it to burning with a brand from his own hearth!

MRS. PATTERSON: We've got to get out of here! All of us! Don't wait to pack. Take the children, quickly ...

MRS. BRECKINRIDGE: Hurry! Didn't you hear? Why don't you hurry?

ESTHER: Because I'm not going. We'll run away, and then ... our husbands will come back ... to what? A ghost village. No. I'm not going.

MRS. PATTERSON: Don't be a fool! What's the point of staying?

ESTHER: To put out the fires ... to help our neighbors rebuild their homes. And if our men should return, and there is fighting, we can cook for them, care for the wounded, stand by them reloading their muskets if need be.

MRS. PATTERSON: Fighting? How could we dare to fight! A few dozen farmers and their women and children against a regiment of redcoats!

ESTHER: Perhaps you noticed the candles. Today is a holiday of ours. Chanukah. The Feast of Lights. I was just telling Joshua the story ...

MRS. PATTERSON: Mrs. Hays, this is no time to ...

ESTHER: ... the story of the Maccabees. A handful of shepherds and farmers ...

MRS. PATTERSON: Mrs. Hays, please!

ESTHER: (Doggedly, calmly going on) ... in Israel, in the village of Modin, there came a regiment of Syrian soldiers—

(The tableau of the story-telling holds at left, and the Chairman takes it up, reading from the diary again.)

CHAIRMAN: "—and I went on, telling the ancient story. A ragged handful of Judeans daring to defend their homes, daring to stand up against the glittering legions of Syria. Judah the Maccabee rallying his regiments of farmers and blacksmiths ... flinging themselves against a crack army with nothing but crude, home-made weapons ... and the dream of liberty. I told it all. How they marched to set Jerusalem free. And then the cleansing of the Temple. And the miracle of the holy oil keeping the light burning ..."

ESTHER: (Taking it up) ... eight days, the oil burned.

And from that time on, wherever they are, on Chanukah, Jews light the menorah and sing of the Maccabees. (Turning to the other women) That's all. That's the story. I'm sorry to have kept you so long. If you're going, you'd better hurry.

MRS. PATTERSON: (A pause ... then softly) Is Bedford Village so different from Modin?

ESTHER: You tell me.

MRS. PATTERSON: (Slowly taking off her shawl, and sitting) I've changed my mind. I think I'll stay ... and watch you light the candles ... (Esther impulsively embraces her. The other women look at each other, and then slowly begin to take off their bonnets and cloaks. Esther turns back to light the first candle, chanting the blessing in Hebrew.)

ESTHER: It's late now. Time to put away this diary and go to bed. My David, wherever you are, I know you would have wanted it to be like this ... with me and the children lighting the menorah and singing the old songs, just as though you were here. Yet I keep reminding myself that no freedom is won without a fight. And who should know that better than I? How does the old Talmudic saying go? "If not I, then who? If not now, then when?" (The stage is in complete darkness by now, except for the one fully lit menorah—for as Esther has been speaking, above, her child has been lighting the rest of the candles.)

My darling, I believe that there will come a time when these dark days will stand with the days of the Maccabees. And wherever there are Jews living in fear and trembling ... when they light their candles ... in Spain— (On a stage level,[*] a woman in Spanish dress lights a menorah.) —In the ghettos of Prague, in the bleak villages of Russia ...

(On another level, another woman in peasant costume lights a menorah—and then a third—so that now four menorahs burn on different levels of the darkened stage.)

When they speak of the Maccabees, they will also speak of Lexington and Concord. And they will know that for simple people to stand their ground and fight for freedom is not a wild dream! (Tableau of the four women hold as—*chorus*, up full, sings *"Mi Y'Malel"*.)

---

[*] NOTE: If it is not possible to light menorahs on different levels, place them at different areas on the stage.

SPEAKER: (As song finishes, fading into background and continuing as a hummed reprise.)

In the pages of history where it tells of how America was born ... in the record of that first lightning flash of independence, alongside the names of statesmen and generals, let there be recorded the names of farmboys and fishermen, housewives and shoemakers, the name of a Jewish mother who remembered the Maccabees. On the anvil of freedom, they hammered out a nation. And Jews among them—trudging westward, peddlers and Indian traders climbing the wild deer trails in the mountains, planting towns out on the great plains. Places bearing their names springing up along the frontier. Gratzburg, Franks Town, Aaronsburg ...

SPEAKER: Beyond the reaches of the Ohio, and west to the Illinois. Upon the cracked, yellow pages of old letters, you find the shape of their hopes, the faint echo of their frontier laughter ...

FIRST PIONEER: April, 1882. Dear Cousin ... We have settled down here in St. Louis. It's a lovely country. Out here in Missouri—the first year you don't believe what others tell you, and the second year you don't believe what you tell yourself. And food ... food is no problem. We've got a thousand things to eat ... every one of them beans. But seriously, you should come out here. I know you think it's further than it is, but you'll find it ain't.

SPEAKER: They were the trail-breakers, carving a nation out of the prairie. The unknown and the anonymous ... those whose names have escaped us, whose faces will never be engraved in monuments. And yet they left behind them something more enduring than stone ...

SPEAKER: They carried the faith of their fathers ... Celebrating Yom Kippur on the banks of the Missouri, Passover in the Sierra Nevadas. Extending a hand of brotherhood to the Indians. Their tradition being the Old Testament belief that all men are equal in the eyes of God. They were pioneers not in spite of being Jews, but *because* of it—their password on the prairie being the old proverb: "If I try to be like someone else, who will be like me?" And so they spilled west, carving a nation out of the wilderness ... (The seder table has been cleared, and now a couple in frontier dress perform a dance in the spirit of the following—)

SOLO

Oh, do you remember sweet Betsy from Pike,*
Who crossed the big mountains with her lover Ike,
With two yoke of oxen, a cheese and a half,
A tall shanghai rooster, and one spotted calf,

CHORUS

Toora dang fol de di do,
Toora dang fol dee day!

SOLO

One evening quite early they camped on the Platte,
'Twas near the road on a green shady flat,
Where Betsy, sore-footed, lay down to repose—
With wonder Ike gazed on his Pike County rose.

CHORUS

They soon reached the desert, where Betsy gave out,
And down on the sand she lay rolling about;
While Ike, half distracted, looked on with surprise,
Saying, "Betsy, get up, you'll get sand in your eyes."

Long Ike and sweet Betsy attended a dance,
And Ike wore a pair of his Pike County pants;
Sweet Betsy was covered with ribbons and rings;
Said Ike, "You're an angel, but where are your wings?"

(Repeat opening verse and chorus to finish.)

SPEAKER: They fought for freedom on the frontiers of Missouri and Kansas as they had fought for it at Bennington and Bunker Hill. But freedom is not a crop to be planted once and then forgotten. The years slip by, and the crop must be sown again, watched and tended, and sown again ... (At left, a woman—Ernestine Rose—has taken her place.)

Out of the shadows of history, on the pages of dusty documents, discover the forgotten names. The year is 1852. The place is Syracuse, New York. The woman is Ernestine Rose. Her family murdered in a pogrom in the ghetto of Poland, she turned toward the beckoning lights of liberty ... (Background: *Chorus* starts to hum "Go Down Moses.")

---

* See "Production Chart" at back of script.

ROSE: We children of Israel cannot but have in our minds always the memory of Moses leading our forefathers out of bondage. We cannot but say that the Negro ought to enjoy or suffer with the prosperity or adversity of his country. Is that any more than any man ought to claim—and ought any man be satisfied with less?

(Chorus: Up full, singing a verse and chorus of "Go Down Moses"—then humming a reprise, fading out ... Ernestine Rose has exited, giving way to an older woman—Mrs. Trager—in Civil War costume, a black gown if possible.)

MRS. TRAGER: Last night, hoping to comfort myself, I turned to my Bible. And there on the page was the story of Solomon's judgment. Oh, dear God, give me a little of the wisdom of Solomon! For I need it to go on living as I live ... here with my husband on our plantation in the South ... and my four sons fighting in the armies of the North ...

SPEAKER: Out of the shadows of history, discover the names. Mrs. Abraham Isaac Trager, of Columbia, South Carolina. Her husband an owner of slaves. A good man, pious and gentle —his slaves calling him Grandpa ... and when he set up his Sukkah, they would say: "Grandpa's building a house to ketch God ..." Mrs. Abraham Isaac Trager. Her husband an owner of slaves, and her four sons fighting on the side of the North. One of them camps this night with Sherman's Army of the Potomac, at the edge of Bull Run ... (Background: The humming has faded out into the sound of cannon firing. Let it establish, then fade down, holding under.)

MRS. TRAGER: (Reading letter) Dear Mother ... I am writing you this on the eve of the battle. I've just learned that the stronghold we're about to attack derives its name from a Jew. In these mountain-passes there once stood a small lodging house, where the travellers used to stop overnight on their way to Richmond. The proprietor was a Jew from Portugal called Menasha. And, bit by bit, it became known as Manassas. And now the whole Army of the Potomac is praying, "Oh, Menasha, what wouldn't we give if you would just admit us to your town tomorrow!"

Dearest Mother ... When I was a little boy, you used to read to me about Moses in Egypt. So perhaps you will understand why I could not find it in me to justify slavery. Mother, believe me, the day will come ... (She breaks down, but forcing back the choked tears, forces herself to go on.)

... the day will come when this bitter war will be nothing but a fading memory. If God spares us, you will see your sons grouped around you once again ... (Weeping—then catching herself and going on determinedly) Give my love to Papa, and assure him that I hold his memory and you dearer than life itself. But I must do what is in my heart ... Your loving son ... Jonathan.

SPEAKER: Is there a poet anywhere looking for an image to describe America? You might do worse than tell of a family named Trager. To tell of four sons who left their plantation home and went to take their places in the battle lines with Lincoln ... And a mother, who wept to see them go, but, being a Jewess, understood why they went.

The hour of agony is long, but it is not forever. There comes a day when the guns fall silent, and peace descends upon the torn fields. The dead lie quiet in the cool earth—and the living turn homeward—(The soldier moves toward Mrs. Trager, pauses a moment gazing at her—and then they move swiftly into a fierce embrace. The tableau of their reunion holding under the following—)

For years the nation carries bitterness like a wound. But slowly, the scar heals over. And the running river of time washes out the old hatreds. (Light blacks out at left.)

The farmers turn back to the land. Wheat coming up once more on the slopes of Gettysburg ... cotton coming up once more on the battlefields of Virginia. These would seem to be quiet days. In the gracious houses of Boston and New York, well-bred ladies turn to writing verses. (Light left comes up on Emma Lazarus—sitting at a small table, scratching absorbedly with a pen—pausing now and then to brood.)

And out of all the well-bred young ladies writing their delicate sonnets, there flashes on with a brilliant gift, a voice lyric as a bird at dusk ... (Emma rises.)

EMMA:
> I behold without regret
> Beauty in new forms recast
> Truth emerging from the vast,
> Bright and orbed, like yonder sphere,
> Making the obscure air clear ...

SPEAKER: A wealthy and fashionable young lady named Lazarus. Emma Lazarus. She has already won the applause and friendship of Emerson and Whittier for her translations of Heine and Hugo ... and for her own romantic songs ... (Waltz music is heard now. Several couples in period dress of the 1870's come on dancing. A partner whirls Emma away with them. Then the music fades down, holding.)

These would seem to be quiet days ... and yet, Emma Lazarus had the curious feeling that beyond the circle of sweet music, another song was rising. Another song, she sensed, not quite so sweet ... (Sound of telegraph key.)

Pogroms flaming in the villages of Russia. Torches flung at the houses of the ghetto, cries of torment rising in the night to echo west across the world, and then to re-echo in the burning verses of Emma Lazarus.

She went to visit the Jewish immigrants in the miserable refuge of Ward's Island. When she returned home, she carried within her the anguish of those faces. And a new poet was born.

EMMA: (Her delivery a marked contrast from the lyric style of her first poem)

> O deem not dead that martial fire,
> Say not the mystic flame is spent.
> With Moses' law and David's lyre
> Your ancient strength remains unbent.
> Let but an Ezra rise anew
> To lift the banner of the Jew!

SPEAKER: And should America ever for a passing moment turn from its tradition of welcoming the oppressed, she wrote a burning reminder— (The lights have gone out, except for a spot on Emma.)

EMMA:

> Give me your tired, your poor
> Your huddled masses yearning to breathe free...
> Send these, the homeless, tempest-tossed to me...

(Light slowly dims out on Emma Lazarus.)

SPEAKER: Standing amidst all the misery of Ward's Island, she foresaw the strength and promise hidden in these immigrants. And the Twentieth Century brought a sunrise of fulfillment. Immigrants weaving cloth in the factories of New Jersey, making shoes in the mills of Massachusetts, planting corn in Iowa and wheat in Texas. Immigrants and the sons of immigrants practicing law in the court houses of the country schoolhouses and the great universities. Across the nation, immigrants and the sons of immigrants standing tall in the American sunlight. Yet, as Emma Lazarus had known, there were the others—the lost and driven of the earth—Jews who needed a homeland of their own—

EMMA'S VOICE: (From offstage) "The idea that I am possessed with is that of restoring a political existence to my people, making them a nation again, giving them a national center ... This is the task which presents itself to me ... I am resolved to devote my whole life to it!"

SPEAKER: Across half a world, at the edge of the Mediterranean, a new nation conceived in liberty ... groping its way to its feet with a stubborn courage that brought back an echo of our own beginnings. The Declaration of Independence in Tel-Aviv striking a memory of our Continental Congress in Philadelphia ... the frontier of the Negev striking a memory of our western territory ... the immigrant camps of Haifa striking a memory of Ward's Island with its horizon of hope ... (During the following, all the cast moves back on stage, taking up positions in semi-circle across background.)

And we reach out a hand to them. And in that simple gesture is all our three hundred years of knowing what it means for a free nation to struggle to its feet. We summon the best that is in us—traditions carried from the voice of Isaiah to the voice of Jefferson, from the slopes of Jerusalem to the slopes of Valley Forge, carried from the wilderness of Sinai to the wilderness of Arizona. (Chorus begins humming softly Lazarus poem.)

Listen to the heartbeat of an American Jew, and Isaac Levy's dream of brotherhood ... and hear the singing echo of Esther Hays' passion for freedom ... and Bertha Trager's love of liberty ... and Emma Lazarus' vision of the future ... and you, woman in New York, going down to cast your vote on election day in the early morning ...

You, woman in Cincinnati, writing a letter to your Congressman regarding the rights of man ...

You, mother in Shenandoah, reaching out to rescue a lonely child in a ghetto, reaching out to help a pioneer in the Negev ...

You, housewife in Seattle, helping to train a student in the Galilee, helping to deliver a baby in the Judean Hills, knowing that new life for freedom anywhere is new hope for America—

You, unknown and anonymous, whose names will never appear on the pages of history books, whose faces will never be engraved on monuments—

You appear at no conferences of statesmen. You lead no armies into battle—

Yet let it be said of you—
Through the shadow and sunlight of your time
You carried the American dream
And left the vivid air signed with your honor!

(*Chorus*, accompanied by all onstage, sings *Third Verse* of *Star Spangled Banner*—up to full finish.)

FINALE

*See Production Chart and Historical Note
on pages 347 and 348.*

PRODUCTION CHART

Episodes	Tableaux	Songs Jewish	Songs American	Dances
Prologue	Speaker vs Chairman			
Eps. I 1654	First Jewish Immigrants to New Amsterdam—1654	Yoheved's Lullaby from "The Gateway to Jewish Song" by Judith Eisenstein		
Eps. II 1655-57	Stand for Equal Rights 1655-57, Asser and Mrs. Levy			
Eps. III 1747	Transition 1680-1763 to First Jewish Colonists	Synagogue Chant		
Eps. IV 1765-1779	Fight for Freedom Revolutionary Period 1775-1779 a. Trader's Act—1765 b. Francis Salvador—1776 c. Esther Hays—1779			
Eps. V 1822-1848	Pioneers—Trail Blazers Opening of Mid-West 1822-25		Betsy from Pike*	Betsy from Pike
Interlude	Westward-Ho			
Eps. VI 1852-1864	Civil War Period a. Anti-Slavery; Ernestine Rose b. Mrs. Trager— Sons at War		Go Down Moses	
Eps. VII 1870-1880's	Immigration— Emma Lazarus			Waltz
Eps. VIII 1950's	Ingathering of Exiles America—Israel			
Epilogue			3rd Verse of Star Spangled Banner	

---

* In "Burl Ives Song Book"—pocket Ballantine Book, p. 234.

HISTORICAL NOTE:

All of the major characters in this pageant were actual people. In many cases, the words they speak here are direct quotations from their letters and diaries, and the episodes are based on events in their lives.

MRS. ASSER LEVY..............Oppenheim; American Jewish Historical Society Publication XVIII. L. D. Scisco: "The Burgher Guard of New Amsterdam:—The American Historical Register, II (1895)

NINE JEWISH TRADERS ....Facsimile, Emmet Collection, No. 230, Manuscript Division, N. Y. Public Library
(refusing to accept goods shipped from Britain)

FRANCIS SALVADOR ....Barnett, A. Elias: "The Jews of South Carolina." Phila. 1905.

ESTHER HAYS ....Solis-Cohen, Solomon: "Note Concerning David Hays and Esther Etting His Wife," AJHSP II 1894.
De Sola Pool, David: "Portraits Etched In Stone," Columbia U. Press, 1952.

CINCINNATI CONGREGATION ...Philipson, David: "The Jewish Pioneers of the Ohio Valley" AJHSP VIII

ERNESTINE ROSE ....Stanton, Anthony and Gage: "History of Woman Suffrage" Vol. I.

MRS. TRAGER ....Henning, Helen Kohn: "The Tree of Life."

EMMA LAZARUS ....Jacob, H. E.: "The World of Emma Lazarus."

GENERAL INFORMATION ....Friedman and Falk: "Jews In American Wars" New York, 1943.

A TWO-FOLD BLESSING
Joseph Krauskopf

Blessed has been the lot of the Jew in the United States, and blessed have been the United States in blessing him. It is a marvelous story, that of the settling of the Jew on the Western continent, and the more we read and study it, the stronger grows the belief that it was the hand of Providence that opened for Columbus and for the Jews accompanying him the portals of the new world, to afford a resting-place at last to the "tribe of the wandering foot and weary breast," and a haven to all others seeking shelter and peace.

Like a chapter of romance reads the answer to the question that Longfellow asks in "The Jewish Cemetery at Newport":

> "How came they here? What burst of Christian hate,
> What persecution, merciless and blind,
> Drove o'er the sea—that desert desolate—
> These Ishmaels and Hagars of mankind?"

THE JEWISH CEMETERY AT NEWPORT
Henry Wadsworth Longfellow

How strange it seems! These Hebrews in their graves,
    Close by the street of this fair seaport town,
Silent beside the never-silent waves,
    At rest in all this moving up and down!

The trees are white with dust, that o'er their sleep
    Wave their broad curtains in the south-wind's breath,
While underneath such leafy tents they keep
    The long, mysterious Exodus of Death.

And these sepulchral stones, so old and brown,
    That pave with level flags their burial-place
Seem like the tablets of the Law, thrown-down
    And broken by Moses at the mountain's base.

The very names recorded here are strange,
    Of foreign accent, and of different climes;
Alvarez and Rivera interchange
    With Abraham and Jacob of old times.

"Blessed be God! For He created death!"
    The mourners said, "and Death is rest and peace,"
Then added, in the certainty of faith,
    "And giveth Life that nevermore shall cease."

Closed are the portals of their Synagogue,
    No Psalms of David now the silence break,
No Rabbi reads the ancient Decalogue
    In the grand dialect the Prophets spake.

Gone are the living, but the dead remain,
    And not neglected; for a hand unseen,
Scattering its bounty, like a summer rain,
    Still keeps their graves and their remembrance green.

How came they here? What burst of Christian hate,
    What persecution, merciless and blind,
Drove o'er the sea—that desert desolate—
    These Ishmaels and Hagars of mankind?

They lived in narrow streets and lanes obscure,
    Ghetto and Judenstrasse, in mirk and mire:
Taught in the school of patience to endure
    The life of anguish and the death of fire.

All their lives long, with the unleavened bread
    And bitter herbs of exile and its fears,
The wasting famine of the heart they fed,
    And slaked its thirst with marah of their tears.

Anathema maranatha! was the cry
    That rang from town to town, from street to street;
At every gate the accursed Mordecai
    Was mocked and jeered, and spurned by Christian feet.

Pride and humiliation hand in hand
    Walked with them through the world where'er they went;
Trampled and beaten were they as the sand,
    And yet unshaken as the continent.

For in the background figures vague and vast
    Of patriarchs and of prophets rose sublime,
And all the great traditions of the Past
    They saw reflected in the coming time.

And thus forever with reverted look
    The mystic volume of the world they read,
Spelling it backward, like a Hebrew book,
    Till life became a Legend of the Dead.

But ah! what once has been shall be no more!
    The groaning earth in travail and in pain
Brings forth its races, but does not restore,
    And the dead nations never rise again.

FROM THE DAYS OF COLUMBUS
Lee M. Friedman

Ever since that day when Columbus first announced in a letter to his Jewish friend, Luis de Santangel, the discovery of America by the expedition fitted out by Jewish gold, manned in part by Jewish sailors, and guided into unknown seas by nautical tables compiled by a Jew, printed by another, and presented to Columbus by a third—ever since that day the Jew has played an honorable and not undistinguished part in the history and development of the Western continents.

THE DISCOVERY OF THE "TU-KEY"
Dorothy Ross

When Christopher Columbus set foot on solid land,
He thought he was in India, the destination planned.
He leaped with great excitement onto the new-found shore,
And stared at all the scenery and mountains that he saw.

Then following behind him, astonished just as he,
His weary, hungry sailors with their backs turned to the sea,
Breathed deeply of the incense that came from fruit and flower,
And dropping to their knees, they blessed this long-awaited hour.

Now suddenly before them appeared the strangest bird,
Of whom not one had ever seen or read or even heard.
"It couldn't be a chicken—it has a spreading tail—"
Said all the sailors staring, as it ambled down the trail.

Columbus grew impatient—the men were hungry too—
"Let's catch and roast the nameless bird, set traps and bag a few!
"We'll truss them and we'll clean them and we'll put them on the flame,
"While Luis checks the records and gives the fowl a name!"

(We know from all the records that Torres was a Jew
Who fled from Spanish terror—but Columbus never knew.)
He took his precious Bible and books of Jewish law,
And looked up beasts and birds and fowl and creatures by the score.

"Old Noah must have had a pair when he filled up the Ark,"
Said Luis as he checked who lived in Adam's Eden Park;
"Perhaps if I read Solomon who spoke to bird and beast,
I'll find out the particulars and then we'll have a feast!"

Columbus snapped his fingers and called Luis de Torres,
Who kept the log, knew languages and did a million chores.
"Say, Torres," said the Admiral, "What would you call this creature—
"With naked head and spreading tail and unfamiliar feature?"

De Torres flipped the pages and nibbled on a cookie.
"I've got it! Yes, I found it! It's referred to as a 'tu-key'—
"King Solomon had many. They played around his zoo,
But he also served them roasted when a King or Queen came through!"

"Hooray!" the sailors chorused, "the mystery is past,
Let's have a tu-key banquet and break our fast at last!"
So someone set the table, Columbus said the Grace—
They gobbled up the tu-key and didn't leave a trace!

And later, much later, when the Pilgrims found the bird,
They called the tu-key—"turkey" because De Torres' notes got blurred;
And we eat it and we stuff it and we thank our Spanish Jew
For tracing it through centuries to Solomon's own zoo!

From Young Judaean

THE FIRST PASSOVER IN AMERICA
Max Ehrlich

PRODUCTION NOTE:

This radio play, originally presented under the auspices of the Synagogue Council of America over the National Broadcasting Company, can effectively be done as a dramatic reading, simulating a radio broadcast.

Obviously, its effect would be enhanced if sound effects and music, as suggested, are incorporated. The director can, however, adapt directions as regards sound and music to available facilities, using recorded music, choral singing backstage or piano accompaniment only.

ANNOUNCER: The First Passover in America!

CHOIR: (Suitable Passover hymn, up for a while, and then down and under for background.)

ANNOUNCER: (Over choir, down under) On ... evening of this week, Jews all over the world will begin the eight-day celebration of the ancient Passover holiday ... one of the oldest festivals of freedom in the history of mankind. And to American Jews, this celebration will mark the 311th (correct to suit exact year presentation is given) observance of the first Passover in America. It was in 1655, when colonial America was still very young, that a sturdy band of Jewish pioneers first participated in this traditional holiday on American soil.

Tonight, we bring you the dramatic story based upon actual fact of 'The First Passover in America.' (Organ theme up for several bars and then down and under)

NARRATOR: The time is August 22nd, 1654. On the high seas, a few miles offshore from New Amsterdam, a tiny sailing vessel dips and ploughs through the waves which threaten to engulf it. Weeks ago, it had started from Holland for the new land. The trip had been stormy and hazardous. Only the superior seamanship of the Dutch captain and his crew had kept the vessel afloat. And then, suddenly from far up in the rigging, comes a glad cry ... (Fade in sound of wind through rigging, the creaking of spars, etc. continuous through scene)

VOICE: (Calling excitedly) Land! ... Land ho! ... (Buzz of eager voices)

CAPTAIN: (Shouting) Ho! Lookout! Where d'ye see it?

LOOKOUT: (Distantly) Over there, Captain! To the West!

CAPTAIN: (Over excited crowd voices, after slight pause)

Ya! Ya! It *is* New Amsterdam! (Then, soberly) Muynheeren, God has been good to us ... ! (Cheer goes up from crowd)

CAPTAIN: Muynheeren ... we have come through a dangerous voyage ... safely ... A higher Power has guided the skill of our hands, and kept alive the courage in our hearts. And for this, I ask you now ... to bow your heads with me ... and give thanks in prayer. (Murmur or quiet assent from crowd. Then silence, except for sound of wind and waves)

CAPTAIN: (He prays) Merciful God! We thank Thee for Thy infinite wisdom and Thy infinite mercy. Thou hast watched over us when the elements raged ... and Thou hast placed Thy blessing on our humble craft and ourselves. For this, we here assembled, thank Thee for Thy compassion and Thy love. Amen. (Murmur of amens. Then voices up for moment and slowly fade)

BARSIMSON: Captain Van Dam!

CAPTAIN: Ya? Oh. Good afternoon, Muynheer Barsimson.

BARSIMSON: Good afternoon. Captain ... when shall we actually be able to set foot on land?

CAPTAIN: Well ... if this wind keeps up, we'll land in the new world in about three hours ...

BARSIMSON: (Half to himself, dreamily) New ... Amsterdam .. ! America!

CAPTAIN: You are anxious to see it, are you not?

BARSIMSON: Yes ... Yes, I am. Captain Van Dam ... as far as I know ... I shall be the first of the people of Israel to set foot in New Amsterdam. The prospect excites me ... a new land ... a land of hope and freedom ... without tyranny!

CAPTAIN: (Slowly) Ya! Ya, I can understand that. (Voice becomes curious) But Muynheer ... there is something I would like to ask you.

BARSIMSON: Yes, Captain?

CAPTAIN: You, Jacob Barsimson, are of the Jewish faith. You do not worship in our manner. Yet when I called for prayer just now, you bowed your head and prayed with the rest of us. This I do not understand ...

BARSIMSON: (Simply) We all worship the same God, Captain. You worship Him in your way ... and I, in mine. A moment ago, you gave thanks to this same Divine Being for having seen us safely through danger ... I, too, was grateful ... and I joined my prayer ... with yours. (Organ up for few bars in narrative theme and then fade under)

NARRATOR: Thus came Jacob Barsimson, the first Jew to set foot in New Amsterdam. A few weeks later, twenty-three of his co-religionists and their families landed in the colony, fleeing Portuguese oppression. They had been dispossessed of most of their worldly goods, but they were sturdy and courageous. They settled down to make themselves hard-working members of the community.

The liberal Dutch people of the colony, in whom the idea of live and let live was inherent, welcomed the new settlers. Peter Stuyvesant, the governor of New Amsterdam, was away on a trip to the Dutch West Indies, and his sheriff, Cornelius van Tienhofen, was in full authority. Tienhofen was narrow-minded and intolerant, hated by his own people, as well as the minority groups of New Amsterdam. He did everything in his power to make the existence of the newcomers intolerable ...

TIENHOFEN: I tell you, Van den Bosch, these Jews must get out! We cannot have them here!

VAN DEN BOSCH: But Sheriff, as head of the Council, I say that we need them here ... they are industrious, hardworking. They obey our laws ...

TIENHOFEN: Ach! Donder! You, Cort Van den Bosch, are advising me? ... Cornelius van Tienhofen? *I* am the Schout ... the governor of New Netherlands in Stuyvesant's absence. I will do as I see fit! I say we do not want these people here! They must go! We want only Dutch!

VAN DEN BOSCH: But van Tienhofen! We have all manner of people here ... Papists, Mennonites, Lutherans, Quakers, Puritans ... They are all part of our community ...

TIENHOFEN: Ya! More strangers! They, too, must get oudt! They are rascals, the whole lot of them!

VAN DEN BOSCH: Excellency, I must warn you. Our people will be angry. We *need* new people here to make our city grow ...

TIENHOFEN: Bah! I am the law! Do you hear that, Cort? I am the law, and not your Council or the people. (Loudly) De Geer!

DE GEER: Ya, Excellency ...

TIENHOFEN: You are my chief deputy in New Amsterdam, is it not so?

DE GEER: Ya!

TIENHOFEN: Then I order you ... you hear, de Geer ...

I order you ... to make these rascals ... the Jews, the Quakers, the Huguenots, the Presbyterians and all the rest ... understand that they are not welcome here. By the sacred spirit of Hendrik Hudson, I'll drive them oudt ... Is it clear what you are to do, de Geer?

DE GEER: It is clear, Excellency! (With delight) Ya! Ya, it is quite clear! (Organ up briefly then strikes dissonant chord)

DE GEER: (Harshly) You! Quaker! You will come with me!

VOICE: Why do you break into my house? Where are you taking me?

DE GEER: To the whipping post!

VOICE: The whipping post? But Deputy, I have done nothing!

DE GEER: You are a Quaker! That is enough. Come! Come, I say! (Sound of whip across body) (Organ strikes dissonant chord)

FILTER VOICE or backstage: Lutheran ... Presbyterian ... Huguenot ... Jew ... Mennonite ... take heed! You are not citizens here ... you are unwelcome strangers! As far as this government is concerned, you have no rights, you are not freemen, you live here under sufferance! (Crowd babble swells up in angry protest, and then down) (Organ up three quick bars)

TIENHOFEN: You there! You two men . !

LEVY AND BARSIMON: Yes? (In unison)

TIENHOFEN: What are your names?

BARSIMSON: Mine is Jacob Barsimson ...

LEVY: And I am Asher Levy ...

TIENHOFEN: Oh! Jews, eh?

BARSIMSON: (Quietly) Yes ... we are ...

TIENHOFEN: (Harshly) Then go and tell your people this: Jews in New Amsterdam are not wanted. From now on, by order of the Governor, you are to be denied all civil and personal rights. You are to be denied freedom to gather in public places, and other rights. You will in every way be prohibited from participating in the life of the community and further, you will be denied the right to worship or to observe any religious holiday! (Music up strong for a few moments and then under)

NARRATOR: The High Sheriff instituted decree after decree against the Jews, and life became almost unbearable for the new colonists. Finally, a Jewish delegation, led by Asher Levy and Abraham de Lucena, visited Tienhofen ... (Music down and out. Fade into buzz of voices which quiet down)

TIENHOFEN: (Irately) Well? Well? You wanted to see me?

LEVY: Your Excellency ... we have come to plead our cause. We have been sorely oppressed ...

DE LUCENA: We have been beaten ... and forbidden to work!

LEVY: Some of our people have been thrown into your prison, although they have committed no wrong ... They were not even given a trial ...

DE LUCENA: We have been driven from our homes by your bailiffs, when we could not pay the grievous taxes you have levied upon us.

TIENHOFEN: (Bursts into roar of laughter) So you don't like it here? Eh!! Gut! Gut! Perhaps you will now leave us, eh?

LEVY: Your Excellency ... we ask only that you allow us to live and work in New Amsterdam in peace. We ask your indulgence to participate in the life of the community, as residents and good citizens. (Murmur of agreement up and down)

TIENHOFEN: You ask! You ask! Muyneheeren, you are impertinent! Insolent! I am in power now, and I govern New Netherlands as I see fit! Ya! As only *I* see fit, and no one else!

LEVY: But Your Excellency!

TIENHOFEN: Silence! I will not be interrupted. You Jews do not belong here! No! The Quakers, the Papists, the Lutherans and all the rest ... they do not belong here. I do not want you here! You will have to get *oudt* soon! Do you hear? Soon you will have to get *oudt* of New Amsterdam! (Angry crowd buzz up and down)

DE LUCENA: Your Excellency ... !

TIENHOFEN: (Peevishly) Well? Have I not made myself clear?

DE LUCENA: Yes ... Yes, you have. But there is one thing more ...

TIENHOFEN: Well? What is it?

DE LUCENA: You have seen fit to turn your face from us, in all respects. This we do not understand, but must bow to the dictate of your authority. Yet we ask one thing which we pray you may grant ... the opportunity to hold religious services ...

TIENHOFEN: Bah! (Sneers) Religious services! Freedom of religion!

LEVY: You do not understand, Your Excellency. In a few months the holiday of Passover will be here. Each year we have observed this sacred holiday, as do Jews in other parts of the world. We beg your indulgence on this point ...

TIENHOFEN: Passover? Oh! So you wish to celebrate your flight from Egypt in the olden times? Well ... I wish to celebrate your flight from New Amsterdam now! So you wish to celebrate the Passover, eh? Well, I say No! No! Dot's my answer, No!

DE LUCENA: Your Excellency, please!

TIENHOFEN: Get oudt! Get oudt of here! I have had enough of these disturbances. I have had enough of troublemakers! I am the authority, in New Amsterdam, and my answer is NO! (Crowd murmur up. Fades into organ for awhile and then fade under)

NARRATOR: Tienhofen was unyielding. The lot of the Jewish pioneers became more and more unbearable. Finally, in desperation they held a meeting at Asher Levy's house to discuss their problems ... (Buzz of voices continuous in background)

VOICE I: We cannot go on like this much longer ...

VOICE II: It's more than anyone can endure. We cannot work ... We cannot worship ... we are not even allowed to stand guard against Indian attacks. If they discover that we are holding even this small meeting, we shall be flogged and thrown into prison!

WOMAN'S VOICE: Let us leave America and look for a new home ...

VOICE I: (Dismayed) But where can we go? We have no money for passage.

VOICE II: And the Passover? What about the Passover? Our fathers, and our father's fathers sat at the table and conducted the Passover ceremony. And now we are to be denied this ...

BARSIMSON: Gentlemen! Gentlemen! (Voices die down)

VOICE: Yes, Barsimson.

BARSIMSON: I have a plan ... although, I admit, its chances of success are doubtful. (Crowd comment—curious. Ad lib: "What's your plan? Tell us about it" etc.)

BARSIMSON: We can write a letter to the directors of the Dutch East India Company which has jurisdiction over van Tienhofen ... yes, and over Peter Stuyvesant himself! We can petition for civil and religious rights. It's our only hope ... (Buzz of agreement from crowd)

LEVY: What do you think of this? Abraham de Lucena?

DE LUCENA: I look upon it with favor, Asher Levy. The Dutch have ever been a liberal people, and lovers of freedom. It has been so in Holland, and the people here have been sympathetic to us, despite the authorities. Certainly it will do no harm. And why knows? A favorable reply may come in time to allow us to celebrate the Passover festival! (Buzz of crowd up ... fade into organ music. Up and out)

NARRATOR: The little group sent the petition off to the Dutch West India Company on the next boat for Holland. (Organ up and under)

NARRATOR: When Tienhofen heard of this, his rage knew no bounds.

TIENHOFEN: Ah! Donder! So they've done it! They've written the Fatherland for help, have they? Well, we shall see! We shall see who is master here ... (Sputters)

DE GEER: Your Excellency!

TIENHOFEN: Ya, De Geer? What iss it?

DE GEER: For weeks you have threatened to expel these people, is it not so?

TIENHOFEN: Ya ...

DE GEER: Then, Excellency, why not do it now? A decree ... a decree of expulsion is all that is necessary ...

TIENHOFEN: A decree? Ya! By the phantom of the Half-Moon, dot iss a good idea! But wait. De Geer! Suppose those stupid burghers of the West India Company in Holland grant the petition of these Jews? Then we will haf trouble.

DE GEER: (Silkily) The West India Company will not trouble itself to answer. They will delegate the handling of it to you, Excellency. And just to make sure, you yourself can write to the directors stating your grievances against these Jews.

TIENHOFEN: (Thoughtfully) You are right, De Geer ...

DE GEER: I have something still further to suggest, Excellency. Something that will be bitter medicine for these Israelites to swallow ...

TIENHOFEN: Ya?

DE GEER: We can expel them on the same boat coming from Holland which they hope will carry an answer to their stupid petition.

TIENHOFEN: (Roars with laughter) Ya! Ya! De Geer! Dot iss a good one! Giff me my quill. This decree I will write now! (Pause) (Scratching of quill on paper) (Organ music up for three bars and out) (Then clanging of town bell)

TOWN CRIER: (Against bell) Hear Ye! Hear Ye! A Decree written and signed by the High Sheriff of New Amsterdam, Cornelius van Tienhofen ... It is so written that the Jews who came last year from the West Indies and from the Fatherland must prepare to depart forthwith from this place. (Bell merges into organ music up and then under)

NARRATOR: This seemed to be the last, final, crushing blow to the Jews of the community. Their only chance was the boat that was soon due from Holland. As the days passed, the prospect looked darker and darker ... It was not only expulsion they faced ... they could not (Fade) even prepare for the Passover. (Slight sound of waves against pier) (Murmur of crowd in background continues)

BARSIMSON: The ship is overdue ... long overdue.

LEVY: It is only two days to Passover, Jacob. If it does not come within that time, then for the first time in our lives, we shall not celebrate the festival ...

BARSIMSON: And even if it does come in time ... there is but a slight chance that our petition will be granted ... (Crowd noises in background)

LEVY: Look at our people. They cannot keep away from the waterfront.

BARSIMSON: Yes Asher. And this waiting ... waiting ... it's getting almost unbearable.

SARAH: (Voice fades in) Jacob!

BARSIMSON: Yes, Sarah?

SARAH: The women are waiting ... What shall we do, my husband? Shall we make matzohs ... the unleavened bread? Shall we fix the bitter herbs, and make the other Passover preparations?

BARSIMSON: (Quietly) Yes.

SARAH: But Jacob! We do not know whether we will be allowed to celebrate the holiday.

BARSIMSON: Make the preparations nevertheless, Sarah.

We shall at least observe it in our hearts. If God is with us, then we shall have the unleavened bread and the bitter herbs at our Seder table, to remind us of our ancestors' sorrow in the land of Egypt ...

SARAH: And if the ship does not come?

BARSIMSON: If the ship does not come, or the answer is unfavorable, then we cannot sit down to our tables and celebrate the story of freedom. But the unleavened bread and the bitter herbs will still be here to remind us of our bitterness in the new land of America ... (Organ up and then under ...)

NARRATOR: One day passed, and then the afternoon of the second day came. A few hours more, at sunset, and Jews all over the world would begin to celebrate the Passover holiday. But the Jewish pioneers in New Amsterdam, their hearts heavy, stood on the docks and stared out to sea ... (Organ out ...) (Fade in slight sound of waves. Crowd buzz in background)

LEVY: It's no use, Jacob. There is no sail on the sea ...

BARSIMSON: (Sadly) The sun has begun to drop toward the horizon. There is no hope, no hope ...

LEVY: The Lord has turned against us.

BARSIMSON: You know, Asher, this will be the first Passover I have missed since I was a little child. And now ... now ... (He chokes with emotion)

LEVY: Come. It is hopeless to wait. Let us all go back to our homes ... (Distantly a church bell begins to ring. Then another and another. Excited crowd buzz rises and gets stronger. All this continues through scene)

JACOB: Asher! Asher! The bells!

LEVY: They're ringing ... and today is not the Sabbath ...

LEVY: They ring the bells on a week day only when they sight a ship. (Excited) Jacob! Look!

BARSIMSON: Where?

LEVY: (Excited) Over there. To the right! See ... it's a sail! A sail! (Crowd uproar. Joyous cries: "It's come!" "A sail!" "The boat's here!")

BARSIMSON: But does it carry an answer to our petition?

LEVY: God grant that it does! But come, Jacob. Come. When the boat docks, we'll go up to the Government House. There *must* be an answer and the captain will bring it there first!

(Organ music ... up strong and then down under)

NARRATOR: In the Council Chamber there was considerable excitement over the mail which the captain of the vessel had just delivered. On one side of the table sat van Tienhofen and his staff; on the other side, headed by Van der Bosch, sat the Council, representing the people of New Amsterdam. And in the anteroom, among others, stood Asher Levy and Jacob Barsimson waiting—but now the voices of the Council can be heard through the thin partition... (Voices up in council chamber... Tienhofen, Van der Bosch, etc. off mike) (Levy and Barsimson up to mike)

TIENHOFEN: Well Muynheeren. I will open these documents from the West India Company at my leisure and report on them later.

VAN DEN BOSCH: No, Your Excellency!! We demand to see them now!

TIENHOFEN: (Apoplectic) You demand? You demand? Ach! Oudt mit you! Stuyvesant is away and I represent the law in New Amsterdam. I will do as *I* please... (Angry crowd murmur through partition up)

VAN DEN BOSCH: Your Excellency! The people are tired of your high-handed methods! You have oppressed the people of our city ever since you have been in power...

TIENHOFEN: (Roars) Silence, Van Den Bosch!

VAN DEN BOSCH: I won't be silent. We represent the people... and we demand that the documents be opened while we of the People's Council are present!

TIENHOFEN: (Reluctantly) Oh, very well, it is better than arguing with you wooden heads... (Sound of envelopes being opened) See, Muynheeren? There is nothing here but drafts, bills of allowances...

VAN DEN BOSCH: Wait! What's this? It's a letter...

TIENHOFEN: A letter?

VAN DEN BOSCH: Yes, Excellency... a letter written to you under official seal... Listen as I read: "To Cornelius Van Tienhofen, High Sheriff of New Amsterdam: We have received communications from the Quakers, Jews, Lutherans, and other sections of your population, protesting your oppressive measures. As long as they continue moderate, peaceful, inoffensive and not hostile to the government, they should be allowed freedom and equal rights. Such have been the maxims of prudence and toleration by which the magistrates of this city have been governed. Follow in the same footsteps ... granting civil and religious rights to all peoples ... and you will be blest!" (Crowd uproar)

LEVY: Did you hear that? We're to be given civil and religious freedom. We can stay in America. We can celebrate the Passover! Praised be the Lord. (Organ music up and then out ...)

NARRATOR: In a typical Jewish household in the little colony of New Amsterdam, we find a family sitting at the table for the Seder. The candles are lit. The matzot are on the table. So, too, are the bitter herbs and wine. (Choir sings traditional Kiddush)

And now, the head of the family, after blessing the wine, holds up the matzoh ... (Passover music. *Hulachma Anyah* chanted quietly in background ... under prayer following)

MAN: This is the bread of affliction which our ancestors ate in the land of Egypt ... let all who are hungry, enter and eat thereof; and all who are needy, come and celebrate the Passover.

And now we fill the second cup of wine ... and the youngest in my household speaks.

CHILD: Wherefore is this night distinguished from all other nights, my father? On all other nights we may eat either leavened or unleavened bread, but on this night we eat only matzoh ... unleavened bread. On all other nights, we may eat any species of herbs, but on this night, only bitter herbs. On all other nights, we do not dip bitter herbs in haroset even once, but on this night we do it twice; on all other nights we eat and drink either sitting or reclining, but on this night we all recline.

MAN: My son ... slaves we were unto Pharaoh in the land of Egypt, and the Eternal, our God, brought us forth from there with a mighty hand and an outstretched arm. And if the Holy One, blessed be He, had not brought forth our ancestors from Egypt, we, and our children, and our children's children, had still continued in bondage to the Pharaohs in Egypt.

CHOIR: (Up strong with *Adir Hu,* then down in background during Narrator's final speech)

NARRATOR: And so, in the little colony of New Amsterdam, the First Passover in America was celebrated three hundred and eleven years ago. So has it been celebrated here, and everywhere, throughout the years, and during this present week.

CHOIR: (Up strong in suitable Passover song for finale.)

Brotherhood Week

Classification	Title	Author	Age Level
1. Choral Reading	Who Are We of the United States?	Ida Rosenfield Rosalie Bissing	10-14
2. Reading	We Believe		12-16
3. Poem	Some Children Are ...	Jo Tenjford Oslo	6-8
4. Psalm Reading	No. 133—How Good and How Sweet		10-12
5. Psalm Reading (dramatized)	Isaiah's Prophecy	Isaiah	13-16
6. Reading	On Loving One's Neighbor	Sefer-Ha-Middoth Adapted by Jacob Kranz	13-16
7. Choral Reading	And No One Asked	Morris Reich	12-16
8. Song	United Nations	Anonymous	8-12
9. Choral Reading	What Is America?	Rabbi Samuel M. Silver	13-16
10. Play	Some of My Best Friends!	Robert Crean	14-16
11. Poem	Where Is Holiness?	Unknown	14-16
12. Spiritual Snog	Walk Together Children	Anonymous	8-16

WHO ARE WE OF THE UNITED STATES?
Ida J. Rosenfield

(Prepared by the 5th and 6th grades of the John Muir School with the assistance of Rosalie Bissing.)

MEDIUM SOLO VOICE: We have been asked to set aside the week of Washington's Birthday as Brotherhood Week.

HIGH SOLO VOICE: Who are we of the United States who need to think of Brotherhood?

LOW GROUP: One-third of a million Indians.

MIDDLE GROUP: One-third of a million Orientals, Filipinos and Mexicans.

HIGH GROUP: Sixty million Anglo-Saxons.

LOW GROUP: Ten million Irish.

MIDDLE GROUP: Thirteen million Negroes.

HIGH GROUP: Fifteen million Slavs.

MIDDLE GROUP: Millions of Italians.

HIGH GROUP: French.

LOW GROUP: Scandinavians.

MIDDLE GROUP: Greeks and Armenians ...

ALL: Millions of us, every color, race and creed—we must all practice Brotherhood.

HIGH SOLO: What are our creeds?

2 OR 3 VOICES FROM MIDDLE: Protestant.

2 OR 3 VOICES FROM LOW: Jew.

HIGH GROUP: Catholic.

MIDDLE GROUP: Quaker.

LOW GROUP: Mormon.

ALL: These are our creeds.

SOLO MIDDLE: And what is meant by freedom of worship?

SOLO VOICE: Thomas Jefferson's Act to Establish Religious Freedom in Virginia, 1783.

ANOTHER SOLO VOICE: Be it enacted by the General Assembly that no man shall be compelled to suffer on account of religious opinions or beliefs—All men shall be free to maintain their right of opinion in matters of religion.

SOLO VOICE: The Declaration of Independence, 1776.

ALL: (Slowly) We hold these truths to be self-evident, that

all men are created equal, that they are endowed by their Creator with certain inalienable Rights, that among these are

HIGH GROUP: Life,

MIDDLE GROUP: Liberty,

ALL: and the pursuit of Happiness.

SOLO VOICE: The Constitution of the United States.

ANOTHER SOLO VOICE: Congress shall make no laws respecting an establishment of religion or prohibiting the free exercise thereof.

SOLO VOICE: (Slow) At this moment in history when the natural rights of man and the spiritual values treasured by *all* religious groups are denied in many parts of the world—the American people reaffirm these rights and values.

HIGH SOLO: What does the word Brotherhood mean to us?

HIGH GROUP: To us, the youth of America—Brotherhood means

MIDDLE GROUP: No matter what color our skin

LOW GROUP: No matter what country we are from

MIDDLE GROUP: We plan together

LOW GROUP: We build together

ALL: For a strong, united America.

WE BELIEVE

WE BELIEVE in the brotherhood of man under the Fatherhood of God.

> that the fabric of America is strong and unique because the threads of many races and creeds are woven into it.

> that every American secures his own greater safety when he stands united with his fellows to uphold and defend the true spirit of democracy.

> in unity without uniformity.

> that we cannot demonstrate to other nations that ours is a better way of life unless all our citizens enjoy the same privileges and assume the same obligations.

> that a man's God-given rights should not be violated because of his race, religion, or national origin.

> that the spirit of Brotherhood Week should season our thoughts and actions every week of the year.

> that the education of every child should encourage his natural inclination toward brotherhood.

WE BELIEVE that we can make this a better country for our children to inherit only if you and I strive unceasingly to stamp out prejudice, bigotry and discrimination.

SOME CHILDREN ARE ...
Jo Tenjford Oslo

Some children are brown
   like newly baked bread,
some children are yellow
   and some are red,
some children are white
   and some almost blue
Their colors are different—
   the children like you!

Some children eat porridge
   and some eat figs,
some children like ice-cream
   and some roasted pigs!
Some eat raw fishes
   and some Irish stew—
Their likings are different—
   the children like you!

Some children say "yes"
   and some say "oui"
some say "ja"
   and some say "si,"
some children say "peep,"
   and some say "booh—"
Their words may be different
   the children like you!

Some children wear sweaters
   and some rebozos,
some children wear furs
   and some kimonos,
some children go naked
   and wear only their queue.
Their clothes may be different—
   the children like you!

Some children have houses
   of stone in the streets,
some live in igloos,
   and some live on fleets.
Some live in old straw huts
   and some in new—
Their homes may be different—
   the children like you!

Some children are Finnish
   and some from Japan,
some are Norwegian
   and some from Sudan.
Oh yes, we have children
   in valley, on pike.
Their countries are different—
   the children alike!

Oh, if they could dance
   and if they could play
altogether together
   a wonderful day!
Some could come sailing
   and some could just hike!
So much would be different—
   the children alike!
      . . . .

Psalm 133
HOW GOOD AND HOW SWEET
(A pilgrim song of David)

O, how good and how very sweet it is
When brothers dwell together as one.

It is like oil poured on the head
And flowing down on the beard.

It is like the sacred oil poured
On Aaron's beard and on his robes.

Welcome as the dew from Mount Hermon,
Dew that descends upon the hills of Zion.

It is this that the Lord commands:
Blessedness and life forever more.

ISAIAH'S PROPHECY

PRODUCTION NOTE:

The following selection from "Isaiah"—"Writings from the Prophets," Chapter II: 1-5 can effectively be dramatized by casting a senior student of dignified commanding presence as Isaiah and costuming him appropriately for the character.

Costume and make-up should be authentically biblical to symbolize the prophet convincingly.

Suitable lighting—the use of a spot with blue gel—would aid in establishing the right mood.

It is important for the player portraying Isaiah to have a mature, resonant voice and imbue delivery of the prophecy with a prophetic quality and dedicated conviction—actualizing that which he foresees.

(In the event facilities and time do not permit these production values, the quotation can be read simply.)*

An arresting voice off-stage announces the introductory passage: "The word that Isaiah the son of Amoz foresaw concerning Judah and Jerusalem." Then, on cue, Isaiah enters majestically, takes center stage and renders the prophecy directly to the audience, as though he were addressing his contemporaries from a mountain-top in Judaea.

ISAIAH

And it shall come to pass in the end of days
That the mountain of the Lord's house shall be firmly established as the top of the mountains,
And shall be exalted above the hills;
And all the nations shall flow unto it.
And many peoples shall go and say:
"Come ye and let us go up to the mountain of the Lord,
And He will teach us of His ways,
And we will walk in His paths."
For out of Zion shall go forth the Law,
And the word of the Lord from Jerusalem,
And he shall judge between the nations,
And shall decide for many peoples;
And they shall beat their swords into plowshares,
And their spears into pruning hooks;
Nation shall not lift up sword against nation,
Neither shall they learn war any more.

---

* If done this way, add the comment that the excerpt—"And they shall beat their swords into plowshares, And their spears into pruning hooks; Nation shall not lift up sword against nation, Neither shall they learn war any more" is carved on a plaque at the entrance to the United Nations.

ON LOVING ONE'S NEIGHBOR

Jacob Kranz

Sefer Ha-Middoth

Love your neighbor as yourself and wish him well. Do not displease God by hating him whom He loves. A father's love for his child is only a drop in the ocean compared with God's love for man. How then, can you slander your neighbor or raise up your voice against him?

If you know in your heart that you are not well disposed toward your neighbor, shut your eyes, do not look at his faults to shame him with stinging reproof. Close your lips; do not rebuke him, lest you destroy your soul.

If your neighbor is guilty of a misdeed, do not hate him for it, since it is quite possible that you in his posiiton would act much worse. Instead, have mercy on him and do all you can for him. Your love and mercy for him should fill you with sorrow and sympathy because of the misfortune that has befallen him. If you have a good heart, you will be sorry for the wrongdoer; you will pray for him and seek to rehabilitate him. If this is not possible, leave him in the care of God who will have mercy on him and direct him in the right path so that he may come to a good end. Seek to love him for the sake of the good he will do in time to come. Enrich your heart with love and friendship.

AND NO ONE ASKED
(Brotherhood Choral Reading)
Morris Reich

READER
In the beginning God created heaven and earth...
And God saw the light that it was good, and God divided the light from the darkness.
And God called the light day, and the darkness He called night;
And there was evening and there was morning, the first day.
And God said:
"Let us make man in our image, after our likeness."
So God created man in His own image, in the image of God He created him.

VOICE
Was he white, yellow or black?
Was he Catholic, Protestant or Jew?

READER
It doesn't say—only that He created man.

CHORUS
Man was created man,
Different from fish or four-footed animal,
Different in color,
But still man, wanting the same things—

VOICE
Food to eat,
A place to sleep,
Land to work, to live on, to build

CHORUS
A better world for his young.
And he got that better world
Because man worked with man.

VOICE
To build a home,
To make the first wheel,
To bring the first fire.

CHORUS
And it was man working with man who built the town and the nation.

VOICE
The little house and the skyscraper,
The wagon and the streamliner,
The arching bridge and the jet.

CHORUS
And no one asked
Was he black or white,
Was he Catholic or Protestant or Jew.
No one—but the sick in mind.
We built a nation, powerful and glorious because man worked with man.

VOICE
The English at Plymouth
The Dutch in New Amsterdam,
The Protestants in New England
The Catholics in Maryland.

CHORUS
And we fought the Revolution
So that man could live with man
In freedom, in peace,
And no one asked at Valley Forge and Saratoga
Was he black or white,
Was he Catholic or Protestant or Jew,
No one—but the sick in mind.

VOICE
When the slaves in the South in their pain and suffering
Cried for freedom, they sang,

SINGERS
"When Israel was in Egypt land,
Let my people go.
Oppressed so hard they could not stand,
Let my people go.
Go down, Moses, 'way down in Egypt land,
Tell ole Pharaoh to let my people go."

VOICE
The American Negro sang of the yearning
Of the white Jew for freedom,
Because freedom belongs to all men,
Not to one color, not to one nation.

VOICE
In the pain and suffering then,
Did the wounded Protestant of Iowa
Fighting in Korea ask,
"Whose blood are you pouring into my veins
So that I may live?"

VOICE
Did the colored gunner cutting his way
Through the fields ask,
"Who made this gun, who filled this bullet?"

CHORUS
No one asked on the fighting front
Is he black or white,
Is he Catholic or Protestant or Jew,
No one—but the sick in mind.

VOICES
(1) I went to a movie last week—
(2) She saw Loretta Young, a Catholic.
(1) And I wore my new cotton dress—
(2) The cotton was picked by a colored man in the South.
(1) I rode down by train—
(2) Every race, every color, every religion was in that train with her.
(1) And met my friend. We were hungry and went out for lunch.
(2) The man who served them was a Swede and a Protestant.
(1) After the movies I came home, turned on the radio, and listened to my favorite programs:
- (3) She heard Eddie Cantor, a Jew;
- (1) Susan Hayward, a Protestant;
- (4) Ann Blyth, a Catholic;
- (4) Marian Anderson, colored.

(1) And I thought to myself what a wonderful world this was with so many different people helping me to be healthy and happy, and how much I owed them.
(2) And she didn't ask once that day,
On the train, at the movies, in her home,
Is he black or white,
Is he Catholic or Protestant or Jew.
No one would—no one but the sick in mind.
The sick in mind,
The sick in mind,
The sick in mind!
Who *are* the sick in mind?

VOICES
(1) In the old days they threw the Christians to the lions,
(4) They slaughtered the Jews in their homes,
They drove the Negroes into slavery.

CHORUS
They were the sick in mind.
And they are the same today.

VOICES
(4) They killed the Polish Catholics in prison camps,
They killed the German Jews on their streets,
(1) They made slaves of Czech Protestants in their factories.

CHORUS
They divide man from man with hate!
They are the sick in mind.
They live in our midst today.

VOICES
(4) They gang up on a Jewish boy,
They won't give a Negro a job.
(2) They build an Iron Curtain around their victims.
They are the sick in mind.

VOICES
(4) Would you get close to a person with a cold?
(1) Would you touch a boy who had scarlet fever?
(4) Will you listen to the one who is sick in mind?

CHORUS
Will you listen to the one who divides black from white,
Protestant from Catholic from Jew?

VOICES
- (4) What are you missing?
- (2) Man divided from man, man fighting against man has taken it from you.
- (1) What have you?
- (2) Man living with man, man working with man gave it to you.
- (1) In all your deeds, in all your thoughts, in all you say, in all you do, remember this—

READER
"And God created man in His own image, in the image of God He created him."

CHORUS
And it doesn't say he was white; it doesn't say he was black,
It doesn't say he was Catholic or Protestant or Jew.
It just says, God created man—that's all of us!

FINALE

UNITED NATIONS*

United Nations make a chain,
Ev'ry link is freedom's name,
Keep your hand on that plow, hold on.

CHORUS:
Hold on, hold on.
Keep your hand on that plow, hold on.

Now the war is over and done,
Let's keep the peace that we have won;
Keep your hand on that plow, hold on!

CHORUS.

Freedom's name is mighty sweet;
Black and white are gonna meet;
Keep your hand on that plow, hold on!

CHORUS.

Many men have fought and died
So we could be here side by side;
Keep your hand on that plow, hold on!

CHORUS.

—*Anonymous*

---

* *The People's Song Book*, edited by Waldemar Hille, published by Boni & Gaer, Inc., New York, includes the music for this song. Please refer to page 59.

WHAT IS AMERICA?

Rabbi Samuel M. Silver

PRODUCTION NOTE:

Various Voices ... or People, are heard in this drama. The number of participants depends on how many people the director wants to use. The same person may enact different roles, or you may use a different actor for each role. Parts may be read and not memorized.

Enter on Stage 4 People

1: What is America?
2: What is this: a quiz?
3: Why do you answer a question with a question?
2: Why not?
4: What is the question again?
1: What is America?
4: America is a land ...
2: The land where my fathers died ...
3: How many fathers did you have?
2: Four fathers ...
1: Your forefathers didn't die here. You come from Montreal.
2: Well, my spiritual forefathers lived here.
3: I think I see what you mean. What was the question again?
1: What is America?
4: Oh ... Let's see: Is the answer, "America is an island?"
1: No.
2: An archipelago ... I like to say that word!
3: No ... it's a peninsula ... no, an isthmus. Did you know there's an island in the Pacific called Christmas Island? ... Suppose it were an isthmus ... wouldn't that be quaint: Isthmus Christmas ... Or would it be Christmas Isthmus? ... Is that the answer to your question? America's an isthmus? Ith it ... I mean, is it?
1: No.
4: What is the answer? I mean, what is *your* answer?
1: I've got several answers ...
2: Oh, one for each day of the week, eh? And two for Sunday?
1: No ... three answers. One of them is that America is a bouquet.
3: What's that again?

2: He said America is a bouquet. Can you put it in a vase? (vahs)
4: It's vase, not vahs.
2: OK, have it your ways, I mean vase. But can you put America in one? What do you mean, America is a bouquet?
1: Simple... Do you know what a bouquet is?
3: Sure... it's a bunch of flowers...
2: Yes, but a bunch of different kinds of flowers.
1: Right you are. America is like that, too. Here, look at this beautiful bouquet (pantomimes by holding up hands to let others admire it)...
2: Oh, look at the marigolds...
3: And jasmines...
4: And nasturtiums...
1: And don't forget the forget-me-nots... And notice that the thing that makes the most beautiful bouquets is the assortment. If you had the same kind of flowers in a bouquet, it wouldn't be much of a much. America is like that, too...
3: Sure... it's simple... Each flower has its own kind of appearance... each flower has its own kind of aroma... Put them all together and they add up to something very lovely...
1: Right... This flower (points to an imaginary one) we could call the Poles...
3: And that one, the Slavs?
4: And that one the Latin Americans...
2: And that one the Hungarians...
1: Yes, and the others the Russians, the Canadians, the French, the Greeks, the English, the Czechs, the Turkeys...
2: You mean the Turks...
1: Yes, but you get the idea...
3: Sure we do... like a bouquet, America embraces them all...
2: They live together in peace...
4: Together they make up a bouquet...
1: America is also a combo...
3: A congo?
2: Why don't you do something about your ears?... He said a combo...
4: What's that? A kind of sandwich?
3: Of course not. I know what a combo is... let's see... Is it animal, vegetable, or mineral?
1: All three...

3: That's a big help ... Can you give me a clue?
1: Sure ... Here, I'll give it to you in a charade. (Pantomimes: strums a guitar, pounds a piano, toots a horn, etc.) ...
2: Oh, I know ... it's a flock of birds ...
4: Oh, cut the corn ... We know what you mean now ... You mean a musical combo ... like a small orchestra.
1: Right ... America is like an orchestra ... Know how?
3: Sure ... I do ... Different people play different things ...
1: Keerect ... give that person 64,000 tons ... A combo or an orchestra depends on something very important ...
2: Money?
4: Music?
3: Television?
1: No ... it depends on variety ... A very important word ... If everyone played the same instrument, the combo wouldn't be a combo ... because combo means combine ... combination, and it would be pretty monotonous ...
2: It would?
1: Sure it would. Let me show you ...
(Here you can have another group come in and simulate musicians ... or you can have the same foursome simulate instruments ... or you can have the group ask the entire audience to join them in the pantomime.)
Let's all play the guitar.
(Group strums ... either the foursome, the group that has come in, or the entire audience.)
2: That's almost good; I mean it's goo ...
1: Now, let's all play the piano ... nothing but pianos ...
(Pantomime of everyone pounding away on the keys)
3: It's pretty for a while, but after a while it does get tiring ...
4: My favorite instrument is the violin ... Can we have everyone fiddling? ... Let me be the conductor ... I've always wanted to lead an orchestra.
(Assumes leadership of orchestra, as everyone pretends to fiddle away for a while) ...
4: Say, you, you got a note wrong. No kidding, though, I see what you mean. Violins are nice, but too many of them. without other kinds of music, is too much of a good thing ...
2: Can't we all be drummers?
(Everyone begins to drum away, in pantomime)

1: (Hands to head) That's enough ... I can't stand the racket ... I've made my point, haven't I?
4: Yes ... America is an orchestra ... different groups make up the band of this land ... If we were all alike, instead of a combo we'd have a monoto ...
2: A what?
4: A monoto.
3: He means ... monotonous ... I get it ...
1: Yes, and we might say that the combo of America is the combo of Catholics, Protestants and Jews ... each one creates his own kind of melody ... and all the melodies synchronize to add up to the religious symphony of America ... If we were all the same, it would be a kind of ... what did you call it?
4: A monoto ...
1: Yes, a monoto ... I mean, well, I can't pronounce it ... America is something else, too. America is a hand.
3: Oh, hand where my fathers died ... What do you mean, a hand?
1: It's simple ... Here's a hand (holds his up).
4: Oh, is that what it is? I thought it was a bug.
2: Maybe you are. OK, that's your hand ... and what do you mean by that?
1: Notice that on my hand there are five fingers ...
2: If you had any more you could go into the circus ...
1: Each finger is separate ... and yet they are part of the same limb, my hand ...
3: Which proves?
1: Which proves that we can have separate groups in our nation, which have movements of their own ... Notice (holds up one finger at a time), and yet they are joined together at the wrist ...
4: I think I'm getting it ...
1: And that's not all. Hold up your fingers, everyone ...
(The others hold up their fingers—the audience could be asked to do so, too) Now, let's try an experiment ... (Pulls one of No. 4's fingers).
4: OUCH!
1: See ... the experiment is a success ... I pulled one finger and he said Ow ...
4: I said ouch ...

1: I mean ouch ... It hurt him ... Now how did he know he was hurt? ...
2: I can explain that question. My brother took physiology. When his finger is pulled, the message goes to the brain and the brain tells the finger it's been hurt ... isn't that right?
1: Yes ... and the whole thing takes only a second ... Now suppose I pulled your finger and it didn't hurt ... suppose you didn't feel it?
3: I guess that would mean that there is something wrong with the brain ...
1: Right you are ... Now, these five fingers are like the different races in America ... you know there are five races ... And they are each separate and different, but they are still part of our wrist and our arm. America is a hand ... Now if you hurt any one of these races ... all of them feel it ...
4: They feel it, providing the message reaches the brain ...
1: Exactly ... if we have brains then we feel the pain when any one else in America is hurt ... If bad things are said about them or if they are hurt, or mistreated ... And if these things happen to other people in our country and we don't feel it, then that means that America's brain isn't working well ...
2: I feel it when someone else is insulted ...
3: I do, too ... I remember how embarrassed I was when someone said something that wasn't nice about some group ... I said: "You ought to be ashamed" ...
1: Now, have I made myself clear? ... America is a bouquet ...
2, 3 and 4: (Holding an imaginary bouquet) ... Of nationalities ...
1: America is a combo ...
2, 3 and 4: Of religions (simulate orchestra)
1: America is a hand ...
2, 3 and 4: Of races ... all members of the human race ...
1: Right you are. (All conclude singing last stanza of "America")

SOME OF MY BEST FRIENDS
Robert Crean

With a discussion guide by
JAMES M. EAGAN

THE CHARACTERS
(All of them young people, in their teens)
THE SPEAKER
CATHERINE
AMY
ANTHONY
PETER

THE SETTING

The play should be performed in an acting area, rather than on a stage. The audience surrounds the acting area, with clearly defined aisles for the entrances and exits of the actors.

There is no scenery.

Use a strip lighting spot at each of the entrances, which creates a strip cross of light which the actor can go in and out of according to the importance of his role at the time he is performing.

(The acting area is empty. The speaker—a forthright young man, or woman—enters down one of the aisles (use No. 3). He speaks in a casual and friendly manner as he passes, saying "hello" and "good afternoon"—or "evening"—to members of the audience as he passes them. He reaches the acting area, pauses for attention, then:)

SPEAKER: (During this speech he walks to center, x's right, then around the edge and should end up at the very end toward No. 4 in the light) Hello, we're about to make a play. Together, in this empty space, we'll make a play. The ingredients are simple. We don't need any scenery or thematic music or luxurious costumes. We need only you and your imaginations. Use your imaginations and see ... that this is not a stage and you are no longer an audience. You are the world and what we will see is ... Life. Our actors are not actors; they are mirrors reflecting you. Shall we begin? (He moves about the area, indicating as he speaks:) We begin in a house not unlike your own. This is the living room ... the stairs ... (Now indicating an aisle through audience:) The front entrance. Furnish this place, in your mind's eye— (He is interrupted by Catherine, a young girl, who rushes down the aisle)

CATHERINE: (Calling, at No. 1—runs to center) Mother! Is anybody home? (She crosses to "stairs," calling upward:) Mother! (The speaker moves closer to audience, speaking quickly)

SPEAKER: (X-ing swiftly up toward No. 2) Quickly! Decorate this place!

CATHERINE: (Crossing between No. 3 and 4) Mother!!!

SPEAKER: This is your home. Place the furniture where it belongs. There ... and there!

CATHERINE: (Breaking down) Oh help me, please! Please, someone help me! (She x's to center, falls to her knees)

CATHERINE: I killed him. I don't know why. I didn't mean to kill him. (Calling:) Mother! Daddy! ... No one's here...

SPEAKER: (To audience) *We* are here. And we've heard this confession, haven't we? But is this a mirror? Can this be a mirror? (With back to Catherine, center:) We don't kill, do we? (He speaks to Catherine, who answers numbly without relating to him. Turning to Catherine) Whom did you kill?

CATHERINE: A friend ... A boy.

SPEAKER: Why did you kill him?

CATHERINE: I don't know. It happened so quickly.

SPEAKER: How did you kill him?

CATHERINE: I took a knife ... and held it in my hand ... and I lifted it ... and ... (She breaks, weeping)

SPEAKER: (Gently, x-ing down to No. 1) Tell us ... We care about people. We're interested. We're listening.

CATHERINE: I can't ...

SPEAKER: (X-ing to her) Yes, you can. Re-create the scene.

CATHERINE: It was ... at a dance.

SPEAKER: (Quietly) Yes. Where was the dance?

CATHERINE: (X's up toward No. 3) In the gymnasium.

SPEAKER: (X's up center stage to No. 2. Quietly, to audience) Quickly, change the scene. A gymnasium!
CATHERINE: No! No, it wasn't there. It didn't happen then. It wasn't at the dance.
SPEAKER: (To audience) Cancel the gymnasium. (X's down to between No. 4 and 1, facing upstage. To Catherine:) Where did it happen?
CATHERINE: Afterwards ... That night. In the car.
SPEAKER: (Cueing audience) A car. Describe the car. A convertible?
CATHERINE: No.
SPEAKER: Describe it. Something we dream about ... A sports car. His high-powered, bright-red two-seater. He got it for his birthday. His parents are wealthy and he—
CATHERINE: No.
SPEAKER: His father's car then?
CATHERINE: No, it wasn't in the car at all. It was at Amy's house.
SPEAKER: (X's to center. To audience) Amy's house. The girl is confused. Do your best.
CATHERINE: (To herself) Yes, that was it. At Amy's house.
SPEAKER: Describe Amy's house.
CATHERINE: (Moves down toward No. 4, turns body around to right) It's just an ordinary house.
SPEAKER: (Moves down to No. 1, turns body around left. Encouraging audience) An ordinary house.
CATHERINE: (Pondering ... walking across to center) We were in the recreation room.
SPEAKER: (Following her to center) (To audience) Recreation room.
CATHERINE: Listening to records.
SPEAKER: What records? Tell us. Perhaps we could sing and recreate the scene.
CATHERINE: I can't remember. (X's to No. 2) A song which goes in one ear and out the other.
SPEAKER: (Following her toward No. 2) Amy, then. Describe Amy.
CATHERINE: (Walking toward No. 3) I can't.
SPEAKER: (Walks to No. 3 ... to 4 ... to 1) What is she like? Who is she? (He points among audience) Is she her? Or

her? Or her? She must have some distinguishing characteristics. Who is Amy?

CATHERINE: (Walks toward center) She's a Jew.

SPEAKER: (Turns right and faces Catherine. Pauses.) Why did you say that? That ... can't have anything to do with it.

CATHERINE: Yes, it has.

SPEAKER: (To audience, with sincerity) Not for us. Never for us. (He turns to Catherine) You see, we don't label our friends. We don't discriminate, not in our world. (To audience) Tell her. Some of our best friends are ... (He is interrupted by a call, as Amy—a pretty young girl—hurries down aisle No. 1)

AMY: (Entering at No. 1) Catherine! Catherine! Let me in! (Speaker draws aside as Catherine rises and allows Amy to enter area)

AMY: Catherine ... (As Catherine begins to weep once more) Don't cry. It wasn't your fault. You didn't mean to do it!

SPEAKER: (Walks to No. 2) (To audience) I believe this is Amy.

AMY: I was there. I saw it all. Nobody is going to condemn you. Catherine, listen to me. It's Amy.

SPEAKER: (Moves toward upper area between No. 2 and 3) I was right.

AMY: I want to help you.

CATHERINE: (Turning on her suddenly) It was your fault!

AMY: My fault?

CATHERINE: You encouraged me! You did it! You're the one who did it!

AMY: (Shocked, hurt) I didn't do anything!

CATHERINE: (Backing away from her) Oh, yes, you did! Oh, yes, you *did!* I shouldn't have been with you in the first place. I shouldn't have gone with you. I was warned by my father. My father warned me that you ... (She stops)

AMY: (Quietly) That I what?

CATHERINE: (Withdrawn) That I should stay with my own group. And ... and not to try to solve the problems of the world.

AMY: I didn't know I was ... A "Problem of the World."

CATHERINE: Oh, but you are.

AMY: (Walks up to No. 2) Why? (Getting no answer, she turns away) I see. (Amy moves away from Catherine, who stands alone)

SPEAKER: (Crosses to Catherine. To Catherine) What group? What did you mean—your own group? (Silence) Look, we're not here to judge you. (Indicating audience) These are not judges. We're here to understand ... You can tell us. What group?

CATHERINE: I don't know. I don't think I ever had a ... "group." At least, I never felt safe and secure and important because I was in a group. (She moves to No. 4, then, to audience:) That's what you're supposed to feel, isn't it? If you're "in" and the rest of the world is "out" ... I guess my father meant *his* group.

SPEAKER: What group is that?

CATHERINE: (Turning body left) The Protestant group, I suppose.

SPEAKER: See here, if you're going to continue dividing everything up like that ...

CATHERINE: But I'm not like that. I'm not like that at all, that's what I'm trying to tell you. It's not the Protestant group, really. It's not narrowed down that way. It's just ... My father's friends.

SPEAKER: How does your father narrow down his friends?

CATHERINE: I don't know. The people he likes, I guess. He's a nice man. He just happens to like the same kind of people.

SPEAKER: What is your father?

CATHERINE: A very nice man.

SPEAKER: Yes, but what is he?

CATHERINE: (Walking fast to between No. 3 and 2 ... Exploding) He's my father! So don't you talk about him! (Turns) He was right! (Starts moving toward audience, walking down to between No. 4 and 1) (To audience) He *was* right, you know. He told me that *she* was a Jew. And that *he* was a Catholic. And he didn't have any hatred in his heart, but I told him, "No, you're wrong, Daddy. It doesn't make any difference. We're all the same." (Quietly) And he said, "I warn you, life is not that simple. You'll find in the long run that you are different and that you will be hurt. Take care of yourself." (She turns to face the Speaker, then turns to point at the audience) Take care of yourselves!

AMY: (Quietly and alone, standing between No. 2 and 1) My father told me to forget the past, to accept all people, and to try to live in peace. But to remember always, "Remember what you are, because *they* will remember." They remember ... (To audience) You remember, don't you? You remember with such great clarity, what she said. I am a Jew.

SPEAKER: (Quietly, between the two) Please ... Please, this will get us no place. Where were we? (Crossing to Catherine) Tell me now, where are we?

CATHERINE: (Dreamily, crossing to between No. 2 and 1) We are at the dance. I had been dancing with him. He left me for a moment and ... and I talked with Amy. (Amy and Catherine move together. A young Negro enters down aisle No. 3)

PETER: (Quietly) I was at the dance, too. I was at the dance. (He enters acting area, looks at the girls and moves aside) I danced with no one.

SPEAKER: (Moves down toward center, but not *in* center) (To audience) Stop now and picture the place. A gymnasium, balloons. An orchestra of kids. Populate the stage with dancers, with happy, laughing, swinging kids.

PETER: (Steps in toward center) I danced with no one.

SPEAKER: (Center, stopping, sympathetic) What's your name?

PETER: (Backs to between No. 3 and 4) Peter.

SPEAKER: I'm sorry. I'm sorry that you ... (Eagerly) You see, we're *not* that way. (Indicating audience) Some of our best friends are ... (The girls interrupt—re-creating a conversation at the dance)

AMY: Stop worrying!

CATHERINE: But I like him, Amy. I like him very much.

AMY: Then it's fine!

CATHERINE: If he likes me.

AMY: I'm sure he does. I can tell.

CATHERINE: How?

AMY: You know the ways. How he looks at you. And other things.

CATHERINE: Maybe he looks at everyone that way.

AMY: (Smiling) I don't think so.

CATHERINE: (Quickly) Of course, it isn't serious. I don't want you to think that.

AMY: Oh, I wouldn't think that. Hold your breath.

CATHERINE: Why?

AMY: He's coming. (Anthony, a young man, enters down aisle No. 4. He looks about for Catherine, including members of audience)

ANTHONY: (Calling) Catherine? Hey, Cathy?

CATHERINE: (Calling) Over here, Tony!

SPEAKER: (To audience, as Tony crosses) You see how he looks at her? He makes his way among the dancing couples. He is young and his heart is in his eyes. (Anthony waves to Catherine as he enters acting area. In so doing, he accidentally bumps Peter)

ANTHONY: Sorry.

PETER: It's okay. (Anthony crosses to Catherine—up toward center)

ANTHONY: (Eagerly) I've been looking all over the place for you.

CATHERINE: (Happily) Have you?

ANTHONY: (Eyes only for her) Yes...

CATHERINE: Tony, this is my friend Amy.

ANTHONY: (Not looking at Amy) I know Amy.

AMY: Hi. (But Anthony and Catherine continue to stare at one another. Amy is unnoticed.)

SPEAKER: (Down to edge of No. 1 with back to the audience) There is a silence. This is the love scene and there is a silence here, although the orchestra continues to play and the couples to dance.

ANTHONY: (Looking directly at Catherine) Hi...

CATHERINE: (Looking at Anthony) Hi...

SPEAKER: (Smiling, to audience) Maybe it's not much of a love scene, but you know how it is. (Amy breaks into the rapport of Anthony and Catherine)

AMY: (Steps into center) I guess I'd better be going.

CATHERINE: You don't have to do that.

AMY: (Stepping in one step further) Two's company.

CATHERINE: (Coming awake, she grabs Amy's arm) It's nothing like that! Tony, tell her to stay. (But Tony's eyes have shifted to Peter, who is watching him)

ANTHONY: (Moves up to Catherine) Why's he staring at me?

CATHERINE: (Looking all around) Who?

ANTHONY: (Indicating Peter) Him.

AMY: His name is Peter. He's in my class.

ANTHONY: He doesn't have to keep staring at people, does he?

CATHERINE: He isn't staring; he's just alone.

ANTHONY: (Still irked, walks up between No. 2 and 3, facing audience) I bumped into him, that's all. He's always standing in doorways or something.

AMY: He's a very nice boy, really.

ANTHONY: (Turns right, toward girls) Does he *want* to get bumped into?

CATHERINE: Tony, don't talk like that!

ANTHONY: He bothers me. (Moves in two steps) I mean, he's always there.

AMY: He's got a right to be there.

ANTHONY: (Walks toward No. 3) Look, nobody's saying anything like that! I'm not talking about his color. I don't have anything against him except he makes me nervous, that's all.

CATHERINE: Why?

ANTHONY: Because he's there.

PETER: (At No. 3) (To audience) I've been here for a long time and I'm going to be around a lot longer.

ANTHONY: A lot of people make me nervous. (To Amy) Like you, right now, for instance.

CATHERINE: Tony!

AMY: I'd better go ...

CATHERINE: Amy! Don't be angry.

AMY: ... And see about the refreshments. (Amy turns to go and as she turns)

ANTHONY: Don't go around telling everybody I hate Negroes, because I don't. Some of my best friends are ...

AMY: 'Bye, Catherine. (Amy crosses away and stands at the edge of No. 4)

PETER: (To audience) Some of *my* best friends aren't even *here*. They didn't get beyond the sixth grade.

SPEAKER: (Crosses up to No. 2) (To audience) The love scene isn't going very well.

PETER: My mother always told me: "You've got to get yourself through high school. Through high school, at least, no matter how much they try to stop you. You show them, son, you show them!"

SPEAKER: (Crosses up to between No. 2 and 3) Of course, we don't have to take this scene as typical. I mean, we've been to a lot of dances, you and I, where the band plays on and the love scenes go on as scheduled.

CATHERINE: Why did you do that to Amy?

ANTHONY: Do what?

CATHERINE: Insult her.

ANTHONY: Did I insult her?

CATHERINE: You know you did.

ANTHONY: Why do you want to hang around with her?

CATHERINE: I like her.

ANTHONY: She's an odd ball.

CATHERINE: Why?

ANTHONY: I've never seen her around with any group I know.

CATHERINE: She doesn't have a group.

ANTHONY: So she's an odd ball.

CATHERINE: You're being mean!

ANTHONY: I'm telling the truth!

SPEAKER: (To them) Can we get on with the love scene!

ANTHONY: I don't want to talk about Amy. I want to talk about you and me.

CATHERINE: I'm not sure I want to. (She crosses away from him, moves toward No. 2)

ANTHONY: (Following her) Look, I'm not being mean to anybody or anything. Right now, I'm thinking about you, that's all. And it makes me nervous.

CATHERINE: Thinking about me makes you nervous?

ANTHONY: (Reluctantly) Yeah ... (She smiles at him, he grins. Then:) Come on. (He leads her away and they stand together, at the edge of No. 2)

SPEAKER: (More happily) You see, he doesn't hate anybody. He doesn't mean to hurt anybody.

PETER: (Crosses two or three steps in toward No. 4) (To audience) He hates me because I'm Colored.

SPEAKER: (To audience) It's not that! It's just, he's always in the way. It's his personality!

AMY: (Moves toward between No. 2 and 1) He dislikes *me* because I'm *Jewish*.

SPEAKER: He wants to talk to his girl, that's all! Two's company. (To audience) If you don't understand that, you're an odd ball. (He turns to others) Can we get on with the love scene? This is a dance, a nice friendly dance.

AMY AND PETER: (They are alone, on opposite sides of the area. Amy turns to face Peter and he, walking toward No. 4, turns left to face her) This dance is hell.
AMY: I would never tell anyone. But for me, this is hell.
PETER: And many other dances have been hell.
SPEAKER: (To them anxiously) You've got the wrong idea. (To audience) You've been to a lot of dances like this one. I mean, they weren't hell? You didn't have to stand in a corner and start to think the world was against you!
PETER: (Crossing to him) Whose side are you on?
SPEAKER: (Baffled) What?
PETER: I said, whose side are you on? I'm beginning to get suspicious of you.
SPEAKER: (To audience) Suspicious of me?
PETER: Are you with me or against me?
SPEAKER: I'm *with* you! (Indicating audience) (crossing down center) Look, if you're suspicious of me, you're suspicious of them, because we're in this together. But we didn't start all this. (Turns) We're innocent bystanders, that's all.
AMY (Quietly): You hate.
SPEAKER: (Walking up to center, turning to Amy) What did you say?
AMY: (Crossing to him) I said, you hate.
SPEAKER: (Comes up to between No. 3 and 2) Not us! (Including audience) Look at us. Do we look like the kind of people who'd hate?
AMY: (Simply) There isn't a single person alive without some hatred in his heart.
SPEAKER: (Turns completely around, back to audience) (Loudly) Can we get on with the love scene!!! (Then) Look, you've got us wrong. We wouldn't be here at all if we hated you. (Down in center) Some of our best friends ...
CATHERINE: (At No. 4, loudly, declaiming) Romeo, Romeo, wherefore art thou, Romeo?
SPEAKER: (Runs toward No. 4) That's the wrong love scene!!! (He stops, confused, then he turns—reasonably—to Amy and Peter) (Comes up to center) Don't you see, you're imagining things, that's all. Now I admit it's difficult for you sometimes. But you're making it worse than it is.
AMY: (Facing center) Do I imagine things? (To audience)

Do I imagine things? Look around you. In your town and in your school ... Where do the Jewish kids hang out?

PETER: (Steps in toward center) (To audience) Where do the Negroes go? (Peter and Amy are closing in on the Speaker)

AMY: With other Jews?

PETER: With other Negroes?

AMY: Or with you?

SPEAKER: (Makes a physical turn, pushing them apart. Peter and Amy go back to their corners—Peter to between No. 4 and 3, Amy to between No. 2 and 1) Now look, we're trying to keep ourselves in balance here. (To audience) Aren't we? I mean, we're trying to make some sense out of this and it's difficult if you're going to go around with a chip on your shoulders. (He turns to pair) It's your parents' fault, don't you see that? They filled you with old-fashioned fears and out-moded defensiveness ... when we don't feel that way at all. (To audience) Do we?

AMY: You're perfect ... all of you.

SPEAKER: I didn't mean it that way, I ... Look, we've got a love scene coming up here. A scene of tenderness and beauty beyond your wildest imaginings. (Indicating) Sit down ... (Amy and Peter sit)

SPEAKER: (Walking around, crossing down edge of No. 1, ending edge of No. 1, facing up) (To audience) Now see, if you can, a moonlit night. Dip deeply into the wondrous vaults of your minds and find the visions deposited there by the hundreds of technicolor movies you have fed upon since your youth. Select from these, the bluest of landscapes and a rhinestone-studded sky. Picture the scene ... and into all this beauty, our young lovers enter ... (Catherine and Anthony turn and walk rapidly toward center)

ANTHONY: I did not!

CATHERINE: You did too!

ANTHONY: You're crazy!

CATHERINE: You're awful to say so!

SPEAKER: The love scene is not going exactly as planned.

CATHERINE: Did I ask you to go steady?

ANTHONY: No!

CATHERINE: Then why did you say you wouldn't?

ANTHONY: I didn't say I wouldn't!

CATHERINE: Oh yes, you did! You just came right out

and said you don't believe in going steady, when nobody even asked you to go steady. It was the farthest thing from my mind ... and who told you not to go steady ... Some *priest!*

ANTHONY: (Completely, and comically, thunderstruck) Priest! How did *he* get in on this?

CATHERINE: Because you're a Catholic and you have to do everything he says!

ANTHONY: Wow! I do not! (Exasperated, he turns to audience) I didn't come out here to talk about religion. *She* started that! I just tried to talk some sense to her and then, out of a clear blue sky ... a technicolor sky ... comes a priest! (Confidentially to audience) Look, I admit I'm a Catholic. What's *that* mean? I turn into a puppet or something whenever I want to think a thought? I'll tell you what it means. It means I'm taught to think about other people, and to love my neighbors, and ... (He stops guiltily as Amy and Peter, moving in toward center and crossing to opposite side of stage, look at him in silent accusation.)

ANTHONY: (To audience) Aw, skip it.

SPEAKER: (Moves to between No. 4 and 1) (To Amy and Peter, as they cross stage in front of him) Sit down. Please sit down.

CATHERINE: I want to go home!

SPEAKER: Wait a minute!

CATHERINE: I want to go home! Something's wrong here! Something's going on I don't understand!

SPEAKER: Nothing we can't fix up if we all try!

CATHERINE: I *have* tried. (She crosses to audience) (To audience) Believe me, I have tried. I've gone out on a limb trying to cross all the lines of religion and color and ... And what do I get for it! (Furiously, she points in accusation at Anthony) Do you know he's an Italian!!!

ANTHONY: I'm supposed to ride in a gondola here! I'm supposed to sing "O Solo Mio!"

SPEAKER: (Moves up toward center) Now wait! Please! Hold it!

CATHERINE: I have tried! I told myself that, despite what my father said, we are all the same.

PETER: I'm supposed to paint my face white here! She wants us all the same!

SPEAKER: (Running toward Peter) We are! We are the same!

AMY: Well, we're *not!* We're *different!* (She crosses to Speaker) Until you admit that, you're just causing trouble, don't you know that?

CATHERINE: (Crosses to Amy) Amy, Let's go home.

SPEAKER: Not yet! (As Amy and Catherine turn and move toward No. 3) We haven't finished the love scene! (Anthony and Peter stand at a distance, looking at one another)

ANTHONY: What are *you* looking at?

PETER: Nothing.

ANTHONY: Fine. (Angrily) Look, I want you to know I love my neighbor and all that, but you've got to stop being in my way all the time. (He turns and crosses up toward No. 2)

PETER: (Looking up toward No. 2) I'm going to be here a good long time. (He turns and crosses out at No. 1)

SPEAKER: (To audience) End of love scene. (The four characters now stand apart, each facing in a different direction)

SPEAKER: (Moves to No. 4, faces audience) I'm afraid the murder scene comes next. You know the setting. The recreation room at Amy's house. Furnish it simply and get it over with. (As Amy and Catherine cross to center, Catherine is lying on the floor with her leg kicking to imaginary music. Amy, kneeling, is putting on a record; she's facing Catherine on her left. Catherine's head is facing No. 4. Anthony is at No. 2. Peter is at No. 3.) The two girls are listening to records. If you could sing something which goes in one ear and out the other ...

CATHERINE: (To Amy) I'm glad I found out. He's horrible.

AMY: You're right. Look how he treated me.

CATHERINE: He's always *seemed* so nice. I don't know what happened.

AMY: (Stands) You found out, that's all. It's good you found out in time. (She begins to dance alone to a rock 'n roll beat. She starts at Catherine's left in the dance and then goes around Catherine to end up at her right. Catherine remains kneeling.)

CATHERINE: (Dejectedly) I don't understand anything.

AMY: (Carelessly) It's his kind, that's all.

CATHERINE: What do you mean?

AMY: His kind are all the same.

CATHERINE: Kind?
AMY: (On Catherine's right) You know. They stick together.
CATHERINE: Who? (Amy stoops and takes Catherine's shoulders)
AMY: You know who ... (A whisper) Catholics.
CATHERINE: Amy!
AMY: Don't pretend. Don't pretend you don't feel the way I do about them.
CATHERINE: (Drawing away) Amy, that's not like you. You don't say things like that.
AMY: (Crosses to No. 1) What about *you?* Be truthful! Tell me the truth!
CATHERINE: (Very disturbed, very unsure) I don't ... I don't hate anybody!
AMY: The truth!
CATHERINE: (Doubting herself) I don't hate anybody ...
AMY: Oh yeah ...? (She turns, almost sadly, and stands with her back to Catherine. Anthony and Peter now move in from their positions toward center.)
CATHERINE: (To herself) I don't hate people because they are Colored or Jewish or Catholics. That's irrational, that's ... I only hate them when they hurt me. I hold out my hand to them and ... they hurt me. (Facing downstage between No. 4 and 1, she looks up to audience) You see, that's how it was. I looked at myself and I looked into my heart and I saw—no matter how I pretend and how much I deny ... (Almost weeping now) I know what I think of them. (She looks to floor) And then ... I took up the knife ... (She makes a complete physical turn to face out No. 1, takes an imaginary knife in her fist.)
SPEAKER: (Moving in) No! No, stop this!
CATHERINE: (Starting to face No. 2) And I lifted the knife ...
SPEAKER: There isn't any knife! Look! You haven't any knife! (Catherine comes to her feet slowly)
CATHERINE: And everything welled up inside me, all the hatred I never thought was there ... And I turned on them ...
CATHERINE: Wop! Dirty Italian! Catholic!
SPEAKER: Stop! (Catherine rushes to Anthony at No. 2 and pounds on his chest with her fist as if it held a knife.)

SPEAKER: No! (Catherine turns on Peter at No. 3, repeating her action. The others stand unmoved.)
CATHERINE: (Pounding on him) Black! Coon! Nigger!
SPEAKER: (Blocking his ears) Stop!
CATHERINE: (Rushing to Amy at No. 1) You kike! Jew! (She begins to weep) Jew! (She turns to audience, the "knife" still in her hand.)
CATHERINE: Oh, God, forgive me ... (Catherine drops the knife, turns, then drops to her knees, facing up to No. 3.)
SPEAKER: (Rushing to her) You didn't kill, you see? They're still standing. You didn't murder anyone.
CATHERINE: With words. I said the words ...
SPEAKER: (Turning on audience) She didn't mean it! You know her and she didn't mean it. (Indicating actors) You see them all? They're just like you, really. They're good ... intelligent ... well-meaning ... (He stops, hopelessly) (The actors stand in a row, numbly)
CATHERINE: (Quietly) Prejudice ... In everyone of us you will find ... prejudice.
SPEAKER: (Eagerly) Not in me!
CATHERINE: And prejudice will hurt, and maim, and kill.
SPEAKER: Not in us! Not us!
PETER: (Quietly) Prejudice is our legacy, come down through history. From the family and village and the nation, prejudice is our inheritance.
SPEAKER: It's the fault of the parents, yes! (To audience) Tell them! We're not to blame!
AMY: We can't pretend we stand together. The differences are all around us. Prejudice is part of us all.
SPEAKER: (Moving into audience) Not in me. Not in us!
ANTHONY: *All* of us! (All four start repeating "He did it! They caused it!" as they walk out) Whenever we are hurt, we cry out: "He did it! They caused it!" Prejudice thrives on our failures.
SPEAKER: (Running to No. 2, to 3, to 4, calling) Stop! Where are you going? (The actors continue moving toward exits)
SPEAKER: (Turning bewilderedly) Where are you going? We haven't finished. (Pursuing them) We have questions! You

haven't answered our questions! (The actors exit. The Speaker walks slowly back to the acting area.)

SPEAKER: It seems we have ended a play ... a play for which there *is* no ending. (He turns and faces audience) Unless *you* have an ending. For this was not a stage, but life. And you are not an audience, but the world.

The stage is then open for discussion.

GUIDE FOR DISCUSSION LEADERS
Prepared by Dr. James M. Eagan,
*Vice President
in Charge of Rearing Children of Good Will Programs*

"Some of My Best Friends" is intended to be an open-ended play which does not present conclusions but which presents problems for discussion. For this reason, audiences should be told in advance that their role is an active one; they are to listen, identify with the characters if they wish, but above all they are to participate actively in the group discussion which follows the play. The intention of the National Conference of Christians and Jews in commissioning the play was to provide the machinery and the setting for lively and thoughtful discussion. The views reflected in the play are not necessarily those of NCCJ, but are purposely included to provoke discussion.

Ideally, the playing cast would be composed of young people who could remain to take part in the discussion which follows the play. The play is designed to produce a somewhat sharp interaction of young persons and adults. One technique found productive is to divide the audience into groups of ten to fifteen and have discussion for twenty to thirty minutes. Each group then returns with one or two questions to be further discussed by the group as a whole, by an "expert" or a panel of "experts."

This method is more conducive to a change of attitude than that of merely giving information alone. In a sense, the form of the play is comparable to the Greek concept in which the audience becomes part of the play, participating as though they, too, were actors. In a small group, it might be possible to stop the play and let members of the audience act out what they consider would be a satisfactory ending for the play. The play could then be resumed to give the author's own open-ended finish.

The play should itself provoke a series of questions which should be the focus of discussion. In case, however, this does not happen, a few questions for discussion are included. These are to be used only as a guide for encouraging the development of further questions.

1. Do we cover up our own prejudices by rationalization? What is the role of "tokenism" in the elimination of prejudice? Is the title "Some of My Best Friends" indicative of hypocrisy? Does it indicate that there can be minor breakthroughs without major breakthroughs in overcoming prejudice?
2. Do the warnings by "father" to stay within the group have an appreciable effect on young people? Do we sometimes tend to live in self-contained and self-imposed ghettoes? What is the effect of this upon community life? To what extent is group cohesiveness necessary?
3. Why are generalizations about any group—Protestant, Catholic, Jewish, Negro, white—dangerous?
4. Do you agree or disagree with the "speaker" that prejudice seems to be the mark of all men? Are we all destined to be prejudiced in one form or another?
5. To what extent does Catherine show the self-inflicted damage done by prejudice? Is this perhaps even greater than the harm done to the victims of prejudice? To what degree does prejudice promote the "murder" of personality? How is it possible to believe in the inherent worth of the individual, his dignity, and be prejudiced?
6. Is the play a characterization of the "gentle people of prejudice?"
7. How do we bring ourselves to admit our own prejudices? How can we diminish scapegoating? How do we become a mirror for prejudice? To what extent are our children reflections of ourselves? What are we going to do to correct all this—in home, school, church, the community? How can we as individuals, as a nation, cease to hate? How can we reconcile the gap between what we preach and what we practice—The American Dilemma?

ACKNOWLEDGMENTS

The stage directions were prepared by Gloria Landis of the Landis Studio of the Performing Arts of Mamaroneck, N.Y.

WHERE IS HOLINESS
National Federation of Temple Youth

Many are the ways of holiness; varied are its paths.
There is holiness in a lab when a vaccine is discovered to destroy disease.
There is holiness when nations meet to beat swords into plowshares.
There is holiness when we strive for purity and harmony in family life.
There is holiness when men of different backgrounds work together for a common future.
There is holiness when men seek justice and struggle for righteousness.
There is holiness when men lift up the fallen and free the captives.
There is holiness when men bring consolation to the sorrowing and comfort to the silent sufferers.
There is holiness when men create lasting poetry or song or philosophy.
There is holiness when men gather to seek Thee, O God, through prayer.
Holy, holy, holy is the Lord of hosts.

· · · · · · · ·

WALK TOGETHER CHILDREN*

Anonymous

Walk together children,
Don't you get weary,
Walk together children,
Don't you get weary,
Oh, talk together children,
Don't you get weary,
There's a great camp meeting in the Promised Land.

Oh, sing together children,
Don't you get weary,
Sing together children,
Don't you get weary,
Oh, shout together children,
Don't you get weary,
There's a great camp meeting in the Promised Land.

Gwine ter mourn and never tire;
Mourn and never tire.
Mourn and never tire;
There's a great camp meeting in the Promised Land.
REPEAT

Oh, get you ready children,
Don't you get weary,
We'll enter there,
Oh, children, don't you get weary,
There's a great camp meeting in the Promised Land.

---

* The music for this song is to be found in *The Books of American Negro Spirituals* (volume 2, page 180), edited by J. W. Johnson and J. Rosamond Johnson, published by the Viking Press, New York.

Supplementary Selections

Supplementary Selections

Classification	Title	Author	Age Level
1. Poem	A Rhyme for Moon Months	Dorothy Ross	6-9
2. Poem	Today's Lag B'omer	Translated by Samuel Dinin	5-7
3. Playlet	Alice in Sunday School-land	Dorothy Ross	5-7
4. Poem	Samson Ha'Gibor	Dorothy Ross	5-8
5. Poem	Joseph the Seer	Dorothy Ross	5-7

A RHYME FOR MOON MONTHS*

Dorothy Ross

TISHRI starts with ROSH HA'SHANAH;
CHESHVAN follows after;
KISLEV bring us HANUKKAH
With dreidels, games and laughter.
TEVET comes before SHEVAT—
That's when trees are planted.
ADAR means that PURIM's come—
NISAN—plagues are counted.
IYAR—Here is LAG B'OMER,
SIVAN—Torah-tended.
TAMMUZ, AV, ELUL, are next,
And the Jewish year is ended!

Many of us use the rhyme "Thirty days has September..." to help us remember how many days there are in each of the 12 months of the year in our common Gregorian calendar.

The rhyme given above helps us learn the 12 months of the Jewish calendar, called "Lunar-Solar" because the year is figured by the length of time it takes the earth to go around the sun and according to the time it takes for the moon to circle the earth.

Every 7 out of 19 Jewish years are "Leap Years," when an extra month is added to make 13 months. The extra month comes after *Adar* and is called *Adar Sheni*—Second *Adar*.

---

* From *Young Judaean*

TODAY'S LAG B'OMER

To forest, to forest with arrow and bow!
To fields full of flowers in gladness we'll go!
There's beauty and greenness and trees row on row!
Today's Lag B'Omer! Today's Lag B'Omer!

The crickets that chirp, the frogs near the sea;
The insects, the flies, the birds in the tree—
All happy, all gay, now sing merrily.
"Today's Lag B'Omer! Today's Lag B'Omer!"

Youths joyous and singing march here and march there
With arrows and bows they roam 'round everywhere.
And sweet is the song that resounds through the air:
Today's Lag B'Omer! Today's Lag B'Omer!

Translated from the Hebrew by Samuel Dinin.

ALICE IN SUNDAY SCHOOL-LAND

Dorothy Ross

CAST OF CHARACTERS
ALICE
PETER RABBIT
TEACHER
PUPILS (boys and girls)

PLACE

Prologue: in front of curtain
Scene: Sunday School class-room in a Hebrew School or Community Center

TIME

9:50 A.M. of a Sunday morning, any year.

PRODUCTION NOTE:

Lights dim in house. The curtain is drawn; spot on curtain. Alice, spotlighted is discovered asleep, sitting on stage apron or platform edge, in center, her feet dangling over edge.

Peter Rabbit comes rushing up the aisle from back of auditorium, carrying child's school-bag. He hastily glances at his watch, then noticing Alice, nudges her.

If possible, Alice and Peter Rabbit should be dressed in costumes, patterned after the illustration-engravings made famous by John Tenniel.

PETER RABBIT
Oh dear, oh dear ... it's getting late,
I know I really shouldn't wait!
(calling)
Alice! Al ... ice! ...

ALICE
(awakens, looks at Peter Rabbit sleepily)
Oh, Peter Rabbit, Peter Rabbit,
Where are you rushing to?

PETER RABBIT
I'm almost late for Sunday School,
And that will never do!

ALICE
Oh Peter Rabbit, Peter Rabbit...
May I come with you?

PETER RABBIT
Why surely, if you hustle up,
Because at ten I'm due.

ALICE
(rises)
But tell me, what is Sunday School?
And wherefore do you hurry?
It seems to me that you're a fool
To go to school and worry!

PETER RABBIT
Dear Alice, come along with me
And just pay strict attention—
For what you'll learn and hear and see—
I haven't time to mention.

>(He leads her through curtain opening. A few seconds elapse. Then curtain is raised, revealing twelve or so pupils—boys and girls—ranging in age from 6 to 9, seated in a typical class-room.)

>(Peter and Alice stand aside, upstage and look on.)

>(Members of class are busy talking loudly. Bell rings. Teacher enters. Class immediately quiets down. Silence.)

TEACHER
Today, we'll have a short review
Of Israel's brave heroes—
And if you fail to answer,
You'll have to get some zeros.

Now, Abraham we know, was one
And Moses was another—
But who was Jacob father of
And just who were his brothers?

>(Several pupils raise their hands. Teacher points to "First Pupil" to answer)

FIRST PUPIL
I know that Jacob was a twin,
And Esau was his brother.
His father's name was Isaac, and
Rebecca was his mother.

He had about a dozen sons,
A tribe each one became;
I'd like to... but I really can't
Call each one off by name.

TEACHER
Now tell me, where does the river Jordan flow?

SECOND PUPIL
In Canaan, on the west.

TEACHER
(addressing class)
Is that correct? Don't hesitate...
This is not a test.

THIRD PUPIL
I'm pretty sure it's on the east.
In fact, I know it's so.
From north to south, is that right?
That's how all rivers flow.

TEACHER
That's true.
Now raise your hand up high
If you can tell me who
Sent soldiers into Palestine...
Whose leader Judith slew?

FOURTH PUPIL
Neba... Beba... Beba—could... NEBUCHADNEZZAR!...

TEACHER
Good!
And who was bravest of the brave?

ANOTHER PUPIL
Why Samson, what a man!
He never drank, he never smoked,
His tribe, I think, was Dan.

TEACHER
Is anybody here today,
Who'd like to say a word
About our Hebrew heroes
Whose names you've often heard?

ANOTHER PUPIL
(declaiming)

Terah was an idol-maker,
Abraham was an idol-breaker,
Jacob was a birthright taker,
And, I think, an awful faker!

TEACHER
Anyone else?

ANOTHER PUPIL
(also declaiming)

There once was a ruler named Saul,
Who, History tells, was quite tall,
    Not heeding instruction
    Led to his destruction
Too bad that his kingdom did fall! ...

TEACHER
Anything else on heroes?

PUPIL
(raising hand, and jumping up—enthusiastically eager)

May I sing a song?
        (sings to music of "Isle of Capri")

'Twas in a field picking wheat that she met him,
'Twas on a bright sunny day, that's the truth;
'Twas in the mid-afternoon that he murmured,
"I am Boaz. Please marry me, Ruth."

    (members of class laugh and applaud)

TEACHER
Name the heroes in a row,
Leave out those you do not know!

           BRIGHT PUPIL (boy)
    1.   2.   3.
ABRAHAM   JUDAH   JEPHTAH
ISAAC   DAN   GIDEON
JACOB   MOSES   SAMSON
JOSEPH   JOSHUA

                GIRL PUPIL
       (raising hand, and simultaneously jumping up)

There are heroines he forgot,
Seems to me, there's quite a lot.

                (counting on her fingers)
    1.   2.   3.
SARAH   JAEL   JUDITH
REBECCA   DEBORAH   ESTHER
RACHEL

                  TEACHER
                  (pleased)

Your History you seem to know,
It's really a delight.
I'm glad to see that everyone
Is so studious and bright!...
We have a guest with us today,
Let's show her something new.
Before the bell rings, let's present...
"The Sunday School Review" (or Revue)

           (Several children rise and cross downstage, forming a
           chorus-line. Each pupil sings a separate stanza. Then
           all join in last stanza)

CHORUS:
ONE... TWO... THREE...
Sunday School for me!
I love to go to Sunday School
To study His-to-ry...

FOUR and FIVE
At ten you must arrive.
Then everybody gets to work
Like bees inside a hive.

SIX, SEVEN, EIGHT...
Don't you dare come late!
It isn't fair to make your class-mates
And your teachers wait.

NINE, TEN, *YOU* ...
        (pointing to members of audience)
And every other Jew,
Should learn our Jewish History,
Just like we pupils do!

    (Pupils who have remained in their seats, join in singing last stanza as reprise)

CURTAIN

SAMSON HA'GIBOR

Dorothy Ross

I am the Hebrew Tarzan
Of rock and iron muscle.
I'll challenge any man on earth
And beat him in a tussle!

The earth quakes when I walk on it;
The skies fade when I bellow.
When enemies approach my camp,
I am a fierce wild fellow!

No rope can bind or tie me in,
No man can guess my power.
I grow more might in every fight,
I'm stronger every hour.

A lion once got tough with me,
I ripped him clean in two.
If you don't fear my strength,
I'll do the same to you.

If you would learn some more of me,
If you would know my fate,
Just take a look in Bible book
I tell you folks, I'm great!
  · · · · · · · ·

JOSEPH THE SEER

Dorothy Ross

I have a robe and I have a globe
And an eye that can clearly see.
I have a mind that can always find
An answer to mys-ter-y!

I have an ear that can clearly hear
The thoughts in your silent heart.
You bring the tale and I never fail,
That is my secret art.

When I did sit in the desert pit,
Where my brothers threw me low,
I didn't weep in the well so deep,
For I knew I would help Pharaoh.

So bring me your dream although it may seem
That Joseph the dreamer won't do.
For I have a robe and I have a globe
And a mind that can see through *you!*

Bibliography

CREATIVE DRAMATICS AND CHILDREN'S THEATRE

Title	Author	Publisher
An Introduction to Dramatics for Children	Dr. Loren E. Taylor	Southern Illinois University
Creative Dramatics for Children	Frances C. Durland	Walter H. Baker and Company
Creative Dramatics in the Jewish Club	Zachary A. Serwer	National Jewish Welfare Board
Children's Theatre	Davis-Watkins	Harper and Row
Children's Theatre and Creative Dramatics	Geraldine Siks and Hazel Dunnington	Univ. of Washington Press
Creative Dramatics	Winifred Ward	Appleton-Century-Crofts
Creative Dramatics	Geraldine Brain Siks	Harper and Bros.
Creative Play Acting	Isabel B. Burger	A. S. Barnes and Company
Creative Power	Hughes Mearns	Doubleday and Company
Creative Youth	Hughes Mearns	Doubleday and Company
Creative Drama in the Lower School	Corinne Brown	Appleton-Century-Crofts
Dramatics for Creative Teaching	Samuel Citron	The United Synagogue of America
Improvisation for the Theatre	Viola Spolin	Northwestern University Press
Let's Make a Play	George Willison	Harper and Bros.
Story-telling and Dramatization	Dr. Loren E. Taylor	Southern Illinois University
Theatre for Children	Winifred Ward	Appleton Century
Twenty-One Years with Children's Theatre	Charlotte Chorpenning	Children's Theatre Press
Plays and Creative Ways with Children	Gertrude Lerner Kerman	Harvey House, Inc.

VOICE AND SPEECH

Title	Author	Publisher
American Dialects	Lewis and Marguerite Herman	Theatre Arts Books
Basic Principles of Speech	Alma Sarett-Wm. Foster	Houghton Mifflin Company
Basic Speech	Jon Eisenson	The Macmillan Company
Foreign Dialects	Lewis and Marguerite Herman	Theatre Arts Books
Everyday Speech	Bess Sondel	Barnes & Noble Inc.
Improving Speech and Articulation	Hilda Fisher	Houghton Mifflin Company
Reading Aloud	Wayland Maxfield Parrish	The Ronald Press Company
Speech	Dorothy Mulgrave	Barnes & Noble Inc.
The Use and Training of the Human Voice	Arthur Lessac	Arthur Lessac
The Improvement of Voice and Diction	Jon Eisenson	The Macmillan Company
Training the Speaking Voice	Virgil Anderson	Oxford University Press
Your Speech and Voice	Bronstein - Jacoby	Random House

ACTING

Title	Author	Publisher
Actors Talk About Acting	Lewis Funke - John Booth	Random House, Inc.
Acting—A Handbook of the Stanislavski Method	Cole - Chinoy - Krich	Lear Publishers Inc.
Acting Is Believing	Charles J. McGraw	Holt, Rinehart & Winston Inc.
An Actor's Handbook	Elizabeth Hapgood	Theatre Arts Books
An Actor Prepares	Constantin Stanislavski	Theatre Arts Books
Actors on Acting	Cole - Chinoy	Crown Publishers
Building a Character	Constantin Stanislavski	Theatre Arts Books
Creating a Role	Constantin Stanislavski	Theatre Arts Books
Emotional Memory (pamphlet)	Robert Lewis	Samuel French & Company
First Steps in Acting	Samuel Selden	Appleton, Century, Crofts
Introduction to Acting	Stanley Kahan	Harcourt, Brace & World
Mask or Face	Michael Redgrave	Theatre Arts Books
Method or Madness	Robert Lewis	Samuel French & Co.
Modern Acting; A Manual	Rosenstein - Haydon - Sparrow	Samuel French & Co.
Six Lessons in Acting	Richard Boleslavsky	Theatre Arts Books
Stanislavski's Legacy	Constantin Stanislavski	Theatre Arts Books
The Actor's Ways and Means	Michael Redgrave	Theatre Arts Books
The Composite Art of Acting	Jerry Blunt	The Macmillan Company
The Craft of Comedy	Seyler - Haggard	Theatre Arts Books
The Craftsmen of Dionysus	Jerome Rockwood	Scott, Foresman & Co.
The Method as Means	Charles Marowitz	Citadel Press
The Stanislavski Method	Sonia Moore	The Viking Press
To the Actor	Michael Chekhov	Harper & Brothers
Strasberg at the Actors Studio	Robert H. Hethmon	Viking Press

DIRECTING

Title	Author	Publisher
Directing Is Fun	Herbert M. Dawley	Samuel French & Company
Directors on Directing	Cole - Chinoy	Bobbs-Merrill
Fundamentals of Play Directing	Alexander Dean - Lawrence Carra	Holt, Rinehart and Winston
General Principles of Play Directing	Brown - Garwood	Samuel French & Company
How to Produce Amateur Plays	Barrett H. Clark	Little Brown & Co.
Practical Stage Directing for Amateurs	Emerson Taylor	
Stage Directions	John Gielgud	Random House
Stanislavski Directs	Nikolai M. Gorchakov	Funk & Wagnalls
The Craft of Play Directing	Curtis Canfield	Holt, Rinehart & Winston Inc.
The Director's Dilemma	Karen Featherman	Walter H. Baker Co.
The Director's Handbook	Frank McMullen	Shoe String Press
The Director in the Theatre	Marian Gallaway	The Macmillan Company

MAKE-UP

Title	Author	Publisher
Hints on the Art of Make-Up	Max Factor	Factor Make-Up Studios
Make-Up	John F. Baird	Samuel French & Co.
Make-Up Magic	Arthur H. Schwerin	Northwestern University Press
Make-Up: The Dramatic Student's Approach	Charles Thomas	Theatre Arts Books
Simplified Make-Up	Le Roy Stahl	Denison
Stage Make-Up	Yati Lane	Denison
Stage Make-Up	Richard Corson	Appleton-Century-Crofts
Stage Make-Up Made Easy	M. H. Benoliel	Walter H. Baker Co.
Technique of Stage Make-Up	Jack Stuart Knapp	Walter H. Baker Co.
The Last Word in Make-Up	Rudolph Liszt	Dramatists Play Service

NOTE: Many theatre make-up manufacturers issue simplified pamphlets on the art of make-up, which are available free, for the asking:

Name	Address
LEICHNER L. LTD.	171 Madison Avenue, New York 10016
MAX FACTOR	Factor Make-Up Studios, 1655 No. McDaddn Pl., Hollywood, California
MINER'S	
M. STEIN COSMETIC COMPANY	430 Broome Street, New York 10013

STAGECRAFT—SCENERY, LIGHTING, etc.

Title	Author	Publisher
Here's How	Herbert V. Hake	Walter H. Baker Company
New Theatres for Old	Mordecai Gorelik	Samuel French & Co.
Play Production	Henning Nelms	Barnes & Noble
Scenery for the Theatre	Harold-Cole	Little Brown
Scene Building, A Primer of Stage Craft	Henning Nelms	Dramatists Play Service
Scene Design & Stage Lighting	Parker-Smith	Holt, Rinehart & Winston Inc.
Stagecraft and Scene Design	Herbert Philippi	Houghton Mifflin Co.
Stage Scenery and Lighting	Selden-Sellman	Appleton, Century, Crofts
Stage Settings for Amateurs and Professionals	Richard Southern	Theatre Arts Books
The Equipment of the School Theatre	Milton Smith	Columbia University Press
The School Theatre	Roy Mitchell	Brentano's
The Simplified Stagecraft Manual	Le Roy Stahl	
The Stage Is Set	Lee Simonson	Theatre Arts Books

LIGHTING

Title	Author	Publisher
A Method of Lighting the Stage	Stanley McCandless	Theatre Arts Books
A Syllabus of Stage Lighting	Stanley McCandless	Stanley McCandless
Home-Built Lighting Equipment for the Small Stage	Theodore Fuchs	Samuel French & Co.
Images in Light for the Living Theatre	Edward F. Kook	Little Brown
Lighting the Stage with Home-Made Equipment	Jack Stuart Knapp	Walter Baker Publishing
Stage Lighting	Theodore Fuchs	Little Brown
Theatrical Lighting Practice	Rubin-Watson	Theatre Arts Books

COSTUME

Title	Author	Publisher
Authentic Costumes for Jewish School Plays	Samuel Citron	Jewish Education Committee
Biblical Costume	Marion Logan Wright	Walter H. Baker Co.
Costumes for Pesach Plays	Walter Herz	Jewish National Fund
Costume in Pictures	Phyllis Cunnington	E. P. Dutton
Costume in the Theatre	James Laver	Hill & Wang
Costuming a Play	Elizabeth Grimball	Theatre Arts Books
Costume Through the Centuries	Jane Oliver	
Costume Through the Ages	James Laver	Simon & Schuster
Costuming the Biblical Play	Lucy Barton	Walter H. Baker Co.
Historic Costume for the Stage	Lucy Barton	Samuel French & Co.
Period Patterns	Lucy Barton	Walter H. Baker Co.
Stage Costume Handbook	Berniece Prisk	Harper & Row
The Bishop Method of Clothing Construction	Bishop-Arch	Lippincott Company
The Costume of the Theatre	Theodore Komisarjevsky	Holt & Co.

PLAY PRODUCTION

Title	Author	Publisher
The Art of Play Production	John Dolman, Jr.	Harper and Bros.
Behind the Footlights	Spaulding-Skillen	Silver Burdett
Book of Play Production	Milton M. Smith	Appleton-Century-Crofts
Fundamentals of Play Production	Emanuel D. Schonberger	
A Handbook of the Theatre	Esme Crampton	W. J. Cage
A Manual of Play Production	A. M. Drummond	
Modern Theatre Practice	Heffner-Selden-Sellman	Appleton-Century-Crofts
Play Production	Henning Nelms	Dramatists Play Service
The Play Produced	John Fernald	Walter H. Baker Co.
Play Production for Young People	Kenneth Nuttall	Transatlantic
Producing the Play	John Gassner	Holt, Rinehart & Winston
The Stage in Action	Samuel Selden	Appleton-Century-Crofts
Theatre Backstage From A to Z	Warren C. Lounsbury	University of Washington Press

STAGE MANAGEMENT

Title	Author	Publisher
Stage Crew Handbook	S. Cornberg-E. L. Gebauer	Walter H. Baker Co.
Stage Management	Hal D. Stewart	Ribman, London
Stage Management in the Amateur Theatre	Harold Melvill	Barrie & Rockliff, London
The Stage Manager's Handbook	Bert Gruver	Drama Book Shop

SOUND EFFECTS AND ACOUSTICS

Title	Author	Publisher
Collected Papers on Acoustics	Walter Clement Sabine	Dover Press
A Handbook of Sound Effects	Frank Napier	Miller (London)
Manual of Sound Recording	John Aldred	Morgan & Morgan
Sound in the Theatre	Harold Burris-Meyer	Theatre Arts Books

PUPPETS AND MARIONETTES

Title	Author	Publisher
The Art of the Puppet	Bil Baird	The Macmillan Company
The Book of Master Puppet	Le Roy Stahl-Effa E. Preston	
Plays Without People: Puppetry & Serious Drama	Peter D. Arnott	Indiana University Press
Presenting Marionettes	Susan French	Reinhold
Puppetry	Janet Evec	Wehman

SONG-BOOKS OF JEWISH CONTENT
(English, Yiddish and Hebrew)

Title	Author-Composer	Publisher
A Purim Songster	A. W. Binder	Bloch Publishing Co.
A Treasury of Jewish Folksong	Ruth Rubin	Schocken Books
Choral Books	Harry Coopersmith	Jewish Education Committee
Festival Songs	Judith K. Eisenstein	Bloch Publishing Co.
Gateway to Jewish Song	Judith K. Eisenstein	Behrman House
Hanukkah Songster	A. W. Binder	Bloch Publishing Co.
Hebrew Songster for Kindergarten & Primary Grades	Harry Coopersmith	Jewish Education Committee
Manginot Shireynu	Moshe Nathanson	Hebrew Publishing Co.
Music for Jewish Groups	Judith K. Eisenstein	National Jewish Welfare Board
Purim, Little Book of Jewish Songs		Hebrew Publishing Company
Purim Songster Materials		Buffalo Bureau of Jewish Education
Purim Songster		Jewish Education Committee
Shire Purim	Zevi Stone	
Songs of Childhood	Eisenstein-Prensky	United Synagogue of America
Songs of Israel	Seymour Silbermintz	Young Zionist Action Committee
The Songs We Sing	Harry Coopersmith	United Synagogue of America
Songs of Zion	Harry Coopersmith	Behrman House
So We Sing	Sara G. Levy	Bloch Publishing Company
The Jewish Year in Song	A. W. Binder	G. Schirmer Music Co.

SONG-BOOKS OF GENERAL NATURE
(suitable for American National Holidays, Brotherhood Week, etc.)

Title	Editor	Publisher
Assembly Songs and Choruses	Condon-Leavitt-Newton	Ginn & Company
A Treasury of American Song	Downes-Siegmeister	Alfred A. Knopf Inc.
Hymns for the Living Age	H. Augustine Smith	Fleming H. Revell Co.
The Book of American Negro Spirituals	J. W. Johnson-J. Rosamond Johnson	The Viking Press
The Lonesome Train	Robinson-Lampell	Sun Music Co.
The People's Song-Book	Waldemar Hille	Boni & Gaer

About the Author

At age 17, Zara Shakow, a native New Yorker, began her career at The Educational Alliance, where she formed a dramatic club for gifted neighborhood children. Even then her major interest was the fostering of young talent, which course she has pursued as teacher-director through the years, having discovered and developed many name players.

A pioneer in the field of Creative Dramatics, Miss Shakow has done inspiring experimental work as Drama Director at YM-YWHAs, temples, recreational centers and creative arts camps. She has organized and directed a number of children's theatres and workshops, and staged many plays with professional and community theatre companies in the United States, Canada, and Israel.

Miss Shakow has traveled and lectured widely. While on the staffs of the Cameri and Haifa Municipal theatres, during a two-year Israeli assignment, she served as Consultant-Adjudicator of dramatic activities for Histadrut's Cultural Division and the Youth Festival, sponsored by the Ministry of Education. Under their auspices, she also conducted seminars on Children's Theatre and related subjects for directors, leaders, and teachers from the kibbutzim and schools. Her book *The Theatre in Israel,* commissioned by Herzl Press, was released in 1964.

Zara Shakow is a member of the Society of Stage Directors and Choreographers, Actors' Equity, the American National Theatre and Academy, American Educational Theatre Association, and the Children's Theatre Conference.